A Whirlwind Passed through Our Country

A WHIRLWIND PASSED THROUGH OUR COUNTRY

LAKOTA VOICES OF THE GHOST DANCE

Rani-Henrik Andersson

Foreword by Raymond J. DeMallie

UNIVERSITY OF OKLAHOMA PRESS : NORMAN

Published through the
Recovering Languages and Literacies of the Americas initiative,
supported by the Andrew W. Mellon Foundation

Library of Congress Cataloging-in-Publication Data

Names: Andersson, Rani-Henrik, author.
Title: A whirlwind passed through our country : Lakota voices of the ghost dance /
Rani-Henrik Andersson; foreword by Raymond J. DeMallie.
Description: First edition | Norman : University of Oklahoma Press, 2018. |
Includes bibliographical references and index.
Identifiers: LCCN 2017049133 | ISBN 978-0-8061-6007-8 (hardback) |
ISBN 978-0-8061-6019-1 (paperback)
Subjects: LCSH: Ghost dance—South Dakota. |
Lakota Indians—Rites and ceremonies. | Lakota Indians—Government relations. |
Wounded Knee Massacre, S.D., 1890. | BISAC: HISTORY / Native American. |
LANGUAGE ARTS & DISCIPLINES / Linguistics / General. |
LANGUAGE ARTS & DISCIPLINES Translating & Interpreting.
Classification: LCC E99.T34 A64 2018 | DDC 978.004/975244—dc23
LC record available at https://lccn.loc.gov/2017049133

RECOVERING
LANGUAGES&LITERACIES
OF THE AMERICAS

A Whirlwind Passed through Our Country: Lakota Voices of the Ghost Dance
is published as part of the Recovering Languages and Literacies of the Americas initiative.
Recovering Languages and Literacies is generously supported by the Andrew W. Mellon
Foundation.

The paper in this book meets the guidelines for permanence and durability
of the Committee on Production Guidelines for Book Longevity
of the Council on Library Resources, Inc. ∞

1 2 3 4 5 6 7 8 9 10

To Raymond J. DeMallie and Douglas R. Parks

Great Spirit, look at us now. Grandfather and grandmother have come. All these good people are going to see *Wakȟáŋ Tȟáŋka*, but they will be brought safely back to earth. Everything that is good you will see there, and you can have these things by going there. All things that you hear there will be holy and true, and when you return you can tell your friends how spiritual it is. Great Father, I want you to have pity upon me.

Ghost Dance Prayer, *Illustrated American*, January 17, 1891

Contents

Illustrations

Figures

Map

Foreword

The Ghost Dance is one of the defining events in Lakota history. The massacre at Wounded Knee continues to fester in the tribal consciousness as a symbol of white America's disregard for the indigenous peoples of the continent. It is a focal point for grief and religious persecution, and a rallying point for protest, as exemplified by the 1973 American Indian Movement takeover of the community of Wounded Knee. For many Lakotas, Wounded Knee is seen as a starting point for cultural resistance in the reservation context. In contrast, non-Indian historians by and large have interpreted the Ghost Dance as the last gasp of resistance on the part of the Lakotas and see the Wounded Knee massacre as resulting from political unrest masquerading as religion. It is usually interpreted as the end of the Indian wars and, by extension, the end of native culture.

Despite the very large literature on the Lakota Ghost Dance, this study addresses a topic that has been sorely neglected. Most scholarship has proceeded on the assumption that there was "a Lakota point of view," neglecting the obvious fact that the Lakotas, like any other group of people, had differing opinions based, for example, on social, religious, and economic factors. Stereotypically, scholars tend to assume that American Indian "tribes" were homogeneous groups.

Using accounts by Lakotas contemporary to the Ghost Dance, or who had firsthand knowledge of it, Rani-Henrik Andersson has mined material largely overlooked by previous scholarship, including documents written in the Lakota language. His retranslations of Lakota voices found in the Eugene Buechel Manuscript Collection are of utmost value in seeking an understanding of the ghost dancers' point of view. While the documents have been published in *Lakota Tales and Texts* by Paul Manhart, Sr., this new translation corrects some of the mistranslations and errors and gives a more nuanced interpretation of accounts by Short Bull, Young Skunk, and Pretty Eagle. Furthermore, his new translation of a text by George Sword, the captain of the Indian police on Pine Ridge Reservation, is of utmost importance, since scholars have used Sword's account ever since to support the argument for the militancy of the Ghost Dance. The new translation places George Sword's text in a broader context and thus offers a far more accurate interpretation. Andersson has also translated several texts published in *Iapi Oaye*, the Dakota language newspaper published by Presbyterian missionaries in Santee, Nebraska. This is also a valuable contribution as these texts give an insight into the voices of Christian Lakotas and Dakotas.

It is also significant to investigate how the opposition between mixed-bloods and full-bloods played out in relation to the Ghost Dance. Their views on the Ghost Dance, while seldom heard, are important as they were following the developments on the reservations close by. Similarly, most scholars have overlooked the voices of Lakota women. Obviously, the lack of materials greatly limits what is possible in this respect, making the texts presented in this study highly important.

Andersson's study places the Lakota Ghost Dance in a wide cultural, religious, and political context by offering careful commentary and annotations for each voice and each document presented in the study. On this basis, Andersson reconstructs a spectrum of Lakota perspectives, from those totally opposed to the Ghost Dance at one end to those who believed in it wholeheartedly at the other. This study yields a treasure trove of new information and offers insights from the point of view of the Lakotas that have to date eluded historical scholarship. This study has long been needed, but no historian had previously risen to the challenge since it requires mastering writings in Lakota and deep knowledge of Lakota history and culture.

Given that interpretations of the Ghost Dance vary so widely and have such importance today, a history of the Ghost Dance religion and the ensuing hostilities from a Lakota perspective that evaluates the surviving evidence objectively has the potential to play a significant role not only in illuminating tribal history but as a contribution to American Indian studies in the broadest sense. *A Whirlwind Passed through Our Country* is an original contribution and one that reflects excellent ethnohistorical scholarship.

Raymond J. DeMallie

Acknowledgments

This book has been a part of my daily life for the past six years. It has challenged, it has frustrated, but it has also brought a lot of excitement and the joy of discoveries. Writing a book is always an arduous journey, but seeing the final text is always a momentous reward. This book has required extreme patience not only from me but also from many other people. I want to thank all the people and institutions that have helped me to achieve this goal.

My first thanks go to my friend Raymond J. DeMallie, my principal teacher in all things relating to Lakota culture and history. His generosity over the past twenty years has been overwhelming. The fact that he agreed to write the foreword to this book speaks for itself and I am so grateful for that. Likewise, Douglas R. Parks, my teacher in the Lakota language, has always been extremely supportive of me and my work.

People who have directly influenced this particular book and who deserve my most sincere thanks include Dr. Justin R. Gage, who has generously shared with me documents that he found in the archives, documents that would surely have eluded me. I am extremely grateful for him. At the time when I was truly struggling with some Lakota language translations, Mr. Timo Oksanen offered his help. Living in Finland, he had learned the Lakota language on his own, just out of interest in the Lakota people, their history, and culture. It was so important for me to be able to run my suggestions by him and get his opinions and support. It is not easy to find someone in Finland who could help you with Lakota language translations! So thank you, Timo. The translation process was also aided by Ray DeMallie, Dennis Christafferson, and David Posthumus. My deepest gratitude to these gentlemen.

I want to express special thanks to my readers Louis Warren and Jeffrey Ostler. They carefully read the manuscript and offered valuable comments and insights. I also want to acknowledge the generosity of Jerome

Greene and Francis E. Flavin, both of whom have helped me in locating valuable documents. Thank you also to Jeremy Johnston, Christina Burke, and Eddie Welch who helped me find some of the illustrations for this book. My research assistants Sara Saikku and Unto Vanhamäki deserve warm thanks.

There are several others who have helped me over the years. If they did not directly influence the writing of this book, their encouragement and friendship have been instrumental over the years. Thank you (in alphabetical order), Nicky Belle, Robert E. Bieder, Kingsley Bray, Donal Carbaugh, Dennis Christafferson, Philip Deloria, Ephriam Dickson, Francis E. Flavin, Markku Henriksson, Pekka Hämäläinen, Sami Lakomäki, Ernie LaPointe, Travis Myers, David Posthumus, Joshua L. Reid, Andrés Reséndez, Rainer Smedman, and Mark van de Logt.

I am also grateful to the faculty and staff at the University of Helsinki, Department of World Cultures. Mikko Saikku, Outi Hakola, and our Fulbright Bicentennial Chairs in North American Studies, and other faculty in Area and Cultural Studies have provided and interesting and stimulating working environment for the past decade. Lars-Folke Landgrén, Varpu Myllyniemi, Maria Colliander, Sonja Pakarinen, and Julija Azbel were always willing to help me out with practical matters and travel arrangements, however weird they were. Thank you for being so flexible.

In addition to the University of Helsinki, I want express my deepest gratitude to the American Indian Studies Research Institute at Indiana University. It has been my second academic home for twenty years now, and I am looking forward to future cooperation. I also want to thank Paul Spickard, who welcomed me and my family to the University of California, Santa Barbara, for the fall of 2016. Writing under the beautiful California sun was easier than in the dusk of October rains in Finland.

This project would not have been possible without proper funding. The Academy of Finland provided me with a generous fellowship for five years. As an Academy of Finland research fellow, despite simultaneously working as the McDonnell Douglas Chair, Professor of American Studies, for two years, I was able to conduct archival research and fieldwork around the United States. The Academy receives my warmest thanks. I also want to acknowledge the help of all the archives, libraries, and their staffs for being absolutely wonderful and always willing to help. Melissa van Otterloo, Daisy Njoku, Mark Thiel, Aaron Marcus, Leif Milliken, Matthew Bokovoy, Odo Muggli, Lina Ortega, Penny Ramon, Sarah Walker, Steven Friesen, and Amy Hague have all been very kind searching for the documents I requested, and also in helping with various copyright and permission issues.

I also want to acknowledge the help of Hayden Ausland in searching for permission to use the Walter Stanley Campbell Collection. I am grateful to Inge Dawn Howe for permission to use Oscar Howe's painting on the dust jacket.

Alessandra Jacobi-Tamulevich deserves very special thanks. From our first conversation, she was always there for me and supported my work. I am, of course, grateful to the University of Oklahoma Press for publishing this book. I wish to thank Bonnie Lovell, my excellent copy editor, and to acknowledge the help of Emily Schuster and Bethany Mowry of the University of Oklahoma Press.

I want to express thanks to my mother and father for their support and for giving me the opportunity to follow my passions; my sister, Aretta, and her friend Sanna have provided various kinds of support over the years. Also, my parents-in-law, Simo and Marjaana, have helped in so many ways.

During the six years of working on this book so much has happened. I have been blessed with two wonderful children. I have been fortunate to have a flexible job. At times writing is absolutely intense, at times less so. This has allowed me to take time to be with my children and watch them grow. Saara, my wife who is always there, who understands me, and who should be named as the coauthor of this book, deserves my deepest gratitude. Her patience and support leave me speechless. Saara, Kaisla, and Aarni, you make my life absolutely wonderful.

Abbreviations

AHP	American Horse Papers
AIWKSC	Reports and Correspondence Relating to Army Investigations of the Battle at Wounded Knee and to the Sioux Campaign of 1889–1890
ARCIA	Annual Report of the Commissioner of Indian Affairs
ARSW	Annual Report of the Secretary of War
BBMG	Buffalo Bill Monument and Grave
BCIM	Bureau of Catholic Indian Missions
EBMC	Eugene Buechel Manuscript Collection
EEAC	Edward E. Ayer Collection
ESRMC	Eli S. Ricker Manuscript Collection
FDP	Florentine Digman Papers
HCIAP	House Committee on Indian Affairs Papers
HCSHL	History Colorado, Stephen H. Hart Library and Research Center
HLDP	Henry L. Dawes Papers
HRMSCA	Holy Rosary Mission Special Collections and Archives
IULL	Indiana University Lilly Library
JRWC	James R. Walker Collection
JWP	Josephine Waggoner Papers
LC	Library of Congress
LFSP	Lebbeus Foster Spencer Papers

LSASPR	Letters Sent by the Agents or Superintendents at the Pine Ridge Agency
MFT	Museum of the Fur Trade
MUA	Marquette University Archives
NARA	National Archives and Records Administration
NCWHMC	Neihardt Collection, Western Historical Manuscripts Collection
NDHS	North Dakota Historical Society
NSHS	Nebraska State Historical Society
RBIA	Records of the Bureau of Indian Affairs
RHPP	Richard Henry Pratt Papers
SCIAP	Senate Committee on Indian Affairs Papers
SFMC	St. Francis Mission Collection
UMC	University of Missouri, Columbia
WHCUOLA	Western History Collections, University of Oklahoma Libraries and Archives
WMCC	Walter Mason Camp Manuscript Collection
WSCMC	Walter Stanley Campbell Manuscript Collection
YCWABL	Yale Collection of Western Americana, Beinecke Rare Book and Manuscript Library

A Whirlwind Passed through Our Country

"I went walking in a beautiful land where the grass was really green."

—*Young Skunk*

"If it was true, it would spread all over the world.
If it was not true, it would melt away like snow under the hot sun."

—*Red Cloud*

"The spirits would not come to me."

—*Dewey Beard*

"I am not going to be foolish and join the dance."

—*Good Voice*

Introduction

This book gives a voice to the Lakotas by presenting more than one hundred Lakota accounts of the Ghost Dance. The Ghost Dance of 1890 marked a critical moment in Lakota history and caused serious friction and divisiveness among the Lakota people. The four quotations above are examples of the various ways in which the Lakotas viewed the Ghost Dance. From the very beginning, however, the perspectives of white Americans characterized the study of the Lakota Ghost Dance, and Lakota views were only briefly incorporated into those narratives. The earliest accounts created a tradition of treating the Lakota Ghost Dance as a military, political, or religious-political movement. Phrases such as "Sioux outbreak," "Messiah Craze," and "Ghost Dance war," so often used in the titles of works on the topic, characterize this approach.[1] The tradition of largely overlooking Lakota views continued into the late twentieth century, when alternative interpretations began to emerge.[2]

1. See, for example, James Mooney, *The Ghost-Dance Religion and the Sioux Outbreak of 1890* (orig. *The 14th Annual Report of the Bureau of Ethnology to the Secretary of the Smithsonian Institution, 1892–1893*, Washington, D.C., 1896) (Lincoln: University of Nebraska Press, 1991); Robert M. Utley, *The Last Days of the Sioux Nation* (New Haven: Yale University Press, 1963); Rex Alan Smith, *Moon of the Popping Trees: The Tragedy at Wounded Knee and the End of the Indian Wars* (Lincoln: University of Nebraska Press, 1975).

2. For newer interpretations see Raymond J. DeMallie, "The Lakota Ghost Dance: An Ethnohistorical Account," *Pacific Historical Review*, 51, no. 4 (1982): 385–405; Jeffrey Ostler, *The Plains Sioux and U.S. Colonialism from Lewis and Clark to Wounded Knee* (Cambridge: University of Cambridge Press, 2004); Sam Maddra, *Hostiles? The Lakota Ghost Dance and Buffalo Bill's Wild West* (Norman: University of Oklahoma Press, 2006); Rani-Henrik Andersson, "Perspectives on the Lakota Ghost Dance of 1890," in *Reconfigurations of Native North America: An Anthology of New Perspectives*, eds. John R. Wunder and Kurt E. Kinbacher (Lubbock: University of Texas Tech

In *The Lakota Ghost Dance of 1890* (2008), I examined the Lakota Ghost Dance from various perspectives: those of the Lakotas, the Indian agents, the missionaries, the U.S. Army, the press, and the U.S. Congress. It was evident that the Ghost Dance filled a religious void in the Lakota society resulting from years of oppression by the whites. Contrary to conventional wisdom, however, the Lakotas did not use the Ghost Dance to start a final uprising against white people. For the Lakotas, as well as for many other Indian tribes, the Ghost Dance was an expression of genuine religious belief. That it led to bloodshed is due to many misunderstandings between the whites and the Lakotas, both on the individual and collective level. The Ghost Dance caused tremendous frictions within Lakota society, as well, and the Lakotas found various ways to deal with the situation.[3]

However, there is still much to unravel about the Ghost Dance from Lakota points of view. For my previous book, I located and studied a number of Lakota accounts of the Ghost Dance that had not been used before. Since the Lakota voice was only one part of that study, much of the material on Lakota perspectives I gathered could only be used in part or had to be left out. In this work I make full use of those accounts as I present and analyze a number of documents revealing Lakota takes on the Ghost Dance. For many scholars and the general public alike, it seldom occurs that the Lakotas did not share a single view of the Ghost Dance. As the anthropologist Raymond J. DeMallie has noted: "Despite the very large literature on the Lakota Ghost Dance, most scholarship has proceeded on the assumption that there was 'a Lakota point of view,' neglecting the obvious fact that the Lakotas, like any other group of people, had differing opinions based, for example, on social, religious, and economic factors. Stereotypically, scholars tend to assume that American Indian 'tribes' were homogeneous groups."[4] Therefore, a more nuanced interpretation of the various Lakota views is still needed.

Press, 2008), 140–51; Rani-Henrik Andersson, *The Lakota Ghost Dance of 1890* (Lincoln: University of Nebraska Press, 2008); Louis Warren, "Wage Work in the Sacred Circle: The Ghost Dance as a Modern Religion," *Western Historical Quarterly* (Summer 2015): 141–68; Louis L. Warren, *God's Red Son: The Ghost Dance Religion and the Making of Modern America* (New York: Basic Books, 2017).

3. For an analysis of the events leading to the Wounded Knee massacre, see Utley, *Last Days of the Sioux Nation;* Ostler, *The Plains Sioux,* 234–360; Andersson, *The Lakota Ghost Dance of 1890;* Jerome Greene, *American Carnage* (Lincoln: University of Nebraska Press, 2014).

4. Raymond J. DeMallie, foreword to this book and personal correspondence with the author, October 2014.

The Story of the Ghost Dance

In 1888 a Paiute Indian, Wovoka, fell into trance and had a vision. In his vision, he met the Great Spirit, who gave him instructions for a new religion. When Wovoka woke up, he started to instruct his people in a new dance. Dancing would bring about a transformation of the earth. There would be a new world where the white man would not hold the Indians down. There would be buffalo and other game, and the dead Indians would be brought back to life. It would, indeed, be an Indian paradise. Wovoka's religion attracted thousands of American Indians around the Great Basin area and beyond, especially on the Great Plains. Soon, the Lakotas living in today's South and North Dakota started to hear rumors of this wonderful new religion. There was a Son of God or Messiah somewhere in the West and he had come upon the earth to help the Indians. The Lakotas, like so many other tribes, wanted to learn more about this religion that the whites called the Ghost Dance.[5]

In order to understand the Ghost Dance among the Lakotas, one needs to recognize the situation in which the Lakotas found themselves in 1889–1890. Famine was a major concern in the spring of 1890 for the Lakotas living on the Pine Ridge, Rosebud, Cheyenne River, Standing Rock, Lower Brulé, and Crow Creek Reservations in North and South Dakota. As part of the compensation for the Sioux Act of 1889, which had divided the Great Sioux Reservation into six smaller reservations, the Lakotas had been promised additional rations, including beef.[6] However, the amount of beef was gradually reduced, causing great anxiety and hardship among the Lakotas. Another major cause for dissatisfaction was the new boundary line between the Pine Ridge and Rosebud Reservations that forced several families, altogether approximately seven hundred people, to relocate. Now they had to

5. For more, see Mooney, *The Ghost-Dance Religion;* Michael Hittman, *Wovoka and the Ghost Dance* (Lincoln: University of Nebraska Press, 1997); Andersson, *The Lakota Ghost Dance of 1890;* Warren, *God's Red Son.*

6. For the recommendations made by the Sioux Commission, see *Congressional Record: Containing the Proceedings and Debates of the 51st Congress, 1st Session,* Sen. Exec. Doc., No. 51, Vol. 4, Ser. 2682, pp. 23–32. Old but still valuable analyses of the 1889 negotiations are Jerome A. Greene, "The Sioux Land Commission of 1889: Prelude to Wounded Knee," *South Dakota History* 1, no.1 (1970): 41–72; Herbert T. Hoover, "The Sioux Agreement of 1889 and Its Aftermath," *South Dakota History* 19, no. 1 (1989): 57–75. A good analysis can also be found in Ostler, *The Plains Sioux,* 217–39.

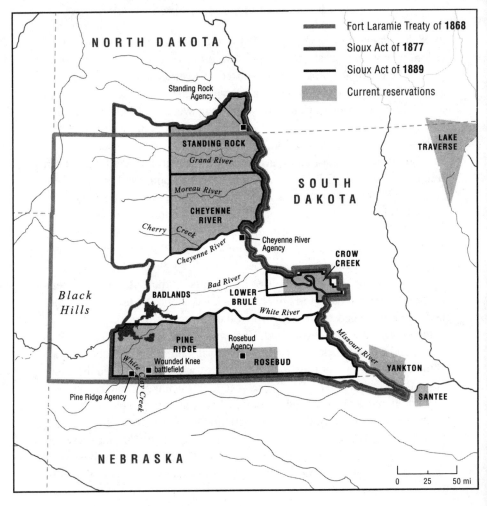

Lakota country, 1890. Map by Erin Greb.

draw rations on Rosebud even if they wanted to live under the Pine Ridge Agency administration. Adding to this, the drought caused Lakota farming attempts to fail year after year. Famine and serious diseases ravaged Lakota reservations. This was the major cause of unhappiness, even unrest, among the Lakotas, and in that sense one of the key factors that increased the interest in the Ghost Dance in late 1889 and early 1890.[7]

In 1889 the Lakotas held a great council that decided to send a delegation to Nevada to meet with the Messiah of the new religion.[8] The Lakota delegation consisted of Short Bull, Scatter, Kicking Bear, He Dog, Flat Iron, Yellow Knife, Yellow Breast, Twist Back, Brave Bear, and Broken Arm.[9] On their way they met people from other tribes who wanted to learn more about the new religion. The Lakotas traveled first to Wind River Reservation in Wyoming. There they discussed the matter with the Arapahos and then continued to Fort Washakie. From there, their journey took them on a railroad to Fort Hall, Idaho where they met with Bannocks, Northern Arapahos, and Northern Cheyennes, who were also on their way to meet the Messiah. From Fort Hall, they boarded a train to Winnemucca, Nevada, and from there, another train to Pyramid Lake and on to the Walker River Agency where they finally met the Messiah.[10]

After returning home in the spring of 1890, they gave their people several accounts of their experiences in Nevada and brought new hope to the suffering Lakotas.[11] News of the Ghost Dance, or Spirit Dance (*wanáǧi*

7. For a thorough analysis of the situation among the Lakotas in 1889–1890, see Ostler, *The Plains Sioux*, 217–39; Andersson, *The Lakota Ghost Dance of 1890*, pp. 19–23; Greene, *American Carnage*, 55–64; Warren, *God's Red Son*, 215–26.

8. For more about Wovoka, see, for example, Hittman, *Wovoka*.

9. There has been extensive discussion on the number of Lakota delegations, although there most likely was only one. Also the names of the delegates vary depending on the source. Even Short Bull gave different names. See part 1, Short Bull accounts. For comparison, see Mooney, *The Ghost-Dance Religion*, 816–24; Utley, *Last Days of the Sioux Nation*, 60–63; William S. E. Coleman, *Voices of Wounded Knee* (Lincoln: University of Nebraska Press, 2000), 10; Maddra, *Hostiles?* 22–23; Andersson, *The Lakota Ghost Dance of 1890*, pp. 31–48; Greene, *American Carnage*, 69; Warren, *God's Red Son*, 182–84.

10. For discussion about the route of the journey, see Mooney, *The Ghost-Dance Religion*, 820; Utley, *The Last Days of the Sioux Nation*, 61–64; Andersson, *The Lakota Ghost Dance of 1890*, pp. 32–38; Justin R. Gage, "Intertribal Communication, Literacy, and the Spread of the Ghost Dance," Ph.D. diss., University of Arkansas, 2015, 234–36; Warren, *God's Red Son*, 182–86.

11. The delegation left sometime in the fall of 1889 and returned in early 1890. For further discussion, see Mooney, *The Ghost-Dance Religion*, 816–24; Andersson, *The Lakota Ghost Dance of 1890*, pp. 31–48; Warren, *God's Red Son*, 182–86.

wačhípi kiŋ), as the Lakotas called it, and its promise of the return of the buffalo and times of happiness, arrived in the spring of 1890, causing great excitement.[12]

The Lakotas of Pine Ridge and Rosebud held the first meetings and ceremonies of the new religion soon after the return of the delegates in April 1890. Lakotas eagerly participated from the beginning. Pretty Eagle and Young Skunk, who participated in the first dances, reported that scores of Lakotas got together to watch the dances, many being drawn into the dance and experiencing powerful visions.

In the visions, the Lakotas met their dead relatives and received messages about the return of happier times. Young Skunk said he had met his dead sister, who showed him a large Lakota village, where people lived like in the past. After waking up from a trance, people wept from happiness and many were convinced that a new world was indeed coming.[13]

The Rosebud Indian agent J. George Wright, however, arrested Short Bull when he heard that his sermons caused the Indians to neglect their farming. Under pressure from the agent, Short Bull promised to stop the Ghost Dance. On Pine Ridge, Agent Hugh D. Gallagher arrested the apostles[14] of the religion who had tried to convince Lakota chiefs to accept dancing. The Pine Ridge Ghost Dance leaders also promised their agents to stop dancing. At this stage, the agents thus managed to prevent the organization of large dances and meetings.

On both reservations, however, the meetings continued in secret. On Cheyenne River Reservation, Kicking Bear, who had traveled with Short Bull to Nevada, was allowed to teach without interruption. He invited all Lakotas to a great dance at Cheyenne River, but once agents interfered on other reservations, the dance did not materialize and interest waned on

12. A better translation for the Ghost Dance would be Spirit Dance. The Lakota word *wanáǧi* refers to the spirits of the departed and the name for the Ghost Dance in Lakota is *wanáǧi wačhípi kiŋ*, the spirit dance. See Andersson, *The Lakota Ghost Dance of 1890*, pp. 29, 46–54. For the effect of the early rumors, see Mooney, *The Ghost-Dance Religion*, 816–24; Utley, *Last Days of the Sioux Nation*, 66–86; Ostler, *The Plains Sioux*, 243–56; Andersson, *The Lakota Ghost Dance of 1890*, pp. 31–48.

13. For first dances, see Short Bull; Young Skunk, Pretty Eagle (pt. 1); Indian agent Hugh D. Gallagher's letter to the SPM, NARA, RG 76, LSASPR, M1282, roll 10, p. 315.

14. The term "apostle" refers to the Lakotas who went to meet Wovoka and who adopted the role of a Ghost Dance leader. This has been the conventional word in research literature. Louis Warren uses the word "evangelist" to emphasize the Christian origins of the Ghost Dance. Warren, *God's Red Son*, 11–12.

Cheyenne River. Kicking Bear then traveled to the Arapahos who were already eagerly dancing.

On other Lakota reservations, the news about a new religion did not create any excitement at this stage because none of the Standing Rock, Crow Creek, or Lower Brulé Lakotas had joined the delegation. The Ghost Dance leaders had not yet reached these reservations to talk about their experiences.

The agents on Lakota reservations were not overly concerned about the Ghost Dance in the spring of 1890. They were too busy with agricultural programs and other routine work. In June all agents downplayed the significance of the Ghost Dance in their reports to the Washington authorities, who had heard rumors about a possible Lakota uprising. These rumors were caused by a few letters from settlers who warned about an uprising. One of the earliest was a letter to the secretary of the interior in late May from Charles L. Hyde, living in Pierre, South Dakota, close to Lakota reservations. He claimed that "the Sioux Indians or a portion of them are secretly planning and arranging for an outbreak in the near future." He got his information from a mixed-blood student at the Presbyterian College in Pierre, who had received communication from his relatives about a Messiah.[15] Even some Lakotas were concerned about a possible uprising. Kaŋǧí (Crow), a Brulé from Rosebud wrote in June in Lakota to a white friend, G. C. Douglas, living in Iowa claiming: "They will fight with the whites, it is said." He did not specifically mention the Ghost Dance as the cause of the possible trouble nor did he mention the Ghost Dance by name. It is impossible to determine what he thought would be the cause of the eventual fighting.[16] Starting in April and May, newspapers warned about the new Indian religion, calling it "the Last Powwow" or simply "the War Dance."[17]

15. Charles L. Hyde to Sec. Interior, May 29, 1890, NARA, RBIA, RG 75, SC 188, box 199. For a good discussion of this letter and its impact, see Gage, "Intertribal Communication," 250–51.

16. Kaŋǧí to G. C. Douglas, forwarded to Secretary of the Interior, June 13, 1890, NARA, RBIA, RG 75, GRBIA, Letters Received, Letter 18612, box 633. Translated by Rani-Henrik Andersson, 2016. The handwriting in this letter is so difficult to read that most of it is impossible to translate. See Gage, "Intertribal Communication," 254–55.

17. See, for example, *Omaha Daily Bee*, April 6, 1890, p. 1; *Washington Post*, April 6, 1890, p. 1; *Washington Post*, April 16, 1890, p. 2; *Chicago Tribune*, April 7, 1890, 9; *New York Times*, April 6, 1890, p. 1.

The agents reassured Washington that the situation on Lakota reservations was completely peaceful. Only the Standing Rock agent, James McLaughlin, reported that Sitting Bull and some other traditionalists were causing trouble. This, however, had nothing to do with the Ghost Dance, and the agent was certain that the unrest would quiet down if Sitting Bull were to be arrested. McLaughlin's comments related to years of disputes between himself and Sitting Bull.[18]

The agents' reports and their lack of action in June show that the Ghost Dance had not yet caused much unrest among the Lakotas. The religion might have completely dissolved, if July had not brought another drought and failed crops. The 1890 crops failed more critically than in the years before, and severe hunger ensued. Some white settlers left their farms and moved to better areas, but the Lakotas could not move.

The government's decision to cut down the Lakota annual rations hit them amidst the famine. Lakotas repeatedly asked for help. Several chiefs wrote to the commissioner of Indian affairs and asked for relief. They explained the direness of their conditions, and how the cut in rations would further deteriorate the situation. They feared that unrest might follow. The Lakotas only wanted to live in peace and receive what was promised to them in treaties and by General Crook who was the main negotiator in the 1889 commission. The government, however, would not change its plans. Only in December did Congress propose additional rations to the Lakotas. This help came too late.[19]

At the end of July, the Lakotas were increasingly dissatisfied. Just then, Kicking Bear returned from his visit to the Arapahos. He said the Arapahos were openly dancing and practicing their new religion. Kicking Bear's return coincided with a time when the Lakotas were growing more des-

---

18. For Sitting Bull's life and his struggles with Agent James McLaughlin, see Stanley Vestal, *Sitting Bull: The Champion of the Sioux* (Norman: University of Oklahoma Press, 1989); Robert M. Utley, *The Lance and the Shield: Life and Times of Sitting Bull* (New York: Ballantine Books, 1993). See also Ernie LaPointe, *Sitting Bull: His Life and Legacy* (Layton: Gibbs Smith, 2009).

19. Little Wound, Young Man Afraid of His Horses, Fast Thunder, in Indian agent Gallagher's letter to Commissioner of Indian Affairs, July 23, 1890, NARA, RG 76, LSASPR, M1282, roll 10, pp. 335–38; *Council Held with a Delegation of Sioux Indians*, House of Representatives Committee on Indian Affairs, 51st Cong., 1st sess., (unpublished hearing, testimony of American Horse, April 15, 1890), IUL, microfiche, card 1, 1–9 (see pt. 2). For more about additional rations to the Lakotas, see *Sioux Indian Appropriation*, 51st Cong., 2nd sess., H. Ex. Doc., no. 36; *Additional Provisions for Sioux*, 51st Cong., 2nd sess., H. Ex. Doc., no. 37.

perate. They were a willing audience, when Kicking Bear spoke about the miracles he had witnessed among the Arapahos, and of the happy future that the Arapahos faced. Short Bull also took advantage of the situation and started the Ghost Dances again.

When the whites were clearly not going to help, increasing numbers turned to the traditionalist, or what the whites generally called "nonprogressive," chiefs. It is, however, extremely important to realize that the terms "progressive" and "nonprogressive" are highly charged terms as they reflect the opinions of the contemporary whites and put labels on Lakotas that are far too simplistic and do not reflect the reality on the reservations. From the Lakota point of view, people acted according to what they believed was best for themselves or for their people. There are many instances where chiefs like Red Cloud or Gall supported efforts such as education that would put them in a "progressive" category. At other times, they might oppose the Indian agents in questions relating to, for example, farming or other assimilationist pursuits by the U.S. government. This would immediately earn them the "nonprogressive" label. This goes to show how problematic and inaccurate it is to use these white-imposed labels when discussing Lakota society in the reservation context. As will be shown below, these labels were even more problematic when used in the context of the Ghost Dance because the contemporary whites used these simplistic categories to describe the Lakotas' attitudes toward the Ghost Dance. Until recently even scholars have followed this oversimplified categorization where "nonprogressive" equals Ghost Dancer, that is, hostile, while "progressive" equals non–Ghost Dancer, or friendly. These categories have been used to promote the thought of the Ghost Dance as being a hostile or warlike demonstration embraced only by the traditionalists. As will be seen below, this categorization is much too superficial. I will use the terms "progressive" and "nonprogressive" in this book, keeping in mind the controversial nature of the terms. I place them in quotation marks to remind the reader that the terms reflect contemporary white attitudes, not mine.[20]

On Pine Ridge, Red Cloud was still the leader of the traditionalists, although he had officially converted to Roman Catholicism. Little Wound and Big Road were among the most influential leaders. "Progressive" chiefs like Man Afraid of His Horses and American Horse were constantly less

---

20. For this discussion, see Mooney, *The Ghost-Dance Religion;* Utley, *The Last Days of the Sioux Nation;* DeMallie, "The Lakota Ghost Dance: An Ethnohistorical Account," 385–405; Ostler, *The Plains Sioux,* 205, 212; Andersson, *The Lakota Ghost Dance of 1890;* Maddra, *Hostiles?* 6, 19–26; Warren, *God's Red Son,* 210–14.

popular. As signers of the 1889 agreement, they were seen as partially responsible for the Lakotas' state of despair.[21]

Soon after the return of Kicking Bear, the Lakotas started dancing on different reservations under the leadership of the Ghost Dance *wičháša wakȟáŋ* (holy men). Despite his Catholicism, Red Cloud gave permission for the dances, although he never actively participated in the Ghost Dance ceremonies. He said the religion would die on its own if it was not true.

Little Wound, whom the whites considered a "progressive" Christian, called for the rapid organization of a dance, so that the Messiah would not abandon them when the time came. At the beginning of August, some three hundred Oglalas began organizing dances in his camp. Other dance camps sprung up across the Pine Ridge Reservation. In August, altogether twelve hundred Oglalas out of the seven thousand Pine Ridge residents were dancing regularly. Many people moved away from their log cabins and erected their tipis to be able to live permanently on the dance sites. The traditional camp circle was revived.[22]

21. See Short Bull Document, BBMG, 3; ARSW 1891, *American Horse, Report of Major General Nelson A. Miles*, 52nd Cong., 1st sess., H. Ex. Doc., no. 1, 136. See also *Council Held with a Delegation of Sioux Indians*, House of Representatives Committee on Indian Affairs, 51st Cong., 1st sess., (unpublished hearing, testimony of American Horse, April 15, 1890), IUL, microfiche, card 1, 1–3; ARCIA, 1891, *Report of Agent James McLaughlin*, 52nd Cong., 1st sess., H. Ex. Doc., no. 1, pp. 126–27; Little Soldier, Shoots Walking, One Bull, WSCMC, WHCUOLA, box 104, folders 5–6, 21.

22. Young Skunk, EBMC, HRMSCA, 1–6; Pretty Eagle, EBMC, HRMSCA, 1–6; Red Cloud's letter to T. A. Bland, December 10, 1890, read in the U.S. Congress, Cong. Rec., 51st Cong., 2nd sess., December 19, 1890, pp. 702–703; Red Cloud, in Charles A. Eastman's letter to Frank Wood, November 11, 1890, NARA, RG 75, SC 188, M4728, reel 1, 1/98–100; Indian agent Daniel F. Royer's letter to Commissioner of Indian Affairs Thomas J. Morgan, November 8, 1890, NARA, RG 94, AIWKSC, M983, roll 1, vol. 1, pp. 62–65; Little Wound, *New York Times*, November 23, 1890, p. 5; *Chicago Tribune*, November 23, 1890, p. 1; *Omaha Daily Bee*, November 23, 1890, p. 1; Little Wound in E. G. Eastman, 1945, p. 30. See Philip Wells, ESRMC, NSHS, box 4, tablet 5. See also James P. Boyd, *Recent Indian Wars: Under the Lead of Sitting Bull and Other Chiefs; with a Full Account of the Messiah Craze and Ghost Dances* (Philadelphia: Publishers Union, 1891), 183; Charles A. Eastman, *From Deep Woods to Civilization: Chapters in the Autobiography of an Indian* (Boston: Little, Brown, 1916), 100; David Humphreys Miller, *The Ghost Dance* (Lincoln: University of Nebraska Press, 1985), 56; William S. E. Coleman, *Voices of Wounded Knee* (Lincoln: University of Nebraska Press, 2000), 48–49. On the life of Elaine Goodale Eastman, see, for example, Kay Graber, ed., *Sister to the Sioux: The Memoirs of Elaine Goodale Eastman, 1885–1891* (Lincoln: University of Nebraska Press, 1985).

On Pine Ridge, Agent Hugh D. Gallagher became worried, and on August 22, assisted by the Indian police, he tried to interrupt a dance, but they met some three hundred Oglalas carrying weapons, ready to defend their religion. The agent had to retreat. For the first time, the Ghost Dancers defied the authorities and were ready to fight against members of the Indian police, their own people. For Gallagher, the Ghost Dance stalled the civilization process of the Lakotas. Other agents shared this view.[23]

The information about the success of the Ghost Dancers spread not only among the Lakotas, but whites as well. Some white settlers living near the Lakota reservations fled from their homes when they heard rumors about Indians gathering arms. Many newspapers reported that the greatest Indian war of all times was about to begin. By the fall of 1890 newspapers were reporting that thousands of Indians were "crazed by the religion" and ready to fight. The rumors were usually exaggerated and distorted. For example, at the end of August, a rumor spread at the Rosebud Indian Agency that soldiers had arrived on the reservation and arrested Lakota women and children. This led to the arming of both traditionalists and "progressives." Armed Indians rode to meet the soldiers, intending to free the women and children. The rumor about the arrival of soldiers, however, turned out to be false.[24]

23. Philip Wells, ESRMC, NSHS, box 4, tablets 1–5; Agent Gallagher's letter to Commissioner of Indian Affairs, August 28, 1890, NARA, RG 75, LSASPR, M1982, roll 10, 387–88; ARCIA, 1891, *Report of the Commissioner of Indian Affairs T. J. Morgan*, October 1, 1891, 52nd Cong., 1st sess., H. Ex. Doc., no. 1, pp. 274–75; Cong. Rec., 51st Cong., 2nd sess., vol. 22, pt. 1, December 12, 1890, pp. 47–48. See Utley, *Last Days of the Sioux Nation*, 91–94; Ostler, *The Plains Sioux*, 274–76; Andersson, *The Lakota Ghost Dance of 1890*, p. 104.

24. See, for example, *Chicago Tribune*, July 12, 1890, p. 1; *Chicago Tribune*, September 26, 1890, p. 1; *Chicago Tribune*, October 28, 1890, p. 1; *Omaha Daily Bee*, July 7, 1890, p. 6; *Omaha Daily Bee*, October 28, 1890, p. 1; *Washington Post*, September 27, 1890, p. 1, *Washington Post*, October 28, 1890, p. 1; *New York Times*, October 28, 1890, p. 3. See also Luther Standing Bear, *My People the Sioux* (Lincoln: University of Nebraska Press, 1975; orig. pub. New York: Houghton & Mifflin, 1928), 221; Miller, *Ghost Dance*, 91–93; Mooney, *The Ghost-Dance Religion*, 92. The historian Jeffrey Ostler argues that newspaper writing and the reports of settlers fleeing did not play a major role in the final decision to send in troops to the Lakota reservations. I agree that there were only a few actual reports of settlers becoming alarmed, and they often had nothing to do with the Ghost Dance. However, as noted above, there were already a few letters warning of a possible outbreak in the summer of 1890. The decision to send troops was also preceded by an army investigation that concluded that there was dissatisfaction among the Lakotas and something needed to be done before an outbreak would occur. The army investigation also noted that the Lakotas were starving and the

During August and September, all agents on Lakota reservations, except for James McLaughlin of Standing Rock, were changed. The new Republican government wanted to get rid of agents hired by the Democrats. Political reasons guided the selection of the new agent on Pine Ridge, Daniel F. Royer. He was entirely unqualified for the job. He had little experience with Indians, and he was close to fearing them. The Lakotas named him Man Afraid of His Lakotas. Only a few days after his arrival, Royer called soldiers to help.

Other agents were not as worried about the Ghost Dance. Rosebud's new agent, Elisha B. Reynolds, was quite indifferent, which Short Bull and his followers were quick to use to their advantage. The new Cheyenne River agent, Perain P. Palmer, was not concerned at all, as things were quiet near his agency. In reality, almost seven hundred Ghost Dancers were gathered along Cherry Creek at Hump and Big Foot's camp to hear the teachings of Kicking Bear. Although Hump had previously worked as an Indian police, he now openly embraced the Ghost Dance. Big Foot had long balanced between the traditionalists and the "progressives." Despite his repeated requests, he had not received more schools on the reservation. Disappointed, he now wanted to hear what the Ghost Dance had to offer.[25]

Moving to the dancing grounds meant the strengthening of the camp circle, and that way, the unity of the nation. Thus, the white goal of crumbling

---

"Messiah Craze" was a symptom of "this ill feeling." From early April, the newspapers had discussed the Ghost Dance in the context of "war dances" and linked it to an uprising. In September and October, this alarmist style of reporting gradually increased (for more on the newspaper reporting see, for example, Andersson, *The Lakota Ghost Dance of 1890*, pp. 193–200). It is obviously difficult to estimate how much attention President Benjamin Harrison paid to the press, but I am inclined to believe that the sensational tone combined with alarming reports by, for example, Agent Daniel F. Royer and the army investigation all played a crucial role in the president's decision to send in troops. I agree with Ostler in that the alarmist tone in news reporting as well as the panic reported by settlers grew dramatically after the military intervention. See Jeffrey Ostler, "Conquest and the State: Why the United States Employed Massive Military Force to Suppress the Lakota Ghost Dance," *Pacific Historical Review* 65, no. 2, (May 1996): 217–48; Ostler, *Plains Sioux*, 289–301; Andersson, *The Lakota Ghost Dance of 1890*, pp. 131–37.

25. For comments on Big Foot, see Joseph Horn Cloud, Dewey Beard, ESRMC, NSHS, box 4, tablet 12, box 5, tablet 30, also published in Richard A. Jensen, *Voices of the American West* (Lincoln: University of Nebraska Press, 2006), 1:191–226. See Forrest W. Seymour, *Sitanka: The Full Story of Wounded Knee* (West Hanover: Christopher, 1981), 53; Andersson, *The Lakota Ghost Dance of 1890*, p. 46.

the power of the chiefs and the traditional structure of the society took a severe blow in the fall of 1890.

————

The ceremony of the Lakota Ghost Dance was never carried out according to a single model.[26] The ceremony had many variations, the songs might be different, and the number of ceremonial leaders varied. Certain characteristics, however, repeated from one ceremony to another, making it possible to create an image of a typical Ghost Dance ceremony.

Preparing for the dance always started with a cleansing ritual, most importantly the sweat lodge ceremony, *inípi* or *iníkaǧapi*. It was conducted in much the same way as in the past. The lodge was built with the doorway facing east, and a sacred path led to the fire where the stones were heated.

Some changes took place in Ghost Dance, however. The Ghost Dancers thought that the people living in the "old camp" (i.e., "real" world) smelled bad or were dirty because of all the murders, suicides, and other trouble ravaging the reservations. For that reason, purification before the ceremony became particularly important. To enable as many people as possible to participate, Ghost Dancers built several larger sweat lodges. They might have two doorways. When a person stepped in the lodge, he carried on his back the burdens caused by the white man. When he exited through the other door at the end of the ceremony, he was cleansed from the burden.

The sweat lodge ceremony thus became a symbol of cultural transformation. It symbolized the universe that had been cleansed of strange elements. It was also a symbolic return to the powers of the past. The dance was often preceded by fasting, and holy men blessed the dance venue. Occasionally the holy men also blessed the dancers by first touching the hallowed ground and then the dancer's forehead.[27]

Most traditional Lakota ceremonies started with the smoking of the sacred pipe, but in the Ghost Dance, the ritual was connected to the preparatory sweat lodge ceremony. The sacred pipe was present in the actual Ghost Dance, but in a different way than in the traditional Sun Dance, for

26. The following description of the Lakota Ghost Dance ceremony is drawn from Andersson, *The Lakota Ghost Dance of 1890*, pp. 54–73.

27. *Illustrated American*, January 17, 1891, pp. 331–23; Boyd, *Recent Indian Wars*, 183–84; Miller, *Ghost Dance*, 59; Mooney *The Ghost Dance-Religion*, 918–19; Ella C. Deloria, *Speaking of Indians* (Lincoln: University of Nebraska Press, 1998; orig. pub. 1944), 81; Raymond A. Bucko, *The Lakota Ritual of the Sweat Lodge: History and Contemporary Practice* (Lincoln: University of Nebraska Press, 1998), 40–41, 255.

example. In the Ghost Dance, a young woman stood in the center of the dance circle, holding the pipe up and pointed to the west, where the Messiah lived. In this case, the person holding the pipe symbolized the White Buffalo Woman, who in the Lakota mythology brought the pipe to the Lakotas.[28]

After the cleansing in the sweat lodge, the Lakotas started preparing for the dance. Symbols, such as circles, stars, and the crescent moon were painted on the faces of the dancers. Preparations might take the entire morning, and the ceremony often started only in the afternoon. Then the dancers gathered around the sacred tree erected in the center of the dance circle. The sacred tree, *čhaŋ wakȟáŋ*, had been an integral part of the traditional Sun Dance, and it symbolized Lakota unity and the center of the world.

Before the beginning of the ceremony, the dancers shared a bowl of meat, symbolizing the disappeared buffalo. In the middle of the dance circle, with the woman holding the pipe, stood another woman, who shot an arrow in each of the main directions, representing the Lakota, Cheyenne, Arapaho, and Crow nations. The arrows were collected and hung on the sacred tree, along with sacrifices such as tobacco or mounted animals.[29]

In the middle of the dance circle also stood the ceremonial leaders and a "foresinger," who started the ceremony with an opening song. During the song, the dancers held their arms raised toward the west. The west was important because the Messiah lived there, but also because the mythical White Buffalo Woman had left the Lakotas for the west. When the song ended, the dancers wept together, took each other's hands, joined in a new song, and started slowly moving from left to right.[30]

28. Mooney, *The Ghost-Dance Religion*, 823–24, 1062–63; *Illustrated American*, January 17, 1891, p. 331; Boyd, *Recent Indian Wars*, 184.

29. Mooney, *The Ghost-Dance Religion*, 823, 915–16, 1063–64; Miller *Ghost Dance*, 60–61. A good description of the Lakota Ghost Dance comes from Special Agent E. B. Reynolds, who was at the venue in September 1890. See Indian agent Elisha B. Reynolds's letter to the Commissioner of Indian Affairs Thomas J. Morgan, September 25, 1890, NARA, RG 75, SC 188, M4728, reel 1, 1/22–26. Another description is in Graber, ed., *Sister to the Sioux*, 32–33. About symbols used in the Ghost Dance, see, for example, Trudy Carter Thomas, "Crisis and Creativity: Visual Symbolism of the Ghost Dance Tradition," Ph.D. diss., Columbia University, 1988.

30. Reynolds's letter to the Commissioner of Indian Affairs Morgan, September 25, 1890, NARA, RG 75, SC 188, M4728, reel 1, 24–26; Mooney, *The Ghost-Dance Religion*, 823, 920–21, 1061. For more about traditional Lakota dances, see, for example, Frances Densmore, *Teton Sioux Music and Culture* (Lincoln: University of Nebraska Press, 1992), 84–151, 468–84.

Slowly the leader of the ceremony increased the speed, alternating between crying and praying toward all directions. As the leader's enthusiasm increased, the other dancers joined him, and the dance became faster. The dancers loudly shouted out the names of their deceased relatives, and vocally expressed their grief. While dancing, they sprinkled soil in their hair to show their anxiety, and gradually provoked themselves to a state where receiving visions became possible.

When the song and dance continued, the excitement grew, and new dancers detached from the circle, screaming and making great leaps in the air, until they fell on the ground with shaking limbs and finally lay still, as if dead. According to one witness, there may have been as many as a hundred dancers lying on the ground at one time.[31]

The Ghost Dance ceremony ended, when enough dancers had fallen into trances. The dancers then sat down in a circle, and the holy men leading the dance started interpreting the visions of the dancers. After a while, the ceremony could start again. There were sometimes three ceremonies a day, and in between the ceremonies, people played traditional games and feasted. The ceremony always ended with an ending song at the request of the leaders. Then the dancers would shake the blankets they had worn to remove the evil power from them. Finally, everyone cleansed themselves by bathing.[32]

Many of the songs referred to ancestors and meeting deceased relatives. Return from a successful war party or bison hunting were also popular themes. Some of the songs referred to the Messiah, or the Father, and the eternal life he promised.[33]

31. Reynolds's letter to the Commissioner of Indian Affairs Morgan, September 25, 1890, NARA, RG 75, SC 188, M4728, reel 1, 24–26; Mooney *The Ghost-Dance Religion*, 915–22; *Illustrated American*, January 17, 1891, p. 329.

32. Pretty Eagle, EBMC, HRMSCA, 1–6; Reynolds's letter to the Commissioner of Indian Affairs Morgan, September 25, 1890, NARA, RG 75, SC 188, M4728, reel 1, 1/25–26; Mooney, *The Ghost-Dance Religion*, 915–21. For traditional games, see Densmore, *Teton Sioux Music and Culture*, 485–91.

33. Lakota Ghost Dance songs can be found, for example, in Emma Sickels, "The Story of The Ghost Dance. Written in the Indian Tongue by Major George Sword, an Ogallala Sioux, Major of Indian Police," *The Folk-Lorist* 1, no. 1 (1892): 32–36; William Powers, *Voices from the Spirit World: Lakota Ghost Dance Songs* (Kendall Park: Lakota Books, 1990), 27–45; Mooney *The Ghost-Dance Religion*, 1061, 1064–70; Wilhelm Wildhage, *Geistertants-Lieder der Lakota: Eine Quellensamlung* (Wück auf Foehr: Verlag für Amerikanistik, 1991), 9–40; Andersson, *The Lakota Ghost Dance of 1890*, pp. 56, 59–60, 71.

Considering the situation of the Lakotas in 1890, it is no wonder that the stories made an impression. In the visions, happy people hunted, danced, played games, and did all the things the Lakotas used to do. In the new world, there were no illnesses or suffering. The traditional lifestyle was coming back. Because this happened in the visions, it was clear that it would also happen in the human world.[34]

The Lakotas had no reason to doubt the message of the visions. Visions had always been integral to the Lakota world, and holy men had always known how to interpret them. Why would it not have been the case now? The countless visions brought new characteristics to the Ghost Dance.

The visions also initiated the new dancing garments that the whites called ghost shirts, or rather Ghost Dance shirts. The Lakota name for the shirts was *ógle wakȟáŋ*, sacred shirt. These simple fabric shirts were special because the Lakotas believed that they brought protection from the bullets of the whites.

At first, the shirts were basic garments decorated with traditional images, but in the fall of 1890, when the U.S. Army came to stifle the Lakota "rebellion," the Ghost Dancers sought protection from the shirts. Facing the power of the army, the Ghost Dancers needed something that would help them face the new threat. The shirts promised to give protection from enemy bullets, thus functioning as a unifying element for the Ghost Dancers. The Ghost Dance shirts served the same way as the shields used in traditional warfare: their protection arose from their sacred power, rather than the materials used. The power of the shirts was based on the symbols that were used to decorate them.[35]

In the fall of 1890, Ghost Dancers were dancing with more fervor and regularity. They believed that the more they danced, the faster the paradise would come. Wovoka had only told them to dance every six weeks, but the Lakotas danced almost daily. This was one of the reasons the whites viewed the dancers with increasing suspicion.

34. Deloria, *Speaking of Indians*, 83; Young Skunk, Short Bull, Pretty Eagle, EBMC, HRMSCA.

35. Pretty Eagle, EBMC, HRMSCA, 1–6. For the origin, development, and significance of the Ghost Dance shirts, see Andersson, *The Lakota Ghost Dance of 1890*, pp. 67–73. See also Clark Wissler, *Some Protective Designs of the Dakota*, vol. 1, pt. 2 (New York: Anthropological Papers of the Museum of Natural History, 1907). For more about Ghost Dance shirts, see pt. 1.

Wild rumors about bloodthirsty wild Indians dancing in religious orgies spread to Washington. The Ghost Dance was increasingly seen as a threat to white safety. A rather usual view until recently has been that the Lakotas changed both the message and the ceremony of the Ghost Dance, because they were militant, hated the whites, and wanted to use the Ghost Dance to start an uprising. Recent scholarship, however, demonstrates that the Lakota Ghost Dance retained its spirituality until the end, and that exterior matters caused the ensuing bloodshed. The traditional Lakota spirituality did not have a doctrine or unified message. As the anthropologist Raymond J. DeMallie has noted, each individual had an impact on the entire belief system through his or her experiences. Although there was a basic structure, the Lakota spiritual world was very flexible. Thus, the changes in the Ghost Dance must also be seen as a part of this constantly changing system of belief.[36] Researchers with Euro-American education and values have not understood the concept of having several ways of practicing a religion at one time.

The Lakota Ghost Dance contained elements that could be interpreted as militant, but only *after* the U.S. Army had been sent to stifle the alleged rebellion. The claims that the Lakotas forgot the Christian teachings of the Ghost Dance are false. The Ghost Dance and its Christian characteristics did not override the old beliefs or sacred powers. The Ghost Dance combined the old religion and Christianity, bringing a new dimension to both. It became part of the Lakota spirituality. The Christian message comes through in the Lakota Ghost Dance, its songs, visions, and speeches by Ghost Dancers throughout the Ghost Dance trouble. The Ghost Dance's foundational principle of resurrection is a purely Christian idea.

The religious message of the Ghost Dance was understandable to both the so-called progressive and traditional Lakotas. That all "progressive" Lakotas did not turn to the Ghost Dance demonstrates the political divisions within the society rather than an outright denial of the religious message of the Ghost Dance. At the same time some Christian Lakotas/Dakotas saw the Ghost Dance as a return to heathenism that would take the Lakota people to destruction (for their comments, see part 4). Although the Ghost

36. See Raymond J. DeMallie, "The Lakota Ghost Dance and the Ethnohistorical Method"; DeMallie, "Lakota Belief and Ritual in the 19th Century," in *Sioux Indian Religion: Tradition and Innovation*, edited by Raymond J. DeMallie and Douglas R. Parks (Norman: Oklahoma University Press, 1987), 34; Andersson, *The Lakota Ghost Dance of 1890.*

Dance was for some "progressive" Lakotas a way to combine old and new, many opposed it, fearing unrest and suspicion caused by the Ghost Dance. In essence, they had a very practical approach to it. This caused a conflict among the Lakotas. The rift that had appeared between the "traditionalists" and the "progressives" during the reservation years deepened.[37]

As dancing intensified during the fall of 1890, agents, settlers living close to the reservations, and government officials in Washington grew more confused. Newspapers and settlers in South and North Dakota and Nebraska called for army troops to come and stifle the revolt, of which increasingly wild rumors circulated across the United States.

Newspapers, in particular, reported in conflicting ways. One day they would write that all Lakotas were ready to go on the "warpath," while the next day they would report about fierce fighting between whites and Lakotas, and yet another day they would say that no violence had occurred. Senator Henry L. Dawes accused the newspapers of spreading terror, when the agents and soldiers reported everything to be peaceful. Senator Dawes, nevertheless, led the Congress in December to discuss the Lakota situation and who really was to blame for possible unrest.[38]

37. Andersson, *The Lakota Ghost Dance of 1890*, pp. 20–23. See also DeMallie "The Lakota Ghost Dance," 56; Warren, *God's Red Son*, 191–93, 210–14. See also Indian agent Perain P. Palmer's letter to Commissioner of Indian Affairs Thomas J. Morgan, November 10, 1890, NARA, RG 94, AIWKSC, M983, roll 1, vol. 1, pp. 30–32.

38. For the army view, see, for example, Miles's telegram to AG, November 24, 1890, NARA, RG 94, AIWKSC, M983, roll 1, vol. 1, p. 219; Miles's telegram to AG, November 25, 1890, NARA, RG 94, AIWKSC, M983, roll 1, vol. 1, p. 235; General Thomas H. Ruger's telegram to AG, November 23, 1890, NARA, RG 94, AIWKSC, M983, roll 1, vol. 1, p. 195; Miles's telegram to AG, November 26, 1890, NARA, RG 94, AIWKSC, M983, roll 1, vol. 1, p. 263; Miles's telegram to AG, November 27, 1890, NARA, RG 94, AIWKSC, M983, roll 1, vol. 1, p. 268. For the opinions of pioneers, see, for example, New England City, N.D., residents' letter to Minister of War Redfield Proctor, November 26, 1890, NARA, RG 94, AIWKSC, M983, roll 1, vol. 1, pp. 246–47; Chardon, Neb., residents' letter (no recipient), November 26, 1890, NARA, RG 94, AIWKSC, M983, roll 1, vol. 1, pp. 252–54; Petition of Citizens of Chadron, Neb., November 26, 1890, NARA, SCIAP, RG 46, box 117, and NARA, House Committee on Indian Affairs Papers (HCIAP), RG 233, box 106. For Senator Dawes's comment, see, for example, Cong. Rec., 51st Cong., 1st sess., vol. 21, pt. 14, December 4, 1890, p. 69; Henry L. Dawes's letter to Electa Dawes, December 2, 1890, LC, HLDP, box 15, Folder–August–December 1890; Henry L. Dawes's letter to Electa Dawes, December 3, 1890, LC, HLDP, box 15, folder–August–December 1890. Newspapers reported on the situation almost daily in the end of November. See, for example, *New York Times,*

On November 20, troops of the U.S. Army arrived on Pine Ridge and Rosebud. The arrival of soldiers early in the morning took the Lakotas by complete surprise. The task of the army was to suppress a rebellion and to protect the local settlers. This was, however, to be done without bloodshed. That is why the troops wanted to avoid disarming the Indians, a move that was expected to meet resistance.

Although the Lakotas had often argued with their agents and caused problems during their reservation years, they had seldom taken matters far enough to warrant the arrival of the military. The power of the U.S. Army was well known and it was feared. The presence of the soldiers on Pine Ridge and Rosebud caused confusion, even panic, among the Lakotas. In fear of possible army action, hundreds of non–Ghost Dancers came near the agency buildings on the reservations to show their "friendliness." On the other hand, some of those considered "progressive" escaped the soldiers and went to the camps of the Ghost Dancers.

The arrival of the soldiers also confused Ghost Dancers. On Pine Ridge, dances continued even more enthusiastically under the leadership of Little Wound, Big Road, and No Water. Little Wound took true charge. On November 20 and 21, warriors under his leadership circled around the reservations, urging everyone to join the Ghost Dancers.

According to the whites, the Lakotas were preparing an attack, but all participating Indians assured the white officials that they were keeping guard only to prepare for a possible attack by the soldiers. The Lakotas told the whites that they would be dancing throughout the winter. They did not plan to attack, but they would defend themselves if needed.

The arrival of soldiers on Rosebud caused eleven hundred Brulés to move with Two Strike and Crow Dog toward the western border of the reservation, where they planned to join the Pine Ridge Oglalas who were with Short Bull's people. Along the way, they were joined by seven hundred

November 27, 1890, p. 1; *New York Times*, November 28, 1890, p. 5; *Washington Post*, November 27, 1890, p. 1; *Washington Post*, November 28, 1890, p. 1; *Omaha Daily Bee*, November 26, 1890, p. 1; *Omaha Daily Bee*, November 27, 1890, p. 1; *Chicago Tribune*, November 27, 1890, p. 1; *Chicago Tribune*, November 28, 1890, p. 2. A good sample of photographs taken during the Ghost Dance are found in John E. Carter, "Making Pictures for a News-Hungry Nation," in *Eyewitness at Wounded Knee*, edited by Richard E. Jensen, Eli R. Paul, and John E. Carter (Lincoln: University of Nebraska Press, 1991). A thorough analysis on the discussion in Congress is in Andersson, *The Lakota Ghost Dance of 1890*, pp. 251–70.

Oglalas, who had lived near the border between the reservations. On Cheyenne River, the message about the arrival of soldiers on Pine Ridge and Rosebud caused Ghost Dancers to unite under the leadership of two chiefs. Altogether some six to seven hundred Minneconjous were dancing almost uninterruptedly in Big Foot and Hump's camp. Both leaders were at this point unconditional supporters of the Ghost Dance religion.[39]

The Ghost Dances had started on the Standing Rock Reservation in October, introduced by Kicking Bear. By November, Sitting Bull led dances in his camp on Grand River, but the dancers were closely watched by the Indian police who were loyal to Agent James McLaughlin. By December, even the U.S. Congress accused Sitting Bull of instigating a revolt and of governing other Indians with terror and tyranny. They believed he commanded as many as five thousand warriors.

General Nelson A. Miles believed Sitting Bull to be the responsible force behind all the unrest and wanted to arrest him. Agent McLaughlin also wanted to arrest Sitting Bull, but he wanted to take care of the matter using the Indian police. He emphasized that he was capable of controlling the Indians on his reservation. He absolutely did not want or need help from the army. He still trusted his Indian police, who had long viewed Sitting Bull as their main rival in the contest over power on Standing Rock.

Many Indians and white visitors to Sitting Bull's camp, however, said that he did not truly believe in the Ghost Dance, although he approved of the dancing. They said that Sitting Bull was trying to obtain a vision that would prove to him that the religion was true. Not having received one, he remained doubtful. Sitting Bull, nevertheless, firmly opposed any violence.[40]

The arrival of the soldiers did not calm down the Indians, as had been intended, but caused the Ghost Dancers to unite, and hundreds of non–Ghost Dancers joined them for fear of the army. On Pine Ridge, the Ghost Dancers had convened in the Badlands. Here, in the Stronghold (*Óhaŋzi*), they hoped they could continue dancing safe from the soldiers.

39. Utley, *Last Days of the Sioux Nation*, 118; Mooney, *Ghost-Dance Religion*, 850–52. For Lakota accounts of the first dances, see pt. 1.

40. See, for example, Reverend G. W. Reed, WMCC, IULL, box 5, folder 1, envelope 41; Missionary Mary C. Collins, WMCC, IULL, box 6, folder 3, envelope 78; Reverend Aaron Beede, Beede Diary, NDHS, vol. 5, pp. 50–53; Bishop Martin Mary in Alexander Berghold, *The Indians' Revenge; or Days of Horror: Some Appalling Events in the History of the Sioux* (San Francisco: P. J. Thomas Printer, 1891), 225–27.

Their fear of the army increased the Ghost Dancers' determination to fight for their religion, and thus had an impact on their acquiring arms for themselves. On the other hand, those Indians who chose to remain near the agencies, tried to show their friendliness in all ways possible. Many wanted to cooperate with the army; for example, some forty Oglalas joined the army as scouts. Thus, the arrival of the soldiers led to an even deeper divide within the Lakota people.

At the same time, the situation in November and December, especially on Pine Ridge and Rosebud, was so flammable that without the arrival of the army, violence might soon have broken out between Ghost Dancers and the Indian police or Ghost Dancers and the whites. In November, about 40 percent of the Indian population on Pine Ridge and 30 percent on Rosebud were Ghost Dancers. On Cheyenne River, the figure was 15 percent, and on Standing Rock only 10 percent.[41]

After the arrival of the army, the role of the new agents diminished on Pine Ridge, Cheyenne River, and Rosebud. The army took almost complete control over the reservations. The newly appointed agents became assistants to the army. The impact of the new agents on the Ghost Dance was mostly restricted to the fact that their incompetence and downright fear was a major factor leading to the arrival of the army to the Lakota reservations.

James McLaughlin, however, became more prominent. He had long wanted to arrest Sitting Bull, but he had no actual reason to do so. When Sitting Bull became the Ghost Dance leader on Standing Rock, McLaughlin got the excuse he was looking for to arrest him. Skillfully using the internal disputes of the reservation to his advantage, McLaughlin manipulated the local commanding army officer to allow him to take care of Sitting Bull's arrest the way he chose.

On the morning of December 15, McLaughlin sent a unit of the Indian police to enter Sitting Bull's cabin and arrest him. Sitting Bull was at first ready to join the policemen, but after coming outside the cabin he hesitated. The situation got out of hand, leading to an exchange of fire, in which Sitting Bull and several other Indians were killed. The U.S. Army unit heard the shots and rushed to the scene. In the ensuing fight, a few more Indians were killed, but most of Sitting Bull's followers escaped. Sitting Bull's death led to increasing disorder on all Lakota reservations.[42]

41. See Andersson, *The Lakota Ghost Dance of 1890*, pp. 76–77.
42. On Sitting Bull's death, see, for example, Vestal, *Sitting Bull*, 280–307; Utley, *The Lance and the Shield*, 291–307.

After Sitting Bull's death, the army was to get the Ghost Dancers to surrender and return to the agencies. On Pine Ridge, General John R. Brooke's negotiation tactic was almost yielding the hoped results, as the Ghost Dancers from Badlands were gradually moving closer to the agency. Just then the news of Sitting Bull's death came, halting the journey. Adding to the confusion, chief Big Foot and his people left Cheyenne River and started the journey toward Pine Ridge. Red Cloud, among others, had invited Big Foot to Pine Ridge, where they planned to discuss ways to calm down the situation. General Miles, however, believed that Big Foot had left on a war party and ordered his troops to "find, arrest, disarm, and destroy him" if needed.[43]

Lieutenant Colonel Edwin V. Sumner, who had been watching Big Foot for some time, had an opposing opinion: He believed that Big Foot wanted peace and was actually fleeing for fear of soldiers. Lakota accounts support Sumner's view. They said the Lakotas had been warned about a possible army attack on their camp. Although such a threat was not real, the Lakota decision to flee was justified. While Big Foot and Lieutenant Colonel Sumner were on good terms, a general lack of trust pained both sides. Thus, the Lakotas had decided to leave before it was too late.[44]

The escape from Cheyenne River was hard on the Lakotas. The temperature was low, and Big Foot was suffering from pneumonia. Still they managed to avoid the troops for several days. Eventually, on December

43. Miles's telegram to AG, December 28, 1890, NARA, RG 94, AIWKSC, M983, roll 1, vol. 1, p. 626; Lieutenant Fayette W. Roe's letter to Colonel James W. Forsyth, December 26, 1890, NARA, RG 94, AIWKSC, M983, roll 1, vol. 2, p. 751; General John R. Brooke's letter to Major Samuel M. Whitside, December 27, 1890, NARA, RG 94, AIWKSC, M983, roll 1, vol. 2, p. 752; Roe's letter to Whitside, December 217, 1890, NARA, RG 94, AIWKSC, M983, roll 1, vol. 2, p. 753; Testimony of Brigadier General J. R. Brooke, January 18, 1890, NARA, RG 94, AIWKSC, M983, roll 1, vol. 2, pp. 740–47. See Andersson, *The Lakota Ghost Dance of 1890*, 152–54.

44. Indian accounts of the Wounded Knee massacre and the events leading to it include Andrew Good Thunder, IULL, WMCC, box 6, folder 14, envelope 90; Philip Wells, Joseph Horn Cloud, Dewey Beard, William Garnett, NSHS, ESRMC, box 4, tablets 1–5, 12, box 5, tablets 22, 30; Statement of the Survivors, IULL, WMCC, box 4, folder 4, envelope 5; James Pipe On Head, 75th Cong. 1st sess., House Committee on Indian Affairs, Published Hearing, March 7, May 12, 1938, IUL, Microfiche, RG 3, card 4, 18–19; Beard in Walker, 165; Dewey Beard et al., in McGregor, *The Wounded Knee Massacre*, 97–100, 109, 111, 117–18, 121–22, 125, 128. See also Donald F. Danker, "The Wounded Knee Interviews of Eli R. Ricker," *Nebraska History* 62, no. 2 (1981); Andersson, *The Ghost Dance of 1890*, 87–96.

28, Big Foot's party surrendered to the unit led by Major Samuel Whitside. The Indians were taken to a camp near Wounded Knee Creek. The army received enforcements overnight, and Colonel James W. Forsyth took charge.

The next day, the Lakotas were to be taken to Pine Ridge Agency, where they had in fact been headed all along. At dawn on December 29, the Indians were gathered for negotiations. They were told to give up all their guns. During the talks, medicine man Yellow Bird started to sing Ghost Dance songs and pray for help from the Great Spirit. The soldiers interpreted this as provocation.

Meanwhile, soldiers were searching the Lakota camp, looking for guns even within women's clothing. Lakota men were in a circle around Big Foot's tent, and soldiers were encircling them. Cannons had been placed on a ridge nearby. During disarmament, the gun of a deaf and mute Lakota, Black Fox, went off. The soldiers opened fire against the men in the circle and the women and children in the camp. Big Foot was immediately killed. In the ensuing bloodbath, about 250 Lakotas were killed. Most of them were women and children.[45]

Many theories have been presented as to the start of the Wounded Knee bloodbath, but most likely the Indians did not intend to oppose the army, but had fled and sought help from Red Cloud's camp. The situation on that morning, however, was extremely tense, and many things happened at the same time: The medicine man started his performance, the soldiers were looking for weapons, and some of the men were already disarmed. The army had surrounded the Indians, the Hotchkiss cannons were pointing directly at the Indian camp, and the army did not want to let the Indians flee again.

45. The army view of the battle is found in, for example, Forsyth's letter to Brooke, December 29, 1890, NARA, RG 94, AIWKSC, M983, roll 1, vol. 2, p. 758; Testimonies of Major S. M. Whitside et al., NARA, RG 94, AIWKSC, M983, roll 1, vol. 2, pp. 656–710. For thorough analysis of the army point of view, see Utley, *The Last Days of the Sioux Nation*, 200–230, and for a more recent analysis, see Greene, *American Carnage*, 191–269. See also Colby, "The Sioux Indian War of 1890–91," 155–57; William F. Kelley, "The Indian Troubles and the Battle of Wounded Knee," *Transactions and Reports of the Nebraska State Historical Society* (Lincoln: State Journal Company, 1892), 4:40–44; Smith, *Moon of the Popping Trees*, 184–96. A good analysis on the number of Lakotas following Big Foot and the victims of Wounded Knee is in Jensen, "Big Foot's Followers at Wounded Knee," 194–212. See also Greene, *American Carnage*, 399–416.

In this context, a significant matter is General Miles's orders to Colonel Sumner to disarm and, if necessary, to destroy the fleeing Lakotas. Commander of the army General John M. Schofield stated repeatedly that disarmament would be a dangerous attempt. It would only lead to suspicion and a battle. It was also against the official U.S. Indian policy. Regardless of that, disarmament was attempted with destructive consequences on December 29, 1890.[46]

The Wounded Knee events were at first lauded within the army as well as in the press. In a few days, however, it was revealed that women and children had been killed without mercy, and the army started to receive heavy criticism.[47] Soon, the events were being referred to as a "bloodbath" and "slaughter." After Wounded Knee, the U.S. Army had a few skirmishes with Indians, but apart from very few casualties, the army fared well in them.[48]

General Miles came to Pine Ridge on December 31 and took charge of the military operations. The goal of the army from then on was to negotiate and tighten the net around the Ghost Dancers. This proved a successful tactic. After two weeks of fighting and negotiations, the Ghost Dancers surrendered on January 15, 1891.

———

The Lakota Ghost Dance differed from the ceremony of other Ghost Dancing tribes, and to outside witnesses it might have looked "wild and barbaric," but the Lakotas never knowingly changed it toward militaristic

46. On the motives of the army and especially of General Miles, see Andersson, *The Lakota Ghost Dance of 1890*, pp. 128–61. See also Greene, *American Carnage*, 192–95, 318–37.

47. See *Omaha Daily Bee*, December 30, 1890, p. 1; *New York Times*, December 30, 1890, p. 1; *Washington Post*, December 30, 1890, p. 1; *Chicago Tribune*, December 30, 1890, p. 1; *Yankton Press and Dakotan*, December 31, 1890, p. 1; *Harper's Weekly*, January 24, 1891, February 7, 1891. The press started to criticize the army only a few days after the massacre. See, for example, *Chicago Tribune*, January 6, 1891, pp. 1, 4; January 7, 1891, p. 1; *Omaha Daily Bee*, January 6, 1891, p. 1; January 7, 1891, pp. 1, 4; *New York Times*, January 6, 1891, p. 5; *Washington Post*, January 7, 1891, p. 1. For more about press reporting, see, for example, Watson, "The Last Indian War," 213–14; Kolbenschlag, *Whirlwind Passes*, 63–74; Andersson, *The Lakota Ghost Dance of 1890*, 240–50; Greene, *American Carnage*, 307–10.

48. For recent reconstructions of events at Wounded Knee, see Ostler, *The Plains Sioux*, 338–60; Greene, *American Carnage*, 215–46. For a thorough classic account of the massacre see Utley, *Last Days of the Sioux Nation*, 201–30.

directions as often claimed. Rather, it changed to reflect the Lakota religious traditions. The Lakota Ghost Dance also evolved to respond to the needs of the Lakotas. Traditional religious ceremonies of the Lakotas had been banned in 1883, and the Ghost Dance presented a possibility of practicing native religions. The Ghost Dance should not be viewed only as an attempt to revitalize a "dying" culture or to bring back the old ways but also as an innovation. The Ghost Dance sought to accommodate and it looked forward.

The historian Louis Warren has stated that for many Indians, including some Lakotas, the Ghost Dance also served as an assimilation strategy, a way to justify life on a reservation and working for the white man, albeit for the most ardent Ghost Dancers, working for the whites was to be only a temporary situation. In the new world promised by the Ghost Dance, there would be no white men—just a world with traditional Indian customs. Still, the Ghost Dance gave Lakotas and other Indians spiritual authority to take up wage work, education, farming, and churchgoing, while allowing them to resist assimilation. The new religion helped them accommodate themselves to new necessities without giving up their Indian identity. Indeed, it provided a psychological means to survive.[49]

The Ghost Dance sought to find a balance between the old way and the new. If the Ghost Dance is viewed only from the Euro-American perspective, it could appear as a "backward" movement. For the Lakotas, the life they were hoping to get back was not a worse way of life than life on the reservation. The white man's progress had not yielded prosperity to the Lakotas, so perhaps the Ghost Dance could be seen as a progressive religion that sought to find a path to prosperity for the Lakotas as well.

Thus, the Ghost Dance that started as a purely religious ceremony led to many controversies between the Indians and the whites, but also to deep problems within the Lakota society. The controversies arose from the inability of two cultures, that of the Lakotas and of the whites, to understand each other. From these misunderstandings grew various personal and collective disagreements that led to the final act in the United States Indian wars.

---

49. Warren, *God's Red Son*, 144–45; Louis Warren, Personal correspondence with the author, February 2017. See also Maddra, *Hostiles?* 61–62.

Editorial Policy and Source Materials

This book presents various Lakota voices of the Ghost Dance grouped in four categories that emerged while I was working with the material. These categories served as tools when I organized this book, but they are artificial and do not reflect the actual situation since many Ghost Dancers were what could be called "true believers" at some point and then abandoned the Ghost Dance, or vice versa. Opponents of the Ghost Dance can also be divided into those who opposed it for purely political and practical reasons and those who opposed it for religious reasons, the latter consisting mainly of people who had entirely abandoned their traditional beliefs and become Christians. Yet, to avoid too simplistic a picture, one needs to note that many Christian Lakotas also began practicing the Ghost Dance. For them, the Ghost Dance was a way to combine Christianity and their traditional beliefs.[50] The documents presented here also demonstrate that the old idea of the Ghost Dance only appealing to the "nonprogressive," that is, warlike, Lakotas is too simplistic and the situation among the Lakotas was far more complex.

As I was working with the material, it soon became evident that there was much more material available from the Ghost Dancers than the non–Ghost Dancers. Clearly those who participated in it were of more interest to newspapermen, anthropologists, and others who interviewed Lakotas during and after the Ghost Dance period. Documents left by Short Bull, for example, are longer and more detailed than those of, for example, Christian Lakotas. For this reason, there is a slight imbalance between the various parts, the ones presenting the Ghost Dancers' voices dominating.

Overall, these categories and the organization of this book turned out to be even more challenging than I had thought. Finally, I decided to divide the book into four parts that allow us to look beyond those artificial categories. The first part, "We the tribe of Indians, are the ones who are living a sacred life," introduces statements by Ghost Dancers, such as Short Bull, describing the ceremony and the visions as well as the events from the

---

50. For this discussion, see DeMallie, "The Lakota Ghost Dance: An Ethnohistorical Account," 385–405; Andersson, *The Lakota Ghost Dance of 1890*, 48–73. Among the standard works on Lakota religion are, for example, DeMallie and Parks, eds., *Sioux Indian Religion*; James R. Walker, *Lakota Belief and Ritual*, edited by Raymond J. DeMallie and Elaine A. Jahner (Lincoln: University of Nebraska Press, 1991).

beginning of the Ghost Dance among the Lakotas to the final surrender in January 1891. The second part, "We did not think we were doing any harm by dancing our religious dances," includes statements by Lakotas who were Ghost Dancers for a while, then abandoned it. Part 2 also tells the story of the Ghost Dance from the point of view of chiefs like Red Cloud, American Horse, Young Man Afraid of His Horses, and Sitting Bull, all of whom were in many ways caught between the Ghost Dancers and the non–Ghost Dancers. Part 2 reveals their understanding of the political and economic factors, such as famine and broken promises, that played a crucial role in the development of the Ghost Dance "trouble" among the Lakotas. Part 3, "They see their relatives who died long before," presents documents that portray the Ghost Dance through the eyes of Lakotas who did not become Ghost Dancers themselves but witnessed it firsthand. This part also includes the stories told by mixed-bloods and white men married to Indian women (sometimes called "squawmen") who lived among the Lakotas and often acted as interpreters to the Lakotas. In part 4, "Messiya Itóŋšni"—"The Lie of the Messiah," Christian and Western-educated Lakotas and Dakotas express their views on the Ghost Dance. Several never-before-published letters written by famous chiefs, but also by less-well-known individuals are published in this study.

One could, of course, argue that statements by Luther Standing Bear or Charles Eastman, for example, could be placed in part 3 instead of part 4, since the two men were very close to the events on Pine Ridge and Rosebud. Luther Standing Bear, especially, was "caught in between" the Ghost Dancers, the non–Ghost Dancers, and the U.S. Army, which would qualify him for part 2 as well. Dewey Beard or Alice Ghost Horse could also be placed in part 2 instead of part 3, if the idea of them being "caught in between" would be the only criterion.

The examples above show that these categories and parts *are* artificial and thus the organization of the book could also look different. Dividing this book into four parts, however, is my attempt to go beyond the traditional "progressive"–"nonprogressive" dichotomy. Another factor that led me to choose the four-part structure was the type of documents. Part 1, for example, highlights statements focusing on the ceremony and visions, whereas part 2 presents mostly letters and statements given during official meetings and councils. I will comment and further analyze these categories in the introductions to each part and in the annotations.

The documents for this study have been collected from various archives, newspapers, diaries, interviews, letters, and reports, which has made this work challenging compared to an editorial project that collects documents derived from only one or two collections. There are also many types of documents, ranging from council proceedings to individual letters, from newspaper clippings to interviews and to oral stories. Thus, a critical look at each source type has been required, for example, in ascertaining the reliability of the source presented here. For that reason, some otherwise interesting texts have been left out of this study.

I am acutely aware of the fact that these documents are not comprehensive; there are most likely more accounts in archives or private collections that I have not discovered. Still, I believe that after reaching a certain saturation point of documents representing the "major" points of view, the "big picture" does not suffer, if one or two accounts are missed. Nevertheless, I have tried to include as many Lakota accounts as possible in this book. I have included accounts that have never been published before, but in order to get as comprehensive a picture of the Lakota voices as possible, I have included texts published previously. For example, Short Bull gave several accounts of the Ghost Dance and many of them have been published, at least in part, in works such as James Mooney, *The Ghost Dance Religion and the Sioux Outbreak of 1890* (1893), Natalie Curtis, *The Indians Book: Songs and Legends of the American Indian* (1907), or more recently in, for example, Richard E. Jensen, *Voices of the American West, Volume I: The Indian Interviews of Eli S. Ricker, 1903–1919* (2006), Sam Maddra, *Hostiles? The Lakota Ghost Dance and Buffalo Bill's Wild West* (2006), and Rani-Henrik Andersson, *The Lakota Ghost Dance of 1890* (2008). I believe, however, that by publishing all these accounts by Short Bull and others in one volume, we can more fully understand their decisions and actions during and after the Ghost Dance. I have compared the texts published elsewhere to the originals whenever possible. If the original document has been blurred or difficult to read, I have made different interpretations than other scholars based on my reading of the original text and my understanding of the Lakota culture. In these cases, I discuss the issues in the annotations.

In a few cases, I have included very short accounts where I felt that they are useful in shedding additional light on the voice of a particular group. I have also included full interviews or discussions between, for example, U.S. military officials and Lakotas. Sometimes there are only one or two sentences directly about the Ghost Dance, but to understand them in the proper context, I have included the entire text.

In order to gain a comprehensive picture of the Lakota situation in 1889–1890, I have included several accounts describing not only the Ghost Dance but also the famine, the loss of land, broken treaties, and lack of work. Several Lakota leaders, both Ghost Dancers and non–Ghost Dancers emphasized that the Ghost Dance was a reaction to the desperate situation among the Lakotas, which makes these accounts extremely important. Interestingly, some of the letters written during the Ghost Dance also reveal that the dance was not the only issue in Lakota lives in the fall of 1890. Letters by Red Cloud, George Sword, and others discuss matters of daily life, houses, freighting and other work, which shows that life went on despite the Ghost Dance.

Because I want to focus on the Ghost Dance and the circumstances surrounding it, I have left out Lakota accounts that focus *solely* on the Wounded Knee massacre or the death of Sitting Bull. A number of official investigations into the Wounded Knee massacre have been conducted over the years, resulting in a wealth of material that describes the tragic event. Some of them have been published before, others not.[51] I believe that it would require an entire study, or a second volume, to properly deal with all these Lakota accounts that describe the Wounded Knee massacre; for this reason, they have been left out of this study. However, in a few cases, where the story of Wounded Knee or the killing of Sitting Bull is integral to the understanding of an individual's interpretation of the Ghost Dance, I have retained parts dealing with those events.

I have also included accounts by mixed-bloods and men married to Lakota women. They were in a unique position to follow the developments on Lakota reservations, and in many occasions, they served either as interpreters or mediators between the Lakotas and U.S. government officials. The voice of women would be extremely important and would shed more light into our understanding of the Lakota Ghost Dance. Unfortunately, only a few women have left written accounts of the Ghost Dance.

An interesting and perhaps the most challenging part of this project has been the translation of Lakota and Dakota language documents. The fact that in writing old Lakota or Dakota no diacritical or accent marks were used has made the translation process complicated. At times one needs to spend considerable time in trying to understand the real meaning of each word or sentence. The challenge has been especially true in texts by Short Bull, Young Skunk, and Pretty Eagle who describe intense religious experiences full of symbolism and *wakháŋ* (sacred) experiences.

To understand the meaning of these documents, I have sought to place them in a wider context of Lakota history, culture, and belief system.

---

51. For this discussion, see, for example David W. Grua, *Surviving Wounded Knee: The Lakotas and the Politics of Memory* (New York: University of Oxford Press, 2016).

Sometimes I have been forced to look beyond the actual words in the text to make the text understandable. Often it is the context of the Ghost Dance ritual, or the Ghost Dance belief system, that provides the clues that make the otherwise difficult text easier to comprehend. For example, in a text written by Elias Gilbert in the *Iapi Oaye* newspaper, the literal translation of one particular sentence would be: "The people sang this and then a hundred danced close by, but they all stood together *opening upward* and they all were really able to cry." That does not make much sense unless you place it in the context of both the Ghost Dance and the Sun Dance, where dancers often danced with their faces turned up toward the sky. The better translation would be: "The people sang this and then a hundred [people] danced close by, but they all stood together *their faces turned upward* and they all were really able to cry." While the original text does not include the word "face" it is implied and adding it to the English translation makes the text more understandable. For the Lakota texts, I use the orthography of the *New Lakota Dictionary*[52] throughout the study. I have also changed the old orthography, for example, for the word Wakan Tanka (Great Spirit) to modern *Wakȟáŋ Tȟáŋka*. I have changed the Lakota names that appear in the documents written in old Lakota to modern Lakota. The documents also contain Lakota names written in English, such as Scatter or Yellow Bird, and I decided not to (re)translate these into Lakota.

I hope I have done justice to the authors or narrators of these documents. For that reason, I have retained some of the traditional Lakota storytelling style in texts by, for example, Young Skunk, Pretty Eagle, and George Sword.[53] Lakota oral narratives include a lot of repetition and so-called sentence-launching expressions like *yuŋkȟáŋ* or *waná* that translate to "and then" and "now." I have kept some of them despite it being somewhat repetitive in English. At the same time, it needs to be noted that most documents, even those written in Lakota, have been written down by white observers. This, of course, means that there might have been misunderstandings in the translation process. Only some letters and the accounts published in the *Iapi Oaye* and the *Word Carrier* newspapers were

52. Jan Ullrich, ed., *New Lakota Dictionary* (Bloomington, Ind.: Lakota Language Consortium, 2011).
53. For an interesting analysis of the process of translating Lakota oral stories, see Delphine Red Shirt, *George Sword's Warrior Narratives: Compositional Processes in Lakota Oral Tradition* (Lincoln: University of Nebraska Press, 2016).

written by the Indians themselves. I have paid considerable attention to possible misunderstandings or misrepresentations that may have occurred between the original authors and their informants, pointing out problems where necessary. I decided to retain commentaries and additions in the original texts made by the narrator or by the person who took down the narrative in parentheses (like this). My own explanations and additions are in brackets [like this] and longer commentaries are in footnotes. In a few cases where several Lakota accounts are interwoven into one narrative, for example, a newspaper interview, I have kept the comments made by the author of the text, but placed them in *italics*.

I provide further information about the authors or narrators, including their Lakota names, in the introductions to each part whenever possible. I also discuss the context in which the text was produced, whether during the Ghost Dance period or afterwards, in the introduction to each document. I have kept the annotations relatively brief, pointing out possible factual errors and explaining cultural, historical, or religious terms. The literature of the Ghost Dance is vast. I have decided for the most part to stay with the relevant classics and most recent studies.

There are a lot of place names and people that appear in these documents. Whenever these require further explanation, I provide it in the annotations. For some people, like Red Cloud or Sitting Bull, there is plenty of information available, but there are many less well-known individuals who are mentioned in the texts and additional information about them is difficult to find. Whenever necessary I have looked at census records and other sources to fill in the gaps. However, when people are not relevant to the overall story or are only mentioned once, there is no note and readers can look, for example, at the census records if they are interested in finding out more.[54]

54. In order to provide birth and death dates for the authors and narrators of the documents, I have looked at the U.S. census records, Indian census records, and other public records that can be accessed, for example, through www.ancestry.com. Another useful site has been www.findagrave.com/index.html that includes a lot of additional information on people. Still I have not been able to find birth dates or death dates for all individuals whose statements are presented in this book. Especially the death dates seem to be difficult to verify. In a few cases I have been forced to leave the death date open. In several instances, the birth dates vary from one census to another. Likewise, names are spelled differently depending on the year of the census, which makes it very difficult to determine the identities of the people in question.

I have used modern spelling for Lakota tribes, i.e. Oglala, instead of Ogallalla, which was common in the late nineteenth century. The word "tepee" is replaced by the word "tipi." Ghost Dance, as a religion, is always capitalized. For a more readable text, I have also slightly edited letters written by the Lakota into more modern English. Some of the Western-educated Lakotas who wrote to their friends or government officials used what could be called "broken English," which is at times very difficult to read. I have, nevertheless, chosen not to use the intrusive "[*sic*]" but have instead made silent corrections. I have also corrected typos, capital letters, minor grammatical errors (such as subject-verb agreement), and added punctuation, especially in the texts originally written in Lakota, where no punctuation existed. There are cases, such as newspaper interviews, where the broken English used by the Indians was published as such. It is not clear in these cases, if this is how the Lakotas actually spoke, or whether they spoke in Lakota but through an interpreter, or whether this style reflects the journalist's idea of "Indian" English. Since English was not their Native language and we do not know how the interview process unfolded, I have, for the most part, left the text as it appears in the original published articles. Even with these slight editorial decisions, this book presents Lakota accounts of the Ghost Dance in the words of the Lakotas themselves.

PART 1

"We the tribe of Indians, are the ones
who are living a sacred life."

This part presents Ghost Dance accounts by those who could be referred to as "true believers," including several accounts by Short Bull (Tȟatȟáŋka Ptéčela, 1845–1915), a leading Ghost Dance *wičháša wakȟáŋ* (holy man) among the Lakotas.[1] Short Bull belonged to the Brulé *Wažáže* band and was a known medicine man and a noted warrior during the wars of the 1870s. Short Bull's role in the Ghost Dance has been much discussed and many contemporary accounts as well as scholars following James Mooney accused him of being the main instigator of trouble. There is no doubt that he was one of the key figures in teaching and spreading the new religion among the Lakotas. He was chosen as the leader of the Lakota delegation that was sent to meet with the messiah, Wovoka. There is also no doubt that he was a true believer in the Ghost Dance, which can clearly be seen in the documents presented here. Short Bull never lost his faith in the Ghost Dance, and as late as 1911 his son John Short Bull wrote letters to Wovoka asking for further instructions about the Ghost Dance.[2] Over the years Short Bull gave several accounts of his journey to the west and his role in the Ghost Dance. While his narrative changed somewhat over the years, the core message remained the same. His religion was that of peace and did not differ in a significant manner from Wovoka's original teachings.[3]

One of Short Bull's companions on his journey to the west was the Minneconjou Kicking Bear (Matȟó Wanáȟtaka, 1846–1904). He was born Oglala, but became Minneconjou through marriage. Marriage also made him a relative of the famous leader Big Foot. Kicking Bear, too, had participated in the wars of the 1870s and was a friend of Crazy Horse. On the reservation he refused to "walk the white man's road." He was considered very "nonprogressive."[4] Unlike Short Bull, Kicking Bear did not seem to be anxious to talk about the Ghost Dance in his later years. Only one lengthy

1. Research literature often refers to Short Bull as an apostle or evangelist, but for the Lakotas, Short Bull was a *wičhása wakȟáŋ*, a holy man or medicine man. For more on Lakota concepts of medicine men and holy men, see Walker, *Lakota Belief and Ritual.*

2. See, for example, Maddra, *Hostiles?* 186–88.

3. For more on Short Bull, see, for example, Wilhelm Wildhage, "Material on Short Bull," *European Review of Native American Studies* 4, no. 1 (1990): 35–41; Maddra, *Hostiles?* 21–22, 35–38, 187–89.

4. Perhaps the best personal information on Kicking Bear can be found in Miller, *Ghost Dance,* 288–89.

account by him has survived. This account gives additional information about the journey to meet Wovoka and the ideology behind the Lakota Ghost Dance. Kicking Bear's role during the Ghost Dance was significant, since he taught the new religion to, for example, Sitting Bull's people on the Standing Rock Reservation. After the U.S. Army arrived on the Lakota reservations on November 20, 1890, and trouble seemed evident, Kicking Bear became the leading warrior, *blotáhuŋka*. He led the skirmishes following the Wounded Knee tragedy and was one of the last Ghost Dancers to publicly surrender to General Nelson A. Miles in January 1891. Like Short Bull, Kicking Bear continued to believe in the Ghost Dance religion even after Wounded Knee. In 1902 he made another visit to Wovoka that clearly demonstrates that he was still interested in learning more. Based on these later visits and letters to Wovoka, Kicking Bear, among others, helped the Ghost Dance to continue and adapt to new circumstances.[5]

Other lengthy accounts that are presented in this part are those of Oglala holy man Black Elk (Heȟáka Sápa, 1863–1950), Oglala Henry Young Skunk (Maká Čhiŋčála, ca. 1866–1935), and Brulé Pretty Eagle (Waŋblí Wašté, ca. 1836–ca.1906), all of whom experienced remarkable visions during the Ghost Dance ceremonies. These narratives are the most complete accounts of Lakota Ghost Dance visions. Pretty Eagle, however, denied being a Ghost Dancer in a letter to former Rosebud Indian agent Lebbeus Foster Spencer. This is perhaps the most striking example of a person who at one point was a devoted Ghost Dancer and then denounced the dance for reasons that remain unknown. Oglala chief Little Wound is another example of a Lakota who led the Ghost Dancers at one point and later tried to negotiate for a peaceful solution. Their vision experiences are included in this part, while their other statements are presented in parts 2 and 4.

Other, shorter, Lakota accounts regarding the ceremony and visions are included in this part. These include statements by Good Thunder (Wakíŋyaŋ Wašté, ca. 1832–?), another member of the Lakota delegation, as well as statements published in the *Illustrated American* in January 1891 by Weasel (Ithúŋkasaŋ, 1863–?) and Little Horse (Tȟašúŋke Čhiŋčála, 1827–?). Good Thunder was perhaps as important as Short Bull in spreading and teaching the Ghost Dance among the Lakotas. More importantly, his accounts

5. See Maddra *Hostiles?* 186–89; Andersson, *The Lakota Ghost Dance of 1890*, pp. 33–34. About the Ghost Dance after Wounded Knee, see, for example, Richmond L. Clow, "Lakota Ghost Dance After 1890," *South Dakota History* 20, no. 4 (1990): 323–33; Maddra, *Hostiles?* 186–87; Warren, *God's Red Son*, 297–325.

as interpreted by George Sword and William Selwyn became the standard references for scholars studying the Ghost Dance ceremony. (For further discussion, see part 3).

Black Elk, the famous Oglala holy man, experienced a strong vision during a Ghost Dance ceremony. In his own words, he was not sure about the new religion at first, but the vision was so familiar to him that he became a Ghost Dancer. Black Elk's life has been of interest to countless scholars and the general public alike. His story was immortalized in *Black Elk Speaks: Being the Life Story of a Holy Man of the Oglala Sioux* (2004; orig. 1932) by John G. Neihardt. During his long life Black Elk participated in the Little Big Horn battle, became a holy man, converted to Christianity, and traveled to Europe. After returning from Europe he became a Ghost Dancer, participated in the skirmishes after the Wounded Knee massacre, later acted as a Catholic catechist, and eventually became a symbol of Native resistance and a keeper of cultural traditions.[6]

Together these accounts present a vivid picture of the Ghost Dance belief system as well as the ceremony. At the same time, many of these documents and those presented in part 2 make a clear connection with the Ghost Dance and the destitute situation the Lakotas faced in the late 1880s. For many, broken promises, hunger, disease, and the Ghost Dance went hand in hand. The Ghost Dance promised to bring an end to the suffering and perhaps it could also help in accommodating the Lakotas to reservation life. The accounts in this part also create a narrative of the development of the Ghost Dance religion among the Lakotas.

6. For Black Elk's life, see *The Sixth Grandfather: Black Elk's Teachings Given to John G. Neihardt*, ed. Raymond J. DeMallie (Lincoln: University of Nebraska Press, 1985); Michael F. Steltenkamp, *Nicholas Black Elk: Medicine Man, Missionary, Mystic* (Norman: University of Oklahoma Press, 2009).

Short Bull

"My people do not want to fight, they want peace."

This account by Short Bull was recorded by George C. Crager in 1891. The original is entitled "As Narrated by Short Bull," and is archived at the Buffalo Bill Museum and Grave, Golden, Colorado.[7] This is most likely the earliest account given by Short Bull. The text is mostly Short Bull's account as dictated to Crager, but at times the narration seems to move from Short Bull to being Crager's own description of Short Bull's words.[8] The document is Short Bull's description of his journey to meet the Messiah, but also an explanation of events leading to the Wounded Knee Massacre and the final surrender. It differs from his account, for example, in the Eugene Buechel collection or the Weygold Collection (see below), as it is a more detailed depiction of his journey west. It also reveals that there were many factions even among the Ghost Dancers throughout the fall of 1890. Short Bull's account, while to a certain extent a defense of his actions, gives valuable information on what was going on among the Ghost Dancers. They had no clear plan about where to go or what to do, let alone starting a major uprising. As they were moving toward Pine Ridge from Rosebud, the people were arguing with each other, finally ending up camping in the Badlands.[9] In the Badlands camp, sometimes called Óhaŋzi in Lakota and Stronghold in English, the Ghost Dancers hoped to be safe from the U.S. military. During their

---

7. Short Bull in "As Narrated by Short Bull," recorded by George C. Crager, 1891, published by permission of Buffalo Bill Museum and Grave, Golden, Colo. (MS [1891]). Published also in Maddra, *Hostiles?* Appendix 1.

8. See Maddra, *Hostiles?* 11–12; Warren, *God's Red Son*, 181–82. The parentheses in the text are by Crager.

9. The journey of several hundred Brulés from Rosebud toward Pine Ridge caused a lot of apprehension in the press, but also among the agents. These people were often described as being on the warpath and extremely hostile. For this discussion in the press, see Andersson, *The Lakota Ghost Dance of 1890*, pp. 200–25. In reality, these people were already dissatisfied as they had been ordered to relocate. See, for example, Maddra, *Hostiles?* 52; Greene, *American Carnage*, 349.

Short Bull, ca. 1891.
Photo: D. F. Barry.
Denver Public
Library, Western
History Collection,
B-567.

stay in the Badlands the Ghost Dancers' unity gradually broke down to such an extent that Short Bull thought his companions would kill him. It is also worth noting that Short Bull says that he asked Agent George Wright for a job as a freighter, but was denied. This demonstrates that Short Bull tried to live up to Wovoka's suggestion of adapting to the white man's customs.[10]

10. For further discussion about working as a central theme in the Ghost Dance and on the Ghost Dance as an accommodation strategy and passive rejection of dependency, see Maddra, *Hostiles?* 61–62; Warren, "Wage Work in the Sacred Circle"; Warren, *God's Red Son.*

In the fall of 1889 I was at Cheyenne [River] Agency and returned to Rosebud Agency in time for the issue [of rations]. I then went to carrying freight for the government between Valentine, Nebraska and Rosebud Agency. I had made one trip and [was] getting ready to make another, when a messenger handed me a letter. I asked for whom the letter was, [and] his answer was, "Take it to the council house." I done so, the council house was full of people as they were dancing "Omaha" [Omaha dance] at the time. I went at night to the council house again, and saw two Brulés searching through the crowd as if looking for someone. One of the men was Eagle Pipe. When they saw me, they pulled off my blanket and placed me in the center of the circle—at this time I did not know what they meant—they then selected Scatter whom they said was to go with me on a great mission. Standing Bear (Brulé) gave me a new blanket and leggings, saying: "We have a letter from the west saying the Father has come and we want you to go and see him (meaning the Messiah). You must try and get there, see him, recognize him and tell us what he says and we will do it. Be there with a big heart. Do not fail."[11] (These were the expressions of the entire council.) It may here be said that those present in the council room were all armed because Two Strike's son had choked one of the Indian police, and a fight was going on outside. I said nothing but thought a good deal. The next morning another council was held and here they told me what my mission was to be. Men and women were assembled and my uncle spoke, saying: "I am not afraid to tell you what this letter contains." It was read and the wind was blowing so furiously that the whole house was filled with dust, but as soon as the reading of the letter began the wind ceased—this gave me confidence.[12] I had faith to go. I had no belief in it before but now my mind was made up. My people know I was a man of truth and could be relied on. I stood up and said: "My brothers, you are all sitting here with your guns; this is not what

11. It is unclear if the person identified here as Brulé Standing Bear is the same person as Luther Standing Bear. In any case, Luther Standing Bear himself does not mention this meeting in his account of the Ghost Dance (see part 4). Most likely he was Luther Standing Bear's father, who at the time was living on Pine Ridge. See Richard N. Ellis, introduction to Luther Standing Bear, *My People the Sioux* (Lincoln: University of Nebraska Press, 1975).

12. William S. E. Coleman says that the letter that was read in the council was the actual letter by Wovoka, later known as the "Messiah letter" and published, for example, by Mooney. Yet Short Bull does not say that the letter was from the Messiah; he states that it was received from the west. In fact, it could not have been the "Messiah letter" as that letter was presented by Wovoka to Southern Cheyennes and Southern Arapahos in the summer of 1890, whereas the "letter from the west" had already been read in the

the Messiah wants us to do, and when I leave here I ask you to drop your arms, follow my trail, watch my movements and have no trouble with the whites or police, be as one, drop no blood; if I have to stay two years I will try and see him myself and bring you his words."

Sore Back arose and said: "My boy, I select you to go west. You ask me to drop my arms and be peaceful and I will do it; I look to you to bring us the good word. Don't think we will shed any blood, we will do right."

Two days after this council Scatter and I started, we went to Pine Ridge Agency, (but before starting High Hawk's brother gave us a buggy). We found at Pine Ridge that Kicking Bear, He Dog, Flat Iron, Yellow Knife, Brave Bear and Twist Back had left two days before for the West and on the night previous Yellow Breast and Broken Arm had left.[13] We were delayed one day at Pine Ridge to have the buggy repaired. We then started off and after hard travelling for two and one half days we caught up with the Oglalas at Sage Creek near Casper Mountains [Wyoming]. Here we also met Man and his two nephews Louis and John Shangrau[14] who were returning to the agency from a trip to Fort Washakie [Wyoming]. We told them we were traveling west to meet the Messiah. We then traveled on to the Arapahos at Shoshone Agency where we stayed until one week after Christmas, when we started on horseback to the end of "Painted Rock" here we boarded a railroad train and arrived at a point where only Chinamen were. The agent at Fort Washakie gave us railroad passes, Sitting Bull[15] gave me 25 Dollars and I sold one of my beaded vests for $10. While we were at Shoshone Agency we danced the "Omaha" and got presents of money. We stayed three days at the Chinaman's town, we then boarded another train travelling one day and night, but owing to a "hot box" we had to get out at the forks of a large creek where we camped for the night; the next morning we walked about 1½ miles reaching a small town, and once more began to travel by

council at Pine Ridge already in the fall of 1889. Coleman, *Voices of Wounded Knee*, 9. For the Messiah letters, see Mooney, *The Ghost-Dance Religion*, 780–81; Andersson, *The Lakota Ghost Dance of 1890*, Appendix 1.

13. Here again the list of participants is different from, for example, Short Bull's account in Buechel. For a list of the members, see introduction.

14. John and Louis Shangrau were mixed-blood brothers from Pine Ridge, who acted as scouts for the U.S. military. For their role in the Ghost Dance, see, for example, Utley, *Last Days of the Sioux Nation*, 140–43, 193–96, 237–39; Maddra, *Hostiles?* 93. See also part 3.

15. This refers to the Arapaho Ghost Dance leader by the name of Sitting Bull. See Mooney, *The Ghost-Dance Religion*, 297–324.

rail. The snow was so deep that plows were used to clear the road which delayed us three days in a small town; on the fourth night the road was open so that we could travel again; after spending the night on the train we came to a creek which was lined on either side by lodges; a town was near so we got off the cars, travelling by foot to this Indian village. The snow was very deep. Two of the men of this camp had been to see the Messiah. The chief of the tribe was the brother of old Washakie, who set up a tipi for us; we stayed nine days and nights, five of which were spent in "Ghost Dancing"—despite the snow, but a rainstorm came up and melted the snow shortly after the dancing began. Here 10 Bannocks came over and took us with them, horses were provided for us at an agency named "Pocktella" [Pocatello]. Here we met two big Indians, one with long black hair and the other with a black beard which looked so strange, they were both holding horses; the bearded man's name was Botee and the other Elks Tusk Necklace. At the request of Washakie's brother, Yellow Breast and myself remained with him, while the others left. We went to his house and here I saw a Dakota woman who was married to a white man. Washakie's brother told me that the Messiah would talk to me, but he wanted to say something to me first—saying: "Once I went to Washington and had a talk with Spotted Tail, Two Strike and Red Cloud (speaking in the sign language). Pay no attention to what some people say, the Messiah will tell you the truth. I shook hands with all the Sioux Chiefs and dropped my arms against them for good and am their friend. Don't be afraid, no one will harm you here, we are all friends—you will not die." Here the Bannocks came in for their rations and they gave us rations too, also horses and took us with them to the other party who had gone on ahead, and we held a council at the house of Elks Tusk Necklace who said: "My heart is glad to see all of you people today, my people here always do as I ask of them; we shake your hands and are glad that fighting we done in the past is dropped. We are friends and hope we will always be so. Now we will go together to the Messiah. He sent for me three times and I went, he has now sent for me again and I will go with you."

After remaining here ten days, over one hundred boarded the cars and travelled from the evening till the next night, where we changed cars to arrive at another agency of the Shoshones.[16] From this point Sitting Bull of the Arapahos, Short Bull of the Sioux, Porcupine of the Cheyennes, and several Bannocks started for the Messiah by rail; after travelling from town to town for two days, we came to an Indian village whose tipis were made

16. This is most likely the Fort Hall Agency in Idaho.

of bark and willows. The chief's name was Owns the People of the Rabbit Skin tribe (their blankets and bedding being made of rabbit skins),[17] the women were dressed like the white women and they lived on fish, they have an agency, their rations are small and one beef suffices for the whole band, they are rich, they fish continually and sell it.

From this point we moved in wagons and other conveyances for one day to the Puites [Paiutes] where we remained thirteen days and then began to travel west, camping on a large creek the first night, and then following the railroad to a station where some young men and women of the "Rabbit Skin" tribe met us who told us to go to the right of a large house in the distance and there remain two days, which was done.

After waiting two days the party started overland, all but one Gros Ventre, a chief of the Rabbit Skins, Two Bannocks and Short Bull who boarded a train at about 3 o'clock in the morning and at sundown reached a white man's village where an agency was. This was the supposed home of the Messiah.[18] They met some Indians who told them the Messiah would come in three days. Short Bull here found out that the letter that was sent to all Indian reservations asking them to gather at this point was written by an Indian.

The spot selected was a lovely one, a heavy growth of willow all around it, and a circle had been cut down in the center with entrances North, South, East and West. Short Bull was put at the West end with a Gros Ventre and Sitting Bull (Arapaho).[19] In this circle were only a few Indian chiefs, all the rest camping outside. In two days the wagon party came, besides every train bringing more and more people to this great gathering, who had been sent for from all parts of the United States. There were Sioux, Cheyenne, Arapahos, Puites [Paiutes], Gros Ventres, Bannocks, "Rabbit Skins,"[20] Indians with rings in their nose and others, names of which Short Bull did not know. Being tired Short Bull laid down but the next day got in a wagon

---

17. "Rabbit Skin Tribe," "Rabbit Skin Wearers," or "Rabbit Skin Blanket Wearers" refer to the Paiutes.

18. Wovoka's home was in Mason Valley on the Walker River Reservation. For Wovoka's family and early life see Hittman, *Wovoka*, 27–62.

19. Placing Short Bull and the others in the west end of the circle signifies respect for these visitors, the west being the direction of, for example, inner reflection, wisdom, power of water and life. In Lakota, the place of honor, opposite the door, in a tipi was called *čhatkú*.

20. Here the term "Rabbit Skins" does not seem to refer to the Paiutes as usual. It is, however, impossible to determine what the reference here is.

and went out to a ridge which would be the spot where the Messiah would arrive; after looking for some time could see no signs of him when finally a messenger arrived, asking for a conveyance to bring the great man in. It was given him, the crowds then mounted their horses to go and meet him, but in a short time the wagon appeared from which direction it came no one knew, it contained two persons. The driver, an Indian, dressed in white man's clothing; and another man who had on a broad brimmed brown hat with two eagle feathers in it, and a striped blanket. The person with the blanket on was the Messiah. Short Bull wanted to shake hands with him but the chief told him not to, saying: "Wait till you go back then he will shake hands with you." At dusk I went out and told all my people to come in. Inside the circle a small tipi was put up for the Messiah. He entered with his face toward the South, the tipi was opened and we all stood before him, everybody crowding to get a glimpse of him. He took off his hat laying it on the ground with the crown down and brim up and said: "How." An old man sat in front of him with his arms extended on his knees and another behind him in the same position, these were his interpreters. While the Messiah spoke these men would stand up and interpret what he said. Short Bull sat directly in front of the Messiah and looked him all over from head to foot.

(At this stage of the story Short Bull went into a trance remaining so for quite a while and then continued). One of these interpreters talked in English to one of the Arapahos named Singing Grass, a son of old chief Friday, who spoke to me in the sign language. The Messiah said: "I have sent for you and you came to see me. I will talk with you tomorrow, today I will talk to these people who have been here so long. We will now pray." Here all who were assembled crowded in with their faces turned toward the west; the Messiah made a speech, but they did not tell me what he said. I got a good look at him, he was dark-skinned, talked in a language similar to Indian and I believe he was an Indian. After he had ceased talking, dancing began in which he joined. Men, women, and all were singing and dancing with hands joined in a peculiar way, knuckle to knuckle, going round and round. Keeping it up for a long time.

The next morning a crier called out for all to assemble as the Messiah was coming. The inner circle was spread over with white sheets for the people to sit on. Everything was quiet. The Messiah stood up and looked toward the west and began to talk (through four interpreters) he said to Short Bull: "I have sent for you to tell you certain things that you must do. There are two chiefs at your agencies and I want you to help them all you can. Have your people work the ground so they do not get idle, help your agents and get farms, this is one chief. The other chief is the church, I want you to help him for he tells you of me; when you get back go to church. All these churches are mine, if you go to church when you get back, others will do the same. I have raised two bodies of men on this earth and have dropped one of them that is the Army; I want no more fighting. Take pity on one another, and whenever you do anything that is bad something will happen to you—I mean fights between the Indians and whites—all over the world one should be like the other and no distinction made; always sing and pray about me, for it is right. Two days from now all nations will talk one tongue (Short Bull thinks he meant 200 or 2 years) the sign talk will be no more. Educate your children, send them to schools." He prayed again and stopped. These are all the words I got from him. While they were dancing the Ghost Dance, I saw white men, women and girls joining in the dance.[21] I saw the Messiah daily for five days, his name was tattooed on the back of his left hand; on the fifth day I shook hands with him and all he said was that "soon there would be no world, after the end of the world those who went to church would see all their relatives that had died (resurrection). This will be the same all over the world even across the big waters."

He advised us to return again in the fall of the following year when he would have more to tell us, but for reasons we did not go.

Our party returned by the same route we came, only one accident occurring, the train was overturned and fell over an embankment but no one was hurt.

When I reached Rosebud Agency everybody looked for me. On the second day after my arrival, I went to the council house to tell them all about what I had seen and heard, but was stopped by Indian police by order of the agent. They arrested me and took me before the agent to whom I told my story. He told me if I would tell this story to the Indians I would be a dead man. I laughed and said it was good, "I wanted to tell the Indians what I have told you but the police stopped me."[22]

When the Ghost Dancing began I did not go there but went afterwards;

21. This is an interesting comment. I have not found other Lakota statements besides Short Bull's suggesting that whites and Indians would dance together. However, there were claims, for example, in the newspapers that some whites, especially Mormons, joined the Paiutes in their Ghost Dance ceremonies. Gregory E. Smoak, "The Mormons and the Ghost Dance of 1890," *South Dakota History* 16, no. 3 (1986): 269–94; Mooney, *The Ghost-Dance Religion*, 766, 792–93; Andersson, *The Lakota Ghost Dance of 1890*, pp. 26–27, 199; Warren, *God's Red Son*, 54–57.

22. For the arrest of Short Bull and the discussion on Agent Wright's actions on Rosebud see Andersson, *The Lakota Ghost Dance of 1890*, pp. 40–41, 104–105.

it was not started by me but by Scatter. Once one of the Indian Police and interpreter Louis Rubadeau insulted me, I did not say much to them but said this: "The Messiah told me not to fight and I will not; you may take a gun and kill me if you want to." Louis Rubadeau said to me: "See if one of the dancers who are in a fit see the Messiah, I[f] you can't do it you will be lost." At this Louis' brother who was nearby, grabbed him and dragged him away. Louis told Turning Bear if "you will kill Short Bull, the agent will give you one hundred dollars, two horses, a cow and a yoke of oxen." *Turning Bear told this to Short Bull who laughed and said nothing. Turning Bear was told to rush into the tipi, grab Short Bull and if he had him help would rush in to assist him to finish the job. This was in May and the Ghost Dancing had well begun.*

One day while a dance was in progress I stood up in the center and told all my people what the Messiah had done and said. The people kept the dancing up with a good will. My funds were now getting low so I applied to the agent for an order to get some freight at Valentine; this was refused me, I was somewhat angered but said nothing. I then went to live with my uncle Hawk Eagle. I lived with him sometime, occasionally visiting the dances and finally participated in them, becoming in time a "regular" dancer—day and night. I kept telling my people of the Messiah and they had faith in him—this was good. While in the ring dancing one day one of the Indian Police, a son of Rope Necklace (a Cut-Off [band member]), caught hold of my shoulder and turned me around [and] said: "You have you [no] ears,"[23] (the dancing stopped) and White Horse told the policeman to go away, as the Messiah's words were right, he only wanted the people to do two things, farm and go to church. We should not fight but be friends. I do not see any wrong in that, it is right and true. Short Bull has told the agent all these things. We sent him to see the Messiah and we believe the words he has brought—he speaks the truth—the Indian police are making trouble and soon plenty of whites will come here and make us trouble. That is all I have to say." And the policeman left and dancing was resumed.[24]

---

23. "Having ears" in Lakota culture signified responsibility and respect. For more, see Raymond J. DeMallie, "These Have No Ears: Narrative and the Ethnohistorical Method," *Ethnohistory* 40, no. 4 (1993): 515–38.

24. The Indian policemen were sent by the Indian agents several times to investigate the Ghost Dance. It is therefore difficult to determine exact dates for the encounter described here. The most famous incident occurred in late August when Agent Hugh D. Gallagher with several policemen entered a Ghost Dance camp. For this incident, see Coleman, *Voices of Wounded Knee*, 50–53; Andersson, *The Lakota Ghost Dance of 1890*, pp. 103–105.

The next day Sore Hip sent for me and I went to him. He told me that he had seen Red Cloud some time ago in reference to transferring a number of families to Pine Ridge Agency and that he was going to see him again and that he would be back in five days, but requested me to go to my home and stay there until he should return, which I done. But while en route from the agency to my home, I was met by a band of Oglalas who had come over for the purpose of dancing. So we camped, all the young men (Brulés and Oglalas) danced the Ghost Dance. Among the young men was a brother of Iron Foot who took quite a lively interest, he said he had seen the Messiah and was much "worked up" over it. (Short Bull does not know if this young man saw the Messiah in person, or if he had only seen him in a trance while dancing the Ghost Dance.)

On the 5th day I went to Black Pipe Creek and waited for Sore Hip, all those who wanted to be transferred to Pine Ridge Agency going along. We met Sore Hip who told us that all had been arranged for our removal and that we were to start in four days. So on the night of the third day those who had no wagons moved to Pass Creek and the main body was to move the next day, but before moving we had a great Ghost Dance that night. In the middle of the night I was awakened by a friend who told me that many of my people were moving toward Pine Ridge Agency which surprised me, and some Indian freighters who had just returned from Valentine sent me word that soldiers were moving toward Rosebud Agency. I did not know why this should be, and it made me angry. One of these freighters, Rescuer son of Elk Road, told me that they were coming to arrest me and if I was not given up they would fire on us all. It was on account of many lies spread by others that I was to be arrested for. Rescuer said all the freighters heard the same, this was in November. I called my people together on Pass Creek[25] and told them to move forward and I would stay here alone, as I did not want them to have any trouble on my account. I want nothing but what was right for myself and my family. I had done as they wanted me to, and now have no rest, day or night. My brother White Thunder and my cousin Thumb had been killed for jealousy and now they want me. "Go on, I will stay here if they want to kill me they are welcome."

25. While camped at Pass Creek, Short Bull was reported to have given a talk to the gathered Ghost Dancers. His talk was published in major newspapers and was referred to as "Short Bull's Sermon." The speech was dated October 30. However, the soldiers arrived at Pine Ridge and Rosebud Agencies on November 20. Short Bull also said that it was November when he camped at Pass Creek. Interestingly, Short Bull does not mention making any major speech while camped at Pass Creek, although he does say that he gathered his people there. For "Short Bull's Sermon," see below.

That night they moved, all save myself and a few young men, my family who were on Pass Creek moved also; that night my brother came to me and said it was all lies that the freighters said, and the next morning some of the young men came back for me and I followed them camping that night on Crow Creek. We broke camp the next morning, moving to Medicine Creek where we rested, camping that night at the forks of Medicine Root Creek. The next morning an Oglala came to us telling us to move our camp to the crossing by American Horse's village, which we done. Having settled our camp we went in a body to the home of Little Wound singing (which signifies a treaty of friendship). An old man known as Issowonie rode around our circle and stopped in the middle saying to us: "My boys, save your powder, guns, bows, arrows and ammunition, for the agency is full of soldiers. Red Cloud says if they do anything we will fight them, and Little Wound says the same; our own people have caused the soldiers to come here by telling lies, American Horse, Charging Thunder, Fast Thunder, Spotted Horse and Good Back told these lies, tomorrow morning we will go to Wounded Knee Creek."

The agent had sent for Little Wound to bring Short Bull and his people to the agency, so Little Wound started with Short Bull and ten Brulés; they halted at the house of Cherry Cedar where they eat [ate] some dried meat, continuing afterward to the agency bluffs and resting. Little Wound going on ahead to the agency, it was sundown when Cheyenne Creek was reached, and afterwards going to the lodge of Twist Back on the agency. While in this lodge, I was called out by some of my young men who told me the Indian soldiers were about to surround us; at this we remounted our horses and rode back to our camp on Wounded Knee Creek. Our people were surprised and feared something was wrong. The old crier then told me to move my people who were poorly mounted to the Badlands, as his people had told him to bring me this word, and should anything happen Red Cloud and the rest would join us there with plenty of horses. The Oglalas brought a large lot of horses to us, saying that they belonged to a white man ("Big Bat")[26] who lived up the creek; we went to him and he told us that "if there is going to be fight he could not take his horses with him as he had so many all over the country and if we wanted to ride them we could." So some of the Brulés did take them; Sore Hip, High Hawk and Chief of the Black Hills

26. Big Bat was a nickname for Baptiste Pourier, who was married to an Oglala woman. For his comments about the Ghost Dance, see part 3.

(a white man who is a judge)[27] came out to us to have a talk. I did not go to the council and don't know what was said. The next morning we moved toward the Badlands and camped there that night. High Hawk and the others returning to the agency, no good being done by them. After we went into camp some half breed Indians came to us, No Ear was in charge asking us for stray horses. They looked through our herd and while picking some out one of our Indians was kicked in the head so we killed the horse that kicked him. The shot caused an excitement in the camp, which only proved to be some wrangling among the Indians. I called them together and bid them to stop, saying "I wanted no trouble. You must stop, you should do right, have no fighting, you have taken and butchered other people's cattle and stolen horses, we will move back to the agency, sell our ponies, pay for these cattle and have no more trouble; the Oglalas must listen to what I say as well as the Brulés, you have plenty of dried meat now, but do as I ask you."

They would not listen but moved toward White River. I again asked them to listen, they had no ears, telling them to go to the agency and that as soon as I got over being mad I would come in too. At this the young men surrounded me, I covered my head with my blanket so I could not see who would kill me for I heard their guns cock, one of them spoke up bidding me to uncover my face so I done it. I told them the reason I covered my face was that I did not care to see who would kill me, and wanted no trouble. The women then came in crying, the warriors left to recall the party who had started for the Agency and brought them back to my camp, which was on the hill by the Badlands. Five of our men were then sent to Cheyenne River to buy sugar and other things for our use and as they neared a house, at the end of which was a haystack, they were fired upon by a party of whites and my nephew Circle Elk, a young boy who had been to school at Carlisle was killed.[28] He could speak English and for that reason was sent with the party. When the four returned all of the young men mounted their horses to

27. The "Chief of Black Hills" refers to Lawrence County Judge John H. Burns from Deadwood. He visited the Ghost Dance camp in late November and upon returning to the Pine Ridge Agency reported that the Indians were preparing for war. See Greene, *American Carnage*, 150.

28. Short Bull is very vague about the date, even the month of this event, but skirmishes between ranchers and Ghost Dancers were reported in newspapers throughout November and December. According to newspapers, the Indians were fighting against the settlers, the cowboys, and the army. In reality, there were only few minor incidents between local ranchers and the Ghost Dancers. See Utley, *Last Days of the Sioux Nation*, 231–55; Coleman, *Voices of Wounded Knee*, 67–71; Andersson, *The Lakota Ghost Dance of 1890*, 200–224; Greene, *American Carnage*, 156, 161–62.

bring back the body of my nephew. I could see them in the distance going backward and forward when finally one of them returned saying they had met a band of Oglalas from Pine Ridge Agency and they had taken away their guns. I told him to go back and return the guns, they had not been sent out to make trouble but to bring back the body of my nephew; he went back to the place and they all came back to the camp. Roaming Walk, who had a "Medicine Pipe" (made of bone) laid it before me to fill and smoke but Porcupine Belly shot it (which means I break the treaty). Crow Dog and Roaming Walk were very much dissatisfied all the time, so we took their guns from them, and some of the Oglalas said they would return to Pine Ridge Agency and kill us all.

The next morning we all assembled on the dancing ground and Knob Arrow said: "Let us ditch this hill and if anyone comes here they cannot get to us." I told them to do as they pleased, but to first get my nephew's body, whereupon some of the young men started, the remainder digging the ditch. They found the body partly burned by prairie fire so it was wrapped up and left. We then went over to where the fire was and were met by white soldiers who fired on us, so we turned back. I then told my people if these soldiers fire on you, fire back and when we got close to them again they fled. (The soldiers here mentioned were Cowboys). Again while a party of my men were out on foot one day they were attacked by soldiers, no one was killed but one was wounded; they had but one gun with them and in their flight lost that. After this my people stole more horses, Lone Bull getting a fine gray horse which he rode.

The next day a delegation of Oglalas came to us from Pine Ridge to make a treaty.[29] Among the chiefs were No Neck, Yankton Charlie, Standing Bear, and Crow Dog.[30] They brought us presents, we killed one of the stolen cattle and made a feast; I told these chiefs that if my people would be allowed to go to Pine Ridge to live and draw rations there, they would all be satisfied to go in. At this Fast Thunder arose [and] pointing to me said: "You are the man who wants to get your people in trouble." To which I asked him: "What do you mean?" He said: "You are trying to have your people fight.

29. Also among the delegation was Louis Shangrau. For his report of the meeting, see part 3.

30. There seems to be a mistake here, since Crow Dog was among the Ghost Dancers and according to Louis Shangrau was almost killed by the Ghost Dancers when he announced that he would go to the agency. Perhaps Short Bull counted Crow Dog as one of those who belonged to the "agency people." See Louis Shangrau in part 3.

Now I ask you to do something wonderful that this Messiah told you to do. If you can do it; I will also believe in him." I then said: "My people do not want to fight, they want peace. I told them what the Messiah said. He did not invest me with any spiritual power, but here is a ghost [dance] shirt. Take any gun and shoot it if you can." He asked for my gun, but I told him to use his own gun and cartridge.

Here young Jack Red Cloud my cousin came between us and said: "Pay no attention to this man. He is crazy, or else he would not speak as he does." I said: "You ask me to stop and I will do it. This shooting at the shirt is only a trick and now I will not let him shoot at it."

The next morning we held a council at which it was decided that we all move in together toward the Agency on the following day, but some starting that same day. The next morning at daybreak the main camp moved, all but Short Bull and his uncle Come Away from the Crowd; during all this time we were being watched by some Cheyenne Indian soldiers, watching all of our movements, but they could not get to us.[31]

That night my uncle and I started to reach our main body that had gone away in the morning, but as we failed to reach them we camped by ourselves on a large hill. At daylight the next day we heard the firing of guns and cannon, so we started off in the direction of the firing and before we got there heard more firing; we met a white man who was driving in the woods after fire wood and we asked him the cause of this firing, he told us it was the soldiers (of whom there were many at the Agency) practicing at targets, and they shoot all the time. So we moved on and as we reached the big hill, we could look down and there saw the village, everything was in a fearful state. Further on were other Indians coming toward the village and it looked as if trouble was near. I went into the village and was there told that Big Foot's (or Spotted Elk's) band had been all killed. I saw my cousin Many Wounds, who was there and confirmed this report in a measure as he himself [had] been wounded in the shoulder; he told me that all his relatives, father, mother, all had been killed, all of their guns were taken from them and then they were fired on, and could do nothing. He continued saying: "I do not know how it happened, I was in my lodge putting on my shirt and leggings when the firing commenced; this will make our hearts bad for a

31. Approximately forty Cheyennes living on Pine Ridge acted as scouts for the army during the latter part of the Ghost Dance trouble. See Utley, *The Last Days of the Sioux Nation*, 119.

long time and we will fight the soldiers." I told him: "It is not right, even if all our relatives are killed we will do right; they blame us when we are not to be blamed. We will now wait and see if the soldiers continue to fire on us. After three days we will try and protect ourselves and families the best we can; I am not to blame; the whites fired on us first, twenty-three of my own relations were killed in this fight, men, women and children; this is like butchery. Why do they kill helpless women and children? This shows the soldiers want us all to die off. When our Indians fought against an enemy of their own color you know what kind of a man I was, I laughed and feared nothing, but now I do not want you to fight, take care of the women and children, I am not looking for trouble, but if I am angered I am the worst among you. I have put all badness from me and want to be a good man. I will go over to where the battle was fought in the morning and see the bodies of my relatives. When I return if the soldiers fire on you, I will remember my old feelings, stand up and be a soldier once more."

The next morning with four others we started for the battlefield. I was looking over the dead bodies and while so doing heard cannons in the distance, in the direction of [White] Clay Creek.[32] I found one of my uncles who had been badly shot in the leg but not dead, who told me this: "All of the Indians had their guns and knives taken from them and as I went to my lodge to get my knife to surrender it, the firing began, I was shot in the leg and have laid here ever since, I do not know where the women and children are." So we "hitched up" four of the wagons we found here and put the horses to them, picking up all that we could find who were not dead (some forty odd) taking them to a deserted house nearby on Wounded Knee Creek. Those whom we thought fatally wounded we left here and with the rest we started for our camp. It began to snow during the night and by morning a heavy snow had fallen, but we started for Wounded Knee about noon; when we reached the house we saw our friends were gone, but afterwards ascertained that they had been taken to the agency by the friendlies in charge of No Neck. During all this time my heart was bad, yet I did not want my people to fight the government. I might have done much harm but always kept my people from it, I wanted no fighting, I wanted to do as the Messiah bid me.

32. After Wounded Knee there were several skirmishes between the Ghost Dancers and the soldiers. See introduction.

Some 10 days afterwards a delegation was sent out to see us from General Miles, asking us to return to the agency so as to save any more bloodshed.[33] General Miles sent to us several times but we paid no attention, but now I told my people: "Pack up everything you have and we will move toward the agency and I hope we will be allowed to live there in peace. General Miles said we shall not be fired on and I believe him; we will surrender our guns and have peace." This message I sent to General Miles. So the next morning we went to the agency. We were asked to surrender our arms, I had a good Winchester rifle, which I surrendered freely and so did my people. General Miles asked me if I had any more guns, I told him I had an old patched up gun the stock and barrel being wrapped with buckskin and not worth anything. He asked me to turn it in, which I done. Some ten days afterwards General Miles asked me to go to Fort Sheridan, with Kicking Bear and some twenty-five others (in all twenty-four men and three women). We started at the same time that a delegation went to Washington to hold a council with the "Great Father."[34] When we reached Chicago we got off the train and were taken to Fort Sheridan. While there we were often visited by General Miles, who with all the officers there made us as comfortable as could be, doing all in their power for us.

In the spring "Long Hair" (Colonel William F. Cody, "Buffalo Bill") came to see us and made us a proposition to join his company across the "big water," we said we would consider the matter, and later on Major John M. Burke came to see us. We held a council and he made us such grand offers to see the "great country beyond the water" with good salary that we all consented to go, and started with sixty of our friends and relatives (from Pine Ridge Agency). Our trip across the water made me somewhat sea sick but as soon as I got on land again was in good health. Ever since I have been with the Company, I have been well treated and cared for, all of the promises made have been fulfilled. Colonel Cody, Mr. [Nathan] Salsbury and Major [John M.] Burke as well as the entire Company are our friends, and do all they can for us in every way. We get good food three times a day, good clothing, warm bedding and plenty of wood. If our people have any

33. General Nelson A. Miles came to Pine Ridge on December 30. He started sending delegations to the Ghost Dancers' camp, which led to their surrender in mid-January 1891. See Utley, *The Last Days of the Sioux Nation*, 255–61; Andersson, *The Lakota Ghost Dance of 1890*, pp. 157–59; Greene, *American Carnage*, 330–32.
34. Among the delegation were Two Strike, Crow Dog, Little Wound, American Horse, Young Man Afraid of His Horses, and High Hawk. Their accounts given in Washington, D.C., can be found in part 2.

complaints it is fixed at once, if we do not feel well, a doctor comes and looks after us. Besides we go everywhere and see all the great works of the Country through which we travel. It learns us much, we see many people who are all kind to us, I like the English people but not their weather as it rains so much.[35]

Short Bull

"An eagle carried me and took me to where my relatives lived."

This narrative was told by Short Bull to Ivan Stars and Father Eugene Buechel in 1915 and later published in Paul I. Manhart, ed., *Lakota Tales and Texts: In Translation*, volume 2, in 1978. The translation, however, contains several errors that affect the interpretation of this and other texts by Young Skunk and Pretty Eagle presented below. This is a new translation by Raymond J. DeMallie, Dennis M. Christafferson, and Rani-Henrik Andersson, American Indian Studies Research Institute, Indiana University, Bloomington, Indiana, from the original manuscript held in the records of the Holy Rosary Mission, Special Collections and Archives, Marquette University Libraries, Milwaukee.[36] This text, like "As Narrated by Short Bull," describes the journey west and the inauguration of the Ghost Dance among the Lakotas. It also gives an insight into Short Bull's Ghost Dance visions. In these visions, he saw the spirits of his dead relatives, just as Wovoka had promised. In one vision he talked to "the Son of God," that is, the Messiah (Wovoka), who gave him further instructions about the Ghost Dance. In his

---

35. Short Bull, Kicking Bear, and the others were taken to Fort Sheridan, Illinois, as prisoners of war. For their imprisonment and subsequent employment in (William F. Cody's) Buffalo Bill's Wild West show, see Maddra, *Hostiles?*

36. Short Bull in EBMC, HRMSCA, MUA. Published by permission of Marquette University Special Collections and Archives. For a different translation, see Paul I. Manhart, *Lakota Tales and Texts, In Translation* (Chamberlain, S.D.: Tipi Press, 1998), 2:509–18. Parts of the new translation was published in Andersson, *The Lakota Ghost Dance*, and with our permission in Maddra, *Hostiles?* Appendix 5.

visions, Short Bull saw a greenish land, a beautiful land inhabited by happy people, including his dead relatives. These themes became very common in the Lakota Ghost Dance tradition. In Short Bull's vision, the Son of God promises that he [the Messiah] will soon truly be with his relatives, but first he will meet them in a vision. Only if the Lakotas do exactly as Wovoka said would the dead come back alive and the new world replace the old that was "worn out." These experiences need to be understood in the context of the Lakota understanding of spirits and visiting the dead in the spirit world through visions. From that point of view, meeting the spirits of the dead in a vision is entirely normal for Lakotas.[37] Importantly, this narrative shows that Short Bull's version of the Ghost Dance is not much different from what Wovoka was prophesizing. Unlike in "As Narrated by Short Bull," Short Bull does not discuss events leading to the Wounded Knee tragedy.

This is the story of the Ghost Dance, in which these men went to the place of ghosts [spirits]; and some of them have died, and I know about it. These are the ones who went to the place of ghosts: Short Bull, Kicking Bear, Brave Wolf, Thunder Horse, Turn Over Back, Scare Them, and Gray Horse.[38]

In the year 1889, in June,[39] we went from Pine Ridge; four of us were from Rosebud, and from Pine Ridge there were three, so we were seven. And after eleven nights we reached Arapaho Agency, Wyoming, and there we rested seven days. And then from there we went to the Bannock (Wabanaka) Agency [Fort Hall, Idaho] and after nineteen nights we reached there and the people came together and held an Omaha Dance, and we took part in it.

37. For more on Lakota concepts of spirits and visions in the context of the Ghost Dance, see Andersson, *The Lakota Ghost Dance of 1890*, pp. 50–67.

38. For comparison, see "As Narrated by Short Bull" above. Going to the "place of ghosts [spirits]" refers to the delegates' journey to Nevada to meet Wovoka. At the same time, it seems that the entire journey was considered a religious experience, or "spirit journey."

39. This date is incorrect; the delegation left most likely in the early fall, perhaps August or September. See Andersson, *The Lakota Ghost Dance of 1890*, pp. 31–32.

Then a man who was said to be holy participated, a Bannock (Banake); he spoke to us as follows: "Three days from here is the place of God [Wakȟáŋ Tȟáŋka], so four tribes will go see him. So, my friends, you will join them, so later when the time is right I will come again and I will speak to you," he said. Thus he spoke to us.[40]

And then the dance ended and then the next morning a man came making an announcement. Then the man in whose tipi we stayed spoke to us as follows: "My friends, there will be a holy dance. At midday there will be a feast," and then he said, "so you will take part in it." So, "Yes," we said.

And then when it was a little past midday again, a crier came and made an announcement. Then that man said, "Now put on red earth paint; we are going to go there." So then we painted ourselves. And then we went with him and all the people gathered in the circle were painted a reddish color. So then we went there and the men and women, too, completely mixed together, were standing in a circle, and there was room so we stood there.

And that man who was said to be holy who had spoken to us stood there in the middle, and he told of his vision, and when he finished they danced. And I did not understand how it was done, so even though I participated in some of the dances, I was not overcome, but for some of them it was different, and they lost their senses and fell into a faint.

And then they rested and sat in a circle and some of those who had fainted came to and five men sat in the center and they came back there and when they sat down a big man, one of those who had revived, told of his experience. So then he stood up and spoke to the people in a loud voice. Well, I counted those who had fainted. There were eleven of them. Well, they all told of their experiences. And then after they finished, we danced for a short while and we stopped.

Then when it was morning that man came and said, "My friends, now they will go together so you should join them. Hurry!" Then we saddled our horses and then we went. We went on a road along a creek and we caught up with them. And then we went with them for six nights and we arrived there at the Rabbit-Skin Blanket Wearers [Paiute] Agency and stayed two days.

40. I have not been able to verify who this Bannock holy man was. However, the Bannocks at Fort Hall played an important role as mediators and aided in the spread of the Ghost Dance. Several Bannock guides were also mentioned by delegates from other tribes, but for some reason they are not mentioned by name. See Mooney, *Ghost-Dance Religion*, 807–808; Gage, "Intertribal Communication," 209, 295.

And from there we went with four Paiutes and after three days we camped; we arrived at the foot of the White Mountains [Rocky Mountains].

Then one of the Paiutes spoke to us as follows: "We will stay here for two days, waiting for two tribes to arrive here; then they will reach us here at midday," he said. Then we stayed right there. And then on the second day some Cheyennes and Shoshones, these two, arrived; there were three Cheyennes and five Shoshones, and so eight [people] arrived.

Well, then we went and they stopped at midday, and when they finished eating they said this: "We will sit on this hill and then he will arrive," they said. And then we went to a hill, the biggest and highest one in the Rocky Mountains. So then I was the last one to join them and then we stopped beneath it. And then we dismounted and we tied our horses to little pine trees. And then we put on red earth paint. And then, one behind the other, we climbed the hill. We climbed to the top. And in the middle there was a huge flat rock and around it was a grove of pine trees, and everything was visible in all directions. And then they sat in a circle.

And one of the Paiutes sat down in the middle where we were sitting and shouted something. After a while a spirit-man [white man; or Wovoka][41] came and stood in the middle of them, but not one of us looked steadily at him. He stood with his head bowed and all at once, surprisingly, he made a speech in the Lakota language. He said as follows:

"My pitiful children," meaning these [gathered], "because you come to me suffering you will hear those things that are right and you will act accordingly," he said. "By means of a dance you will see again those of your relatives who died long ago, but only if you do it properly will you truly see your people. And because the Father told me these things, remember me! Behold me, my sons, I myself was killed long ago by the white men, and therefore now there are many holes in me. They went away, and now they honor me," he said, "but because you Indian people are suffering, I am paying you this visit so in the future you and your relatives who have died

41. The Lakota word used here is *wasicun* (*wasičuŋ*), which usually refers to a white man. However, originally the term in Lakota referred to special spirits, especially those of war. Thus, the word in this context could also refer to a spirit or a spirit-man. That would make more sense, and Short Bull used the English term "spirit-man" in his account (see below) that was published in Natalie Curtis, *The Indian's Book: Songs and Legends of the American Indians* (New York: Dover, 1950; orig. publ. 1907), 45–47. The original 1907 text can be accessed through https://ia600209.us.archive.org/12/items/offeringindianlore00burlrich/offeringindianlore00burlrich.pdf. For the discussion on the use of "spirit-man," see Ostler, *Plains Sioux*, 251.

will see one another. From this time on, by dancing and [doing] those things that I will say, you will live well.

"My beloved sons, do not murder one another! Whoever commits murder does evil. And love one another! And take pity on one another! If you act in this manner, I will give you more concerning the ceremony. And those people should take sweat baths. While you are dancing you must not eat any at all of the white man's food! And fast! And you must not wear any metal. And while you dance you must dance with your eyes closed. If you think about one of your relatives who died long ago you will see him.

"Well, it is not possible for you Indians and the whites to become the same as long as your generations continue. Therefore, my Father made you of a different nature and also gave you a country.[42] And he will see any bad things that you do, so from this time on whatever you do, I will watch over and keep. The Indians are far below because my Father made you last. Now I will help you and you will live well. In the future these things will be fulfilled. Behold! There is a village. These are your relatives of past generations so you will go there," he said, and turning around he looked to the west, so we looked there.

Then there was a village of people and many were walking about and the village was smoky. And some were coming this way on horseback. And on this side there was a hill so they were coming up on the other side. Then he said as follows: "You will be with them, but then you will not [yet] truly be with them; then [later] you will see your relatives, so then you will see them in the normal way," he said, "and from now on, do not forget this visit! And whatever the whites with whom you will live want, do it accordingly! This will not be for long. Well, I give you these things, so remember them well!"

He sang:

My son, hold my hand!

My son, hold my hand!

You will grow up, you will grow up.

My Father says so, my Father says so.

He sang:

My Father says so, my Father says so.

---

42. The expression "as long as your generations continue" could also be translated as "as long as your people continue to live." For further discussion of the idea of Indians and whites not being the same, see Part 4.

I am bringing a pipe to you

So you will live.

My Father says so, my Father says so.

"Well, my sons, do not overdo these things! And do them properly! Everyone close their eyes!" he said. So I sat there with my head bowed and I sat with my eyes closed. And then I looked. Then he was gone, so, "Look there!" I said. Then one of them looked up furtively, pointing behind, so I looked that way. Then he was standing high up. And the land and that village of people too were slowly disappearing. So those whom I had joined were crying.

"Come on! Now we will go down," I said. And then they stopped crying, so we went together back to where the horses were tied and we sat down there in the shade of the pine trees. And then I asked them, "Did you understand clearly what he said?" "Yes," they said. Then I asked the Cheyenne named Porcupine, "My friend, did you understand what Father said?" Then, "Yes," he said. Then I asked a Shoshone and he too said they understood him. So I told them how we understood him and when I finished they all said it was right.

So again I spoke as follows: "When you return and arrive home, will you dance?" Then, "Yes," they said. So before that, the Blue Clouds (Arapahos) and Bannocks, those two tribes, already knew about it and danced.

So then we went back and we arrived at the Paiute Agency. And we stayed there four days and from there again we went back and arrived at the Bannock Agency and we stayed there six days. And from there we went to Pine Ridge, South Dakota; we arrived there and at White Clay we told our story. There in the middle of a flat prairie a dance ceremony was to be held by Brave Wolf and High Horse. And among those who took part there was Kicking Bear.

And from there we returned to Rosebud, and at once we danced. And those who longed for their relatives and danced in earnest fainted. And then when I was first about to be overcome, suddenly something flashed in my face, a bright light that turned blue. And then I really felt that I was going to vomit and so I was frightened and lost consciousness. And it seemed that I was brought down in a land of green grass and I set out walking and I went up a big hill and stood on the top.[43]

---

43. When Lakota men went on a vision quest, they often selected a secluded area on a high hill or butte. Quite often people experiencing visions in the Ghost Dance also ascended a hill, perhaps symbolizing a vision quest.

Then beyond there was a big village of only tipis and so I went there. Then a horseback rider came from there, galloping fast, and reached me. Then it was my father as a very handsome young man, and speaking, he said this to me: "Alas! I see you, my beloved son, but you smell bad, so go back home, and when you get there, wash yourself and come back! So you will go among the lodges and there we will see you," he said.

So therefore I turned around. Then that was all. I came to. Then I was actually sitting in the middle of the dance circle. Right there I came to and I was very sad. Anyone who was overcome and fainted told about what he learned and did not lie. So then I myself told of my experience. And then we finished. So then I went swimming and washed myself thoroughly.

And in the morning we danced again. Then again I was overcome. And all at once I fainted and again I was standing on top of a hill. Then there was a man standing there so I went to him. Then it was the Son of God, the one who we came back from visiting, who was standing there, so I went to him, but, in the village beyond, the center of the camp circle was buzzing, and the man said this: "My son, you have not related my words properly. So these customs that I tell you about, I have established for the future, so therefore tell them to the people! And under your clothes, always paint your bodies like this! And wear this! And do not forget! By means of these, in the future you will see one another. So behold! These and their people have come together here crying and talking sorrowfully. So I want you to live well, but in the future, when the time is near to see one another, you will hear the sound of the land. And this earth is now completely worn out, so you will live in a new land. So rejoice!

"So listen now to these things that I tell you and remember them well! I am the one, so by and by you will pray to me for things and I will hear it.

"Well, you want to see your relatives, so go there!"

Thus he spoke to me so then I went straight there. And from the hill I went toward the village. And then as I neared it, a rider came galloping from the village and came near me and dismounted. Then it was my father as a small young man and he said, "My beloved son," and he hugged me around the neck and said, "we live in that big tipi over yonder, so we will go there." So then I went there with him. And then we arrived at that tipi. And then I went inside. And there were no women there. Nine important young men[44] were sitting inside and they said "Hau!" and they made room for me

---

44. The literal translation for the Lakota words *wičháša tȟáŋka* is "big man," but it can also refer to grown-up men, middle-aged men or important men.

at the place of honor [opposite the doorway] and I sat down there. And they gave me a wooden dish of pemmican and put it in front of me and I took it, ate, and gave the dish back to them.

And then an important man spoke to me as follows: "Grandson, I am your grandfather, and these are your grandfathers, one after the other. And we are without women. Father decreed it so. We of one blood are gathered together here. The people of the village are all camped here. And those in the tipi next to where we live are your grandmothers, so go there! They will see you," he said.

And none of the men with him in the tipi said anything; they sat in silence. And so then I came outside and went to the other tipi. And then there were only women there, twelve of them, and so I went inside. And so a woman hugged me around the neck and said, "Grandson, these are your grandmothers, and we are not with your grandfathers, and this is what Father decreed so this is how we are," she said. And she said, "Grandson, eat this!" She gave me some honeycomb tripe and a marrowbone so I took them and ate. And none of the other women said anything. So I ate it up and I started back and I went up and stood on the hill.

Then I started to wake and I came to lying right there in the middle of the dance circle and I was very sad and I stood up at the sacred tree and the people sat around me. And so I told them what I had seen and what had been told to me and I instructed them to do things properly.

Well, that is the way it was, and because of it there was fighting, but there was nothing about that in the ceremony. Twelve times I fainted and each time an eagle carried me and took me to where my relatives lived and with great joy I saw all my fathers, mothers, sisters, and brothers.

Well, that is the way it was and more than this cannot be told. This was the Indians' religion, so in the future the people and the ghosts [spirits] would see one another and in the future the Indians would be strong because of the things that he would give them. These are the things I know.

Short Bull—Chases Insect[45]

45. Short Bull has signed this text with his name and another name, Chases Insect (Wabluška Kuwapi) [Wablúška Khuwápi]. I have been unable to verify the meaning of this second name. It was customary for the Lakotas to change their names several times during their lives. Whether this was an example of such change, I cannot determine.

Short Bull

"We the tribe of Indians, are the ones who are living a sacred life."

In October 1890, Short Bull allegedly gave a speech to the crowd gathered at Pass Creek on the border of the Rosebud and Pine Ridge Reservations. By this time several hundred Brulés from Rosebud were on their way to Pine Ridge. They stopped at Pass Creek where a Ghost Dance was held. Short Bull's speech was published in newspapers like the *Chicago Tribune* and the *Omaha Daily Bee* in late November and later in the report of General Nelson A. Miles in the annual report of the secretary of war in 1891. The speech was initially part of a telegram by an unnamed officer to General Miles on October 19.[46] It was often described as "Short Bull's Sermon" and was interpreted as his declaration of war. In other texts by Short Bull, he does not mention such a speech at Pass Creek at all. In fact, this speech is mostly likely a fabrication, but I want to include it here as so many scholars have used it as a proof of the militancy of the Ghost Dance. I will analyze the text first in the context of the Lakota Ghost Dance practices and then point out the problematic issues. In this speech, Short Bull makes several references to Lakota traditional beliefs. He discusses the flowering tree, a central symbol for the Lakota that was also present in Black Elk's vision.[47] Short Bull also discusses sacred shirts, that is, Ghost Dance shirts, which would protect the wearers. This is often interpreted as being a sign of a warlike twist in the Lakota Ghost Dance. Yet Short Bull refers only to the fact that bullets would not cause any harm and that soldiers and other whites would be dead. This is in line with other accounts of the Ghost Dance teachings. It is also vital to understand that in the traditional Lakota belief system a person could become invulnerable through personal sacred experiences. His *wóthawe* (power or medicine) could protect him. Thus, what Short

---

46. Short Bull in *Omaha Daily Bee*, November 22, 1890, 1; *Chicago Tribune*, November 22, 1890, 2; ARSW, 1891, 52nd Cong., 1st Sess., H. Ex. Doc., No. 1, 142–43.
47. For an analysis of Black Elk's vision and the flowering tree, see Black Elk's account below.

Bull describes, is an innovation derived from Lakota traditions. Even if the newspapers at the time interpreted this as a certain sign of war, in the context of Lakota traditions, invulnerability is not strange or uncommon. Short Bull says that the shirts would protect their wearers only if the whites attacked the Indians, further emphasizing the protective nature of these garments.[48] It is, however, worth noting that here Short Bull says that those who do not believe would be "blown away." In several other documents (see below) it becomes evident that the nonbelievers would indeed not make it to the new world (for comparison, see Kicking Bear, below). In this account, Short Bull says that the dancers should be naked. This is the complete opposite of the Ghost Dance teachings. Other historical sources, Indian and white, do not report such practices. Short Bull also says that he will start the wind to blow and advance the coming of the new world, thus taking on himself the role of the Messiah. He also says that when soldiers sink into the earth, the Indians can do whatever they want with them. These statements are in stark contrast to any known teaching by Short Bull or any other Ghost Dance leader. "Do not listen to white men" is also contradictory to other Short Bull accounts. These words reflect more the views of the *Chicago Tribune* correspondent than the views of Short Bull. Thus the authenticity of this text can indeed be questioned.[49]

My friends and relatives: I will soon start this thing in running order. I have told you that this would come to pass in two seasons, but since the whites are interfering so much, I will advance the time from what my Father above told me to do so.[50] The time will be shorter. Therefore you must not be afraid

48. See Andersson, *The Lakota Ghost Dance of 1890*, pp. 73–74. Also George Sword, who opposed the Ghost Dance, emphasized that the shirts were used as protection, saying, "whoever they have as enemies and point their guns to shoot is not able to do it." For George Sword's account, see part 3.

49. For the discussion about the authenticity of this text see, for example, Ostler, *Plains Sioux*, 295–97; Warren, *God's Red Son*, 187–89.

50. According to Wovoka's original doctrine, the cataclysmic event was supposed to take place in the spring. It was usually interpreted as referring to the spring of 1891.

of anything. Some of my relations have no ears, so I will have them blown away. Now there will be a tree sprout up, and there all the members of our religion and the tribe must gather together.[51] That will be the place where we will see our relations. But, before this time, we must dance the balance of this moon, at the end of which time the earth will shiver very hard. Whenever this thing occurs, I will start the wind to blow. We are the ones who will then see our fathers, mothers, and everybody. We the tribe of Indians, are the ones who are living a sacred life. God, our Father, himself has told and commanded and shown me to do these things. Our Father in Heaven has placed a mark at each point of the four winds; first, a clay pipe, which lies at the setting of the sun and represents the Sioux tribe; second, there is a holy arrow lying at the north, which represents the Cheyenne tribe; third, at the rising of the sun there lies hail, representing the Arapaho tribe; and fourth, there lies a pipe and nice feather at the south, which represents the Crow tribe. My Father has shown me these things, therefore we must continue this dance. There may be soldiers surround you, but pay no attention to them, continue the dance. If the soldiers surround you four deep, three of you on whom I have put holy shirts will sing a song, which I have taught you, around them, when some of them will drop dead, then the rest will start to run, but their horses will sink into the earth; the riders will jump from their horses, but they will sink into the earth also; then you can do as you desire with them. Now you must know this, that all the soldiers and that race will be dead; there will be only five thousand of them left living on the earth. My friends and relations, this is straight and true. Now we must gather at Pass Creek, where the tree is sprouting. There we will go among our dead relations. You must not take any earthly things with you. Then the men must take off all their clothing, and the women must do the same. No one shall be ashamed of exposing their persons. My Father above has told us to do this, and we must do as he says. You must not be afraid of anything. The guns are the only things we are afraid of—but they belong to our Father in Heaven. He will see that they do no harm. Whatever white men may tell you, do not listen to them. My relations, this is all. I will now raise my hand up to my Father and close what he has said to you through me.

---

51. Short Bull refers to the Lakota sacred tree that symbolizes the unity and the center of the Lakota people. Andersson, *The Lakota Ghost Dance of 1890*, p. 95.

Short Bull

"Who would have thought that dancing could make such trouble?"

Short Bull gave this statement to ethnologist Natalie Curtis and it was published in *The Indian's Book* in 1907.[52] This account is a shorter version of Short Bull's trip to Nevada, but more importantly gives an insight into his understanding of the Ghost Dance. In this text Short Bull forcefully denies all hostile intentions and laments that "in this world the Great Father has given to the white man everything and to the Indian nothing," hoping that matters would be different in the other world.

Who would have thought that dancing would make such trouble? We had no wish to make trouble, nor did we cause it of ourselves. There was trouble, but it was not of my making. We had no thought of fighting; if we had meant to fight, would we not have carried arms? We went unarmed [to] the dance. How could we have held weapons? For thus we danced, in a circle, hand-in-hand, each man's fingers linked in those of his neighbor.[53]

Who would have thought that dancing could make such trouble? For the message that I brought was peace. And the message was given by the Father to all the tribes. Thus it happened: I journeyed to the land where the sun sets, and then I went to the spirit-land, where I saw the spirit-encampment. I drew near and stood outside the spirit tipi. A spirit-man came out and stood beside me. He spoke to me and said: "Behold, I give you something holy!" Then he said: "Whence do you come from?" And I answered: "I come from Rosebud." Then said the spirit-man: "Go we together in a cloud, upward, to the Father."

So we rose in a cloud to where were other camps, and there we saw those who wear the blanket of rabbit skin [Paiutes]. As we passed through the camp of these, there came toward us a man and his wife. Said this one of the rabbit robe: "I would speak with you now. Behold, I tell you something for you to tell to all the people! Give this dance to all the different tribes of

52. Short Bull in Curtis, *The Indian's Book*, 45–47. The original 1907 text can be accessed at https://ia600209.us.archive.org/12/items/offeringindianlore00burlrich/offeringindianlore00burlrich.pdf. See also Maddra, *Hostiles?* 228.

53. Dancing hand in hand was a new innovation in Lakota culture. Never before had men and women danced together in a circle holding hands. This, however, had a great symbolic meaning as the dance circle symbolized the sacred hoop and the unity of the Lakota people. See Andersson, *The Lakota Ghost Dance of 1890*, pp. 55–57.

Indians. White people and Indians shall all dance together.[54] But first they shall sing. There shall be no more fighting. No man shall kill another. Hear me, for I will give you water to drink. Thus I tell you, this is why I have called you. My meaning, have you understood it?"

Thus spoke he of the rabbit-blanket, and holy red paint he gave to me. In the spirit-camp I had seen those who had died, and when I came homeward there came with me two spirit companions invisible to all but me. These journeyed with me and stayed ever with me. I heard their counsel. Alone in my tipi I dreamed, and saw visions, and communed with the spirits. And I went forth and taught the people and told them of the Father's word and of the help that should come to the Indians. There were others who taught us [as] well as I. The Father had commanded all the world to dance, and we gave the dance to the people as we had been bidden. When they danced they fell dead [in trances] and went to the spirit-camp and saw those who had died, those whom they loved—their fathers, their mothers, and their little children. Then came trouble. Yet in our dance we harmed no one, nor meant we ill to any man. The Father had commanded, so did we.

Is true, all men should love one another. Is true, all men should live as brothers. Is it we who do not thus? What others demand of us, should they not themselves give? Is it just to expect one friend to give all the friendship? We are glad to live with white men as brothers. But we ask that they expect not the brotherhood and the love to come from the Indian alone.

In this world the Great Father has given to the white man everything and to the Indian nothing. But it will not always be thus. In another world the Indian shall be as the white man and the white man as the Indian. To the Indian will be given wisdom and power, and the white man shall be helpless and unknowing with only the bow and arrow. Four ere long this world will be consumed in flame and pass away. Then, in the life after this, to the Indian shall all be given.

54. The idea that the whites would be participating in the Ghost Dance was not common and does not appear in other accounts by Short Bull. However, there were reports that Mormons may have participated in some of the ceremonies in Nevada. For Mormon influence, see Mooney, *The Ghost-Dance Religion*, 766, 792–93; Hittman, *Wovoka*, 84–86; Smoak, "The Mormons and the Ghost Dance of 1890," 269–94.

Short Bull

"I was called by Jocko Wilson."

Judge Eli S. Ricker interviewed many Lakotas in the early twentieth century. These interviews are in the holdings of the Nebraska Historical Society, but they were edited by Richard Jensen and published as *Voices of the American West: The Indian Interviews of Eli S. Ricker* in 2006.[55] Jensen notes, however, that there is no evidence to show that Ricker ever met with Short Bull. Rather he got Short Bull's account from James R. Walker, the physician on the Pine Ridge Reservation from 1896 to 1914.[56] Indeed, the text in the James R. Walker collection is word for word the same as the text in the Eli S. Ricker Collection.[57] In any case, in this account Short Bull continues with the same tone as in the other texts presented here, although he is somewhat vaguer in dates and places. Perhaps Ricker or an unidentified interpreter added a side text saying that Short Bull "wants to prove that he was not the cause of the trouble of 1890–91." Ricker also notes that

> Dr. Walker describes Short Bull as an open, generous and kind hearted man who attends with diligence to his own business, frequenting public places only when necessity makes this necessary, and remaining quietly at home most of the time. He's one of the few real chiefs remaining. When any person for whom he has special regard comes to his house he bestirs his followers in a truly lively and commanding way to provide the most appropriate entertainment for the

55. Short Bull in ESRMC, NHS, tablet 1. Published also in Jensen, *Voices of the American West*, 1:189–90. I have followed the transcribed copies of the Eli Ricker Collection tablets held at the American Indian Studies Research Institute at Indiana University and compared those to the ones published in Jensen, *Voices of the American West*. The original Ricker Collection tablets are very difficult to read and present tremendous editorial challenges as noted by Jensen in his introduction to *Voices of the American West*, 1:xxii–xxvii. I am therefore grateful for the American Indian Studies Research Institute for allowing me to use the transcribed copies.

56. See Jensen, *Voices of the American West*, 1:189.

57. See Short Bull in Walker, *Lakota Belief and Ritual*, 142–43. The original is in The James R. Walker Collection, Colorado Historical Society. I have used the copies and transcripts made by Raymond J. DeMallie and held at the American Indian Studies Research Institute, Indiana University.

visitor; and in all the respect in which it could be expected of him he proves himself the real gentleman. His face always wears a smile, telling unmistakably that nature made him gentle and benevolent.[58]

Short Bull refers in the document to the idea of the world being filthy and smelling bad. As noted above, this was a common concept in the Lakota Ghost Dance, but here Short Bull explains why: "These murders and suicides are that which now stinks." This is a clear reference to the problems of reservation life and to the peaceful aims of the Lakota Ghost Dance. People should no longer fight or kill each other.

He saw a woman. It was told that [the] woman gave birth to a child and this is known in heaven. This was told to him and he wanted to see the child when they heard this. This man professed to be a great man, next to God; [the Messiah] told them that he wanted to be their intermediator, and that they should dance and be together, and he would be with them. He [the Messiah] had a look. He said has [how] many nights and days it would take to do [and] that he knew all about it. He said Indians [are] like grass and flowers; they learn, and they sing and pray. He said: "Do nothing wrong." He said the people can't take anything away when they die.

Whiskey is bad. Who drinks, they cause murders and suicides. Across the ocean is a great church where he came from. "That church belongs to me. You may go as you please. But one church, one belief, one faith. When you listen to me when I pray or teach from my church all good people will come with me. The whole world will sing. The whole earth is now filthy and stinks. These murders and suicides are that which now stinks. You say, 'Father! Oh Father! Is that you?' All that will say, say that the Father, God, will look at you. Those that have done wrong he will shake the earth. This part of the earth will get it."

[I] first heard of this man at Rosebud, in the year that Red Shirt's sister committed suicide.[59] I did not see the child. I do not know where it was born.[60] I was called by Jocko Wilson[61] to go, and I went to see him. I went

58. See Jensen, *Voices of the American West*, 1:190.
59. This was in 1889 according to the No Ears winter count. See Walker, *Lakota Belief and Ritual*, 142–43, and endnote 48 in part 2. No Ears winter count in Walker, *Lakota Society*, 151.
60. The reference to the child is ambiguous. Perhaps it means the Christ.
61. Jocko Wilson means Wovoka, also known as Jack Wilson. See Hittman, *Wovoka*.

to the Rabbit Blanket Indians [Paiutes]. I went in March.[62] I was a long time in going. I first went to the Arapaho Agency. I do not know how long I was there. I was six days [at] Pocatello. I went to the Bannocks and was there nine days. Then I got on the train. I was on the train two days, and the third day in the evening I came to the fish eaters, and I was there eight days.[63] There were many whites and Indians there. I left there on train, and on the hills above Pocatello, there was an accident. Big river washed out bridge, and train [was] upset. I came to Arapaho Agency [Wind River Reservation]. Came from Arapaho Agency on horseback. To my home it took 14 days. Red Star went. At Rosebud [I] heard that this man had sent representative[s] to Rosebud and Pine Ridge and told them to have Short Bull come over there. He wanted a man who would be straight and would not lie. Rosebud Indians called a council and tried to pick out a man to go and they chose me. There was a paper at Rosebud that called for such a man, made by the Oglala chiefs.[64]

I first heard that this was a holy man. Said that God's daughter gave birth to a child and we should go and see it. I do not know where. I did not see this woman. All I saw was the man and his wife. Dance for five days; first pray and address. The other four all dance.

Short Bull

"The ghost shirt is *wakȟáŋ*."

This text by Short Bull is a follow-up to the text above and can also be found in the James R. Walker Collection in the History Colorado Stephen H. Hart Library and Research Center.[65] This brief text gives instructions for the Ghost Dance ceremony and notes that the Ghost Dance shirts

62. In the statement Short Bull gave to Eugene Buechel, he says the delegation left in June. See above.

63. The Fish Eaters are most likely the Pyramid Lake Paiutes, who call themselves Kuyuidika, "Eaters of the Cui-Cui Fish." See Walker, *Lakota Belief and Ritual*, endnote 49, pt. 2.

64. This seems to refer to the letter that Short Bull also mentioned in "As Narrated by Short Bull." However, Short Bull says that the letter was written by the Oglala chiefs. It was not directly written by the Messiah as suggested by historian Michael Coleman. See above.

65. Short Bull in JRWC, HCWHL. I have used the copies and transcripts made by Raymond J. DeMallie and held at the American Indian Studies Research Institute, Indiana University. See also Walker, *Lakota Belief and Ritual*, 143.

are sacred and bulletproof. Clearly Short Bull still, at the time of the interview with Walker, believed that the shirts had power.

First: purification by sweat bath. Clasp hands and circle to left. Hold hands and sing until a trance is induced, looking up all the time. Brought to pitch of excitement by singing songs prescribed by the Messiah. Dressed as prescribed. Froth at mouth when in trance. They must keep step with the cadence of the song. The[y] go into trance in from ten minutes to three quarters of an hour. Each one described his vision. Each vision is different from others. Men, women, children have visions.[66]

The ghost shirt is *wakȟáŋ*. It is impervious to missiles.

Short Bull

"Take off your rings, earrings and all metal when you dance."

The original version of this account by Short Bull was written in German by ethnographer Frederick Weygold in 1909. It is deposited in Die Oglala Sammlung Weygold in Hamburischen Museum für Völkerkunde, in Hamburg, Germany. The original is written in German and I have relied on an English translation made by Wolfgang Haberland and published in *Sonderdruck aus Mitteilungen aus dem Museum für Völkerkunde Hamburg Neue Folge* 7 (1977).[67] According to Haberland, in the summer of 1909, "Weygold talked to Short Bull through Bissonette,[68] he could not make Short Bull say a Ghost Dance prayer, but he later sent one in

66. It is noteworthy that according to Short Bull even children were having visions during the Ghost Dance ceremonies. That was not common in Lakota traditions, and for example Robert P. Higheagle states that children were not allowed to enter the dance circle. For his account see part 3.

67. Short Bull in Die Oglala-Sammlung Weygold im Hamburgischen Museum für Völkerkunde; Teil 4. Published by permission of Hamburgischen Museum für Völkerkunde. An English version can be found in Wolfgang Haberland, "Die Oglala Sammlung Weygold im Hamburischen Museum fur Völkerkunde [Weygold's Oglala Collection in the Hamburg Museum of Ethnology]," Mitteilungen aus die Museum für Völkerkunde, 1977, 37–38.

68. This refers to interpreter Joseph Bissonette (1879–1957), a fur trader who had married an Oglala woman and a Brulé woman. He was well respected, for example, by Red Cloud. See Catherine Price, *The Oglala People: A Political History: 1841–1879* (Lincoln: University of Nebraska Press, 1996), 20.

a letter to Weygold."[69] However, Short Bull told Weygold about his role in the Ghost Dance. Bissonette simultaneously translated Short Bull's speech into English, and Weygold translated it into German. Therefore, mistakes could have taken place. According to Weygold, Short Bull felt that the whites misunderstood him, and Weygold believed this was true. Short Bull was considered a gentleman by all whites, although they did not always understand him. According to Weygold, many Indians blamed Short Bull for the Wounded Knee affair, so he felt the need to defend himself. His life was a complex combination of Indian and white habits, but his religion and the ceremonies, especially, were purely Indian. Weygold also states that in 1909 when he interviewed Short Bull, he was still a believer in the Ghost Dance.[70] Weygold says:

> He [Short Bull] was selected from Rosebud to go to Nevada in order to find out everything about the Messiah. Many did not want to choose him, but he HAD to go.[71] He told them (the Ghost Dancers): 'Paint your faces, you must have good hearts, close your eyes and keep your heads bowed in order to find the right way of thinking.'

At first glance, this text by Short Bull seems truly defensive. Yet most people who consider it as such have ignored the possibility that this was actually what Short Bull *really* thought and told his people. If the initial assumption is that Short Bull twisted Wovoka's message into one with militant overtones, this—and other accounts by him—seem more defensive than they actually are. Like Wovoka, Short Bull urges children to go to school, and others to attend Mass and take jobs. Short Bull also notes that wearing any metal in the dance might have harmful effects.[72] Short Bull clearly wants people to understand that he and his message had been misunderstood and he was unjustly portrayed as a

69. Weygold in Haberland, 37.
70. Ibid.
71. Capitalization original.
72. Many scholars have interpreted this feature of the Lakota Ghost Dance as some-how being a sign of militancy. Yet, if the Ghost Dancers were not allowed to carry metal, how could they then carry arms, as often suggested? There is clearly a contradiction in this line of reasoning.

troublemaker. Perhaps that is why he felt that he needed to defend his point of views; he did not need to defend his actions or his interpretation of the Ghost Dance. Instead, he needed to defend himself against *unjust* accusations. In this and other accounts there are suggestions that those whites who believed in the Ghost Dance might survive and join the Indians in the new world. Yet Short Bull says here and in other accounts that the Indians and the white people are made different. "The Great Spirit made us Indians and we are not to take the ways of any other people," he says and continues that "many misunderstood this." This is an interesting concept as it emerges in several documents presented here, even in some of the accounts written by Christian Lakotas who objected to the Ghost Dance.[73]

The story is as follows:

I told them to stay in this position in order to listen and focus on what I had to say. I said, your children should go to school and the older people should attend Mass and pray. They should work and farm, and build houses and take the advice of the good, wise white men. Do not kill each other; in the olden times there were many wars and bloodshed and because of that there was a bad smell. I told this to the old people, who could make use of their experiences. They should listen to my words and then I would say a prayer. Take off your rings, earrings and all metal when you dance, if you wear anything of metal there will be harmful effects. I want to tell you all (the Messiah says the following): "The white people know about the prayers. I tell you, you should pray and then dance. All the people of the world, even the whites, who have understanding and heart, will join us in our way of praying. From where the sun comes up and where it goes down, all the people should be together in this way of praying. From all this, one terrible thing will come. (I think there is a mistake here. I believe it should say that, if people do not follow this way, something bad will happen.)[74]

The Indians and the whites should take pity of each other. "The man who sent me (the Messiah) said that the people should pray as he has told them to. When someone does not follow this, many bad things will come upon him. This is what Wovoka told to the people: "I have given up the white man's ways." Then he took a stick and threw it away from the people. This is what it means: "We Indians did not understand the white man's language

73. See part 4.
74. The insertions in parentheses are Haberland's.

that well." And the whites escaped us and we Indians did not understand why. And I told the Indians to give up the white man's ways and not follow them anymore. The Great Spirit made us Indians and we are not to take the ways of any other people. I think that many misunderstood this.

Short Bull

"I had seen the Holy Man, and he had told me to live in peace."

The following document is taken from *The Red Man* periodical published in 1915. The article was entitled "Short Bull's Story of the Battle of Wounded Knee" and was written by Courtney R. Cooper, a reporter for the *New York Sun*.[75] I decided to publish it here in its entirety since Short Bull's accounts are interwoven with the author's own writing. The article gives a very sentimental description of the Ghost Dance and it clearly states that Short Bull is attempting to exonerate himself of all the blame for the trouble. Despite the author's sentimental tone and paternalistic views, Short Bull's basic message does not differ from his other accounts. What is noteworthy in this text is that Short Bull blames Lakota chiefs Red Cloud, American Horse, Two Strike, and others for instigating trouble and then blaming him for it. This reflects the factionalism among the Lakotas. While other documents by Short Bull portray him as being at odds with, for example, the above-mentioned leaders, this is the strongest accusation. Short Bull says bluntly that they "wanted war." One is left to wonder what really took place when this interview was taken down in 1915.

It was in a South Dakota blizzard that I found him huddled in his flapping tent, far out upon the Sioux reservation of Pine Ridge. The marks of the warrior were absent, a frayed fur overcoat covered the somewhat undersized form that once had known the dancing bustle and the ghost shirt, and

---

75. Short Bull in Courtney R. Cooper, "Short Bull's Story of the Ghost Dance and Wounded Knee," *The Red Man* (February 1915): 205–12. Published also in Peter Cozzens, *Eyewitnesses to the Indian Wars, 1865–1890: The Long War for the Northern Plains* (Mechanicsburg, Pa.: Stackpole Books, 2004), 630–636. *The Red Man* was published by the Indian students at the Carlisle Indian school in Pennsylvania from 1910 to 1917.

cotton gloves shielded the wrinkled hands which held once the war club and the rifle.

Under the banking of the tent, the wind sifted its snow; the old stovepipe rattled; in a corner, huddled and shivering, sat a wrinkled squaw, awaiting in stubborn silence the return of the sun. From a rope at the top of the tent—the tipi of earlier days had vanished—hung a few shreds of jerked beef left from the rations of the agency. It was a home of poverty and of hopelessness, the home of Ta Ta La Slotsla,[76] Short Bull, blamed for a quarter of a century for an Indian war, which called forth half troops of the United States and cost lives by hundreds—the war of the Messiah.

So to explanation. Consult history and there comes the story of a strange, an unknown being who, in 1890, incited the Indians to rebellion; who, in personification of Jesus Christ, gave the promise that once again the prairies should be the Happy Hunting Grounds of the red man, where again would roam the elk, the antelope and the buffalo, and that the white man would vanish into the eastern seas. Consult history and it tells the story of how the representatives of the Indian tribes from Canada to Oklahoma journeyed to Pyramid Lake, Nevada, that they might hear a message of war and hatred; of how the ghost shirt, supposedly impervious to bullets, was fashioned; and particularly of how it was Short Bull of the Sioux who spread the news and brought about the war which followed.

Therefore, it was because of this history that they had told me upon the reservation not to talk to Short Bull. He would say nothing. He would be taciturn. He would be evasive, for what could he say, now that his fabled ghost shirt had been riddled with many an army bullet, now that the white man had built cities where the buffalo were to have grazed, and the Indian braves who were to have driven their enemies into the eastern ocean had lain these twenty-three years in their trenches atop the battlefield of Wounded Knee? No, Short Bull would be hardly the man to care to talk. And yet we entered—Horn Cloud, the interpreter, and myself.[77] There went forth my message, the question of the cause of the war of the Messiah. A smile of greeting from the little man beside the rickety, rattling stove, an outstretching of arms; a cry from the squaw in the corner. The little man in the frayed overcoat had risen, his eyes glistening, his face alight.

"How kola!" *he called.* "How kola! Was' te—was' te!"[78]

---

76. This name is a corruption of Tȟatȟáŋka Ptéčela.

77. The interpreter was most likely Joseph Horn Cloud, himself a survivor of Wounded Knee.

78. *"Kȟolá"* is "friend" in Lakota and *"wašté"* means "good."

And there can be no Indian greeting of more friendliness. I tried to answer in what little Sioux I had learned. It was impossible. Short Bull—he who is blamed for a war—was talking excitedly, gesticulating. Horn Cloud turned.

"He says you're the first man who ever asked that," *came from the interpreter.* "He say to thank you—maybe now he get to tell the truth."

And so there was something wrong with history? I smiled at that, but when I spoke of it to Horn Cloud, he smiled also and shook his head. Evidently there was a great deal wrong with history, at least from the standpoint of the man blamed for a war. Evidently—but Short Bull had doffed his coat now and was standing with outstretched arms. His face had grown suddenly serious.

"Ask the white man," *came through the interpreter,* "whether he comes through friendship or through curiosity. Ask the white man whether he will hear the story of Ta Ta La Slotsa and remember it as he tells it. Ask the white man whether he wants to hear the truth and nothing but the truth from Short Bull—Short Bull who saw the Messiah."

A silence except for the flapping of the tent, the shrill of the wind. I nodded. Short Bull raised his arms.

"Tell the white man to forget what he has read in history, for my story is different. Tell him that I deny I caused the war of the Messiah. Tell him that I preached peace, not war."

And so a new phase of history came forth. There was a conference. Horn Cloud was telling the little man to begin at the beginning. Once again, Short Bull raised his arms.

"There was starvation in 1888 and 1889," *he said slowly.* "The tipis were cold for want of fires. Up on the Rosebud Agency, where I lived, we cried for food, as they did down here at Pine Ridge. The white man had forgotten us. We were going toward the sunset. Then, one day—it seemed we all heard it at once—there came a message that the Messiah was soon to come to us. The white man had turned him out, long ago. Now he was coming to the Indian. We danced for joy. The Messiah perhaps would bring us food and warmth and clothing. There was a letter, too, from Red Cloud on Pine Ridge. Red Cloud said, too, that the Messiah was coming and to choose the hard-hearted [stouthearted; brave] man of the tribe to meet him. I was that man."[79]

79. Here again Short Bull makes the point that he was the man selected by Lakota leaders, including Red Cloud, to investigate the Ghost Dance. This gave him the authority to talk and teach about it.

The little Indian swallowed hard and looked at the ground. The inter-preter turned. "He means brave-hearted," *came the explanation.* "How!"

Short Bull heard the command to continue. He folded his hands. "There were twelve of us, each from a different tribe. One by one we traveled to the head of Wind River and met. The Messiah was in Nevada at Pyramid Lake. Some of us had horses. Others walked. We did not care for fatigue or for hunger. One must suffer to see God. We traveled on. We reached Pyramid Lake. And then—"

"How!"

It was the command of Horn Cloud again. Short Bull smiled the least bit.

"Some way we all knew where he would come and when he would come, at sunset by the great rocks. So we waited. I had not believed. They had taught me in the parish churches not to believe too much. So I stood there and watched and looked here and there to see where he would come from. I looked hard and rubbed my eyes. He had not come at all. He was there. Just as if he had floated through the air."

Short Bull was biting his lips the least bit. Horn Cloud turned from him and faced me.

"I know that happen," *he explained in his Indian English.* "Big rocks—see? The Messiah, he get on a wagon and have it pulled up so it'll be hid-den by them rocks. Then he jumps out from behind the rocks like he floats through air—see? Wait!" *A moment of Indian gutturals, then a smile from Horn Cloud.* "Short Bull, he say he go behind rocks next day and see a wagon there."

And so, in this little explanation of an Indian interpreter came the first glimpse of the truth about the so-called Messiah—some street-corner ora-tor with a great scheme and with the spirit of the faker to carry it through. The questions went on. Short Bull, looking into the past with all the super-stition of the Indian, hesitated and moistened his lips.

"He was the Holy Man. His gown was like fire. It caught the sun rays and sent them back to the west. It glowed like the fire of a feast. It changed colors. All over the robe there were crosses, from his head to feet. Some of them were in white—some were in red. We could not see much, for he looked at us and we were afraid of him. He raised his arms, and there seemed to be fire all about him. We fell down and worshipped. And when we raised our heads, he was gone."

They had fallen and worshipped, worshipped with all the superstition and all the faith of the Indian race, worshipped a man in a changeable silk robe who had come mysteriously from behind a pair of great rocks by aid of an unseen wagon. But Short Bull was continuing.

"There was a little house by the side of the lake, and we went back there. We did not talk much. We were afraid to. The next morning, a little white boy came to us and told us his father was ready to see us and talk to us down in the willow grove by the lake. We . . ."

But I had interrupted. "His father?"

"The Messiah had a little boy," *came from Short Bull.* "The little boy said the Messiah was his father."[80]

And so this fanatic of Pyramid Lake had given God a grandson in his masquerade. But the Indians had not doubted it. How could they? It had been many years since the Messiah had been on earth. The Messiah was the Son of God; therefore, why not a grandson? And so they went to the willow patch, still trusting.

"So we went to the willow patch"—*Short Bull was in the past now, his face brightened by a wonderful memory*—"and he was here, just as we had seen him the night before. He talked to all of us, but he talked to me the most. He came close to me. He laid his hand on my forehead, and I thought that fire had gone through me. He held my hands, and they turned numb. His hands were hot when they touched me. When they left me, they were cold—cold like the wind outside. Then he talked. 'A long time ago,' he said, and he talked slowly, as if it hurt to remember, 'I came among the white people. But they did not like me. They sent me away. They crucified me."

Short Bull raised his hands and pointed to his palms. He raised his beaded, moccasined feet and pointed there. He bared his breast and patted it above his heart.

"He was the Holy Man," *he almost shouted, and there was a strange, an awed something in his voice.* "I saw. He showed me. Here, and here, and here—where they had nailed him to the crucifix! He was the Holy Man!"

Horn Cloud, educated and somewhat worldly, turned, wondering. "What [do you] make [of] that?" *he asked.*

And there was only one answer—reality, self-imposed torture, such as few men can stand, or the acid burns that are known to every professional faker the world over. But it would have done no good to tell that to Short

---

80. This is the only reference to Wovoka's son that I have found. Wovoka did have three daughters and two other children, who died young. Wovoka's son Timothy died at the age of six or seven. He was alive in 1892 when James Mooney met him, describing him as being four years old. So perhaps Short Bull met him. It needs to be noted that Father was the usual term to address Wovoka, the Ghost Dance Messiah. About Wovoka's family, see Hittman, *Wovoka*, 27–46, 201–206.

Bull. Nothing could take away the glamour of the vision. He had seen God. Besides, Short Bull was talking again.

"But after the Holy Man said that, he smiled and shook his head. That was a long time ago that the white people did that, and now he didn't care. Now he had come back to bring peace. He said, 'I have come back to bring you news. You have fought with the white man. That is wrong. I want you to go back to your tribe and tell them what I have said. You must say that the white man and the Indian shall live in peace. You shall say that the Indian must learn the white man's way and the white man's religion. There may be trouble. Stamp it out like a prairie fire. They may try to kill you, Short Bull, and even if they should, do not fight back. You must live in peace. Your children must go to the white man's school, and your children's children must grow to become the husbands and the wives of the white woman and the white man. And some day there will be no Indian. There will be no white man. You will all be one, and then will be peace.[81] Listen to me and listen to each other. I am the Holy Man. I am the Messiah. Listen to the white man and the white man shall listen to you. Do as I say, and on earth you will be together—and in heaven you will be together. And then there shall be no nights, no sleeps, no hunger, no cold. You shall be with me!'"

And even as he spoke, the words by jerks and fragments, there was an oratory in the recital of the little man, a resemblance as he quoted to the forms of the Scriptures. He continued, "'You have come unto me,' the Holy Man said, 'to learn the news. I have told it to you, and now you must journey forth to tell it to the others who wait by the tipis. Tell them to be merciful unto each other. Tell them the Father says to do no harm, but to live in

---

81. This, of course, contradicts other Ghost Dance accounts that emphasize the disappearance of whites and the survival of the Indian believers. This may be a later-born attempt by Short Bull to defend his religion. At the same time, this can be seen as one of the features of the Ghost Dance that emphasized assimilation into white society, seen in both Wovoka's and Short Bull's other texts. Still, in many Ghost Dance accounts presented here, the Ghost Dancers emphasized that whites and Indians cannot be the same. The historian Louis Warren has noted that the idea of racial blending and the disappearance of racial divisions in the Ghost Dance could be "seen as a counterpoint to contemporary white scientific and religious prophesies of an all-white world . . . racial transfiguration—the conversion of dark-skinned pagans to believers, who then miraculously acquire a white skin—was a hallmark of Christianity in the 19th century US. The idea that only good people would survive as Indians could be an Indian version of just this belief. That after the millennium only believers will populate the earth, and there will be no racial or tribal differences to separate them." Louis Warren, personal correspondence with author, February 2017. See Warren, *God's Red Son.*

peace.' And he told this to each one of us. To me he told it in Sioux. He told it to the others in their own language. Could any man but God have done it? There is no man who can talk all the languages. He taught us to dance, and he says this is the dance we must perform. He showed us his robe and told us that we should worship him by wearing robes like this. He told us that we must throw away the rifle and the war club. 'Live in peace,' he said, 'and let the white man live in peace with you.' And that was all he said. Pretty soon he was gone, and we turned and came home. Yes, that was all."

But history had interfered. History tells a different story of the Messiah—of someone who desired war between the white man and the Indian; of someone who told of the coming back of the Happy Hunting Grounds; of the return of the buffalo and the antelope and the elk, and the fading of the white man from the land. The questions came. But Short Bull only smiled.

"Yes, history say that," *he answered,* "but history lies. It was not the Messiah." *His face suddenly hardened. His hands clenched.* "It was the men who have made us suffer, who have brought the wrinkles to these cheeks and the trembling here!"

He held out his hands. His voice rose high. "I went home—and all before me there was singing and happiness. They had heard of [the] Messiah. All down through Pine Ridge, they sang and danced, and pretty soon Red Cloud and American Horse and Fast Thunder sent for me to come home. I knew what they wanted. They wanted war. They did not want to do as the Holy Man said. And so I went. I talked to them and they laughed at me. Then they brought me the ghost shirts to bless. I blessed them— and then—then," *the muscles of Short Bull's face were drawn tense,* "then they went back to their people and told them I had said that bullets would not pierce the ghost shirts. They went back and told their people I had brought a message from the Messiah, but that I could not give it directly. They told their people I had said the white man was to be driven out and that there must be war. But I did not know then. When I heard it was too late. All through the reservations, they were dancing now—and dancing for war—because American Horse and Fast Thunder and Red Cloud wanted war. They had blamed it all on me—and yet I only told what the Messiah had ordered me to tell. I begged them to listen to the Holy Man— to hear the news he had sent and live in peace with the white man. I did not want war; I did not want it! The Messiah had told me what to do, and I was trying to do it. I had told my people we should dance for the Messiah when the grass turned brown, but the police from the agency came out and told me to stop. Then they told me soldiers were coming. And then Fast Thunder and American Horse and Red Cloud called for me to come to Pine Ridge and fight the white man. But I said, 'No! No! The Messiah had said there must be no war.' Old Two Strike moved his camp from the Little White River toward Pine Ridge, but I stayed. The Brulés moved from the Rosebud toward Pine Ridge, but still I stayed. I had seen the Holy Man, and he had told me to live in peace. Then the young men of the Rosebud came to me and ordered me to follow Two Strike. I followed. They talked to me about cartridges, but I would not help them get them. I did not want war; I wanted to do what the Messiah had told me. We went to the Badlands. They told me that now I must fight against the whites. I cried out to them, 'No! No!'"

The little man was striding up and down the narrow space of his tent now. The squaw was wailing in a corner.

"'No! I keep calling to you; you do not hear me. I try to tell you that there shall be no war; you will not listen. You say the white soldiers will kill me? Then they can kill; I will not fight back. Once I was a warrior, once I wore the shield and the war club and the war bonnet; but I have seen the Holy Man. Now [there] is peace; now there shall stay peace. You chose me as the hard-hearted [stouthearted; brave] one to journey to the sunset to see the Messiah. I saw him, and I brought you his message. You would not hear it. You changed it. Now, I am silent.'"

There was a long pause. The death song from the old squaw in the corner rose high and shrilling, as shrilling as the wind of the blizzard without. Short Bull folded his hands.

"The next day I saddled my horse. I rode away. I came to the pine hills and looked out in the distance. They were fighting the battle of Wounded Knee. I kept on. They fought the battle of the missions, and they blame me for it—me, who saw the Holy Man. They were jealous; I was a hard-hearted [brave] man, and I was a chief. They did not like me, so they blame me for a war—my own people, my people who had sent me to the sunset that I might talk to Him, the Holy Man!"

So there is the story of Short Bull, whatever history may say. This is the story told me by that wrinkled, little heartbroken old Indian who lives in the past, standing there in the willow patch, listening to the message of the Messiah.

Short Bull

"You told us to quit the Ghost Dance and we will quit."

Short Bull and Kicking Bear delivered the following letter during the period of intense negotiations between the Ghost Dancers and the U.S.

Army.[82] It is a response to General John R. Brooke's request that the Indians come to the Pine Ridge Agency. By mid-December the Ghost Dancers were gradually moving toward the agency, but the killing of Sitting Bull on the Standing Rock Reservation on December 15 halted their movement and the negotiations had to be started again.

To Chief of Indian Scouts
From Short Bull & Kicking Bear

We don't want to fight. You told us to quit the Ghost Dance and we will quit my friend. I understand that you said in that case all the soldiers would go home. I am very anxious that that should be done—in that case my movements will be slow and careful in settling down again at the agency and, after we have settled down on White Clay Creek, I do not want any more soldiers to come back again my Friend. I shake hands with you with a good heart.

I am Short Bull.

Kicking Bear

"And our hearts sang in our breasts and we were glad."

This account by Kicking Bear was originally included in Agent James McLaughlin's letter to the commissioner of Indian affairs, Thomas J. Morgan, in October 1890, and later published as a part of McLaughlin's memoir, *My Friend the Indian*.[83] Kicking Bear provides us with another

82. Short Bull and Kicking Bear to Chief of Scouts, copy in Jerome A. Greene Collection, Arvada, Colo. The original letter is deposited in the National Archives, Washington, D.C. The letter is also published in Greene, *American Carnage*, 160. I am grateful to Dr. Jerome A. Greene for sending me a copy of the letter.

83. Kicking Bear in James McLaughlin to the Commissioner of Indian Affairs, October 17, 1890, NARA, RG 75, SC 188, M4728, roll 1, 3–33. See also James McLaughlin, *My Friend the Indian* (Lincoln: University of Nebraska Press, 1989; orig. pub. 1910), 185–89. Warren K. Moorehead summarized Kicking Bear's experiences in his article "The Red Christ" in the *Illustrated American* on December 13, 1890. Moorehead has mistakenly attributed the account to Kicking Horse, but it is clearly Kicking Bear's story, even though it is heavily edited by Moorehead. See Warren G. Moorehead, "The Red Christ," *Illustrated American*, December 13, 1890, p. 9.

view of the journey to the west. His account is not as detailed as Short Bull's. Kicking Bear describes a vision in which he is shown his dead relatives, the buffalo, and a new earth where white men were not allowed to live. Interestingly, Kicking Bear says that only Indians who believed in the new religion would survive the transformation of the earth. The rest would be left wandering in despair, but, according to Kicking Bear, they could enter the new world if they started believing. This is an interesting parallel to Christianity where sinners can repent and redeem themselves (for comparison, see Short Bull). Kicking Bear also refers to an "Evil Spirit" that fights with the Great Spirit for the "souls" of the people. This, too, is a reference to Christian concepts.[84] Kicking Bear, like Short Bull, also offers a solution to the Ghost Dance believers in case they encounter the U.S. Army; the powder used in the guns would simply not work. This, much like the Ghost Dance shirt, is an innovation grown out of fear of military intervention; the Ghost Dancers needed something to keep them united under the growing threat posed by the whites who were interfering with their religious ceremonies. Kicking Bear also promised that all Ghost Dancers killed by the whites would only "go to the end of the earth" and then be resurrected.[85] Kicking Bear arrived at Standing Rock on October 9, 1890. He went to Sitting Bull's camp on Grand River and told Sitting Bull's people about his experiences. Agent James McLaughlin sent the Indian policemen to see what was going on. After some hesitation, they escorted Kicking Bear off the reservation.[86] One of the Indian policemen, One Bull, related to McLaughlin what Kicking Bear told Sitting Bull's people. According to McLaughlin, the following is Kicking Bear's account "word for word."[87]

84. The devil or evil spirit was translated as *wakȟáŋšíča* by, for example, Christian missionaries.

85. For more, see Andersson, *The Lakota Ghost Dance of 1890*.

86. For the policemen see, for example, McLaughlin, *My Friend the Indian*, 190–91; Utley, *Last Days of the Sioux Nation*, 97–98; Coleman, *Voices of Wounded Knee*, 73–75.

87. McLaughlin, *My Friend the Indian*, 185.

My brothers, I bring you the promise of a day in which there will be no white man to lay his hand on the bridle of the Indian's horse; when the red men of the prairie will rule the world and not be turned from the hunting grounds by any man. I bring you word from your fathers the ghosts [spirits], that they are now marching to join you, led by the Messiah who came once on the earth to live with the white man, but was cast out and killed by them. I have seen the wonders of the spirit-land, and have talked with the ghosts [spirits]. I traveled far and am sent back with a message to tell you to make ready for the coming of the Messiah and return of the ghosts [spirits] in the spring.

In my tipi on the Cheyenne [River] reservation I arose after the corn-planting, sixteen moons ago, and prepared for my journey. I had seen many things and had been told by a voice to go forth and meet the ghosts [spirits], for they were to return and inhabit the earth.[88] I traveled far on the [railroad] cars of the white men, until I came to the place where the railroad stopped. There I met two men, Indians, whom I had never seen before, but who greeted me as a brother and gave me meat and bread. They had three horses, and we rode without talking for four days, for I knew they were to be witnesses to what I would see. Two suns had we traveled, and had passed the last signs of the white man, for no white man had ever had the courage to travel so far, when we saw a strange and fierce looking black man, dressed in skins. He was living alone, and had medicine with which he could do what he wished. He would wave his hand and make great heaps of money; another motion, and we saw many spring wagons, already painted and ready to hitch horses to; yet another motion of the hands, and there sprung up before us great herds of buffalo. The black man spoke and told us that he was the friend of the Indian; that we should remain with him and go no farther, and we might take what we wanted of the money, and spring wagons, and the buffalo. But our hearts were turned away from the black man, my brothers, and we left him and traveled for two days more.[89]

On the evening of the fourth day, when we were weak and faint from our journey, we looked for a camping place, and were met by a man dressed like an Indian, but whose hair was long and glistening like the yellow money of

88. It is interesting that Kicking Bear says that he was told by a "voice" to go forth and look for the Messiah, whereas Short Bull makes it quite clear that he was chosen by the council of Lakota leaders to go to Nevada (see above). So the two Lakota Ghost Dance leaders began their journeys from different premises.

89. I have not been able to determine who this black man was. It might refer to the same Bannock holy man mentioned by Short Bull.

the white man. His face was very beautiful to see, and when he spoke my heart was glad and I forgot my hunger and the toil I had gone through. And he said: "How, my children. You have done well to make this long journey to come to me. Leave your horses and follow me." And our hearts sang in our breasts and we were glad. He led the way up a great ladder of small clouds, and we followed him up through an opening in the sky. My brothers, the tongue of Kicking Bear is straight and he cannot tell all that he saw, for he is not an orator, but the forerunner and herald of the ghosts [spirits]. He whom we followed took us to the Great Spirit and his wife, and we lay prostrate on the ground, but I saw that they were dressed as Indians. Then from an opening in the sky we were shown all the countries of the earth and the camping-grounds of our fathers since the beginning; all were there, the tipis, and the ghosts [spirits] of our fathers, and great herds of buffalo, and a country that smiled because it was rich and the white man was not there. Then he whom we had followed showed us his hands and feet, and there were wounds in them which had been made by the whites when he went to them and they crucified him. And he told us that he was going to come again on earth, and this time he would remain and live with the Indians, who were his chosen people.

Then we were seated on rich skins, of animals unknown to me, before the open door of the tipi of the Great Spirit, and told how to say the prayers and perform the dances I am now come to show my brothers. And the Great Spirit spoke to us saying: 'Take this message to my red children and tell it to them as I say it. I have neglected the Indians for many moons, but I will make them my people now if they obey me in this message. The earth is getting old, and I will make it new for my chosen people, the Indians, who are to inhabit it, and among them will be all those of their ancestors who have died, their fathers, mothers, brothers, cousins and wives—all those who hear my voice and my words through the tongues of my children. I will cover the earth with new soil to a depth of five times the height of a man, and under this new soil will be buried the whites, and all the holes and the rotten places will be filled up. The new lands will be covered with sweet-grass and running water and trees, and herds of buffalo and ponies will stray over it that my red children may eat and drink, hunt and rejoice. And the sea to the west I will fill up so that no ships may pass over it, and the other seas will I make impassable. And while I am making the new earth, the Indians who have heard this message and who dance and pray and believe will be taken up in the air and suspended there, while the wave of new earth is passing; then set down among the ghosts [spirits] of their ancestors, relatives, and friends. Those of my children who doubt will be left in undesirable places, where they will be lost and wander around until they believe and learn the songs and the dance of the ghosts [spirits]. And while my children are dancing and making ready to join the ghosts [spirits], they shall have no fear of the white man, for I will take from the whites the secret of making gunpowder, and the powder they now have on hand will not burn when it is directed against the red people, my children, who know the songs and the dances of the ghosts [spirits], but that powder which my children, the red men, have, will burn and kill when it is directed against the whites and used by those who believe.[90] And if a red man die at the hands of the whites while he is dancing, his spirit will only go to the end of the earth and there join the ghosts [spirits] of his fathers and return to his friends next spring. Go then, my children, and tell these things to all the people and make all ready for the coming of the ghosts [spirits]."

We were given food that was rich and sweet to taste, and as we sat there eating, there came up through the clouds a man, tall as a tree and thin like a snake, with great teeth sticking out of his mouth, his body covered with short hair, and we knew at once it was the Evil Spirit. And he said to the Great Spirit: "I want half the people of the earth." And the Great Spirit answered and said: "No, I cannot give you any; I love them all too much." The Evil Spirit asked again and was again refused, and asked the third time, and the Great Spirit then told him that he could have the whites to do what he liked with, but that he would not let him have any Indians, as they were his chosen people for all future time. Then we were shown the dances and taught the songs that I am bringing to you, my brothers, and were led down the ladder of horses and rode back to the railroad, the Messiah flying along in the air with us and teaching us the songs for the new dances. At the railroad he left us and told us to return to our people, and tell them, and all the people of the red nations, what we had seen; and he promised us that he would return to the clouds no more, but would remain at the end of the earth and lead the ghosts [spirits] of our fathers to meet us when the next winter is passed.

90. Kicking Bear says here that the invulnerability of the Ghost Dancers was an idea that came directly from Wovoka. Thus it would not have been developed by the Lakota Ghost Dance leaders alone. Wovoka, however, denied ever saying anything about invulnerability or the bulletproof dance shirts. The Lakota Ghost Dance shirts were most likely a cultural innovation born out of visions and the shirts assumed their bulletproof nature only after the military arrived on Lakota reservations. (For Lakota accounts of the shirts, see below). It is worth noting that the Kiowas, for example, associated invulnerability with the Ghost Dance. See Benjamin Kracht, *Kiowa Belief and Ritual* (Lincoln: University of Nebraska Press, 2017).

Grand Council, Pine Ridge, Kicking Bear addressing the crowd, January 17, 1891. Photo: Northwestern Photographic Company. Denver Public Library, Western History Collection, X-31474.

Kicking Bear

"We do not want to fight. We did not begin to fight."

Kicking Bear was interviewed by Colonel Leonard W. Colby in the spring of 1891. This account was included in Colby's "The Sioux Indian War of 1890–91," published in 1892.[91] Here Kicking Bear, like so many others, complains about broken promises, bad agents, and the resulting destitution. He notes that the Lakotas did not start the fight and did not want to fight. They were looking to live in peace, learn to work, and send their children to school. While Kicking Bear's words could be interpreted as defending his actions during the trouble, one needs to remember that those were the exact instructions given by Wovoka to all Indians who visited him.[92]

My people have much to complain of. Our rations are too small. The Great Father promised us plenty. He sends us bad agents who rob us. Our land is poor and we can raise nothing. The buffalo, deer, elk, and antelope are all gone. We want more meat. We are hungry. We do not want to fight. We did not begin to fight. We want to be like white men and have our children go to school and learn to work. If the Great Father will do as he promised us, we will live in peace and be happy. Our Great Father said when he took our land that we should have plenty of meat and coffee and sugar, and have so much money every year, but we do not get it; and when the agent robs us they send soldiers. We want the Great Father to know this.

Good Thunder

"I saw the prints of the nails on his hands and feet."

Good Thunder, one of the members of the Lakota delegation, gave the following account to Elaine Goodale Eastman, the wife of Charles

91. Kicking Bear in L. W. Colby, "The Sioux Indian War of 1890–91," *Transactions and Proceedings of the Nebraska Historical Society* (Fremont, Neb.: Hammond Bros., 1892), 187.
92. For a thorough analysis of Wovoka and his message, see Hittman, *Wovoka;* Warren, *God's Red Son.*

Eastman.[93] Good Thunder's account is in "Little Sister to the Sioux," Elaine Goodale Eastman's memoir manuscript in Smith College's William Allan Neilson Library (Northampton, Mass.). It was later published in *Sister to the Sioux: The Memoirs of Elaine Goodale Eastman, 1885–1891*.[94] She came to Pine Ridge in the early 1880s to work as a schoolteacher. In the fall of 1890 (most likely November), she toured the Cheyenne River and Standing Rock Reservations, staying in the camps of Big Foot and Sitting Bull. In her memoir, she reflects upon how badly the Indians were suffering from hunger, but also how openly the people of Big Foot and Sitting Bull welcomed her. Of her meeting with Big Foot she writes: "Little did I dream as we drove gaily out of the peaceful, pretty settlement . . . followed by the cheerful barking of dogs and the laughter of children, and hearty goodbyes of our kind hosts, that our next meeting—only a few weeks later—would be a tragic one."[95] Next, her journey took her to the camp of Good Thunder where she took the following notes from Good Thunder's speech. In this account, Good Thunder refers to the Messiah as the Son of God, once crucified by the white men. The nail prints in his hand and feet were visible signs of the cruelty. Like others who saw the Messiah, Good Thunder describes him as a man of great beauty, although the exact appearance varies depending on the storyteller. Now the Messiah had come to save the suffering Indians. There has been extensive debate on whether Wovoka

93. For more about Alexander Eastman and his Ghost Dance statement, see part 3.

94. Good Thunder in Elaine Goodale Eastman, "Little Sister to the Sioux" (type-script), undated, Sophia Smith Collection, Smith College, William Allan Neilson Library, Northampton, Mass., box 8, folder 1. Copyright by the Board of Regents of the University of Nebraska. Published here by permission of University of Nebraska Press. Published also in Eastman, *Sister to the Sioux*, 143–44. A shorter version can be found in Elaine Goodale Eastman, "The Ghost Dance War and Wounded Knee Massacre of 1890–1891," *Nebraska History* 26, no. 1 (1945): 26–42.

95. Eastman, "Little Sister to the Sioux" (typescript), undated, Sophia Smith Collection, Smith College, William Allan Neilson Library, Northampton, Mass., box 8, folder 1.

claimed to be the Son of God or only a messenger. Many Lakotas seem to have believed that he was indeed the son of the Christian God.[96]

With three others I traveled a long time to find the Christ. We crossed Indian reservations and passed through white men's towns. On a broad prairie covered with Indians I saw him at last. We could not tell whence he came. Suddenly he appeared before us—a man of surpassing beauty, with long yellow hair, clad in a blue robe. He did not look at us or speak, but read our thoughts and answered without speech. I saw the prints of the nails on his hands and feet. He said that he had come upon the earth once before. Then he had appeared to the white people, who had scorned him and finally killed him. Now he came to red men only. He said their crying had sounded loud in his ears. They were dying of starvation and disease. The Messiah said he had come to save them. He had thought to come in three days [explaining to Eastman he meant three years] but their cries had so moved him to pity that he would come tomorrow [meaning next summer]. He would gather together the souls of all Indians who had died and they would be with the living in paradise, once more hunting the buffalo, dressing in skins, and dwelling in skin tents as of old. The souls of thieves and murderers must wait for some time outside. The people offered him a pipe, tobacco pouch, and moccasins. Three birds—an eagle, a hawk, and a dove—attended him.

Pretty Eagle

"I danced the dance with my eyes closed."

The following two stories by Pretty Eagle were recorded by Father Eugene Buechel in 1915 with Ivan Stars as the interpreter. A somewhat different translation has been published in *Lakota Tales and Texts*, edited by Paul Manhart. I and Raymond J. DeMallie made the new translation from the original in the Eugene Buechel Manuscript Collection.[97] In these stories Pretty Eagle describes his first visions during ceremonies at White Clay Creek. These accounts are remarkable because they

96. For this discussion see, for example, Andersson, *The Lakota Ghost Dance of 1890*, p. 38; Warren, *God's Red Son*.
97. Pretty Eagle in EBMC, HRMSCA, MUA. Published here by permission of Marquette University Special Collections and Archives. For a different translation, see Manhart, *Lakota Tales and Texts*, 532–39.

describe the Ghost Dance ceremony in great detail, including the visions and trances experienced during the ceremony; the second version stands out especially since it is a firsthand account of how the Ghost Dance shirts came about. There are several explanations for the origin of the shirts, but this and Black Elk's story give an insight into Lakota thinking and support the argument that the shirts were not "made for war," as many contemporaries and historians accused. In fact, to understand the significance of the Ghost Dance shirts, one needs to look for clues in Lakota traditions. The invulnerable Ghost Dance shirts were painted with sacred, protective symbols, similar to those used in shields and other protective garments. They would help the wearer in case of trouble.[98]

Story 1

They danced right there at the flats at White Clay Creek.[99] Now one morning they held a council so [to decide] that they will dance. And then they stood in the center of the camp and I joined them. And now they danced, so I joined in. And it was said that they would dance a really long time. And they sang two songs. Then they sang a third. Suddenly a light fell on my face and then I felt as though I would die. And then I did not know where I was going. So for a long time I did not remember anything [being unconscious]. And suddenly, at that time I remembered I went downhill together with someone.

So I went along with him into dense woods. And then the one I went with said this: "From here on you will go alone," he said, and so I looked at him. And then he came and stood right there and he said: "On the other side of the woods there is a camp!" So then I went along. Now I went through the woods. And then beyond [the woods] was a big and really pleasant camp. So I went as if nothing had happened and I went to the three men who came to the center. And then one said this: "Come and stand here and say something if you will!" he said. So, "Where do we live," I asked. Then he said: "You don't live here, so your older sister with your father, they live over there in

98. Recent works discussing the origins and the meaning of the Ghost Dance shirts include Ostler, *Plains Sioux*, 279–87; Andersson, *The Lakota Ghost Dance of 1890*, pp. 62–73; Warren, *God's Red Son*.

99. In Manhart, *Lakota Tales and Texts*, 2:532, the translation says White River, but Makȟásaŋ Wakpála is White Clay Creek.

that tipi." So I went there near the tipi, then at that time, someone came out and he came toward [me] and he came to me and then it was indeed my father and he said this: "*Huŋhuŋhé*, my son![100] I take pity of you, now you have come to me, so you will live right here," he said and hugged me.

So I went with him to the tipi and we went inside. My older sister sat alone inside and now I went close to her. Then she stood up and hugged me, saying: "My younger brother, you will stay right here." I sat down close to her and at once she gave me something to eat and I ate it. I sat right there a really long time. During that time my sister sat there with my father who sat silently the whole time, and so outside there seemed to be enemies [some commotion]. Then my father went outside and returned inside again and said: "My son, one man that lives in the old camp came but he smells really bad so he was told not to go inside, so he went home and did not go inside," he said.[101] Now I sat as if nothing was the matter and my father went again outside and said: "My son, go out, we will go to the other side of the camp," so I came out. So I went behind him and as I looked around there were many people walking around and I saw nobody on horseback and the men were almost invisible as far as their legs and I could only see their bodies. The hands of those who were walking were really black. So I went with my father and I looked at him and he too became affected and I did not see the one who was walking and my father knew how I was thinking and said thus: "My son, you cannot see [the soles of] the feet of the old camp's men."

We went to a really big tipi in the center of the camp. A man stood outside and said this: "Wait a little. Stand here," he said and then he stood there putting his head inside for a long time. Then he drew it back and said: "Even if you do well, still not one old camp man should come here. The Father thus forbade it. So go home from here. But first . . . ," he said.[102] So I went back with my father and again we came home and arrived there and my older sister sat right there so we arrived there. And my older sister said this: "My

100. *Huŋhuŋhé* expresses a wide range of emotion, such as pleasure, surprise, and sadness, depending on the tone. Here the tone is sadness. Manhart's translation is: "How sad! my son, whom I pity . . ." See Manhart, *Lakota Tales and Texts*, 2:533.

101. The "old camp" refers to the life outside the vision. In that world the people smelled bad because of all the terrible things that were going on. That is why the Lakota Ghost Dancers purified themselves in the sweat lodge before the ceremony. For further discussion, see Young Skunk below. For the use of the sweat lodge in the Ghost Dance, see introduction to this volume and Andersson, *The Lakota Ghost Dance of 1890*, pp. 54–55.

102. The idea is that the time for the coming of the new world was not yet at hand. The visions gave people a glimpse into that world, but before they could truly enter the new world, they had to dance and pray.

younger brother, they say that you will not be able to stay right here so you will return home. Yet we will not see you for a very long time," she said. "So from here on, whenever you want to see us here and when you will sleep, we will remember [you]. Soon I will see you often for many days and [you] will speak to mother. The mother that I love will soon come here," she said, "and my younger brother, whenever you are suffering we will look out for you and the people will do as the Father said, and whenever the old camp man comes here for four days, from then on he will be washed and then he will be camping among the people," she said, "and well, my younger brother, now you should go home, but I will take you," she said.

Now I came out and she came out with me and I started out in the direction that I had come from. My sister came after me and even if I walked very fast she gradually caught up with me. Thus, I was on that hill that I had come down [from] and now again I came back uphill and came on top. And suddenly it felt like I fell into a hole. And then at that time I remember very little as they crowded around me to care for me, and my older brother said this: "My younger brother, are you conscious?" so "yes," I said. Then he said: "This is the second time we take care of your body and now they danced for a long time and they dispersed," he said. So as my mother was crying, I became really sad and my mother, older sister and my father, those were right there behind [me]. Then again they told me to return home and they said my older sister will soon see me, so I felt really sad and the people were camping really pleasantly and doing really well and I did not at all think of coming here and I forgot about you [them?]. They said that my older sister will come too, so when she said, "Be alert and mother will soon go," I got really sad and as I was walking around, I spoke with them thus and when I finished I asked them how long I was lying down and standing. And right there, at the flats where they danced, I lay and so they stopped me, he [older brother] said.[103]

And then they took me inside and then in the morning they said they would break up the camp and, finally, as I was not yet recovered they said

103. This paragraph is very unclear. It is almost impossible to determine who is the subject and who is the object. It is not quite clear in the text when the description of the vision experience ends and when Pretty Eagle is back in the "real world." It seems that during Pretty Eagle's vision he was becoming very sick, perhaps close to dying, and having breathing problems. The people had to really take care of his physical body while he was "gone" on his journey in the spirit world. For comparison, see Manhart, *Lakota Tales and Texts*, 2:535–36.

they would carry me home and now it seemed it [the sickness] would be really bad. Then at that time they said I was gasping for breath [breathing again], so they rejoiced and from then on myself I was happy. Well, this is the way I know it and I believe it was done in a very sacred way.

I am Pretty Eagle.

Story 2

I went to a sacred dance on the White Clay Creek on the flats there. There was going to be a dance and the people gathered and they formed a circle. Then they danced and I joined in. Then again, I was overcome. Again, I died and was unconscious for a long time and then I again remembered.[104] I stood in the middle of the flat. The grass was very green and I climbed up and I was standing with someone. Then he said: "Look at this, make shirts in this way and give them to them [the Ghost Dancers]! And so those will come traveling this way and they will not hinder them," he said.[105] So when I looked there, an eagle was flying off spreading his wings and on both sides there were stars. And a sun was attached to the back of the eagle.

And it went flying off. And again it reached there and said this: "Make four in this manner: two for men and two for women," he said, "and those who will wear them, will soon arrive traveling and they will come on their own accord," he said, "so do it well," he said. And now it [the eagle] flew to the west and right there, I turned around and I came to. There again, I was sitting in the middle of the dance circle and right there I woke up. And then they questioned me and so I told about it. "This evening I will paint two shirts and two dresses," I said and they will announce it, "and right there, those who come, those who will come in front and they will speak to me," I said. And then, right there two young men and two young women came and they wanted to wear them. "Soon, when they have finished, bring them the two shirts and dresses," I said.

104. Both Pretty Eagle and Young Skunk use the same term *wéksuye*, "I remembered." Here it refers to waking up from a trance and remembering the vision experienced during the trance.

105. Both Young Skunk and Pretty Eagle refer several times to those who "travel" or are called "travelers" or "visitors." In this sentence, I believe that "those who will come traveling" refers to the Ghost Dancers who will wear the Ghost Dance shirts as they travel to the spirit world.

And then again we danced, but I danced watching and was not over-come. Whoever was overcome cried out. And they stood and those who fainted told about it.[106] And then they broke up. And in the evening those young men and women arrived and came to me. So they put up a tipi in the center [of the camp]. And inside they spread out sweet grass. And there I painted the shirts and the dresses: on the upper part of the back I painted an eagle; and then on both shoulders I painted stars; and on the chest I painted the moon. And then in the evening I finished. And early in the morning, there was going to be a dance again, so they gathered. And now, again, Brave Wolf acted as a leader.[107] And then they were going to dance so they proclaimed this to the gathering: "I come from the Father. And then that traveler they spoiled and in the future, put them aside and do it well!" he said.[108] And he cried out and we danced and those who I made shirts for, those then were overcome and moved about and both of them fainted. And here and there, they fainted. And then they came to and they sat down and told about it. And again we danced and the two women were overcome and again they fainted. And then they woke up. And then they told about it, those two young women told this: "An eagle came to me and took me to the camp [in the spirit world]," they said, "and again he came to me," they said.

And then, again when we danced, I was overcome and then again I became unconscious. And once again, when I came to my senses, then I remembered that I stood on a hill with a man. Then he said this: "My son, I will give you this song so therefore, I called you quickly," he said. And then as I stood there, I heard this song:

My Father said this, so sing it.

Those things that grow on the earth are mine

Those things that grow on the earth are mine

Father said this, so sing it, so sing it; Father said this, so sing it, so sing it.

106. It was a common feature in the Ghost Dance that those who experienced visions told about them publicly, an innovation in the Ghost Dance context. The Ghost Dance evolved through these experiences, and songs as well as the Ghost Dance shirts were born from these stories. See Andersson, *The Lakota Ghost Dance of 1890*, pp. 48–73. Traditionally, visions were private affairs, only to be discussed with a medicine man. See, for example, Black Elk in DeMallie, *The Sixth Grandfather*, 111–42, 215–44.

107. Brave Wolf was one of the delegates who traveled to see Wovoka.

108. This part of the text is unclear. Perhaps the word "traveler" refers here to Christ, who journeyed from heaven back to Earth and was "spoiled" by the white men. In other places the "traveler" or "visitor" refers to the "spirit journeys" that people experienced during visions, the "traveler" or "visitor" being the one who visits the spirit world.

"Well my son, whatever grows out of the earth in the future will be like this," he said and he shook the land with his foot, "Well, my son, that is why I invited you, go home and do like this," he said and he turned around and he flew off. And then all at once he shone and disappeared. And then I turned back there and then again I woke up in the middle of the dance circle. So again those who fainted told about it, so there I joined in, and I brought back that song and so I told about it and sang it. And so it was and many were overcome and fainted. And some were overcome for a long time. Then the dance lasted a long time and for a long time they recovered. I sat there and one was overcome for a very long time, so I sat watching him. And then he was babbling something incomprehensibly, so I watched him. Then I would again see this eagle with outstretched wings at his head. And then it was gone and the one lying fainted, it seemed like it came for him, I thought. Then he told about it: "An eagle came for me," he said.

And then when they all were finished telling about their visions, they danced again and I danced the dance with my eyes closed and it seemed like those sounds like buffalo hoofs galloping and then again little by little the sound of bird wings were mixed together and it seemed that the buffalo really bellowed and grunted, and it was like a buzzing noise and the dance songs disappeared and were soon gone. And more were really overcome and quickly I looked, but thus they were dancing and they were only ordinary people and my heart was beating fast and I was shaking.

And then at last they danced and stood still. And those who fainted then told about it. And when they stopped and when they were to finish there were still some lying fainted; Short Father (a priest)[109] went there and saw it. And now Short Father knows about it.

So I know this about these things, and now I do this for him. Little by little as I danced [with] my eyes shut, I knew nothing, although I believed it then.

I am Pretty Eagle.

---

109. Short Father refers to the Jesuit missionary Father Joseph Lindebner. He was stationed at the Holy Rosary Mission on the Pine Ridge Reservation. He was instrumental in, for example, Black Elk's conversion to Catholicism. See, for example, Paul P. Steinmetz, Sr., *Pipe, Bible, and Peyote among the Oglala Lakota: A Study in Religious Identity* (Syracuse, N.Y.: Syracuse University Press, 1998); Steltenkamp, *Nicholas Black Elk.*

Young Skunk

"I went walking in a beautiful land where the grass was really green."

This account by Young Skunk is part of the Eugene Buechel Collection like the Pretty Eagle and Short Bull texts.[110] Young Skunk actually gives three different stories relating to his various visions that he received during the Ghost Dance ceremonies. These texts give detailed descriptions of Young Skunk's visions and were very difficult to translate. Yet, despite some inaccuracies, these texts give a wonderful insight into the "doctrine" and ceremony of the Lakota Ghost Dance. Young Skunk, like Short Bull and Kicking Bear, notes several times how the world has become filthy and how people "in the old camp," or old world, smell. Interestingly, he experiences this smell firsthand in a vision, as the people in the spirit world look at him strangely because he smells. When he wakes up from his trance, he sees a "grayish world" where people smell, and he feels very sad. In his visions, his relatives tell him that there will soon be a new world that will be green and filled with happy people. However, he is told that it is not yet time for him to join his relatives, but by doing the right things his vision will come true. Young Skunk also describes how the dancers gather in a circle, raise a sacred cottonwood tree, and how people gradually take each other by the hand, start dancing, and fall into trances. Young Skunk, like Pretty Eagle, describes how important it was for those who "died" to relate their experiences to others after they woke up.

---

110. Young Skunk in EBMC, HRMSCA, MUA. See also Manhart, *Lakota Tales and Texts*, 519–32. I have retranslated this text from the original in the *Buechel Collection* with the help of Raymond J. DeMallie and Timo Oksanen in 2015–2016. Published by permission of Marquette University Special Collections and Archives.

Story 1

I joined the sacred dance at the flats there at White Clay Creek.[111] And then a man named Brave Wolf was going to lead it, they said. And then, one day they camped there and there were many people and the Cheyennes also camped [there].[112] And in the morning a camp crier came and said: "Those of you who will dance must eat no meat of any kind throughout the afternoon, but any chokecherries you have, you can eat, it is said, and then when the sun is about to set, you will dance."

And then those who were going to dance did so, and therefore I did so also. And then in the afternoon that crier came again and he said: "Those of you who will dance, come to the center!" Then many people came out of our tipis and I joined them. And then in the middle of the flats a cottonwood tree was raised, and a red blanket was tied on it, and several men sat there, and then all around them people stood there in a circle.[113] And then that man who was the leader stood by the sacred tree. And that man came along the circle of people and had them hold one another by the hand and he said this as he went along: "From now on whenever you dance you will hold on to one another. And you will only dance [with] your eyes shut, and you will not peek," he said, "and you will hold on firmly to one who is affected and then when he is really affected, you will hold him and take him to the center," he said, "and you will all sing as you dance," he said. "And first that one calls out and then he stops and then he sings and when he stops singing you people will really cry," he said. As he went along he said: "If you love your relatives, cry for them," he said as he went around the circle.

He comes, he, he, he comes he, he, he comes he he

He said this–ye, he said this

He said this ye-ye

The Father said this, he said, yo-yo-yo

111. Manhart has it as White River, but the correct translation is White Clay Creek (see above).

112. There was a large Cheyenne population (517 in 1890) on the Pine Ridge Reservation. A group of Cheyennes had come to Pine Ridge in 1879, followed by their relatives in 1881 and 1883. See, for example, Greene, *American Carnage*, 62.

113. The sacred cottonwood, *čháŋ wakȟáŋ*, was an essential part of the Lakota Sun Dance and symbolized the unity and the center of the Lakota people. For discussion of the Ghost Dance ceremony and the symbolism related to it, see Andersson, *The Lakota Ghost Dance of 1890*, pp. 54–67.

> You will see your relatives, he said
>
> This is why he said, he said ye-ya
>
> The Father said so, he said yo-yo.

When he finished the song, the people were crying and when they stopped crying they danced. In a very large circle and eyes shut we danced.

And then some of them were affected but I was not affected. So they rested and they sat down. And some lay in the middle as though dead. And some also lay on their backs. And after a little while those who lay as dead in the center, they came to and stood up and one after another they told how they died and where they went and then they finished speaking.

And then again we danced a little while and suddenly as I danced with my eyes shut, a light fell on me and my heart beat fast and I felt as though I was going to be affected but regardless I danced. And then I had pain in my liver and could not breathe, I became affected and once was dying of suffocation and my hands too were clenched, so I remember nothing. And then someone went following a path, so I went behind him and he went uphill so I went, and he went and stood on a hill and I went up and stood [there]. And then he said: "Go from here! It is not far from here." So then I went further on and in a little ways there was a hill so I went up it and stood. And then beyond there was a hill and a horseback rider was coming downhill and beyond the sky was full of smoke. So then he came closer. And then it was a woman who came and she came to me. And then it was my older sister who died long ago.

And that's the way it was; she came to me and said: "My younger brother, you came, so I came to meet you," and she hugged me by the neck and cried so I cried too, and she stopped crying so I stopped too. And then she said: "My younger brother, eat this and then go home from here," and she gave me some pemmican and she said: "My younger brother you smell very bad so you may not go to the camp [in the spirit world]!" And she said: "My younger brother, you people of the old camp really smell, so even though many come visiting over here they cannot go to the camp! And when you return here, do not wear any metal. So when you come here again you will go to the camp and you will see your child and your grandmother too," she said. And she kicked her horse, turned around and disappeared. And meanwhile I came to my senses and the dancers were resting. I woke up and stood up. And then the man who was the crier called me and said: "Come back over here!" so I went toward him and got there. And then he said: "Well, you will tell what you experienced," so I told how an eagle took me and how I arrived as a visitor [to the spirit camp].

Well, it was the first time I fainted, so I learned things from it and I was really anxious to go back again [to the spirit world].

I am Henry Young Skunk.

Story 2

They camped in a circle at the flats there at White Clay Creek during the sacred dance. And in the afternoon they danced and I joined. And again I was affected and I was really frightened and remembered nothing. And again I went with someone and he took me to a hill. And there beyond, there lay a land where all the leaves and the countryside were green. And there the people camped in a circle and at the center stood a crowd, so I came out to see. And the one who I went with said: "So go!" and so I looked [at him]. And then an eagle went flying in another direction, and it flew in the direction that I came from and I myself went into that green land.

And then I went, approaching the camp. And then a horseback rider came and she came over to me. And then again it was my older sister, and again she dismounted and hugged me. "My younger brother, those [in the camp] I love them," she said and cried. Thus I too cried again and then we stopped and she said: "My younger brother, come with me!" And thus I went and we went to a tipi at the end of the camp. And there was a really great circle and in the middle there was a really great crowd and they moved around in wild excitement. And we went to a tipi a little beyond the circle. We went on the side of the circle and the women and men too really looked at me. And so we arrived at a big tipi. As we arrived, there were only women sitting and they made room for me at the place of honor. And so I sat down and they all sat their heads bowed down and my sister sat close to me. And a big [grown-up, or middle-aged][114] woman sat close to me at the left-hand side.

She said: "My grandson, do not think that from here we will see them [dead relatives] soon. They tell you a story [about the Father] in this way; that is why our hearts will be sad for a long time and the journey is not as it used to be. And thus many will be allowed to see their own relatives; the Father has pity for the Indians, thus the men in the old camp really pray for the generations to walk accordingly. Again thirteen times, one by one, they returned to pray and in the future it might also be so, but the Father will be

---

114. A literal translation for *wiŋyaŋ tȟáŋka* is "big woman," but it also can mean a mature woman, adult or grown-up woman.

sad.[115] Well, my grandson, you will come here three times, but this is all that I declare to you. And soon your grandfather too may speak to you in this manner, but it will not be yet. Well, my grandson, eat now," she said and a pounding mat full of pemmican was brought to me. And so I ate and the fat too. Thus I ate it up. So I gave back that pounding mat and said, "Grandmother, I will go home now," and started off for home and looked ahead. And whenever I looked ahead there was a camp so far in the distance and there lay a land that smelled really good and the grass was really green. And then I looked to the north.

And again there was a fine camp and a fine horseback rider traveling. Thus I saw and then I was on my way home, and how I was on my way home I do not remember. So the dancers were sitting and I woke up right there, and looked. And then it was not the beautiful land that I saw; there was a grayish land. And it was sad. I really trembled and the men sitting around me smelled really bad and were really dirty. So now as I was conscious, I spoke and told them about those things that I knew. And again it will be three times [that he would visit the spirit world], I said and then suddenly I was a normal man again and recovered from being afraid and trembling and I felt really cold.

So that is what I know, and I think it is true and I believe it and by now that is how I think it will be. So that is all that I know.

I am Henry Young Skunk.

Story 3

They camped there at White Clay Creek, among the flats there was going to be a sacred dance and again I joined. And one day there was going to be a dance and they went together in the center and there was a really big crowd; thus they came in a row, facing one way. And thus they went in the center and the one who was acting as a leader came to the center and he said: "Hehehe, the Father told me that we do not do it [the Ghost Dance] in the right way. And thus the traveler, Father, said we will stop for a while, but once again really go slow for this last month," he said, "so do the dance

---

115. The meaning of this paragraph is unclear. It does refer to the common Ghost Dance belief that the time of the new world is not yet at hand, but by acting properly it will soon come. Still, I have not been able to determine what the number 13 stands for in this context.

really well and have pity [on each other]. And the Father says do not overdo it! So in the future this traveler will again receive you.[116] So listen to him! And whenever you dance, then dance with your eyes closed! And so one by one you will see your relatives," he said.

And now, "He he he-hi he he," he said, "Father look toward here, many of them listen to you, they will go, so he will have pity on them and they will see their relatives."

Father says this, he says it, yo yo

Father says this, he says it, yo yo, he says it ya yo

That he says, he says, he says

You will see your relatives, he says!

He sang this song and when he stopped they all really cried. And then we danced and at first some were affected, then they rested. So they sat down, they sat down in the circle and several of those who had died [fainted] talked about it and finished [talking]. And then again we danced and now a little longer, then again I was affected and was really frightened and soon remembered nothing. And then at that time I remembered, I went walking in a beautiful land where the grass was really green. And I arrived to a camp that had a good supply of food and there [people] were really walking about, so I came along the tents of the camp circle and over there outside there stood an older woman, so I went and asked a question. And then she knew this beforehand and said this: "Now it is not the time for you to come here; he went over there to the tipi on the other side of the camp, he went thereto and he went inside," she said.[117] Thus I went across the camp circle, but all those walking about were really afraid of me and they only went downwind [from me], so I went toward them. And the horses were lying nearby all together. And now I went inside. And then, a man was sitting inside all alone and as I arrived he said nothing and I stood inside and so I returned outside and stood there. And over here I saw a woman first, then she came and commanded me, implying that it was not the time for me to come here, I thought.

116. Here again the word "traveler" comes up. I am inclined to think that in this particular sentence the "traveler" is a term that refers to the Messiah or the Father.
117. It is not clear who she is referring to.

And then a man came from inside and said this: "Nephew, you come here not understanding, thus I said nothing," he said, "and now they went far away to pick berries, so they are out somewhere," he said. So I went back again the same way [from which I came]. And then a woman came along the way and said this: "My grandchild, come, we will go home, this is where we live," she said. So she started for home and so I saw her although her legs were not [entirely] visible;[118] my thoughts were clear, yet I did not see clearly. So I went back with her and there was a tipi painted red, so I went back inside with her and inside someone's voice was heard. So I went back inside with that woman. And then one woman sat inside and at the left side of the tipi only five young women were sitting and on the right side almost only older women were sitting. And then I sat down near a woman. She said: "My grandchild, I will give you something, but those who want to see their own relatives, whenever they dance, they should paint a stripe around their faces; only before these the Father brings them back and he asks them to do this and so I will give you one thing, but first you eat and then [I give it]," she said and she gave me pemmican. And I ate and I ate it all up. And then she gave it to me and said: "Well my grandchild, you understand this, so do not overdo it, then they will do the paint in vain," she said and she gave me red paint and I took it and I came back [to my senses]. Thus I came back to my senses.

Then I got up behind the dance [circle] and I was really shaking. I held the red paint on my left side [in my left hand]. So I remember. And then I recalled that the grandmother gave it to me. And then many died [fell into trances] and those they spoke about it, and myself when it happened to me, I told about how I had traveled, and whenever I told about the red paint, then they really wanted to put it on. And when the dancers had rested, I put on paint on twelve women and men too. And now at the dance, those whom I painted were all affected and they were dead [in trances] for a really long time and they saw their relatives well and they talked well. And they all said that an eagle carried them and they did not see the Father, but they indeed saw their relatives.

And so this dance adjourned and they broke up the gathering and the dancers camped really far away. Again and again they would dance, so one day they went to the center of the [circle] and there was a really big crowd. Then right there Kicking Bear and Brave Wolf together were acting as lead-

---

118. This sentence implies that the woman was floating in the air only partly visible. See also account by Pretty Eagle.

ers. Then Kicking Bear was first affected for a very long time and he recovered at last and the people stood there waiting. And now he spoke and he said this:[119] "Hehehe, my relatives have pity on each other! Lately the Father said we have done wrong and therefore we will see them [dead relatives] further on [in the future]. The Lakotas killed Sitting Bull because of this dance, it is said. So we break the rules we [the Messiah?] made for us, he said.[120] And thus from here on as long as this dance is not stopped, we will dance, but there will be no brave deeds.[121] So my boys, listen! We will do it well. Well now, because of the white men, this community [reservation] is shrinking badly.[122] Now, [my] Father is the one who decide[s] the strength; he has not yet given it to us. So over here among the Oyúȟpe [band], we will hold this sacred dance, but I will do it well and Brave Wolf does it here too, and he does it well. Very well, whenever you dance, dance [with] your eyes closed. So now stand up!" And thus they stood up, then he called out four times in a really loud voice:

> He came, he-e, he came, he-e, he came, he-e, he came he-e
>
> Father pity me, many want to see you
>
> And those they want to see their relatives, have pity on them
>
> He came bringing this song
>
> You shall see your relatives
>
> The Father says so, say it yo yo, say it
>
> The Father says so, say it yo yo.

When he stopped they all really cried and when they stopped they danced. This is the really beautiful song that they sang first:

> My son, hold me by the hand
>
> You will prosper, ye ye
>
> Father says this, yo

---

119. Manhart's translation attributes the following speech to Brave Wolf, but the original manuscript clearly states that the speaker is Kicking Bear. For comparison, see Manhart, *Lakota Tales and Texts*, 528.

120. This is perhaps a reference to Wovoka's message that forbade fighting and killing.

121. Kicking Bear seems to say that since there will be no fighting, no brave deeds will be done.

122. This is a reference to the Sioux Act of 1889 that split the Great Sioux Reservation, resulting in white settlers encroaching on Lakota lands.

My son, hold me by the hand

You shall prosper ye ye. The Father says this yo!

So now they sang it a second time and again a light fell on me. And again I had that feeling that vomit came toward my throat and it was becoming tight and I was really frightened. So I remembered nothing. And again I went up on to a hill. At that time I remembered. Then suddenly a man came up close to me and he said to me: "My boy, once again I bring you to the Father; from then on your relatives are alive, you will go over to them, I myself watch over the path, but I will close the door whenever the Father says nothing further," he said. And then I went with [him] and we went up that hill. And then there was a man who stood above the ground, it seemed to me. And then that man who had brought me said: "Go and stand before him! He is your Father," he said. Thus I went and stood before him. "Now my son, I love you [people], but now again I give you this traveler[123] so that you will go to your relatives, and the Indians from all over the country come back crying. Thus soon I will examine this in a different manner, so I will do accordingly, so report it! And now go," he said. And so I went straight on, and I went to a real camp, but at first I did not see that man who I came with. So now I arrived near that camp. And then someone came from there and arrived. It was my younger sister and again she came toward me and thus she hugged me around the neck and said: "My younger brother, let us go! We will go to our home," she said. And so we went toward home and we went home through the [circle of] tipis and I saw no fires built in the tipis nor did anybody come out. So now I went inside one tipi and the land where I first came to [in previous visions] was not there. So I arrived in this land along a creek where the leaves were green and at that time a camp extended a ways along the creek and the tipis were all alike and there was no smoke. And now then I went inside and again I sat down at the place of honor and looked around the tipi and it smelled good inside and two young women sat inside and they did not look up at me at all, they sat silently, their heads bowed. And then my older sister gave me food, a piece of meat, fat. So I took the food she gave me and I ate and I ate it all up. Then my older sister said thus to me: "My younger brother, soon the Father will stop these visitors [visits] and the people will be very sad hearted. For the last two gen-

---

123. Here the word "traveler" seems to refer to the man who brought Young Skunk in front of the Father, as if he were a mediator between the Father and those visiting the spirit world.

erations the difficulties have been prolonged. So my younger brother, when you will go home, hold on to this," she said and I took something that she gave me and I came to my senses.

And again after they danced a little, they sat resting; at that time I woke up. And again the land where I woke up was really bad and I looked to and fro and my heart was really sad. And now many of those who died [went into trances] spoke and I myself stood up in the center and thus I walked around telling about these things. And I held in my hand what my sister gave me and looked at it.

Thus it was medicine, small and very yellow and it smelled good and the smell was pleasing to them. And they told me the medicine was nothing. So it was not clear how I should use it. So I said nothing and again when we danced, I was again affected and I remember nothing; I stood on a hill together with my younger sister who cried and said this: "My younger brother, whenever you want to see me, then burn this medicine," she said, "and so you will lie down and the men in the old camp smell really bad and the Father takes those men here and there, so I take it and give it to you. Well it is so, he says! But your meat [body] will be different. The Father gives you an eternal life, so in the future you will have a different kind of body, he said. It is so," she said, so I looked at her again. Then I do not know what happened, and I was standing right there all alone. So I turned around and started back home. And here in the countryside the dancers were sitting and I walked there into the center. At that time I remembered. I stood up at once and thus told about my experiences.

And then this dance was finished and they broke up the gathering and we arrived home. Then one evening I remembered and was going to lie down, but then I did not lie down, so I burned incense [the yellow medicine] and then lied down. Then at once my younger sister stood outside laughing and said this: "My younger brother, I came, but thus they walk all over camp," she said, "and along with them I bring along this small thing," she said. And she gave me a piece of pemmican and, "Well my younger brother, now I will go home," she said and at once she went and I watched her. And she went home over the tree tops and so she went and disappeared. So at dawn I spoke in our tipi and they listened and now this was the second [account] of what I know. Well this is how it was.

I am Young Skunk.

Little Wound

"I would like to see my relations who have been dead a long time."

This account by Little Wound was received through Lone Wolf and appeared in the *Illustrated American* on January 17, 1890, in an article entitled "Ghost Dances in the West."[124] The article was written by archaeologist-anthropologist Warren King Moorehead, who arrived at Pine Ridge in November 1890. Altogether he wrote five articles about the Lakota Ghost Dance, four of them as "special correspondent." His first article, entitled "Red Christ," described the Ghost Dances although he had not at the time even seen one.[125] Little Wound, who later denied believing in the Ghost Dance, relates his vision experience that promised to bring about the new world. He also discusses the blessed medicine shirts, that is, Ghost Dance shirts that would protect the wearer. It is also worth noting that toward the end of the vision, Little Wound is allowed to smoke the sacred pipe, which could be seen as a symbol that validates the Messiah's teachings.[126] While Good Thunder (see above) referred to the Messiah as the Son of God, Little Wound goes a little further, referring to the Messiah as God, but simultaneously calls him Great Spirit and Wakȟáŋ Tȟáŋka. Little Wound had become an Episcopalian a few years earlier and this account combines his Christian and Lakota beliefs into one new belief—the Ghost Dance.

When I fell in the trance a great and grand eagle came [and] carried me over a great hill, where there was a village such as we used to have before the whites came into the country. The tipis were all of buffalo hides, and we

---

124. Little Wound in Warren K. Moorehead, "Ghost Dances in the West," *Illustrated American*, January 17, 1891, pp. 330–31. Published also in Boyd, *Recent Indian Wars*, 189–91.

125. For an analysis of the *Illustrated American* and Warren K. Moorehead's reporting from Pine Ridge, see Karen A. Bearor, "The *Illustrated American* and the Lakota Ghost Dance," *American Periodicals*, 21, no. 2 (2011): 143–63.

126. For the significance of the sacred pipe, see, for example, Walker, *Lakota Belief and Ritual*, 82, 87–90; Joseph Epes Brown, *The Sacred Pipe: Black Elk's Account of the Seven Rites of the Oglala Sioux* (Norman: University of Oklahoma Press, 1989).

made use of the bow and arrow, there being nothing [of] the white man's manufacture in the beautiful land. Nor were any whites permitted to live there. The broad and fertile lands stretched in every direction, and were most pleasing to my eyes.

I was taken into the presence of the great Messiah, and he spoke to me these words: "My child, I am glad to see you. Do you want to see your children and relations who are dead?" I replied: "Yes, I would like to see my relations who have been dead a long time." The God then called my friends to come up to where I was. They appeared, riding the finest horses I ever saw, dressed in superb and most brilliant garments, and seeming very happy. As they approached, I recognized the playmates of my childhood, and I ran forward to embrace them while the tears of joy ran down my cheeks.

We all went together to another village, where there were very large lodges of buffalo hide, and they held a long talk with the great Wakȟáŋ Tȟáŋka. Then he had some squaws prepare us a meal of many herbs, meat, and wild fruits and *wasná* (pounded beef and chokecherries). After we had eaten, the Great Spirit prayed for our people upon the earth, and then we all took a smoke out of a fine pipe ornamented with the most beautiful feathers and porcupine quills. Then we left the city and looked into a great valley where there were thousands of buffalo, deer, and elk feeding.

After seeing the valley, we returned to the city, the Great Spirit speaking meanwhile. He told me that the earth is now bad and worn out; that we needed a new dwelling place where the rascally whites could not disturb us. He further instructed me to return to my people, the Sioux, and say to them that if they would be constant in the dance and pay no attention to the whites he would shortly come to their aid. If the high-priests would make for the dancers medicine shirts and pray over them, no harm could come to the wearer; that the bullet of any whites that desired to stop the Messiah dance would fall to the ground without doing anyone harm, and the person firing such shots would drop dead. He said that he had prepared a hole in the ground filled with hot water and fire for the reception of all white men and non-believers.[127] With these parting words I was commanded to return to Earth.

127. Pretty Eagle (see above) also noted that all holes and bad places would be filled up, and George Sword (see part 3) mentioned a hole in the ground that would contain water that would cover the Earth.

Little Wound

"There was my mother and father and brother who had died long ago."

In December 1890, Little Wound gave an interview to Captain Marion P. Maus. The interview was published in *Harper's Weekly* magazine under the title "The New Indian Messiah." [128] Maus writes about Little Wound at length and notes that he "claims to have seen the Messiah sitting in a *wickiup.*"[129] Little Wound never met Wovoka so this account is a description of a vision experience, but Maus does not elaborate on that.

The Messiah had long hair down to his shoulder, and when I first saw him he seemed about twenty years old; the next day he appeared thirty; the next, forty; and the next, an old man. He said: "Come with me and I will show you your dead relatives," and suddenly I heard a noise like that of a railroad train. I was carried through the air, and came to a field with a small house on it. I went in, and there was my mother and father and brother who had died long ago. My father and brother were both killed years ago fighting the white man. They came up to me crying, and I shook hands with them.

Weasel

"We . . . trusted to the Great Spirit to destroy the soldiers."

This account by Weasel also appeared in the *Illustrated American* on January 17, 1890, in "Ghost Dances in the West" by Warren K. Moorehead.[130] In this short but interesting account Weasel gives an insight into what happened among the Ghost Dancers when they received news of the soldiers' arrival. Instead of talking about fighting the soldiers, the Ghost Dancers prepared to flee if necessary. This supports Short Bull's account above. Weasel also noted that they trusted

128. Little Wound in Marion P. Maus, "The New Indian Messiah," *Harper's Weekly*, December 6, 1890, p. 947.
129. See Maus, "The New Indian Messiah," 947.
130. Weasel in Warren K. Moorehead, "Ghost Dances in the West," *Illustrated American*, January, 17, 1891, p. 333. Also published in Boyd, *Recent Indian Wars*, 194–95.

the Great Spirit to destroy the soldiers and that no arms were carried by the dancers contradictory to many contemporary accounts.[131] Weasel's story about a girl trying to gash herself with a knife was a common story among the Ghost Dancers at the time.

While dancing I saw no visions, but the other Indians told me to not think of anything in particular, but keep my eyes fastened upon the holy men, and soon I would see all that they saw.

The first large dance held was on Wounded Knee Creek under the guidance of Big Road. I attended this one, but did not observe Two Strike in the audience. We had been dancing irregularly for several weeks when a runner came into camp greatly excited, one night, and said that the soldiers had arrived at Pine Ridge and were sent by the Great Father at Washington. The holy men called upon the young men at this juncture not to become angry but to continue the dance, but have horses ready so that all could flee were the military to charge the village. So we mounted our ponies and rode around the hills all night singing our two songs. Never before in the history of the "Dakotas" (the name by which the Sioux call themselves, meaning "allies") has a dance like this been known. We did not carry our guns nor any weapon, but trusted to the Great Spirit to destroy the soldiers.

Question: "Did you ever see the medicine-shirt worn?"

Weasel: "Yes, they wore blessed shirts that night. The holy men had said prayers over these garments, and they were bullet proof. One girl tried to gash herself with a butcher knife on the arm, but the blade was bent and the edge turned, so powerful was the medicine in the shirt."

Little Horse

"The earth . . . was now worn out and it should be re-peopled"

This text portrays a vision experience by Little Horse and was interpreted by Weasel for Warren K. Moorehead and published in the *Illustrated American* on January 17, 1891.[132] Here we can again see the merging

---

131. For the discussion about arms carried during the Ghost Dance, see Andersson, *The Lakota Ghost Dance of 1890*, pp. 64–65.

132. Little Horse in Moorehead, "Ghost Dances in the West," 332. Also published in Boyd, *Recent Indian Wars*, 193–94.

of Lakota traditions with Christian teachings. Two holy eagles,[133] messengers from the spirit world, take Little Horse to the Messiah, who shows scars from nails in his hands and feet and a wound in his side. Little Horse, like Good Thunder (above) and many others, clearly thought of the Messiah as Jesus, once crucified by the whites and now back on earth to help the Indians. The idea that the world was "worn out" or was smelling bad due to violence and misery is brought up again.

Two holy Eagles transported me to the happy hunting grounds. They showed me the great Messiah there, and as I looked upon his fair countenance I wept, for there were nail prints in his hands and feet where the cruel whites had once fastened him to a large cross. There was a small wound in his side also, but as he kept himself covered with a beautiful mantle of feathers this wound only could be seen when he shifted his blanket. He insisted that they [the Indians] continue the dance, and promised me that no whites should enter his city nor partake of the good things he had prepared for the Indians. The earth, he said, was now worn out and it should be re-peopled. He had a long beard and long hair and was the most handsome man I ever looked upon.

Anonymous Woman

"I was carried into the beautiful land."

This typical vision experience was related to Warren K. Moorhead by an anonymous woman and was published as part of Moorhead's article "Ghost Dances in the West" in the *Illustrated American* on January 17, 1890.[134]

I was carried into the beautiful land as others have been, and there I saw a small but well-made lodge constructed entirely of brushes and reeds.[135]

---

133. In Lakota traditions, the eagle symbolized the unity of the Lakota people and the crow acted as a messenger from the spirit world. Both birds frequently appeared in Ghost Dance visions.

134. Anonymous woman in Moorehead, "Ghost Dances in the West," 332. Published also in Boyd, *Recent Indian Wars*, 193.

135. Interestingly, she describes a typical Paiute lodge, not a tipi, as in most Lakota vision experiences.

These were woven closely together and resembled the fine basket work that many of our squaws make during the winter. The tipi was provided with a stonewall, which is composed of small, flat stones laid up against the walls to the height of three or four feet. In this lodge the great Wakȟáŋ Tȟáŋka dwelt and would issue forth at noon. Promptly at the time when the sun was above me, the lodge trembled violently and then began its descent toward the earth. It landed near the dance ground, and there stepped forth a man clothed in a blanket of rabbit hides. These are [This was] the Messiah and he had come to save us.

Two Lance

"We are simply to pray and trust in the Messiah."

Two Lance's comments were published in the January 24, 1891, issue of the *Illustrated American*.[136] Although the paper does not mention the author, "the special correspondent" was Warren K. Moorehead.[137] Two Lance discusses the basic themes of the Lakota Ghost Dance: he forbids violence and says that they should rely on prayers instead. Still, the tone of this text makes me wonder if it is more of a construction of Moorehead's imagination than the actual words by White Lance. For example, the sentences "This is to us a very strange doctrine, as you will admit. We have been accustomed to fight, not to pray" strike me as very strange, almost as if the Lakotas had never prayed before. Even though the Ghost Dance included many Christian elements, the sentence "Be repentant for your sins" is more likely Moorehead's own interpretation than a translation from Two Lance's Lakota words.

Brothers, if you listen to my words attentively you will profit thereby. We have returned from the country of the Utes bringing good news for the Dakotas [Lakotas]. Many, many winters ago the Great Spirit sent His Son upon the earth to teach men to do right—to be good. Instead of listening

136. Two Lance in "Why the Indians Fight: A Startling Story of Famine and Fraud," *Illustrated American*, January 24, 1891, pp. 392–93.
137. See Bearor, "The *Illustrated American* and the Lakota Ghost Dance," 143–63.

to the words of the holy Visitor, the wicked white men killed Him.[138] He has appeared to be a good and righteous man in the land of the Utes, and told him [them] that he would soon come upon earth again; but this time for the salvation of the Indians, and not the whites. The whites are to be overwhelmed, so the Messiah said, by a great earthquake or storm. In the terrible convulsion of the earth, all Indians who are not prepared to welcome their Lord will meet with the same fate as the whites. Therefore, O my people, I exhort, nay, command you to do all that the good man says, in order that you may not suffer the death of our despised enemies.

The holy Teacher further says that the overpowering of those who have oppressed us is not to be accomplished by force of arms, that no weapons are to be used. We are simply to pray and trust in the Messiah, and dance as he shall command. This is to us a very strange doctrine, as you will admit. We have been accustomed to fight, not to pray. Therefore we must be all the more careful to obey every command of the new Saviour, or we will displease Him.

In conclusion, I have but to urge upon you to watch very carefully every motion of the dance which we are about to execute for you, and, when you have learned the songs and the movements, join in with us. Be repentant for your sins, pray the great Wakȟáŋ Tȟáŋka to look down upon you in pity, to give you food and clothing. Be sincere, be earnest, and He will hear our prayers.

Anonymous Man

"Let us worship the Great Spirit in our own way."

Father Florentine Digman, a Catholic missionary at the St. Francis Mission on the Rosebud Reservation, wrote a lengthy description of his meeting with Ghost Dancers in his diary on September 30. He also described his encounter in a letter to his superior, Father J. A. Stephan, on October 2, 1890.[139] Father Digman called the Ghost Dance "a new

138. Two Lance mentions the "Holy Visitor," meaning the Messiah, that is, Jesus, in other words, Wovoka. See Young Skunk above for further commentary about the terms "visitor" and "traveler."

139. Anonymous man in FDP, September 30, MUA, BCIM, History of St. Francis Mission, 1886–1922, SFMC. Published by permission of Marquette University Special Collections and Archives. A slightly different, shorter, version can be found in Florentine Digman to J. A. Stephan, October 2, 1890, MUA, BCIM, series 1–1, roll 10.

kind of sacred dance and prayer."[140] He visited a Ghost Dance camp on White River and discussed the Ghost Dance with several dancers. According to Digman, they were peacefully disposed, but refused to give up the Ghost Dance, arguing that they needed to have a "free council" of Lakotas to make a decision like that. Digman notes that one man "made a very good remark" about why the Lakotas believed in the Ghost Dance. The following remark by this anonymous man explains in a somewhat ironic tone that there were many Christian denominations on the Lakota reservations, all claiming to be better than the other. Now the Lakotas had their own prayer, and they wanted to be left alone. When Agent Wright, who accompanied Digman, asked the Indians why they were "bent on dancing," a Ghost Dancer replied:

This is our way of worshipping the Great Spirit, who has taught us so. You are a Blackrobe [Jesuit]. We know you speak the truth. For this reason chief Spotted Tail had asked the Great Father to send Blackrobes as teachers for his people. But instead he sent us Whiterobes [Protestants], saying they are alike. Now you white folks have different prayers. The Blackrobe's prayers and that of the Whiterobe's and you quarrel [with] each [other] saying the other is not right. We Indians do not want that strife. Let us alone then, and let us worship the Great Spirit in our own way.

Anonymous Ghost Dancers

"I have seen the Great Father but he was not talk to me because I stink."

The *New York Times* ran an article on November 22, 1890, that described a Ghost Dance ceremony. The reporter witnessed the ceremony with the Lakota scout Half Eyes, mixed-blood scout Jack Russel, and Major John Burke.[141] The first brief quotation is interesting, as it evokes the common

---

140. Many of the Catholic missionaries did not condemn the Ghost Dance as such. Father Francis M. Craft even noted that it was quite "edifying." In fact, the Protestant clergy condemned the Ghost Dance in much harsher words. See Andersson, *The Lakota Ghost Dance of 1890*, pp. 166–91.

141. Anonymous Ghost Dancers in *New York Times*, November 22, 1890, pp. 1–2.

idea that the Messiah will not yet talk to the people because they stink. That idea is also present in the vision experiences of Young Skunk and Pretty Eagle.

All of a sudden one of the warriors in the ground heat [rose] to his feet and exclaimed: "I have seen the Great Father [Messiah] but he was not talk to me because I stink." *And the other warrior good [got] up and cried:* "I have seen the Great Father but he will not talk to me because I have no ponies!" *A squaw was the last to get up upon her feet. In a shrill voice she cried out:* "I have seen the Great Father. He sent an eagle which picked me up and carried me to a faraway mountain. The Great Father told me that the whites would be driven from the country, that the Indians would rule the land and the buffalo and deer return."

Black Elk

"Under the tree that never bloomed I stood and cried because it faded away."

John G. Neihardt interviewed Black Elk first in 1931 and again in 1944. The original manuscripts and other materials are in the Neihardt Collection, Western History Manuscript Collection, University of Missouri, Columbia. Raymond J. DeMallie edited these documents for publication as *The Sixth Grandfather: Black Elk's Teachings Given to John G. Neihardt* (1985).[142] As Black Elk's account has been fully published before, I debated whether to include it here at all. However, Black Elk's role as a spiritual leader during the Ghost Dance was so important that his story has to be included here too. I have followed Raymond DeMallie's edited version, but added a few comments when it seemed necessary. As a young boy, Black Elk received a vision that set him on his path to become a holy man. As the Ghost Dance was taking hold of the Lakotas, Black Elk had just returned from a tour in Europe

---

142. Black Elk, NCWHMC, UMC. I have used Raymond J. DeMallie's transcript notes with his permission. Published also in DeMallie, *The Sixth Grandfather*, introduction, 256–82.

with Buffalo Bill's Wild West show. He was devastated about the poverty that had taken hold of his people on the Pine Ridge Reservation. Black Elk doubted the Messiah's teachings at first, but then a vision reminded him of the powers he had received in his boyhood vision. He believed that his mission was to bring the people back together through the Ghost Dance into the sacred hoop. In his boyhood vision, he saw a tree in full bloom, which represented the prosperity of the Lakota people. During a Ghost Dance ceremony, he saw this tree in the center of the dance circle and again in a vision: "When I saw the tree in the vision it was in full bloom, but when I came back the tree was wilted and dead. If this world would only do as it is told by this vision, the tree would bloom," and the Lakotas would prosper again. As a Ghost Dance leader, he participated in making the sacred Ghost Dance shirts and he depended on their power during the battles following the Wounded Knee massacre. Yet because he was wounded in one of the skirmishes, he realized that he had forgotten the real vision that gave him power. Had he relied on his boyhood vision, he would not have been wounded, he believed. Still, in Black Elk's words, the Ghost Dance was going to give his people "a place in this earth where they would be happy every day and that their nation might live," and it would bring them "back into the hoop."

When I came back [from Europe] [143] my people seemed to be in poverty. Before I went some of my people were looking well, but when I got back they all looked pitiful. There had been quite a famine. I returned in 1889. While I was gone I had lost my power, but as soon as I returned I was called out to cure a sick person and just then my power returned.[144]

At this time people were all talking about the land they had sold to Three Stars [General Crook] as a result of a treaty [the Sioux Act of 1889]. This fall I had another brother who went out on a show which went all over the world. He started out on this show.

---

143. The italicized insertions in brackets in this document were made by Raymond J. DeMallie and the texts in parentheses are part of the original text. The insertions in brackets without italics are mine.

144. Black Elk refers to his time in Europe (1886–1889) with Buffalo Bill's Wild West show. See *The Sixth Grandfather*, 245–55.

This fall I heard that there were some men named Good Thunder, Brave Bear, and Yellow Breast who had gone and seen the Messiah. It was toward the west right around Idaho somewhere. There was a sacred man there. These three men had gone to see this sacred man and they came back that following fall [1889] and reported that they had seen the Messiah and actually talked to him and that he had given them some sacred relics.[145] They had had the meeting at the head of White Clay [Creek] and the people gathered together there to hear what these men had to say about it. I did not go over there, I just heard of it, that's all. These three men had brought some sacred red and white paint that the sacred man had given them. This paint was broken up into little pieces and distributed among the people.

These people told me that these men had actually seen the Messiah and that he had given them these things. They should put this paint on and have a Ghost Dance, and in doing this they would save themselves, that there is another world coming—a world just for the Indians, that in time the world would come and crush out all the whites. But if you want to get into this other world, you would have to have this paint on. It should be put all over the face and head [*show them this ceremony to be performed*], and that this Ghost Dance would draw them to this other world and that the whites would have no power to get on so that it would crush them. In this other world there was plenty of meat—just like olden times—every dead person was alive again and all the buffalo that had been killed would be over there again roaming around. This world was to come like a cloud. This painting and Ghost Dance would make everyone get on the red road again. Everyone was eager to get back to the red road again.[146]

This sacred man had presented two eagle feathers to Good Thunder, one of these three men. The sacred man had said to him: "Receive these eagle feathers and behold them, for my Father will cause these two eagle feathers to bring your people back to him." This is all that was heard this whole winter. At first when I heard this I was bothered, because my vision was nearly like it and it looked as though my vision were really coming true and that

145. Black Elk's time frame seems to indicate that there was first one delegation and later in the fall of 1889 another. The official delegation left in the fall of 1889 and returned in April 1890. Yet it is not impossible that some Lakotas visited, for example, the Shoshones in Idaho earlier. Intertribal visitation was quite common in the late 1880s. For this discussion, see Andersson, *The Lakota Ghost Dance 1890*, pp. 31–34; Gage, "Intertribal Communication," 157–220; and Warren, *God's Red Son*, 182–84.

146. In Lakota tradition, the red road represents all things good—peace and prosperity—while the black road is a symbol of war and destruction. Hence, the red paint was also very sacred. See DeMallie, *The Sixth Grandfather*, 119–28.

if I helped, probably with my power that I had I could make the tree bloom and that I would get my people back into that sacred hoop again where they would prosper.[147] This was in my mind but I still worked on as clerk in the store.[148] I wanted to see this man personally and find out and it was setting firmer in my mind every day.

It was now the spring of 1890. The winter of 1889–90 I heard that they wanted to find out more about that man. So Kicking Bear, Short Bull, Bear Comes Out and [Mash the] Kettle and a party started out to find out more about this sacred man and see him if possible. These fellows came home in the spring of 1890. I did not hear of the news that they had. But I heard that at the head of Cheyenne Creek, north of Pine Ridge, Kicking Bear had held the first Ghost Dance. From the rumors and gossips I heard that this Messiah was the son of the Great Spirit that had come out there. Then the next thing I heard was that they were dancing below Manderson on Wounded Knee. I wanted to find out things, because it was setting strongly in my heart and something seemed to tell me to go and I resisted it for a while but then I could no longer resist, so I got on my horse and went to this Ghost Dance near Manderson and watched them dance.

They had a sacred pole in the center. It was a circle in which they were dancing and I could clearly see that this was my sacred hoop and in the center they had an exact duplicate of my tree that never blooms and it came to my mind that perhaps with this power the tree would bloom and the people would get into the sacred hoop again. It seemed that I could recall all my vision in it. The more I thought about it, the stronger it got in my mind. Furthermore, the sacred articles that had been presented were scarlet relics and their faces were painted red. Furthermore, they had that pipe and the eagle feathers. It was all from my vision. So I sat there and felt sad. Then happiness overcame me all at once and it got a hold of me right there. I was to be intercessor for my people and yet I was not doing my duty. Perhaps it was this Messiah that had pointed me out and he might have set this to remind me to get to work again to bring my people back into the hoop and the old religion.

147. Black Elk refers to his boyhood vision where he saw a tree in full bloom, which represents the Lakota people. His task in life was to keep the tree flowering, that is, the Lakotas prospering. The sacred hoop, *čhaŋgléška wakȟáŋ*, also symbolized the unity of the Lakota people and it was enacted, for example, in the form of the camp circle, *hóčhoka*, or in the Ghost Dance circle. See Walker, *Lakota Society*, 21–23.

148. This was most likely a store in Manderson. See, DeMallie, *The Sixth Grandfather*, 257.

Again I recalled Harney Peak in the Black Hills [*the center of the earth*].[149] And I remembered my vision that the spirits had said to me: "Boy, take courage, they shall take you to the center of the earth." When they took me here, they said: "Behold the universe, the good things of the earth. All this behold it, because they shall be your own." Then I saw people prospering all over. And I recalled my six grandfathers. They told me through their power I would be intercessor on earth for my people. They had told me that I should know everything so therefore I made up my mind to join them. What I went there first for was to find out what they had heard, but now I changed my mind and was going there to use my own power to bring the people together. The dance was [*all*] done that day, but the next day there was to be another dance, so I stayed all night for another one.

The fall before [1889], I regret to say that I lost my father and I was fatherless on this earth and I was supporting my mother at that time; and while sitting there I could recall my father watching that dance and I made up my mind to communicate with my father about the other world. So that night I had it deeply in my heart that I was to be in there to make the tree bloom. So I dressed up in the sacred clothes. I told no one that I was going to join them but I got ready for the next day. (After dancing this Ghost Dance, they fall over and faint and see visions.)

Before the dance was on the next morning I got among them around the sacred pole. Good Thunder, an uncle of mine (Good Thunder later married Black Elk's mother), took me in his arms and took me to the sacred stick, offering a prayer for me here. He prayed thus: "Father, behold me, this boy your ways he shall see, and the people shall know him." (Then Good Thunder began to cry.) Just then I happened to think of my father and my sister and brothers which I had lost the year before. I couldn't keep the tears from running out of my eyes and so I put my head up to keep the tears from running out. I was really sorry and cried with my whole heart. The more I cried, the more I could think about my people. They were in despair. I thought about my vision and that my people should have a place in this earth where they would be happy every day and that their nation might live, but they had gone on the wrong road and they had gone into poverty but they would be brought back into the hoop. Under the tree that never bloomed I stood and cried because it faded away. I cried and asked

149. Harney Peak in the Black Hills was considered to be the center of the world and thus vey sacred. It was the place where Black Elk was transported in his boyhood vision. See DeMallie, *The Sixth Grandfather*, 98. Harney Peak was named Black Elk Peak in 2016.

the Great Spirit to help me to [make it] bloom again. I could not stop crying no matter how much I tried.

Then I had a funny feeling of shivering over my body and this showed that it really was the real thing. Everyone knew my power and with my own will to make that tree bloom, I joined the people there. Kicking Bear held one of my arms on one side and Good Thunder held the other arm and I was ready for the dance now. The song we sang next was:

Who do you think he is that comes?

It is he who seeks his mother.

Father has said this.

(To be said in the other world to someone coming there from here.)

At the first dance I had no vision, but my body seemed to be raised off the ground while I danced and I had a queer feeling. We danced all day. When I went back after the dance, I thought about the other world and that the Messiah himself was with my people over there, and perhaps my tree was actually blooming over there and my dream was really coming true. I thought to myself that I would try my best to know more about this. While I was thinking this, it occurred to me that in my vision I had seen beautiful things and in the center of the earth I had seen everything and perhaps this land of my vision was where the people were going and that we would disappoint the white race and only my people would live.

The next morning we danced again. As we started out to dance Kicking Bear offered a prayer saying: "Father, behold me, these people shall go forth today. They shall see their relatives that they may be happy over there day after day and there will be no end to that happiness." Then all the dancers around began to wail and cry. As we started to dance again some of the people would be laughing and some would be crying. Some of them would lie down for a vision and we just kept on dancing. I could see more of them staggering around panting and then they would fall down for visions. The people were crying for the old ways of living and [that] their religion would be with them again.[150]

It took quite a while for me to get in this condition. They sang all sorts of songs. Then I began to fear that my breath was coming up while we were

---

150. The U.S. government had forbidden all traditional religious ceremonies in 1883. The Ghost Dance brought religious ceremonies back to Lakota lives.

dancing. The first feeling I had was that my legs seemed to be full of ants. We always danced with our eyes closed. Then we heard wailing of women and people were lying around all over as though they were having visions. It seemed as though I were swaying off the ground without touching it. This queer feeling came up [farther] and it was in my heart now and I was panting. It was not a fear. It seemed that I would glide forward like a swing and swing back again. Of course it took me quite a while. I was panting hard and I must have fallen down, for they let me go.

All I saw was an eagle feather in front of my eyes at first. I felt as though I had fallen off a swing and gone out into the air. My arms were outstretched and right before me above I could see a spotted eagle dancing toward me with his wings fluttering and the shrill whistle he made. I could see a ridge right in front of me and I thought I was going to hit that ridge, but I went right over it. I did not move at all, I just looked ahead. After I reached the other side of the ridge I could see a beautiful land over there and people were camping there in circle[s] all over. I noticed that they had plenty, and I saw dried meat all over. I glided over the tipi. Then I went down feet first and lighted on the ground. As I was going down to the center of the hoop I could see a tree in full bloom with flowers on it. I could see two men coming toward me. They were dressed with ghost shirts like I was dressed. They came and said to me: "It is not yet time to see your Father, but we shall present to you something that you will carry home to your people and with this they shall come forth to see their loved ones."[151] I could see fat horses all over and the wild animals ranging out over the country and hunters were returning with their meat. I was very happy to see that and I'm hungry for some of that meat right now. They told me to return at once and I was out in the air again and I glided the same as before back.

When I got right above the dance place, they were still dancing the Ghost Dance. I hoped to see that tree blooming [*but the day following it was not blooming*] and it was just seemingly faded. I went down to my body then and I could hear the voices. Then I got up from my vision. Whenever a man comes to, they ask you what you have seen. So most of the people came over there to see what I had dreamed. I told them the exact vision I had had.

---

151. It seems to be typical of the visions that those visiting the spirit world were told that the new world was not yet to be reached. Thus, the dancers received instructions in visions on how to perform the dance correctly to make the new world come about. On several occasions, phrases like "you are not doing it correctly" and "do it well" indicate that the instructions given by the Messiah had to be followed precisely. The visions, then, functioned as heralds for future events. For comparison, see the Young Skunk and Pretty Eagle documents above.

What I brought back was the memory of what they had shown me and I was to make an exact copy of it. This Ghost [Dance shirt] was to be used always in the Ghost Dances. So I started the Ghost [Dance] shirt.[152]

That evening we got together at Big Road's tipi; the chief dancers came. They decided there to use my ghost shirts. So the next day I made Ghost Dance shirts all day and they had to be painted by me. The first two shirts I made were made according to the Messiah vision. In this vision I saw everything old-fashioned and the only things that spoke to me were the two men in the vision and I was told to take the way they were dressed home to my people. So when I came back to earth I made these shirts accordingly. When I saw the tree in the vision it was in full bloom, but when I came back the tree was wilted and dead. If this world would only do as it is told by this vision, the tree would bloom. I made the first two shirts according to what I saw in the vision. The first one I made was for Afraid of Hawk. I made another one for the son of Big Road. I got a stick to resemble the one I had seen in my vision and painted it red with the sacred paint of the Messiah. I put one spotted eagle feather on top of the stick. I worked all day making shirts. I spent the evening making the sacred stick. I wanted all the people to know the facts of this vision.

I decided to go to the dance. Every time we danced Kicking Bear and Good Thunder were on either side of me. As we proceeded to the place where we were to dance, we stood in a straight line facing the west. I was to perform the ceremony. They all looked forward for me to take part, because they all knew I had had a better vision than they had. We began to pray: "Father, behold me! The nation that you have and the nation that I have, they are in difficulty. The new earth you promised, I want my nation to behold it!" After the prayer we stood with out [our] right hands raised to the west and we all began to weep. Right there as they cried some of them fainted before they had danced. They all began to pant and fall down before they had danced. The ones who did not faint got into a circle and started to dance. We sang this song:

Over here they have said, over here they have said.

Father, in tears I have said.

The Wasichu[153] have said.

---

152. Pretty Eagle also claimed that he made the first Ghost Dance shirts. See above.

153. The word *wašíču* or *wašíčuŋ* usually refers to a white person, but here it could again refer to a person with spiritual power or a guardian spirit, which would make much more sense in this context.

A Sioux Ghost Dance shirt. Gift of the New Hampshire Historical Society. Buffalo Bill Center of the West, Cody, Wyoming, NA.204.2.

As we danced around I felt the same feeling that I had before—as though I had my feet off the earth and was swinging. I just hung on to the men, for I was in fear. They let go and again I glided forth. The same thing happened; I ascended into the air again and there was a spotted eagle in front of my eyes and I could hear the shrill whistle and scream of the eagle. I was gliding again prone through the air with my arms out. I was right on a ridge again and as I neared it I could hear strange noises, [a] rumbling sound. Right below that ridge there was [a] flame coming up. As it began to flame up, I glided right over it. I glided over the fifth circle village and glided over the sixth circle village. I landed on the south side of this sixth village.

As I landed there, I saw twelve men coming toward me and they stood before me and said: "Our Father, the two-legged chief, you shall see." Then I went to the center of the circle with these men and there again I saw the tree in full bloom. Against the tree I saw a man standing with outstretched arms. As we stood close to him these twelve men said: "Behold him!" The man with outstretched arms looked at me and I didn't know whether he was a white or an Indian. He did not resemble Christ. He looked like an Indian, but I was not sure of it. He had long hair which was hanging down loose. On the left side of his head was an eagle feather. His body was painted red. (At that time I had never had anything to do with white men's religion and I had never seen any picture of Christ.)[154]

This man said to me: "My life is such that all earthly beings that grow belong to me. My Father has said this. You must say this." I stood there gazing at him and tried to recognize him. I could not make him out. He was a nice-looking man. As I looked at him, his body began to transform. His body changed into all colors and it was very beautiful. All around him there was light. Then he disappeared all at once. It seemed as though there were wounds in the palms of his hands.

Then those twelve men said to me: "Turn around and behold your nation, your nation's life is such." The day was beautiful—the heavens were all yellow and the earth was green. You could see the greenward of the earth [the plains]. The men that I saw were all beautiful and it seemed there were no old men in there. They were all young. There were no children either, all were about the same age. Then twelve women came and stood in front of me. They said: "Behold them, your nation's life is such. Their ways of life you shall take back to the earth." The women were dressed beautifully with ornaments of all kinds. As they finished speaking to me I heard singing in the west (where the sun goes down). When I heard this song I learned it. I prepared myself to come back and before I started the twelve men took two sticks and pounded them into the ground and they said: "Take these, you shall depend upon them." One of the sticks was painted white and the other was painted red. They were about a yard high.

Then these men said: "Make haste!" As I advanced it seemed as though the wind went under me and picked me up. I could see plenty of meat there—buffalo all over. I was hungry and they should have fed me then. The wind went under me and took me up there. I was up in the air then with outstretched hands. I had to go over a big river now and the village in circles was on the other side of the river. This was a very fearful, dark river,

154. By the time of the Ghost Dance in 1890, Black Elk had actually become acquainted with Christianity. For example, while in Europe he wanted to travel to Jerusalem to see the place where Christ was crucified. DeMallie, *Sixth Grandfather*, introduction.

rushing with foam in it. On this side nobody was living. As I looked down there were men and women. They were trying to cross this river, but they couldn't do it so they were crying about it. They looked up to me and said: "Help us!" I came on and glided over them. Of course when I came over the river I heard the strange rustling and rumbling sounds and the flames also, but I just glided over them. I saw my people again and I just figured that I had brought something good for them. When I came down I came back to my body again. This was the vision I had. All the people there were eager to hear of what I had to say and they all gathered around me. Lots of these people are still alive. These visions that I have told to the people they still remember.

At this time there was quite a great famine among the people and some of them really believed in this Messiah business and were hoping that this land of promise would come soon so that they would be through with the poverty. Many of them wanted to know more about this. I told my vision through songs. As I sang one song, there were older men [*than I*] there to tell what they meant to the others. Before I told this everyone took out his pipe filled with kinnikinnick to make offer[ing]s to the sacred man that I had seen. Then I told my vision in song and I sang this song three times. I sang a song the words of which were the same as the one the man on [beside] the tree had said, and the melody of it was that which I heard above the sixth village in my vision. [*I sang this song three times and*] the fourth time I sang it the people all began to cry, because the white man had taken our world from us and we were like prisoners of war.

I went to the sixth village in the vision because in the flaming rainbow of the first vision I had seen six grandfathers—the powers that the earth got from these six powers.[155] I saw two men first in the vision and now I saw two men in the Messiah vision also. Here on earth I had six children; three have died. In my first vision, I had seen twelve riders and again I saw twelve men in this vision. It represents the twelve moons in the year. This village might represent six generations from the first and perhaps in the sixth generation the tree will bloom as in my vision.

At this time, I think my nephew, Mr. [John G.] Neihardt, would have cried too, because they had nothing—they were starving and had no guns. They had this hard time because the whites were killing off all their rela-

---

155. In Black Elk's boyhood vision, the grandfathers took him to their tipi in the clouds. The grandfathers represented the powers of the different directions. Black Elk became the Sixth Grandfather, representing the below, the power of the earth. See DeMallie, *The Sixth Grandfather*, introduction, 111–42.

tives-like [the game animals]. Just to look at the people would make anyone lonesome. Some of them just fell over as they were lean and poor and all this because of the white man's treachery. Everyone who was there when they heard the translation of the song, everyone cried. I realize now that I had prophesied. The Big Foot massacre occurred and I saw them wailing. They were shedding tears for the old ways and old religion. When the people had this they were never feeling bad. They were always happy. Through the four-leggeds [buffalo and other animals], Indians reared their children.

I noticed how the twelve men in the vision were dressed and I made six sacred shirts according to what these twelve men wore. I took six copies of the fashion of the twelve women that I'd seen in my vision. The Brulés were camped here too. We invited them over. I made six more of these outfits for the Brulés after making them for the Oglalas. The Brulés were camping at this time at Cutmeat Creek.

At this time every once in a while I would get dizzy as a result of this vision. Every time I danced I never fainted again, but the dizziness would affect me. I would think I was going to but I did not. Later I had a vision again but not much. The last vision I had was in a Ghost Dance again. I was back here again. The only thing I saw was toward the west I saw a flaming rainbow that I had seen in the first vision. On either side of this rainbow was a cloud and right above me there was an eagle soaring, and he said to me: "Behold them, the Thunder-being nation, you are relative-like to them. Hence, remember this." During the war I was supposed to use this rainbow, and the Thunder-beings but I did not do it. I only depended on the two sticks that I had gotten from the vision. I used the red stick.

It seems to me on thinking it over that I have seen the son of the Great Spirit himself. All through this I depended on my Messiah vision whereas perhaps I should have depended on my first great vision which had more power and this might have been where I made my great mistake.

(Black Elk was considered the chief Ghost Dancer. [One] might hear that Black Elk had made [created] it, but he did not, only he had so much power that he became the most important Ghost Dancer.)

I was the leader in every dance. Soon I had developed so much power that even if I would stand in the center of the circle and wave this red stick, the people would fall into swoons without dancing and see their visions. The Brulés had wanted me to come because they thought they might get some power from me. I took a special trip over there for this purpose. I made six shirts and six dresses for them. I was over there four days and we were dancing every day. I told the Brulés what I had seen in my vision of the Promised Land. I told them everything that I had told the Oglalas. In the center was the sacred tree and on either side were the six dressed in sacred clothes. Everyone raised their right hand toward the west and I recited that prayer and waved the sacred [*red*] stick. Then they all began to cry and some of them began to have their visions before the beginning of the dance even. After the dance I stood right in the middle by the tree and talked to the people making this speech concerning the Messiah (Wanekia [Wani-kiya]—"Make Live"), son of the Great Spirit.[156] In olden times way back the sacred men would make an offering to the Great Spirit saying: "Great Spirit, our grandfather, mercy may you have on us and make us live."

I returned from the Brulés to the Oglalas with lots of things to bring home with me. Before I left I heard that there were soldiers here at Pine Ridge already. When I left, the Brulés all followed me. It seemed that I just drew them along with me. I knew that they were depending on me, so they just followed me. Still my people were dancing right below Manderson on the Wounded Knee [Creek]. There was a big camp here. Next morning it was reported that the soldiers were coming over here, so we broke camp and started west across the country to Grass Creek. We broke camp there and moved from here to White Clay [Creek] where we set up camp. Over at Medicine Root Creek the largest part of the Brulés were camping. Some chiefs came over from Pine Ridge to White Clay Creek north of Pine Ridge—Fire Thunder, Little Wound and Young American Horse. These men brought a message in behalf of the soldiers that this matter of the Ghost Dance should be looked into, that there should be rulings over it, but they did not mean to take the dance away from us. We moved camp from White Clay Creek and we moved nearer to Pine Ridge and camped here. We had a meeting over this Ghost Dance, but I did not attend it. I knew that Good Thunder and Kicking Bear were at the meeting. There were many soldiers there now. We were dancing nearly every day and I heard that this is what the agent said to the people. He had made a ruling that we should dance three days every month and during the rest of the time we should go out and make a living of some kind for ourselves. This was all he said to them.[157]

156. *Wanikiya* means to save one's own, or savior, but it can also mean the Savior, Messiah, Christ.

157. There were several discussions between Agent Royer, General John Brooke, and the Ghost Dancers in late November and early December. The most important took place at the Pine Ridge Agency on December 6. It is not clear if Black Elk refers to this meeting, but it is interesting that the agent gave them permission to dance for three days a month as long as they found work to do for other days. This is not mentioned in any of the agents' reports or correspondence. Considering how worried the agents in general

When these men brought the news back, we were all satisfied with it and we agreed to do it. While I was sitting in a tipi with Good Thunder a policeman came over from Pine Ridge. He said: "I was not ordered to come, but I came over anyway just for an errand for the good of you and Good Thunder." He said, "I have heard that you two will be arrested and also Kicking Bear."[158] Of course I did not want to flee and I was going to take it as it came. If it was the will of the Great Spirit it was all right with me. The Brulés were coming and Good Thunder suggested that we go out and meet them. So we saddled up that evening and started out. We came through White Horse Creek and followed it down to the mouth of Wounded Knee [Creek]. We followed this creek down about six miles below Manderson. There was a big camp of Brulés here.

Early in the morning the crier announced that we would have a meeting with the Brulés. When the people got together this is what I told them: "My relatives, there is a certain thing that we have done. From that certain sacred thing we have done, we have had visions. In our visions we have seen and we have also heard that our relatives that have gone before us are actually in the Promised Land and that we are also going there. They are with the Wanekia. So therefore the Wasichu [*wašíču*, or whites] if they want to, they may fight us, and if they fight us, if we are going to we will win; so have in your minds a strong desire and take courage. We must depend upon the departed ones who are in the Promised Land that is coming and who are with the Wanekia. We should remember this. Because in the first place our grandfather has set the two-leggeds on earth with the power of where the sun goes down" (meaning that the two-leggeds have the Thunder-beings' power).[159]

Some more Brulés came over soon after this time from the Porcupine and Medicine Root Creeks. From Wounded Knee camp we followed the

---

were about the collapse of order and daily routines on the Lakota reservations, this offer from Royer sounds unlikely. For the reactions of Lakota agents to the Ghost Dance, see introduction to this volume and Andersson, *The Lakota Ghost Dance of 1890*, 100–127.

158. Agent Daniel F. Royer recommended in a letter to the acting commissioner of Indian affairs on November 25, 1890, that sixty-six men should be arrested. Black Elk was on that list as number 65. Daniel F. Royer to Commissioner of Indian Affairs Thomas J. Morgan, November 25, 1890, NARA, RG 75, SC 188, M4728, roll 1, 31–33.

159. The Thunder-beings were the most powerful entities in the Lakota belief system. Black Elk, for example, received his powers directly from them. The term "two-legged" refers to human beings and birds, who according to Lakota traditions are related. See DeMallie, *The Sixth Grandfather*.

Wounded Knee [Creek] down toward White River. That same evening of the day that I had talked, my mother was over there at the camp. We moved camp again to Red Hawk's place. When we camped here, some of the Oglalas turned back. A Black Robe [*Catholic*] priest came here and some of them turned back with him. Later this priest was stabbed at the Big Foot massacre.[160] From here we moved camp to a place called High Pocket's place southwest of Cuny Table in the Badlands. (Cuny Table is called by the Sioux the Top of the Badlands.) Then again some chiefs came from Pine Ridge with many people.

American Horse and Fast Thunder came over to where I was and asked me to put this Ghost Dance aside quietly (in other words, stop it). Just then Kicking Bear and Good Thunder and Big Road came in. I knew there was trouble now, so I consented to do this. Then we moved camp, as the chiefs had come after us. The Brulés interfered and kept us from moving, as they did not want us to go. The soldiers' band [*akičhita*] of the Brulés tried to stop us and we tried to go anyway and they hit many of us. We had quite a little struggle here and Good Thunder, Kicking Bear and others were trying to quiet them down. Somehow they induced Kicking Bear to go back to the Brulés, although he was going to go with us. Then we left them peaceably. Then we camped on White River. We started and moved north of Oglala to White Clay Creek. Some of the Brulés went with some of the Oglalas, but more of them stayed in the camp at Cuny Table. Later, the Brulés and Oglalas who stayed back went to the Onagazhee [*ohanzi*], [*ohánži*], "Place of Shelter," on top of the Badlands.

We moved camp to the Cheyenne River north of Pine Ridge. Most of the Oglalas were camping around Pine Ridge. I was out looking for horses and when I returned I learned that two policemen had come after me to be on their side as a scout. Two days later I learned that the soldiers were marching toward Wounded Knee. This was in the Month of the Popping Trees—December. I heard that Big Foot was coming from a young man who had come there. Rough Feather, I heard, was going to get Big Foot, who was coming from his camp near the mouth of Medicine Root Creek on White River. At that time there were some soldiers camping somewhere around

---

160. The Catholic priest was Father Francis M. Craft. He was stabbed during the Wounded Knee battle, but he survived. For Father Craft's life and work, see Thomas W. Foley, *Father Francis M. Craft: Missionary to the Sioux* (Lincoln: University of Nebraska Press, 2002); Foley, ed., *At Standing Rock and Wounded Knee: The Journals and Papers of Father Francis M. Craft, 1888–1890* (Norman: Arthur H. Clark, 2009).

there on the other side of the river. Rough Feather went over there in order to get Big Foot. He wanted them to come in a southeasterly direction, but they did not do it. They wanted to follow up Medicine Root [Creek]. They followed it to the head and then scouts for the soldiers saw them here at the head of Medicine Root. The scouts represented this to the soldiers and from here it was represented to Pine Ridge. On this same evening the soldiers went toward where Big Foot was camped at the head of Medicine Root. Big Foot's camp came to the creek of Porcupine Butte where the soldiers met them and they nearly had a fight here.[161] The soldiers brought Big Foot back to Wounded Knee. That evening the soldiers gathered around where they had camped. The soldiers had them well guarded all night.

It was December 29, 1890, the next morning. They carried Big Foot over to the officers, for he was sick.[162] They told the rest of Big Foot's people to bring their guns over there. Everyone stacked their guns and even their knives up in the office [at the officers' headquarters]. The soldiers were searching all the tipis for weapons. There were two men near Big Foot's tipi who wore blankets made out of white sheets, with just their eyes showing. Some of them had probably hidden their knives. The officer who was taking the guns from them went up to these men and pulled their white blankets apart and one of them had his gun concealed inside the sheet. He proceeded to the other one and opened it and just as he was going to get his gun, this man shot him. This man's name was Yellow Bird. This fellow did not want to give up his gun, and did not intend to shoot the white man at all—the gun just went off.[163] Of course the soldiers were all around there already with their [wagon] guns on the hill north, across the flat east, and across the creek. The Indian scouts were behind the soldiers on the south. Yellow Bird and the white officer were wrestling with this gun and they had rolled

161. Some Lakotas later noted that if they had wanted to fight the soldiers, the best time for them to do so would have been at this moment instead of at Wounded Knee, which is an indication that they did not plan any resistance at Wounded Knee as claimed by many at the time. Andrew Good Thunder who was among the Lakotas scouting ahead of the main group said: "We agreed not to fight but get in line and go toward them abreast and if they [soldiers] began firing we would charge and wipe them out." Andrew Good Thunder, WMCC, IULL, box 4, folder 14, envelope 90.

162. Big Foot had pneumonia.

163. The debate of who fired the first shot has continued for decades. Most likely the first shot was fired by a man called Black Coyote, not Yellow Bird. See Utley, *Last Days of the Sioux Nation*, 212–13; Ostler, *Plains Sioux*, 343–51; Andersson, *The Lakota Ghost Dance of 1890*, pp. 92–94. For the most recent contribution to this discussion, see Greene, *American Carnage*, 222–30.

down together on the ground and were wrestling with it. Dog Chief was right there where they took the guns and was standing right by these men while wrestling. This man was a friend of mine and he saw the whole thing.

Big Foot was the first Indian that was killed by an officer before the [*wagon*] guns began [*to shoot*]. They had carried Big Foot over to where the guns were being given up and immediately after the shot of Yellow Bird the officer shot Big Foot. Yellow Bird went into a tipi nearby and killed lots of them [soldiers] probably before he died. The Indians all ran to the stacks of guns and got their guns during a lull while the soldiers were loading again. A soldier ran up to tear the tipi away to get at Yellow Bird, but the latter shot at them as they came up and killed them. They fired at the tipi and the soldiers' guns set it afire and he died in there.

The night before this I was over in the camp at Pine Ridge and I couldn't sleep. When I saw the soldiers going out it seemed that I knew there would be trouble. I was walking around all night until daylight. After my meal early that morning I got my horse and while I was out I heard shooting over to the east—I heard wagon guns going off. This was a little distance from the camp and when I heard this gun I felt it right in my body, so I went out and drove the horses back to the camp for I knew there was trouble. Just as I got back with the horses there was a man who returned from Pine Ridge and had come back because he had heard this. He said: "Hey, hey son, the people that are coming are fired upon, I know it."

I took my buckskin and saddled up. I had no gun. The only thing I had was the sacred red stick. I put on my sacred shirt. This was a shirt I had made to be worn by no one but myself, which had a spotted eagle outstretched on the back of it, a star on the left shoulder, the rainbow diagonally across the breast from the left shoulder downward toward the hip. I made another rainbow around the neck, like a necklace with a star at the bottom. At the shoulder, elbows, and wrists were eagle feathers. And over the whole shirt I had red streaks of lightning. This was a bullet-proof shirt. I painted my face red. I had another eagle feather thrust through my hair at the top of my head. Of course I was going out by myself, and I could see that there were some young men following me. The first two men who followed me were Loves War and Iron White Man. I asked them where they were going and they said they were just going over to see where the firing was. I told them that I was going there to fight for my people's rights and if they wanted to, they could come along. So they went with me and about this time some more older men came.

I just thought it over and I thought I should not fight. I doubted about this Messiah business and therefore it seemed that I should not fight for it, but anyway I was going because I had already decided to. If [I] turned back the people would think it funny, so I just decided to go anyway. There were now over twenty of us going. As we neared there was a horseback coming toward us. He said: "Hey, hey, hey, they have murdered them!" Just then right before us I could see a troop of soldiers coming down a canyon. They stopped their horses and asked me what to do, so we decided we'd first see what we could do and then we'd do it. We started out and at the head of the gulch we went along the creek and got on top of the hill at the head of the gulch now called Battle Creek.

In the morning when the battle started, I could hear the shooting from Pine Ridge. With about twenty other young men, I started out to defend my people. When we got on the hill at the head of the draw about two and one-half miles west of the monument [at Wounded Knee grave site], we could see some Indians being captured by two small troops of soldiers. This was at the head of the draw. I could hear the cannons and rifles going off down there and I could see soldiers all over the hills on each side of the draw. I then depended on my Messiah vision. As we faced them we sang a sacred song which went like this:

A thunder-being nation I am I have said. (twice)

You shall live. (four times)

Then I said to the men whom I had led here: "Take courage, these are our relatives. We shall try to take the captives back. Furthermore, our women and children are lying dead. Think about this and take courage."

I had good eyes at this time and I could see cavalrymen scattered all over the hills. After I had said this to my young men I proceeded down on horseback and they followed me. Right by the yellow pine in the head of the gulch there was an Indian wounded through the legs by the name of Little Finger. Another man was following me, Iron White Man, and we put this wounded man behind [him on] his horse. At the very end of the gulch this wounded fellow fell off. Then another Indian came along and we asked him to take him over to a safe place. We took him across the hills northwest to safety. At the head of the gulch I saw a baby all alone. It was adopted by my wife's father. Its name was Blue Whirlwind. I was going to pick her up but I left her for she was in a safe place.

We started north toward where the horses are and we stopped right this side of the horses. We started out straight north under the first white clay spot a little ways up the hill. To the north was a troop of cavalry and about one hundred yards to the east was another troop of soldiers (by the pine trees). Two of my men went to where the captives were and there was another Indian riding a black horse standing right this side of the captives. Just as the two men got to where the soldiers were and got to where the black horse rider was standing, the farthest troop over there fired on us first and shot right across the draw as we retreated. Then after a little bit the main body of the men said: "Take courage, it is time to fight!" As the cavalrymen fired, the horses stampeded across the hills here.

Then the body of Indians charged down this draw toward the captives. I could feel the bullets hitting me but I was bullet proof. I had to hang on to my horse to keep the bullets from knocking me off. I had the sacred bow with me and all I had to do was to hold the bow toward the soldiers and you should have seen the soldiers run! They saw they couldn't hit me so they ran eastward toward the monument. The other boys were not bullet-proof so they had to get behind the hill back there. I was alone. Every time I pointed the bow at the soldiers they couldn't run fast. If I had had a gun I could have killed a lot of them. When they got over the hill they peeped out ready to shoot. Just as I got up to them about twenty yards away, they shot at me and missed me. The soldiers on the other side came down the creek and lay down ready to shoot and they pumped away at me but they didn't hurt me. I proceeded back to where my men were. I had to hold my bow in front of me in the air to be bullet-proof but just as I had gotten over the hill after completing my charge, I let my bow down and I could feel some bullets passing through my Ghost Dance shirt near my hip. You could see the marks of the bullets on the shirt. I got shot but not much. I could only feel a bullet graze my body, was all. Then I made another charge, as the soldiers had crept over by this time. (After I had made the charge the other young men came and got the captives while I had the soldiers chased away.) Then as I charged again you could hear the bullets whizzing by me.

In this draw there was another Indian. Then right in here I was surprised to see two boys about fifteen years old who had repeaters and who had evidently done quite a lot of damage. They killed lots of soldiers lying around. These two boys followed after the soldiers and had lots of ammunition. After this we made the soldiers retreat. As I charged they all fell back and they all gathered together in a little bunch over the hill there. These two boys were the bravest of all of us, for they were not bullet-proof but they did not get a scratch—they were lucky. One of my men was shot and two got wounded—one broke his leg and the other broke his arm. They retreated so fast that we just pulled up and went along after them. The battle started at about ten o'clock and we fought all day here. We went back to Pine Ridge just after dark. It was about fifteen miles by the old road. When the soldiers gathered on the hill they began to go back on that ridge over there. After the soldiers did their dirty work over there they began to march up Wounded Knee [Creek]. The soldiers wanted to fight yet, but we did not care so much about charging at them. I wanted to see the place where Big Foot and his people got killed and as I followed down the draw I could see men and women lying dead all along there. Soldiers and Indians afterwards were here and there. [*Then as I got nearer there were more of them lying there.*] Right at the beginning of the draw there were many Indians and there were more soldiers further down.

This was a good day—the sun was shining. In the evening it began to snow. It was a very bad snow. The day was cold even though it was sunny. That night the snow covered us and we all died [really suffered] from the cold. As I went down toward the village, I could see children dying all over—it was just a sight. I did not get as far as Big Foot's body though. Somehow I did not use my first vision, but I used the power of the vision about the Messiah. I was not sorry, I was not feeling bad about it, but I thought there will be a day. I was not sorry about the women and children because I was figuring on dying and then I would join them somewhere. I just thought I would probably die before this thing was over and I just figured that there would be a day when I could either take revenge or die. I did not recall the vision that I should have recalled at this time.

There was a big Stronghold between Manderson and Oglala where all the people gathered and after I gathered them there, I recalled the first vision and therefore I gathered them here and I prayed and sent voices to the spirits above and I said:

Yeah hey! (four times)

Grandfathers, behold me and send me a power for revenge.

(While fighting here the women were in the Stronghold.) Just as I said that (it was a clear day with no clouds; January—snow on the ground), in the west there appeared clouds and there was a thunderstorm in the winter. After this the people all depended on me. The people and chiefs got together and made me commander of all the Sioux there in the Stronghold. When they made me commander, I made some sacred herbs. They brought all their guns to me and had me make them holy. When I got through blessing the guns, the next day there was a treaty and there was peace. Chief [Young Man] Afraid of His Horses came back from the agency and said there was peace. He was the big chief then and next was Red Cloud.

(At this time I had no children and maybe if I had been killed then I would have been better off.)

After the battle [*December 29, 1890*] we went back on the north side of Pine Ridge [Agency] where the hospital now is and as we were standing here the soldiers at Pine Ridge shot at us. We went back because we thought there was peace back home. The Indians fled from our camp at Pine Ridge and there was no one at home. The camp we left in the morning had been deserted. We were pretty hungry so we peeked in from tipi to tipi and we saw something cooked to eat, and so we had something real to eat. This was Red Crow and myself alone. As we were feasting there about three feet apart we heard some shots and just then the bullet went right between us and threw dust over our plates. We kept on eating anyway and had our fill and we got on our horses and went the way the people had fled. Probably if I had been killed there I would have had papa [dried meat] in my mouth.

The people fled downstream [White Clay] and we followed them down. It was now dark. We followed them up all night and finally we found their camp below the stream which is east of Oglala. The people had no tipis, they were just sitting by their fires. They had fled without their tipis. I went among them and I heard my mother singing a death song for me. I followed the voice and found her in a little log house which they had found and moved into. Mother was very glad to see me, as she thought I had died over there. Of course, I did not sleep the night before and I had fought all day and then there was a war party that went out, but I did not go as I was very tired and wanted to sleep that night. Some of the Brulés and Oglalas were gathered here now.

I got up at daybreak the next morning. This morning more war parties went out to Pine Ridge to fight. A man by the name of He Crow and I went east of the White Clay Creek staying as far from it as possible, because we could see all over the country from here and we could see just where the trouble was all the time. This war party had met the soldiers right where the [Holy Rosary] Mission is today and we could hear the cannon go off here.[164] We proceeded toward this. We went to the White Clay Creek and crossed it, following the creek up on the west side and we could now hear the gunshots plainly. We then proceeded west following the ridge to where the fight was going on. Right from the ridge we could see that the Indians were on either side of the creek and were pumping at the soldiers who were

---

164. This was the battle of Drexel (Holy Rosary) Mission, on December 30, 1890. See, for example, Utley, *Last Days of the Sioux Nation*, 237–40.

coming down the creek between the Indians. As we looked down we saw a little ravine and across this was a big hill and we went down the ravine and got on the big hill. The men were fighting right here. They sent a voice to me saying: "Black Elk, this day is the kind in which to do something great!" so I said, "How!" [*Yes!*] I got off my horse and started putting dirt all over myself. I had a rifle and I proceeded up the hill and right below here the soldiers were firing and they told me not to go up, that they were pretty good riflemen there. I got on up the hill anyway and I was in very close range of the enemy. Then I recalled my vision, the north where the geese were; then I outstretched my hands [*and my rifle*] and then made the goose sound. They pumped away at me from the creek then, but not a single bullet came near me—they couldn't hit me.

As I went back down the hill again I heard them say: "They are gone!" So I got on my horse and started down the north side of the hill and right there a buckskin rider went past me; his name was Protector. He went past me to look at them and just then they fired so he came back again. I did not expect them to be so close and I went up there right away and they were about one hundred yards from me and they began to shoot at me. I proceed toward them anyway. If I had kept on I would not have gotten hit, probably; some of them started to flee toward the creek and I turned around and as I fled toward the hill I could hear the bullets hitting my clothes. Then something hit me on the belt on the right side. I reeled on my horse and rode on over the hill. I was riding my buckskin then. I should have kept on coming like that with my hands up. I was in fear and had forgotten my power. I had forgotten to make the goose sound there and to keep my hands up. I doubted my power right there and I should have gone right on imitating the goose with my power and I would have been bullet-proof. My doubt and my fear for the moment killed my power and during that moment I was shot.[165]

Protector ran up to me and grabbed me for I was falling off my horse. I said: "Let me go, I'll go over there. It is a good day to die so I'll go over there." He said: "No, nephew." Protector tore his blanket up and wrapped it around my wound. This kept my insides from falling out. Then Protector told me to go home and said: "You must not die today, you must live, for the people depend upon you."

The soldiers were now retreating and the Indians were fighting harder.

---

165. It is interesting that here Black Elk says that if he had relied on his earlier vision he would have been bulletproof. He is not seeking power and protection from his Ghost Dance vision or Ghost Dance shirt; instead, he turns his attention to his "real" vision. Perhaps this indicates that he had some doubts about the Ghost Dance.

The Mission was there then and there were lots of Indian children in there. The priests and sisters were all over there praying.[166] That building now has many shots in it. A man by the name of Little Soldier brought me back to the camp near the Stronghold.[167] When I got back the people were on top of the Stronghold. Old Hollow Horn was a bear medicine man and he came over to heal my wound. Of course he was a powerful medicine man and my wound began to heal and I was able to walk in about three days.

I heard the soldiers were coming now and I caught up my buckskin. My mother asked me not to go but I went anyway. About sixty men of us started out on a warpath east. We heard that the soldiers from the battlefield were marching through Wounded Knee to White River and were coming to the Stronghold. The soldiers were now at Black Feather's place. We Indians followed Little Grass Creek down and got on the west side of the river on a hill and saw the soldiers down on White River. We got off our horses and we saw some Indians coming on the other side on the north. The soldiers began to corral the wagons and were preparing themselves to fight. We proceeded down toward the Indians on the other side. They saw us and they fired on the soldiers because they took courage by seeing us coming. As we neared the Little Grass Creek, flowing into White River on the south side, right above was a little knoll. The soldiers [were] across the creek. As we looked over the bank of the creek we saw some soldiers' horses coming to the water with harnesses on. I said: "Fire at them and I will go and get the horses." The Indians fired at the soldiers and I got the soldiers' horses and drove them southward. Then they saw me and began to pump on me. I got back with five horses and they killed two of their own horses. There was a little gulch there and I got away with five of their horses. When I got out of bullet range with the horses I caught the best horse—a bay horse with a bald face. I turned mine loose and from there I drove the rest of them back.

About this time there was a whole detachment of cavalry coming up the river. I knew there were a lot of them, so I hurried with the horses. Just then I met a man running on foot without a horse. The Indians on the north side had retreated up the river. About that time they had come up to where

166. Father Emil Perrig was inside the mission and wrote about the fighting in his diaries. See Emil Perrig Diary, December 28–January 10, 1891, MUA, BCIM, HRMC.

167. This is an interesting comment, as the Ghost Dancers had left the Stronghold in the Badlands before Wounded Knee and did not return there. Instead, they camped close to the Badlands along the White Clay Creek. Perhaps Black Elk refers to this camp as "a stronghold," since the Ghost Dancers had made some fortifications on this camp too.

I was. This man on foot was Red Willow. His horse had played out. He said: "Cousin, I am on foot." So I caught him a roan horse with a halter on dragging a rope—a soldier's horse. About that time the soldiers were very near us and you could see the bullets coming and the dust kicking up. Then there was another man whose horse played out, so I caught him a brown horse and gave it to him. I was a Wanekia[168] just then, saving these two men by giving them horses. There was hard fighting now since the cavalry came up. The soldiers had come around and stopped the men in front. The soldiers were not crack shots so several fellows got away. Two of the men got wounded but they got home alive even though they were badly wounded. One of them was Long Bear, but I don't remember the other one's name.

After we got into the badlands the soldiers let us go so we came back to the Stronghold that night. The next morning I got up early and myself, One Side, Poor Buffalo, and Brave Heart, we all started out east again and we came to where Manderson is at present. When we were there we could see the soldiers coming up the creek toward Manderson. They were cavalrymen coming back after that fight. On either side of them there were scouts and we had one on the other side of the hill on the west side of the store and hid there. I wanted to shoot, but the other three men didn't allow me to. I said: "Let's stay here and kill at least one." They said they would kill us if we did. We had quite an argument. So the three men led me away on my horse to stop me. We came past this sacred butte [*near Black Elk's home*] up through this little cut and went over to Grass Creek. There we[re] a lot of cattle there, so we butchered three of them and took the meat back to the Stronghold on White Clay. As we were on top the Stronghold we could see Sioux hiding along the rocks, guarding the Stronghold all night. They were guarding all around the camp. They asked us if the soldiers were coming and we told them that everything was all right now. That day that we had butchered there was a soldier lieutenant and some scouts that came over there and they surrounded him and killed him. We thought that the scouts would probably report this and there would be a surprise attack so we were on guard all night and did not sleep any.

The next day I went on the highest point and asked the people to gather there. The announcer announced it and the crowd came. This day I remembered my six grandfathers, although I had completely forgotten my vision for a spell before this. I had some white paint with me, so I told them to bring their weapons that I might make them sacred [*to do their great dam-*

---

168. *Wanikiya* also means a person who saves another in a battle.

age]. I put a little bit of white paint on every gun that they brought and when that was done everyone stood facing the west, pointing their weapons toward the west.

Then I thus sent a voice: "Hey-a-a-a-a (four times). Grandfathers, the six grandfathers that I thus will recall to you today, behold me! And also to the four quarters of the earth and its powers. Thus you have said if an enemy I should meet that I should recall you. This you have said to me. Thus you have set me in the center of the earth and have said that my people will be relative-like with the Thunder-beings. Today my people are in despair, so, six grandfathers, help me."[169]

About this time we could see a storm coming up (in January, in the middle of winter), but the Thunder-beings appeared with lightning and thunder. The people all raised their hands toward the Thunder-beings and cried. The Thunder-beings followed the White Clay up and went toward Pine Ridge. We were well prepared now and were going out again for revenge. Revenge is sweet. We got ready and just then [Young Man] Afraid of His Horses came over to make peace with Red Cloud who was in our bunch then. [General] Miles had told [Young Man] Afraid of His Horses to come over and make peace. We had gathered there at this time. Red Cloud got up and made this speech: "Boys, this is a hard winter. If it were in the summer we would keep on fighting; but, boys, we cannot go on fighting because winter is hard on us, so we should make peace and I'll see that nobody will be hurt."

After that meeting Afraid of His Horses wanted to talk to me, Good Thunder, Kicking Bear, and Short Bull. We went over to a tipi and Afraid of His Horses began to speak: "Relatives, if this were in summertime it would not be so hard. If this were [not] winter, my people at Pine Ridge would have joined you and we would have had to fight to a finish, but I don't want my and your people to make us kill each other among ourselves. I don't care how many the soldiers are, without the Indian scouts they cannot fight and the army will be helpless. So, relatives, if this were in the summer I would have joined you and had it to a finish. But this is winter and it is hard on our children especially, so let us go back and make peace."

We all agreed. I wanted revenge anyway. I knew that when those clouds had appeared the Thunder-beings had talked to me. I did not want to have peace, but the people insisted so we broke camp the next day and went down from the Stronghold and camped several places and got to Pine Ridge where we camped on the northwest side. That day we were going to camp right in

---

169. Here again Black Elk relies on his power vision instead of the Ghost Dance vision.

Pine Ridge. People gathered here—hundreds on horseback. Then Kicking Bear and High Hawk (Brulé) were among these young men who were going around among the young men. They came to me and made me stand at a certain place. They put another man by my side—his name was Lick His Lips. Another one was brought here named Red Willow and another man whom I do not know. These were supposed to be the great warriors and they told the people that we were commanders of the Indian army and we were to take the lead. The men on foot were first, then the horsebacks followed. Then the wagons followed the horsebacks. We had started toward the office at Pine Ridge. We were now inside where the guards were and we could see soldiers all around. As we went down there, the soldiers that were coming stood in two bodies on either side of us and were ordered to present arms. We went right through the middle of them. There were many soldiers there. We went through Pine Ridge and went in front of the office; the officers saluted us. We went to a place on White Clay Creek and camped. The next day we were supposed to make peace. We made a law that anyone who should make trouble in the fort [agency] should be arrested and tried and if found guilty he would be punished.

Two years later I was married.

PART 2

"We did not think we were doing any harm
by dancing our religious dances."

This part presents documents by several Lakotas who in many ways were caught between the Ghost Dancers and non–Ghost Dancers. At the same time this part demonstrates how complicated the situation on the Lakota reservations was. It highlights the diverse approaches to the Ghost Dance, but also shows how many difficult, often contradictory issues, ranging from devastating famine and daily reservation politics to internal divisions and power struggles, complicated the situation for the Lakotas. For many, the Ghost Dance became yet another cause for divisiveness, instability, and uncertainty.

The part opens with accounts by chiefs Little Wound, Two Strike, Crow Dog, and Big Road. They give valuable insights into the Lakota Ghost Dance since they were at first strongly involved in the dance, experienced strong visions, but later, after the arrival of the military, gave up the Ghost Dance. They talked about the Ghost Dance to newspapermen or government officials during the "trouble" and continued to do so after Wounded Knee. Despite abandoning the Ghost Dance, they emphasized its religious and peaceful nature, comparing it to the practices of Christian churches. They pointed out on several occasions that the trouble was caused by the destitution on the Lakota reservations, not by the Ghost Dance.

Little Wound (Tȟaópi Čik'ala, ca. 1835–1899/1901) was an Oglala chief of the Khiyúksa band. His father, Bull Bear, was killed by Red Cloud in the early 1840s, which created tremendous tension among the Oglalas that continued into the Ghost Dance era. Little Wound was a prominent warrior during the 1860s battles. On the reservation, he converted to Episcopalian Christianity.[1] During the Ghost Dance he played a major role as one of the leading Ghost Dancers. However, he was also one of the first Oglala leaders to abandon the new religion when trouble started to become evident. The following accounts by Little Wound portray him as a leader very much concerned with the problems his people faced and as a man trying to find a balance between his traditional beliefs and Christianity, the old and new ways of life. These documents also reveal that he gave mixed accounts of his own participation in the Ghost Dancing.

Big Road (Čhaŋkú Tȟáŋka, 1834–1897) was an Oglala chief of the Oyúȟpe band. He fought at Little Big Horn and possibly surrendered with Crazy Horse. Like Little Wound, he at first embraced the Ghost Dance, but then abandoned it. Two Strike (Núm Kaȟpá, ca. 1831–1915) was one of the

---

1. For a brief life sketch on Little Wound, see Josephine Waggoner, *Witness: A Húŋkpapȟa Historian's Strong-Heart Song of the Lakotas*, edited by Emily Levine (Lincoln: University of Nebraska Press, 2013), 456–58.

most influential Brulé chiefs on the Rosebud Reservation. After Spotted Tail's death in 1881, the leadership on that reservation was often in dispute. Gradually Two Strike emerged as one of the leaders of the "nonprogressive" people. During the Ghost Dance he became the major leader of the Rosebud dancers. Crow Dog (Kȟaŋǧí Šúŋka, ca. 1832–1912) was also labeled as very "nonprogressive" by the white officials. He gained notoriety by killing Spotted Tail in 1881.

These documents are followed by those of Red Cloud and Sitting Bull, who were arguably the most well-known Lakota chiefs at the time, at least from the white point of view. Their involvement in the Ghost Dance was of great concern to the local Indian agents, settlers, newspapermen, and even to the U.S. Congress. Both men were accused of instigating trouble; Sitting Bull especially was singled out as the one individual preparing to take his men on warpath.[2] The discussion about their role in the Ghost Dance has continued among historians, recent scholarship showing quite clearly that neither was an active Ghost Dancer. In many ways, both men were caught between the dancers and those who did not dance. Sitting Bull wanted to get to know the religion but was never convinced about it. He never got a vision that would confirm its truth. However, he let his people dance.

Red Cloud never attended a Ghost Dance but allowed his son Jack Red Cloud to become a dancer. Do these decisions make Red Cloud and Sitting Bull Ghost Dancers? Perhaps not, but their actions might indicate their sympathies toward the Ghost Dance. The documents presented in this part help us understand their views on the Ghost Dance and their rationale in accepting or denying it.

Red Cloud (Maȟpíya Lúta, ca. 1822–1909) rose to fame during the wars of the 1860s as one of the great Lakota chiefs who forced the U.S. Army to abandon several forts on the Bozeman Trail and to sign the Fort Laramie Treaty of 1868. This treaty created the Great Sioux Reservation. Red Cloud settled on the reservation in 1872 and from then on, he tried to look for ways to negotiate a path between the "white man's road" and the traditional Lakota way of life. This task was very difficult to achieve and gained him many enemies. By the time of the Ghost Dance he was approximately sixty-eight years old and nearly blind.[3]

2. See Andersson, *The Lakota Ghost Dance of 1890.*

3. For Red Cloud's life, see James C. Olson, *Red Cloud and the Sioux Problem* (Lincoln: University of Nebraska Press, 1965) and Robert W. Larson, *Red Cloud: Warrior-Statesman of the Oglala Lakota* (Norman: University of Oklahoma Press, 1997).

Sitting Bull (Tȟatȟáŋka Íyotake, ca. 1831–1890), although a medicine or holy man, gained early fame on the warpath against traditional Indian enemies, but his greatest moments came during the wars of the 1870s. He was one of the leaders of the Lakota, Cheyenne, and Arapaho alliance that defeated Colonel George A. Custer's Seventh Cavalry at the Little Big Horn in 1876. After the battle, he went to Canada where he stayed until 1881. Later he settled on the Standing Rock Reservation and ended up having an almost decade-long battle over power with Indian agent James McLaughlin. McLaughlin finally used the Ghost Dance as an excuse to attempt the arrest of Sitting Bull, leading to the holy man's death on December 15, 1890.

After Red Cloud and Sitting Bull, this part introduces the voices of several Indian policemen who were involved in the arrest and killing of Sitting Bull. The stories of Henry Bullhead (Tȟatȟáŋka Pȟá, ca. 1846–1890), Gray Eagle (Waŋblí Ȟóta, 1851–1934), John Loneman (Išnálawičhá, 1850–ca. 1920), and Grover Eagle Boy (Waŋblí Hokšíla, ca. 1862–1939) are more closely related to the actual events surrounding the attempted arrest and death of Sitting Bull, but they also discuss the Ghost Dance.[4] Their voices are included here because they help us to understand the volatile situation on the Standing Rock Reservation and the policemen's complicated position relative to the Ghost Dancers and the non–Ghost Dancers. All three men were veterans of the war of 1876 and had been Sitting Bull's followers. They had been with him in Canada, but after settling on the reservation decided to take up the policeman's uniform. As John Loneman pointed out, he decided to drop all "heathenish" practices when agent James McLaughlin offered him a job. Working for the agent placed these men at the center of the power struggle between McLaughlin and Sitting Bull.

These stories are followed by accounts of several chiefs who bitterly opposed the Ghost Dance—Gall, John Grass, American Horse, and Young Man Afraid of His Horses. Oglala chief American Horse (Wašíču Tȟašúŋke, 1840–1908) was known as a very "progressive" leader even before the reservation years. He strongly opposed the Ghost Dance and was actually threatened by some Ghost Dancers, who entered his home and destroyed his property. Young Man Afraid of His Horses (Tȟašúŋke Kȟokípȟa Kȟoškálaka, also Tȟašúŋke Kȟokípȟapi, 1836–1893), like

<hr>

4. For brief biographies of Bullhead and Gray Eagle, see Waggoner, *Witness*, 311–12, 439–41. John Loneman appears in the 1920 Indian census, but I have not been able to determine his exact year of death.

American Horse, was one of the leading "progressive" chiefs among the Oglalas. Still, he was part of the initial council that decided to send Short Bull on his journey west to learn more about the Ghost Dance. For most of the Ghost Dance period, he was away from the reservation on a visit to the Crow Indians in Montana. However, upon returning on January 8, 1891, he played a major role in convincing the Ghost Dancers to surrender. As one of the most influential Lakota chiefs, his voice during, and especially after, the Ghost Dance is very important. His role as a mediator between the Ghost Dancers and the government was crucial. Gall (Phizí, 1838–1894) and John Grass (Pȟeží, 1837–1918) were the leading chiefs opposing the Ghost Dance on the Standing Rock Reservation. For several years, they were at odds with Sitting Bull. During the reservation years, Gall had become a devout Episcopalian and remained so throughout the Ghost Dance.[5]

Several lengthy documents in this part bring together many of these chiefs presenting their commentaries as part of a larger interview or a meeting. The first is an interview published in the *Washington Evening Star*, January 23, 1891. It is published here in its entirety because editing or breaking it into individual accounts would disrupt the narrative. Similarly, accounts by Lakota chiefs given to the secretary of the interior, John W. Noble, and the commissioner of Indian affairs, Thomas J. Morgan, during conferences held in Washington, D.C., in February 1891 are published here in full. The comments by the chiefs deal with matters of reservation life, hunger, education, religion, and they discuss those issues in relation to the Ghost Dance.

This part also includes letters and statements by lesser-known chiefs and individuals, such as the Brulé Hollow Horn Bear (Mathó He Oȟlóǧeča 1850–1913), the Hunkpapas Many Eagles (Waŋblí Óta, 1834–1912?),[6] One Bull (Tȟatȟáŋka Waŋžíla, 1853–1947), and Old Bull (Tȟatȟáŋka Eháŋni, ca. 1849–1935),[7] and the Oglalas Rocky Bear (Íŋyaŋ Mathó, 1836–1909) and Fast Thunder (Wakíŋyaŋ Lúzahaŋ, 1839–1904?).[8]

5. For more on John Grass and Gall, see Larson, *Gall*; Waggoner, *Witness*, 320–23, 422–26.

6. The last Indian census showing Many Eagles is for the year 1912.

7. The U.S. census Records give varying birth years for Old Bull, ranging from 1841 to 1851.

8. The last Indian census for Fast Thunder is from 1904.

Little Wound

"We fear another winter like the past would render our people desperate."

On July 23, 1890, Little Wound gave the following statement to Agent Hugh D. Gallagher at a meeting held on the Pine Ridge Reservation. Gallagher forwarded it to the commissioner of Indian affairs.[9] This document explains the Lakotas' impoverished conditions. Little Wound warns that if the suffering continues, there might be serious trouble in the near future. Later in the summer and early fall, the Ghost Dances started in earnest and Little Wound joined the dancers.

We would like you to write down what is said here in order that the Great Father may hear our words. We often have talks with you but what is said is not taken down and apparently goes for nothing. We had a big council last night among ourselves and agreed upon what we would say to you today. If I was addressing you it would not be necessary to take it down, but I am going to speak to the Great Father just such words as all of these people wish me to say for them. Therefore we wish you to write our words and send them to him and when you get a reply you can let us know and we will all gather here and listen to his words.

Some years ago we were like drunken or crazy people. We were fighting and killing not only the whites but our own people. We were induced to give up that kind of life upon promises made us by the Great Father through the representatives he sent among us to make a treaty of peace.[10]

Had we known then how the government intended to treat us we would never have signed this treaty. What do they intend to do with us? That is what we would like to know. Look at these people around you, see their sunken cheeks and emaciated bodies. Many of these you will notice have drooping heads and an expression of unconcern in their faces that shows plainly the ravages of hunger has reduced them to the verge of idiocy. This has been a hard winter upon us. Many of our children died from hunger. Surely the Great Father did not know this or he would not have taken away

9. Little Wound in Hugh D. Gallagher to the Commissioner of Indian Affairs Thomas J. Morgan, July 23, 1890, NARA, RG 75, LSASPR, M1282, roll 10, 335–36.
10. Little Wound refers to the Crook Commission of 1889.

a million pounds of our beef.[11] Great Father, you promised us plenty to eat. You said this should be the biggest and most important agency and even if small agencies should suffer we would always have plenty. We would like for you to give us back the beef you took from us last winter. We fear another winter like the past would render our people desperate causing trouble that would give us a bad name.

Little Wound

"Our dance is a religious dance and we are going to dance until spring."

On November 20, 1890, U.S. Army troops entered the Pine Ridge Reservation. By that time Little Wound had been singled out as one of the main instigators of trouble. Among his accusers was Agent Daniel F. Royer. Little Wound was also portrayed in many newspapers as a man ready to go on the warpath.[12] Little Wound replied to his accusers with this letter published by many newspapers under the title "A Letter of Defiance." It was originally included in a letter by John M. Sweeney, the teacher at Day School No. 8 at Medicine Root District, Pine Ridge, to Agent Royer.[13] Sweeney had discussed with the Ghost Dancers and noted:

11. In August 1890, the annual appropriations for all Lakotas were reduced as a result of the census made by Special Agent A. T. Lea, which showed the number of Lakotas being fewer than expected. This is a good example of why the Lakotas often fiercely opposed censuses. The cut in rations was made even though the Sioux Commission (Crook Commission) of the previous year recommended that the rations should be kept on the same level as earlier. For the Sioux Commission recommendations, see 51st Congress, 1st Sess., *Senate Executive Document*, No. 51, vol. 4, ser. 2682, pp. 23–31.

12. For portrayals of Little Wound in the press, see Andersson, *The Lakota Ghost Dance of 1890*, pp. 204–207, 214–16, 221–22.

13. Little Wound in John M. Sweeney to Agent R. F. Royer, November 22, 1890, MS 3176, EEAC, Newberry Library, published by permission of Newberry Library; Little Wound as quoted in *New York Times*, November 23, 1890, p. 5; *Chicago Tribune*, November 23, 1890, p. 1; *Omaha Daily Bee*, November 23, 1890, p. 1. There are minor differences in the papers. The papers also published a response by Agent Royer, who claimed that the letter signified Little Wound's hostile intentions.

Dr. Royer, Little Wound and a number of people from Yellow Bear Camp have commenced dancing on this creek this morning Nov. 20, and if I am allowed to express my opinion, I think that he will continue to dance until he is stopped by force. He is a very obstinate man and of ungovernable temper and he is carried away with the dance craze seeming to believe firmly the absurd doctrines which are preached at these dances. . . . It is a positive fact that the Indian dancers are all well-armed and have plenty of ammunition and my opinion is that they have been preparing for trouble sometime. Indians whom I have talked with have told me that they would all fight if it became necessary and they seemed to think that the Great Spirit will assist them so that they can easily overcome the whites.[14]

Little Wound himself notes that the Ghost Dance was a religious dance and he could not understand why the soldiers had arrived.

I understand that the soldiers have come on the reservation. What have they come for? We have done nothing. Our dance is a religious dance and we are going to dance until spring. If we find then that the Christ does not appear we will stop dancing; but, in the meantime, troops or no troops, we shall start our dance on this [Medicine Root] creek in the morning. I have also understood that I was not to be recognized as a chief any longer. All that I have to say to that is neither you nor the white people made me a chief and you can throw me away as you please, but let me tell you, Dr. [Daniel] Royer that the Indians made me a chief, and by them I shall be so recognized so long as I live. We have been told that you intended to stop our rations and annuities. Well, for my part, I don't care; the little rations we get do not amount to anything, but Dr. Royer, if such is the case, please send me a word so that me and my people will be saved the trouble of going to the agency. We do not intend to stop dancing.

14. John M. Sweeney to Agent R. F. Royer, November 22, 1890, MS 3176, EEAC, Newberry Library.

Little Wound

"If this is a good thing we should have it."

Little Wound gave the following account to former agent Valentine T. McGillycuddy.[15] During October and November 1890, a number of Ghost Dancers left the Pine Ridge Agency area to live in the Ghost Dance camps. In late November and early December, General John R. Brooke sent several delegations to the Ghost Dancers to induce them to return to the agency. As the dancers finally agreed to come to the agency, Little Wound was one of the negotiators for the dancers. The council was held at the Pine Ridge Agency, and Agent Daniel F. Royer and General John R. Brooke represented the government.[16] On location was also former agent Valentine T. McGillycuddy, who later reflected on the council and reproduced Little Wound's words. Little Wound interestingly denies being a Ghost Dancer, but in a clever way asks how the Ghost Dance is different from what the Christian missionaries have been teaching the Lakotas for several years. So when General John R. Brooke asked Little Wound if he was a Ghost Dancer, his reply was an emphatic no:

No, my friend, over sixty winters have passed over me and I am too old for dancing, but now that you have asked me that question I will tell you what I know and have heard about the Messiah and the Ghost Dance. There have lived among my people for many winters the holy men of missionaries whom the Great Father has sent to us to teach us your religion, and how much better it is than ours. They bring with them the holy book, the Bible, from that book they tell us wonderful stories, they tell us of the man who went into the den of wild animals, and was not harmed because his Great Spirit protected him. They tell us of the men who went into the fiery furnace, hot enough to melt bullets, but their hair was not even singed.

Then they tell us a wonderful story, of how many ages ago the white

15. Little Wound as quoted in Valentine T. McGillycuddy, WSCMC, WHCUOLA, box 107, folder 7. Published by permission of University of Oklahoma Libraries. Published also in Vestal, *New Sources*, 87–89.

16. Utley, *Last Days of the Sioux Nation*, 134–45; Coleman, *Voices of Wounded Knee*, 160–62; Ostler, *The Plains Sioux*, 313–20.

men's brains got to whirling, they lost their ears, they would listen no more to the Great Spirit, and they strayed off on the wrong road, and finally the Great Spirit sent his Son on earth to save them. He lived with those white men for over thirty winters, and worked hard to get you back on the road, but you denied Him, and you finally nailed Him up on a great wooden cross, tortured and killed Him. He was known as the Messiah, and when He was dying on the cross, it was promised that He would come again some time to try and save the people. These things the missionaries tell us.

About two moons ago there came to us from the far North, from the Yellowstone country, a young Cheyenne, named Porcupine, with a strange story.[17] He had a vision—in it he was told to go to a large lake, in the Northwest (Walker Lake, Nevada) and there he would meet the Messiah.

He told me that the Messiah was a tall white man with golden hair and whiskers, and blue eyes, a well-spoken man, and he said: "Porcupine, I am the Messiah; my father the Great Spirit, has sent me a second time to try and save the people, but when I was here before, they denied me and killed me. When the spring time comes with the green grass, I am going to visit the different Indian people, and the whites. But this time I have arranged a certain dance and signs, and in my travels if I am so received I will stop with them and try and help them. If I am not received in these signs, I will pass them by. Now Porcupine, I will give you these signs and this dance, and you go ahead of me and teach them to your people."

Now whether Porcupine really saw the Messiah, or only had a pleasant dream, I do not know. I got my people together and said: "My friends, if this is a good thing we should have it; if it is not, it will fall to the earth itself. So you better learn this dance, so if the Messiah does come he will not pass us by, but will help us to get back our hunting grounds and buffalo."

Then the old chief turned to me with these words: "My friend Little Beard [McGillycuddy], if the Messiah is *not* coming, and by his coming he will again make us a strong people and enable us to hold our own in this land given us as a home by the Great Spirit, and the white man is not afraid of that, *why* have these soldiers been brought here to stop the dance?"

Additional from Chief Little Wound: "I try hard to see goodness in the White Man's religion, and why he killed the Messiah, for if our Great Spirit, Wakȟáŋ Tȟáŋka, the Great Mystery, were to send his Son on earth to help

17. See Porcupine's account, June 28, 1890, RBIA, RG 75, SC 188, M4728, roll 1, 1/16–20. For more on Porcupine, see Mooney, *Ghost-Dance Religion*, 812–13; Gage, "Intertribal Communication," 245–46, 395–96.

us, we would feel honored, build a great house for him, and try and keep him with us forever."

Little Wound

"Who, then, proves that paleface liar?"

Little Wound finally came to the Pine Ridge Agency in mid-December, but only a few days after his arrival, he entered Agent Daniel F. Royer's office enraged by the idea of sending Indians to bring in those still in the Badlands.[18] Little Wound referred to a promise made earlier that never again should Lakotas be pitted against each other in the service of the U.S. military. Now, however, General Brooke employed the same tactics to get the Ghost Dancers to come in. While this text does not discuss the Ghost Dance, it gives valuable insight into the volatile situation among the Lakotas. It also explains how the divisive politics employed by U.S. government officials, the Indian agents, and the army affected Lakota society during the final weeks of the Ghost Dance.

Little Wound: This thing should not be. It makes nothing more or less than the breaking of another pledge given us in apparently the best of faith and with the greatest emphasis by the white rulers. The pledge [of] which I speak is [the one made] 14 years ago. The white faces must remember it surely. The Indian never forgetting. In 1876 when at Fort Robinson [Nebraska], the War Department asked us to go out for those bad Indians who were making trouble then. We did so on the promise that never would we be asked to do so again but here, notwithstanding that promise made and received in the name of the Great Spirit, we are now asked to again go out and get Indians whose hearts are bad. Does the white man think that right or wrong? Has he no longer left to him any knowledge of truth and lying?

Royer: I have nothing to do with this asking you and your men to go out on such a mission.

Little Wound: Who, then, proves that paleface liar?

18. Little Wound in Charles Cressey, *Omaha Daily Bee*, December 20, 1890, p. 1.

Royer: Go and ask General Brooke!

Little Wound: Never, never, never. Never would I go and see him, no, no!

Little Wound

"All we want is what is right."

After the troubles were settled, Little Wound gave another account to L. W. Colby.[19] Here he again returns to the famine and broken promises, reiterating that the fighting was not caused by the Indians. He also alludes to the old feud between him and Red Cloud.[20]

Red Cloud is not my friend and he has talked much against me. We are holding councils and trying to settle all the difficulties. The Great Father does not know our troubles. The agents have stolen from us and made themselves rich. We do not get the pound and a half of meat or beef promised us. We do not get our coffee, sugar and flour. The agents lie to us and lie to the Great Father. I will go to Washington and tell them how we are treated. The Wounded Knee battle was very bad. The Big Foot Indians were driven into the fight, and they fought brave, but they were killed. The soldiers were too many. They fought for their lives and did not want to be made prisoners and have their guns taken away, and the soldiers killed them and their wives and children. Our hearts are all sad about those that were killed. General Miles is our friend. All we want is what is right. We want our children to go to school. We want to live in houses and have farms, and have our money. We want what the Great Father promised us. We want the government to do right, and we will not fight. We have money and we have property in the hands of the government, and the government agrees to take care of us, but we are hungry and can get nothing. We do not want to be beggars. If we had our lands and our money that the Great Father has promised us, we would take care of ourselves.

19. Little Wound as quoted in L. W. Colby, "The Sioux Indian War of 1890–1891," 186.

20. For this feud see Olson, *Red Cloud*, 19–22; Larson, *Red Cloud*, 58–61.

Crow Dog

"The Indians are not to blame. We did not want war."

Crow Dog, like Little Wound, gave an interview to L. W. Colby in early 1891.[21] In his description of Crow Dog, Colby writes that he is "the most notorious Indian sub chief of the Brulés . . . [a] small, inferior looking Indian, with one withered arm, but he is a man of brains and iron nerve" and he "killed Spotted Tail." In the actual interview, Crow Dog explicitly states that they intended no harm, but that they had been robbed of their treaty rights and did not want to be treated as slaves. For Crow Dog, this unfairness clearly justified their anger but also their actions during the Ghost Dance, that is, their breaking of the reservation rules and leaving for Pine Ridge.

The Indians are not to blame. We did not want war. We had many things to contend with. My tribe came to the Oglalas on a friendly visit and did not intend to fight. General Miles says that the Great Father does not know that we have been robbed and that we shall have what was promised, and that we shall go and see the Great Father and tell him about it. When they took our lands they said our children should be educated and that we should have plenty each year, but we have not received it, and we are hungry. We want what was promised. We want to do right, but we do not want to have our guns taken away and be treated as slaves!

Two Strike

"We were afraid of the soldiers."

The following comment by Two Strike was originally reported by Father John Jutz in a letter to Father J. A. Stephan on December 14, 1890.[22] Father John Jutz and Jack Red Cloud visited the Ghost Dancers' camp as General John R. Brooke's emissaries. The council was held on November 5, and Two Strike was the main speaker for the Ghost Dancers. Others

21. Crow Dog in Colby, "The Sioux Indian War of 1890–1891," 188–89.
22. Two Strike by Father John Jutz to Father Joseph A. Stephan, December 14, 1890, MUA, BCIM, series 1–1, roll 20. Published by permission of Marquette University Special Collections and Archives.

present were Turning Bear, Short Bull, High Hawk, Crow Dog, Kicking Bear, Eagle Pipe, Big Turkey, and High Pipe. The Lakotas again emphasized that government dishonesty caused the problems. They were especially bitter about the inaccurate census count conducted by A. T. Lea and the new boundary line between the Pine Ridge and Rosebud Reservations.[23] Father Jutz was not at all certain that the Ghost Dancers would listen to his arguments, but he describes Two Strike as being very friendly and polite. Still, the tensions were high. After Jutz had promised that no harm would be done to those who come to Pine Ridge Agency for negotiation, tensions subsided. According to Father Jutz, the Indians told him about their concerns quite openly.[24] When Jutz asked the Ghost Dancers why they were staying out there in the Badlands, they replied:

(1) We did not like, that the white men came to [disturb?] us. (2) We were afraid of the soldiers. (3) We want to stay here at Pine Ridge Agency and get our rations here. (4) We fear to be punished, because we killed cattle, but we are sorry for it. *I answered to all these reasons in such a way, that they were full satisfied, and* [they] *told me how:* our hearts are good again, since you have spoken to us such good and important words, we will do, what you will tell us to do.

Two Strike and Crow Dog

"If we stop now we will be punished."

The newspapers reported eagerly on Father John Jutz's mission. An article was published in the *Omaha Daily Bee* on December 6, and in the *New York Times* on December 7, 1890. The article was written by Charles

23. For A. T. Lea and the census, see Andersson, *The Lakota Ghost Dance of 1890*, pp. 105, 141, 196–97, 223, 261, 276–77. For the boundary dispute, see introduction above.

24. Father John Jutz to Father Stephan, December 14, 1890, MUA, BCIM, series 1–1, roll 20. The peace mission of Father Jutz was also noted by Father Emil Perrig in his diary. Father Emil Perrig Diary, MUA, BCIM, HRMSCA. See also Coleman, *Voices of Wounded Knee*, 158–59; Ostler, *The Plains Sioux*, 317–18; Andersson, *The Lakota Ghost Dance of 1890*, 179, pp. 220–21; Karl Marcus Kreis, *Lakotas, Black Robes, and Holy Women: German Reports from the Indian Missions in South Dakota, 1886–1900* (Lincoln: University of Nebraska Press, 2010), 142–46, 160–66.

Cressey of the *Omaha Daily Bee* under the title "Mission of Father Jute," whereas the *New York Times* entitled it "The Hostile Camp Visited."[25] The article describes the council held at the Ghost Dancers' camp in the Stronghold in the Badlands. It is quite interesting that the newspapers quoted Two Strike in more detail than Father Jutz's own description of the meeting. It is somewhat unclear how Charles Cressey got his information. The newspapers also reported on how well the Indian Stronghold was fortified and how well prepared they were for war.[26]

Two Strike: We object to the recent census returns made by Mr. Lee [Lea]. His enumeration, as he is now making it would not give food sufficient for us to live on. They down list, many less, for each tipi than these tipis contain. We are to receive food according to that enumeration. We shall starve; we know we shall starve, if the Great Father chooses to lay a trap to cheat us: we shall have one big eat before the starving time comes. After that we shall fight our last fight, the white man shall see more blood more dead by us from our guns than ever before. Then we will go to the last hunting ground happy. If the white man did not mean to cheat us out of food the Great Father never would have sent soldiers. There is no need of soldiers if the Great Father intended to be fair with us. We know he intends cheating less by the way the census man is now putting down figures that lie and by which we are to be fed.[27]

The Great Father has done another wrong. He put a new line, a new boundary line, between Rosebud and Pine Ridge Agency, which makes many of us leave our homes and give them to others. The Great Father broke the old treaty when he did this. We can no longer believe the Great Father. He says to us: "children you shall never be moved again unless you want to move," and then he goes right away and moves us. We are done with promises; now we make a promise that we will fight and the Great Father will find that we will not break our promise. We will now be very plain

25. Two Strike and Crow Dog in *Omaha Daily Bee*, December 6, 1890, p. 1; *New York Times*, December 7, 1890, p. 14. See Kreis, *Lakotas, Black Robes, and Holy Women*, 160–66.

26. Andersson, *The Lakota Ghost Dance of 1890*, pp. 220–21.

27. The U.S. Congress discussed Lakota rations and A. T. Lea's report in December 1890. Senator Henry L. Dawes, who was considered one of the best experts on Indian affairs in Congress, said that Lea's report was correct and therefore the cut in rations was justifiable. Senator Dawes even read aloud Lea's letter where the agent said that the

with you, Christian father, and tell you another thing, something of which you may have already thought. It is this: we are not coming in now and will not lay down our rifles because we are afraid of the consequences. We have done wrong: we know it. If we stop now we will be punished. The Great Father will send many of us to this big iron house to stay many moons. We would die. No, we will not go and give up. We know the Great Father better than he knows us or cares to know us.

Crow Dog: Hold your hands up to the Great Spirit and tell us as though you were about to start on a journey to the last hunting ground of the red man, whether what you said to us from General Brooke be true and that we will not be harmed if we come in simply to talk to Gen. Brooke.[28]

Two Strike

"We only wanted . . . to be allowed to worship the Great Spirit in our own way."

As a member of the Lakota delegation to Washington in 1891, Two Strike met with Thomas A. Bland of the Indian Defence Association and gave Bland his interpretation of the Ghost Dance and the "trouble." Bland published his account as part of his own report, "Brief History of the Military Invasion of the Home of the Sioux," under the subtitle "The Immediate Cause of the Troubles: What Two Strike Says About It."[29] Bland notes that during

the recent visit of the Sioux delegation to Washington, I obtained through Louis Richard and other interpreters, a brief statement of the

---

Indians had more than enough and only the "most gluttonous . . . eat up their rations often a day or two before issue day." A few senators, however, challenged Senator Dawes, saying that Lea's report was incorrect and the Lakotas were not getting what was promised to them. For this debate, see Andersson, *The Lakota Ghost Dance of 1890*, pp. 251–62.

28. The Lakota delegation came to the Pine Ridge Agency for negotiations on December 6.

29. Two Strike in Thomas A. Bland, "A Brief History of the Late Military Invasion of the Home of the Sioux," pt. 2 (Washington, D.C.: National Indian Defense Association, 1891), 7–8. Thomas A. Bland was the founder of the Indian Defense Association. He corresponded with several Indian leaders, including Red Cloud. Unfortunately, Bland's papers have not been systematically archived.

origin of the recent troubles from Two Strike, who, as is well known, was the commander-in-chief of what was called the hostile party.[30]

Two Strike's comments were also published by L. W. Colby.[31] In his description Two Strike compares the Ghost Dances to the white man's churches and praying to Christ. The only difference, he thought, was that the Lakotas were dancing around a pole as they prayed. He also points out that they never attacked any white people, stole cattle that belonged to the whites, or left their reservation, but admits that they stole cattle from Indians. They felt that it was cattle bought with government money for the Indians, so they could use it just as well. Two Strike ends by saying that if there had been no soldiers there would have been no trouble.

We have been suffering for food and other things, which the government promised to give us for our lands which we sold in 1868 and 1876;[32] and we were disappointed at not getting pay for the land we sold to the government last summer. We had come to fear that the government would let our wives and children starve, for rations were getting less and less all the time. Last spring we heard of a great Medicine Man out in the far West who had been sent from the Great Spirit to help the Indians. From what we could learn of him he was like the white man's Christ. We sent one of our men out to Montana [Nevada] to see this new Messiah. He came back and told us that it was all true what we had heard; and that he had seen the new Messiah and talked with him, and he said that he had come to restore the Indians to their former state. Some of us believed this good news, and we began to hold meetings. These meetings are what the white people call "Ghost Dances." We pray to the Great Spirit, and dance around a pole, or post, while we pray. We did not think we were doing any harm by dancing our religious dances, and praying

30. Bland, "A Brief History of the Late Military Invasion of the Home of the Sioux," pt. 2, p. 7.

31. Two Strike in L. W. Colby, "The Sioux Indian War of 1890–91," 174–75.

32. In 1868 the Treaty of Fort Laramie established the Great Sioux Reservation with an enormous area mostly in today's Wyoming and Montana as unceded Indian territory. After the Little Big Horn battle and the surrender of the Lakotas, the Sioux Act of 1877 was passed. As a result, the Lakotas lost the Black Hills area. For recent works discussing this issue, see Jeffrey Ostler, *The Lakotas and the Black Hills: The Struggle for Sacred Ground* (New York: Penguin Books, 2011).

to the Great Spirit to send the Deliverer to us quickly. We had no thought of going on the war path against the government or our white neighbors.

One day a white man employed at a trader's store at the agency came up to my camp and told me the soldiers were coming to stop the dance. This scared us so that we put our women and children into wagons and got on our ponies and left our homes. We went to Pine Ridge and asked Red Cloud and his people to let us have [a] home on their reservation. They said we might stay, but in a short time we heard that the agent at Pine Ridge had sent for soldiers to come and make us stop dancing. Then we went to the Badlands and some of the Oglalas who had joined our dance went with us. We went there to keep away from the soldiers. We did not want to fight; we only wanted to be let alone, and to be allowed to worship the Great Spirit in our own way. We did not go off the reservation, nor rob any white man of his property. We did take some cattle on the reservation which we knew belonged to the Indians, for they had been bought by the government with the Indians' money.[33] We did not mean to fight unless the soldiers came to the Badlands to break up our dance and take our guns away from us. If the soldiers had not come to our country there would have been no trouble between us and the government.

Two Strike

"My heart is good. I am for peace."

In another interview with L. W. Colby in January 1891, Two Strike continues his accusations against the government.[34] He blames the agents for robbing the Lakotas. Like many Lakotas, Two Strike hoped that the civilian agents would be replaced by army officers. The Lakotas trusted the soldiers and believed that officers would never cheat them.

We were driven to fighting. We did not fight first. Our agent treated us bad, so we came over to Pine Ridge. Big Foot and his wives and children were all murdered at Wounded Knee. The soldiers took away their guns and cut them down like grass, and fired big guns at them, and so we proposed to

---

33. The Ghost Dancers caused in total $98,383.46 worth of damage. See Eli R. Paul, "Dakota Resources: The Investigation of Special Agent Cooper and Property Damage Claims in the Winter of 1890–1891," *South Dakota History* 24, no. 3–4 (1994): 212–35.
34. Two Strike in Colby, "The Sioux Indian War of 1890–91," 186–87.

fight. General Miles said we could get our guns back again if we gave them up. We believe General Miles, and many of my people will give up their guns. He has given us beef. One hundred and forty of my people with Yellow Robe have gone to Rosebud Agency. I want to go to Washington and see the Great Father and tell him how the agent starved us and did not give us what the Great Father promised when he took our lands from us. My heart is good. I am for peace; I am not for fighting, but we had rather die fighting than be disarmed and then killed. The army officers are our friends. They do not steal from us. We believe what they say.

Big Road and No Water

"We will obey the Great Father in Washington."

An interview with Oglala Chiefs Big Road and No Water was published in the *Omaha Daily Bee* on November 25, 1890.[35] In this interview by the *Bee* correspondent Charles Cressey, Big Road and No Water explain that they were "hounded on by hunger and famine." This, "rather than religious enthusiasm has excited the Indians," writes Cressey.[36]

Big Road: We much think good of you. You print paper. Paper tells us what [how] the Great Father want us to act. But some papers say we Injun[s] bad, no, we not bad. Paper say bad, but they say not [do not say] right. We will obey the Great Father in Washington. He cannot [wants] us to stop dance, then we will stop. We like [the] white man, he say we know [do not] like him. White man [is] wrong to say that.

Question: Why did you not stop dancing when Agent Royer told you to, weeks ago?

Big Road: Indian police tell us stop. We [do] no[t] believe [the] Indian police. Great Father say stop, we stop.

Question: Do you still believe that if you keep on dancing the buffalo and other game will come back as in the old days?

No Water: No, no. Buffalo he never come on prairie again; white mans shoot him too much.

Question: Have your people stopped dancing?

35. Big Road and No Water in *Omaha Daily Bee*, November 25, 1890, p. 1.
36. Cressey, *Omaha Daily Bee*, November 25, 1890, p. 1.

No Water: All stop—no dance no more.

Question: Why?

No Water: Great Father [does not] like it.

Question: Who told you?

No Water: We know. You paper man now tell white man just as we tell you. Do not be [have] bad heart to Indian[s]. Tell everybody we like [the] white man; this [is] all we say now.

Big Road

"Our hearts are not bad, but we have some rights."

Big Road was also interviewed by L. W. Colby in January 1891.[37] Like Crow Dog and Two Strike, he argues for certain rights the Lakotas were entitled to according to the Sioux Act of 1889. Those rights had not been met. Big Road also emphasizes that the Lakotas had not killed any white neighbors or stolen any of their cattle. "The Indian should stand for their rights," argues Big Road and continues his powerful argument, saying that an Indian who is starving has the right to complain and has the right to dance just as the white man does.

When I promise something I do it; when the Great Father promises he never does it. Yet they say the Indian is a bad man. The Great Father should have good agents, and he should not lie to us. His agents rob us and starve us, and do not give us anything that they agreed to. They promise us good things—money, clothes, tools, and plenty going of food for our good lands, and they said they would teach us to farm, but they lied. I do not lie like the white men. The Great Father should not let his agents steal. The Indians should stand up for their rights. They have a right to food and money, and clothing, and everything that was promised them [in the Sioux Act of 1889]. The Indian have not stolen from the white neighbors, but they [the whites] have stolen our cattle and horses. The Indians have not killed our white neighbors, but they have killed our women and children. We did not want to fight. The Indian who is starving has a right to complain, has a right to dance the

37. Big Road as quoted in Colby, "The Sioux Indian War of 1890–91," 190.

same way as a white man. Let the Great Father do right by us and there will be no trouble. Our hearts are not bad, but we have some rights.

Red Cloud

"Some have told I have seen the dance [but] I have not been near it."

This statement by Red Cloud appeared in the *Omaha Daily Bee* on November 22, 1891.[38] The *Bee* correspondent Charles Cressey was on Pine Ridge and he wrote almost daily dispatches from there. His writings were also published by other newspapers. Cressey has often been discredited for spreading unfounded rumors, but he also wrote articles that objectively described the situation on the reservation.[39] In his introduction to this interview, Cressey depicts Red Cloud as a statesman and a wise human.

I hope that the great council [Congress] that assembles in Washington in December will help us more.[40] On this reservation I am the chief. We don't object to the soldiers being here. I haven't been to see the dance. My eyes are sore, but as soon as my eyes get well I am going to see it and try to stop it. If we can't stop it now, we can in the spring. There would be no trouble from the soldiers. Some have told I have seen the dance [but] I have not been near it, not seen it. When we made our treaty we were not to have troops here. But if the Great Father has ordered them here I suppose it is right—if there is trouble—that they should be here. My name is Red Cloud, and that is all I have to say about this question.

---

38. Red Cloud in *Omaha Daily Bee*, November 22, 1890, p. 1.
39. Andersson, *The Lakota Ghost Dance of 1890*, pp. 223–24, 248, 290–92.
40. The U.S. Congress had been on recess since October, but reconvened in December. On December 6, Congress started to discuss the Lakotas and the Ghost Dance. See Coleman, *Voices of Wounded Knee*, 130–45, 150–53; Andersson, *The Lakota Ghost Dance of 1890*, pp. 251–70.

Red Cloud

"If it was true, it would spread all over the world."

This brief comment by Red Cloud was published in *Harper's Weekly* in an article by Marion P. Maus under the title "The New Indian Messiah" on December 6, 1890.[41] This quote, although brief, has been used in countless works of the Ghost Dance and is important as such.

If it was true, it would spread all over the world. If it was not true, it would melt away like snow under the hot sun.

Red Cloud

"There was no hope on Earth, and God seemed to have forgotten us."

The following comment by Red Cloud about the start of the Ghost Dance was published in James P. Boyd, *Recent Indian Wars: Under the Lead of Sitting Bull and Other Chiefs; with a Full Account of the Messiah Craze and Ghost Dances*, in 1891.[42] This dramatic testimony illustrates the situation and logic of many who took up the Ghost Dance. However, it is difficult to determine when and if Red Cloud really made this speech, as Boyd does not quote any source.

We felt that we were mocked in our misery. We had no newspapers and no one to speak for us. We had no redress. Our rations were again reduced. You who eat three times each day, and see your children well and happy around you, can't understand what starving Indians feel. We were faint with hunger and maddened by despair. We held our dying children and felt their little bodies tremble as their souls went out and left only a dead weight in our hands. They were not very heavy, but we ourselves were very faint, and the dead weighed us down. There was no hope on Earth, and God seemed

41. Red Cloud in Maus, "The New Indian Messiah," *Harper's Weekly*, December 6, 1890, p. 947. Red Cloud's comment also appears in a slightly different form in a letter by Charles Eastman to Frank Wood (see pt. 3).
42. Red Cloud in Boyd, *Recent Indian Wars*, 181.

to have forgotten us. Someone had again been talking of the Son of God, and said He had come. The people did not know; they did not care. They snatched at the hope. They screamed like crazy men to Him for mercy. They caught at the promises they heard He had made.

Red Cloud

"It looks as if they have come to fight, and if it is so, we must fight."

Dr. Valentine McGillycuddy served as the agent for the Oglalas from 1882 to 1889. During that time, he and Red Cloud battled fiercely over authority on the reservation. Dr. McGillycuddy arrived at Pine Ridge on December 1890 to try to settle the troubles on behalf of the governor of South Dakota, Arthur C. Mellette. According to McGillycuddy, he could have helped a lot, but the U.S. Army did not let him do so. Still he discussed the situation with Lakota leaders and his discussion with Red Cloud can be found in the Walter S. Campbell Collection.[43] It was also published in Stanley Vestal, *New Sources of Indian History*. In McGillycuddy's words, "The old chief turned to me with the following words":

I see it now, and if we had in those days listened to him [McGillycuddy] we would not have this trouble now. Little Beard [McGillycuddy], we have not behaved half as badly as we did in your day, but you never sent for troops. Why have these soldiers been brought here, coming in the night with their big guns? It looks as if they have come to fight, and if it is so, we must fight, but we are tired of war, and we think of our women and children, and our property, our homes, our little farms, and our cattle we are raising. Can you not send these soldiers away, and if you will, we give you twenty-five of our young men you can take as hostages, and everything will be settled in one sleep.

43. Red Cloud in McGillycuddy, WSCMC, WHCUOLA, box 107, folder 7. Published by permission of University of Oklahoma Libraries. Published also in Vestal, *New Sources*, 82–83. A slightly different account was published in Julia B. McGillycuddy, *Blood on the Moon: Valentine T. McGillycuddy and the Sioux* (Lincoln: University of Nebraska Press, 1990; orig. pub. 1941).

Red Cloud

"It must be apparent that there is no room for us to go to war."

The following letter was sent by Red Cloud to Thomas A. Bland of the Indian Defense Association on December 10, 1890.[44] Bland apparently forwarded the letter to someone in the U.S. Congress, as it was read aloud when the House of Representatives discussed the situation on the Lakota reservations on December 19. It sparked a lengthy debate on the Lakotas' living conditions. When the Lakota situation was discussed in the Senate, several noteworthy senators, including Henry L. Dawes, affirmed to the Senate that everything had been done according to treaties and the Lakotas were not suffering. The "nonprogressive" chiefs like Red Cloud and Sitting Bull were causing trouble and excitement, not the U.S. government or Indian agents.[45] In this letter Red Cloud denies ever seeing a Ghost Dance, but gives an insider's view on how the Brulés came to Pine Ridge to seek better living conditions and how they became known as the "wild Indians." He notes that the Oglalas unanimously invited them to Pine Ridge, but that he personally has no responsibility or authority over them. They were afraid of coming to the agency, because they had destroyed Oglala property. Red Cloud also gives his view on the devastating starvation on the reservation, with 217 people having died during the previous year.

44. Red Cloud to Thomas A. Bland, December 10, 1890, in Bland, "A Brief History of the Late Military Invasion of the Home of the Sioux," 19–21. Read in the House of Representatives, December 19, 1890, Congressional Records, 51st Congress, 1st Sess., vol. 21, pt. 14, pp. 702–703.

45. For further analysis of the congressional debate, see Andersson, *The Lakota Ghost Dance of 1890*, pp. 251–70; Heather Cox Richardson, *Wounded Knee: Party Politics and the Road to an American Massacre* (New York: Basic Books, 2010).

Pine Ridge Indian Agency, S.D.
December 10, 1890

My Dear Friend: I am very glad to hear from you and to get the strip of newspaper written by our good friend, Alonzo Bell, in my defense. You were very good to send it to me, and it makes my heart glad to see that he has written to the newspapers all those sensible words of justice in behalf of us poor Indians, but it would make my heart more glad to see him face to face.

You know I am the same all the time. I am true and have not changed. I am the constant friend of the whites, and all that has been said about my preparing my people for war is false and a lie, for they do not desire nor intend to go on the warpath. The soldiers are here and treat us very well. We have no fault to find with them.

My people (the Oglalas) are all here now; they came at the request of the military. Since they all arrived we had several open councils among my people only, which resulted in a unanimous agreement to stop the Ghost Dance; and, so far as the dance is concerned, I can truly say that I never had anything to do with or encouraged it, never having seen one.

You ask me how I and my people have been treated by the agent here. It is the business of the government agent here to treat every one of us Indians fair and alike. For some time our rations have been falling off gradually. I have never been told that that was the wish of the government. None of the treaties made by the government with us since 1868 have been fairly fulfilled, but our rations have been cut down more and more every year and former delinquencies were not made good.

The past two seasons have been so dry that we could raise little or nothing, and the rations were so scant we were obliged to kill our own cattle to keep us all from starving to death. A great many had no cattle, and those that had were obliged to help them; therefore we cannot increase our stock cattle. In consequence of these hard times many of my people got weak and sick from the want of a proper quantity of food, 217 of them dying since the fall of last year from starvation. All the whites along the railroad and about here who are not in the employ of the government treat my people and myself well. I have no fault to find with any of them. We frequently go to Fort Robinson and Oelrich; the people of those places have fed and treated us well. If it had not been for the United States soldiers, I do not know what would have become of us. My good friends Mr. Nicholas Janise [Janis] and Joseph Bissonette witnessed nearly all of our treaties arranged with the government since 1868. They also know of most of the councils I have had with my people since that time, and that I have always kept my word with the government, ever counseling my people to do the same.

My country is divided into four districts. In each of them we have schools and churches.[46] All my people have houses which they built themselves, like white men, and it is unreasonable to suppose such people as mine, established as they are here, would go to war with the United States government, to whom they have to look for the very necessities of life, to say nothing of the fact that my country is surrounded with railroads and white farmers and towns. It must be apparent that there is no room for us to go to war. Now, I will speak of the Brulés. Last July some of them asked my people in council to allow them to be transferred from the Rosebud Agency to this agency. We told them we would confer with our agent (Colonel Gallagher) about it. This we did, and the agent called for our vote, when we all raised our right hands in agreement to the transfer. We then requested him to notify the Commissioner of Indian Affairs of our wishes. There were two hundred and fifty lodges of Brulés who wanted to be transferred.[47]

A lot of those Brulés came here and told me that their rations had been stopped since last July, and their ration tickets taken away from them, consequently they have had to rove about the country to get a living the best they could. I have nothing to do with these people, but since Spotted Tail was killed they have had no head man, and it appears to me that they have not had a capable agent either since that time. The young men, having no ruler over them to check or discipline them or teach them anything about good government, have done about as they pleased. Now, those two hundred and fifty lodges of Brulés who were seeking the transfer referred to and living

46. Red Cloud refers to the Pine Ridge Reservation, which was divided into White Clay, Wounded Knee, Porcupine, and Medicine Root districts. For details about schools and churches operating on Lakota reservations in 1890, see ARCIA, 1891, 52nd Cong., 1st sess., H. Ex. Doc., no. 1, *Reports of the Indian Agents in South and North Dakota.*
47. Red Cloud refers again to the border dispute and the relocation of the Brulés. See introduction.

quietly on this reservation, and while moving in here, at the request of the present military commander, were overtaken by a lot of those unruly young Brulés from Rosebud, thus increasing the party to about four hundred lodges. This is the band now looked upon by the whites as wild Indians. I am not responsible for them, for they are not my people, but the fact is that a large number of them are afraid to come here now because of their depredations on my people's land and property. I have not heard of their having done any mischief outside of this reservation.

As a proof of my good will toward the whites and for the interests of our homes, I have furnished two hundred of my people as soldiers and police to assist the United States government.

All my words in this letter are true.

Your friend,

Red Cloud.

P.S. I have already told you that all my people have homes and good homes like white men, therefore they have no good warm skin tipis like they used to have, but those they have are made of thin cotton and were made two years ago, a few were made last year but they are most all worn out. The clothing and bed clothing is very scant also.

So my friend you will appreciate our suffering from cold, because I cannot allow my people to go to their comfortable homes while the government officials desire them to stay here.

I am not speaking for myself but for my people, as I live here in my own house. I hope the government will not detain my people here much longer as many of my old and very young people will perish.

Red Cloud

"I being in danger of my life between two fires, I had to go with them."

Red Cloud sent the following letter to Thomas A. Bland on January 12, 1891.[48] He was clearly still shaken by the events following the Wounded

---

48. Red Cloud to Thomas A. Bland, January 12, 1891, in Bland, "A Brief History of the Late Military Invasion of the Home of the Sioux," 21–22.

Knee massacre, as he had been forced to join the fleeing people. After Wounded Knee the Indians on Pine Ridge and Rosebud were contemplating a full-scale war. Before heading again toward the Badlands they fired a few shots at the Pine Ridge Agency buildings. According to some witnesses, Red Cloud had barely time to lower an American flag that was flying by his house before he was forced to join the fleeing people. In the camp of the refugees, tensions mounted quickly as some wanted to surrender, while others did not. Red Cloud finally escaped on January 7, 1891.[49] It must have been a shock to the aging chief that his own people made him go against his will and threatened to kill him if he did not obey. Red Cloud had indeed been caught between the Ghost Dancers and non–Ghost Dancers.

Pine Ridge, January 12, 1891

T. A. Bland,

Dear Friend: I have received your kind letter of justice to us poor Indians, and it made my heart feel very good that you show my letter to my friends and to Congress. Since then I have trouble. Chief Two Strike and his people Brulé Sioux, 145 family lodges and some Oglalas was camped near my house, when the news came about Big Foot and his people. Some young men of the Brulés on horseback went to fire on the agency. It caused great excitement. The Brulés and others all stampeded, and the Brulés forced me to go with them. I being in danger of my life between two fires, I had to go with them and follow my family. Some would shoot their guns around me and make me go faster. We [were] all going down White Clay Creek, 15 miles, and met Short Bull, Brulés, coming in from Badlands. There were 150 lodges. When they learned about Big Foot's people being killed they all feel very bad. All then went in cannon [the canyon] and fortified [it], and hold [held a] council, and made a law, that no one should go back to the agency. All [would] rather die together. I tried my best for them to let me go back, but they would not let me

49. Utley, *Last Days of the Sioux Nation*, 250–59; Andersson, *The Lakota Ghost Dance of 1890*, pp. 95–98.

go, and said if I went they would kill me. But three nights ago I and
my family and He Dog and White Hawk and families, all made our
escape very late in the night while they [were] all asleep, and we got
all right to the agency, and I reported all about it to General Miles.
Our escape we hope [will] have [a] good effect on them now, they
[would] all [be] moving on their way to surrender.[50] And we [are]
all hoping everything will be made agreeable to General Miles and
to the Indians. My people, the Indians of this agency, have always
been peaceable and well disposed toward white people, always ready
to listen to the words of the Great Father, knowing it was for our
good. While I was with the Brulés, the soldiers and Cheyenne scouts
camped near the mouth of White Clay River, and I heard an officer
from there was coming to talk with the Brulés. I sent my son-in-law
to warn him to turn back, but after that one of Big Foot's young men
shot the officer dead.[51] And it made me very sorry for him. General
Brook[e] had sent a large delegation of Indians of this agency to
Badlands to bring in Short Bull, but when they met the stampeding
from here they all turned back. All the above is a true statement.

Your friend,

Red Cloud

Red Cloud

"I am certainly on the right side of this great trouble."

In January and February 1891, Red Cloud sent several letters to the
commissioner of Indian affairs, Thomas J. Morgan. In his letters, he
usually did not discuss the Ghost Dance; rather he requested permission

50. Red Cloud's escape did indeed cause disintegration in the camp as more people
followed his example in the days that followed. For more on the situation in the camp,
see accounts by Short Bull and Black Elk in part 1.

51. This is a reference to an incident on January 7, 1891, where the young Lakota
Plenty Horses shot Lieutenant Edward Casey. Plenty Horses had attended Carlisle
Indian Industrial School in Pennsylvania for five years, and after returning home he felt
like an outsider. By shooting Casey he wanted to prove that he was still a Lakota. He
was tried but was acquitted as his act had been committed during wartime. Utley, *Last
Days of the Sioux Nation*, 257–58, 265–66.

to come to Washington, D.C. He sent the following letter to William J. Pollock, who forwarded it to the commissioner.[52] In the letter he, however, also discusses the situation following the Wounded Knee massacre. He reiterates that he was forced to join the fleeing Ghost Dancers. It seems that he not only felt threatened by the dancers but also that his authority had been violated. He wants to assure the commissioner that he wanted to get out of the Ghost Dancers' camp and was at no point planning any violence. Perhaps this letter also reveals how he felt marginalized at the time when the other chiefs were invited to Washington for discussions.

Hon. W. J. Pollock
Pine Ridge, February 5, 1891

My Dear Friend,

Your letter of January 31 to hand and on reply would say I am glad
to hear from you so promptly. My eyes are now in good condition
and if you can assist me in any way in getting permission to come to
Washington, I wish you would do it. I want to come for [the] same
reason one particular one is this: On the 29th day of December
when the Indians from Rosebud and other places made an attack
upon the agency I was resting quietly in my house and before I
could do anything in the way of stopping the outbreak my home
was completely surrounded and I was compelled against my wishes
to go with the troublesome Indians and I assure you I made every
honorable effort to get away from them but they said they would kill
me if I made an attempt to escape away. My horses were shot down
to prevent me making my escape. My enemies in the meantime were
making every point against me [that] they could to Commanding
General [Nelson] Miles [that] I was the leader of the hostile Indians.
You know and have always known my friendly feelings toward the
whites and my great desire to live like them and do as they requested
me to do, but for these bitter enemies that are continually trying

52. Red Cloud to William J. Pollock, forwarded to the Commissioner of Indian Affairs Thomas J. Morgan, February 5, 1891, NARA, RBIA, RG 75.4, GRBIA, Letters Received, Letter 5164, box 703.

to down me in my old age, I would not be placed in [the] situation I am now in. I of course, as many others have done before me, I have made mistakes in not doing something I should have done and done what I should not have done. But be that as it may, I am certainly on the right side of this great trouble and will continue to be there. I want you to see if they have any idea of letting me come to Washington. You can go and have a talk with the Commissioner and see if he feel[s] kindly toward me and will let me come. I of course I would like to bring some others with me so that I will have someone to consult with, who were here during this trouble. I would like to come as soon as the commissioner thinks best for me to come. Genl. Miles told me just before leaving here [that] he would call me to Washington in about one month. Hoping you will attend to this matter and let me hear from you as soon as possible.

I am your red friend,

Red Cloud

Sitting Bull

"If they cannot do so, I will return and tell my people it is a lie."

Kicking Bear introduced the Ghost Dance to Sitting Bull and his people on October 9, 1890. After that, dances became regular in Sitting Bull's camp. Yet, according to some Indian accounts, Sitting Bull himself did not get a vision that would have confirmed to him that the new religion was true.[53] Despite being skeptical, he wanted to learn more about the Ghost Dance. During a meeting at his camp on November 18, Sitting Bull asked Agent James McLaughlin for permission to go west to learn about the new religion.[54] The agent denied his request.

---

53. It is not certain that Sitting Bull ever participated in a Ghost Dance ceremony as a dancer or sought a vision, but there is enough evidence to safely say that he was interested in the new religion and wanted to know more. For this discussion, see Andersson, *The Lakota Ghost Dance of 1890*, pp. 65–66.

54. Sitting Bull as quoted in McLaughlin to the Commissioner of Indian affairs Thomas J. Morgan, November 19, 1890, ARCIA, 1891, pp. 330–31. See also Utley, *The Lance and the Shield*, 288–89.

Father [Agent McLaughlin], I will make you a proposition which will settle this question. You go with me to the agencies to the West, and let me seek for the men who saw the Messiah; and when we find them, I will demand that they show him to us and if they cannot do so, I will return and tell my people it is a lie.

Sitting Bull

"You should say nothing against our religion, for we said nothing against yours."

The lengthiest document explaining Sitting Bull's views on the Ghost Dance is a letter he dictated to his son-in-law Andrew Fox a few weeks after the above-mentioned agent's visit.[55] In the letter he again explains to Agent James McLaughlin his views on the situation and why he needed to learn the truth behind the Ghost Dance. He told the agent that, if not allowed to go west, he had also been invited to go to Pine Ridge where he could learn more about the religion. Interestingly, Sitting Bull says that he knows what the agent tells the newspapers about him and that he knows that the agent dislikes him. According to Sitting Bull, the agent thought that he kept the people from becoming civilized.[56]

I want to write to [you a] few line[s] today and to let you know something. I [held a] meeting with all my Indians today, and [I am] writing to you this order. God made you, all the white race, and also made the red race and give they [gave them] both might and heart to know everything in the world: But white high[er] than the Indians. But today, our Father, is helps [helping] us the Indians. So we all the Indians knowing [So all we Indians believe]. So I think this way. I wish no one [to] come to [me] in my pray[ers] with

55. Sitting Bull as dictated to Andrew Fox, December 11, 1890, WSCMC, WHCU-OLA, box 114, folder 6. There is also an interview of Andrew Fox in a question-and-answer form in box 105, folder 5. Published by permission of University of Oklahoma Libraries. Also published in Vestal, *Sitting Bull*, 283–84. In *Sitting Bull*, Vestal provides the letter in full, both verbatim in "poor" English and as a free rendering made by himself. The letter can also be found in McLaughlin, *My Friend the Indian*, 215–16. For more on this letter, see Utley, *The Lance and the Shield*, 394, footnote 11.

56. For more on the troubled relationship between Agent McLaughlin and Sitting Bull see Vestal, *Sitting Bull*; Utley, *Lance and the Shield*.

their gun or knife. So all the Indians pray to God for life, and try to find a good road, and do nothing wrong in their life. This is what we want, and to pray to God. But you did not believe us. So you must not say anything about our pray [religion], because we did not say anything about your pray [religion]. Because you pray to God. So [do] we all the Indians. While we both pray [to] only one God to make us and you my friend today, you think I am fool[ish]. And you take some wise men among my people and you let the white people know back East. So I know that, but I think that is all right, because I am fool[ish] to pray to God. So you don't like me. My friend, I don't like it myself when someone is fool[ish]. I like him. So you are the same. You don't like me because I am fool[ish], and if I were not here, then the Indians would be civilized, but because I am here, all the Indians are fool[ish]. I know this is all you put down on newspapers back East. So I [am] seeing [in the] paper, but I think it is all right. When you were here in my camp, you gave me good words about my pray [religion], but today you take [it] all back from me. And also I will let you know something. I got to go to Pine Ridge Agency and to know [about] this pray [Ghost Dance]. So I let you know that. The policemen told me you [are] going to take all our ponies, [and] guns too. So I want you [to] let me know [about] that. I want answer back soon.

Sitting Bull

Sitting Bull

"They must learn this religion *wočékiye*."

Just two days before being killed, Sitting Bull visited John Carignan, who was a teacher at the Grand River Day School close to Sitting Bull's home. Carignan related his discussion with Sitting Bull to the Episcopal missionary Aaron Beede, who wrote it in his diary. The following conversation is taken from Beede's diary.[57] Carignan noted that the Indians did not call the dance "Ghost Dance," but *wóčhekiye*, "worship"

57. Sitting Bull in Aaron Beede Diary, 2:242, NDHS. Published by permission of North Dakota Historical Society Archives.

or "prayer." He said there was nothing to be concerned about and that he had taken a journalist to Sitting Bull's camp. The Indians allowed Carignan and the journalist to witness a Ghost Dance ceremony, the journalist even taking a few photos with his camera. Carignan says that Sitting Bull was very much concerned about Agent James McLaughlin and the welfare of his people. According to Carignan, Sitting Bull says that he wanted to learn more about the Ghost Dance and wanted to go to Pine Ridge to do exactly that. Agent McLaughlin did not allow him to go. Carignan believed that "Sitting Bull was sincere in his religious belief; he seemed anxious to learn more about the coming Messiah; his object in going to Pine Ridge was not to defy the reservation authority, but to learn more about this new religion."[58] Carignan also quoted an anonymous Indian. He asked that if there once had been a flood, why it could not happen again—an interesting comment clearly referring to Christian teachings of the great flood. According to Carignan, on "Saturday before he [Sitting Bull] was killed Monday morning he came to see me and wanted me to intercede with the agent, McLaughlin, to have the beef rations sent out there for his people during the winter."[59] Sitting Bull said:

I am going down to Pine Ridge to learn more about this religion. I start Monday [and] I am worried about my people while I am gone. The distance to the agency is long and it may be cold and stormy. So I want the beef sent out here. My people w[ill] send a man in for the small things, but I want the beef to be sent out here."

I told him: "I don't think Mr. McLaughlin will do it. He might be willing, but I think the Indian Bureau is not willing, because you keep up the *wočé-kiye* and so keep the children out of school."

Sitting Bull replied: "I do not want to keep them out of school. I want them to go to school, but they must learn this religion *wóčhekiye*[60]—as soon as they have learned this religion they shall go back to school."

58. John Carignan in Aaron Beede Diary, 2:242, NDHS.
59. Ibid.
60. Underlined in the original.

One Indian said to Mr. Carrignan: "You believe there was a flood of water once, and so why is it strange to believe there would be a flood of soft mud role [roll] this way from the Rocky Mountains?"

Sitting Bull and Gray Eagle

"I could not give up my race as it is seated in us."

The following discussion between Sitting Bull and Gray Eagle took place only a few days before Sitting Bull was killed. The original text is in the Walter S. Campbell Collection, Western History Collections, University of Oklahoma, Norman, Oklahoma.[61] Gray Eagle, who was Sitting Bull's nephew, acted as a judge on the Standing Rock Reservation and as a messenger for the agent and the Indian police force. He tried to convince Sitting Bull to stop Ghost Dancing in his camp. For Gray Eagle, Ghost Dancing signified Sitting Bull's reluctance to accept the prevalent situation and the realities of reservation life. Sitting Bull clearly understood the risks, but wanted to continue on his chosen path. The political division on Standing Rock is evident in this discussion; the Ghost Dance was one more divisive issue, which in Gray Eagle's mind had the potential to cause trouble. Gray Eagle told Sitting Bull the he "must not take up this dancing as it wasn't doing him any good but if he would take up good regulations he would get along good. And have to get along with your government and work and not spend your time dancing."[62] The following discussion between the two illustrates the differing political views of the situation. Sitting Bull clearly says that he cannot deny his people the right to dance, that he could not give up his people. Gray Eagle relates the discussion as follows:

Gray Eagle: Brother-in-Law, we've settled on reservation and we're under jurisdiction of [the] government. We must do as they say—we must

---

61. Sitting Bull and Gray Eagle in WSCMC, WHCUOLA, box 106, folder 54, pp. 52–53. Published by permission of University of Oklahoma Libraries. See also Vestal, *Sitting Bull*, 277–84.

62. Gray Eagle in WSCMC, WHCUOLA, box 106, folder 54, p. 51.

cut out the roaming around. Live as they say and [you] must cut out this dancing.

Sitting Bull: Yes you are right, but I could not give up my race as it is seated in us. You go ahead and follow what [the] white man says, but for my part, leave me alone.

Gray Eagle: If you're not going to obey and do as the whites say, you are going to cause a lot of trouble and [it will] cost your life. I have sweared [sworn] to stay by [the] government and we have been friend[s] a long time, but if you are not going to [do] as [the] white [men] say, we will not be together anymore.

Sitting Bull

"I did not start this Ghost Dance."

Walter S. Campbell interviewed many Lakotas about Sitting Bull's life, including his arrest. The following is Grasping Eagle's report of Sitting Bull's words when he was told that he was to be arrested.[63] Like Little Wound, Sitting Bull was very displeased about the fact that Lakotas were being used against each other. In addition, only a few days before his arrest, he had a vision in which a bird told him that his own people would kill him.[64]

Why should the Indian police come against me? We are of the same blood, we are all Sioux, we are relatives. It will disgrace the nation, it will be murder, it will defile our race. If the white men want me to die, they ought not to put up the Indians to kill me. I don't want confusion among my own people. Let the soldiers come and take me away and kill me, wherever they like. I am not afraid. I was born a warrior. I have followed the warpath ever since I was able to draw a bow. White Hair (McLaughlin) wanted me to travel all around (with Buffalo Bill) and across the sea, so that he could make a lot of money. Once was enough; I would not go [again]. Then I would not join his

63. Sitting Bull as quoted by Grasping Eagle in WSCMC, WHCUOLA, box 114, folder 6. Also published in Vestal, *New Sources of Indian History*, 309–10. Published by permission of University of Oklahoma Libraries.

64. See Vestal, *Sitting Bull*, 278; Utley, *The Lance and the Shield*, 290; Andersson, *The Lakota Ghost Dance of 1890*, pp. 84–86.

church, and ever since he has had it in for me. Long ago I had two women in my lodge. One of them was jealous. White Hair reminds me of that jealous woman. Why does he keep trying to humble me? Can I be any lower than I am? Once I was a man, but now I am a pitiful wretch—no country, no fast horses, no guns worth having. Once I was rich, now I am poor. What more does he want to do to me? I was a fool ever to come down here. I should have stayed with the Red Coats in the Grandmother's country.[65]

I did not start this Ghost Dance; Kicking Bear came here of his own accord. I told my people to go slow, but they were swept into this thing so strong nothing could stop them.[66] I have not joined the sacred dance, since I was told to stop, a way back.

Sitting Bull

"If they became civilized, I shall go down."

Episcopal missionary Mary C. Collins spent considerable time among Sitting Bull's people during the 1880s and she became Sitting Bull's friend. The following comment by Sitting Bull is from Mary Collins's article that appeared in the November 1890 issue of the *Word Carrier* newspaper.[67] This statement, however, is very different from any other left by Sitting Bull and most likely reflects the opinions of Mary Collins more than those of Sitting Bull. Sitting Bull clearly states on many occasions that he wishes children to go to schools and become educated. That does not sound as if he wanted to keep his "people in a savage condition," as claimed by Collins. Collins's article is very negative, even hostile, toward the Ghost Dance and also Sitting Bull. For her, the Ghost Dance meant a return to savagery and it also signified that her own

---

65. For Sitting Bull's life in Canada from 1877 to 1881, see James H. Howard, *The Canadian Sioux* (Lincoln: University of Nebraska Press, 1984).

66. It must be realized that while Sitting Bull was a major political and spiritual leader among the Standing Rock Lakotas, in terms of the traditional Lakota leadership structure, he had no authority to decide over other people. So it might actually be true that some of his people would not have stopped dancing even if Sitting Bull told them to. See One Bull in WSCMC, WHCUOLA, box 104, folder 11. See also Andersson, *The Lakota Ghost Dance of 1890*, p. 84.

67. Sitting Bull in Mary C. Collins, *Word Carrier*, November 1890, p. 31.

efforts to civilize Sitting Bull were suffering a blow. In another interview with Collins, Sitting Bull made a brief statement that "our own religion is best for us," which has been used as an indicator that he refused to accept both Christianity and the Ghost Dance.[68]

They did not regard my wishes in selling the lands and opening the reservation.[69] I will be chief. I can only be chief by keeping the people in a savage condition. If they became civilized, I shall go down.

Sitting Bull

"We have abandoned the white man's houses."

The *New York Times*, like many other newspapers, was constantly reporting about the possibility of Sitting Bull leading a major uprising in November and December 1890.[70] The following article contains a statement allegedly directly from Sitting Bull.[71] According to the paper, two Indian scouts were sent from Fort Yates to Sitting Bull's camp to "ascertain if the Indians were on warpath." They met Sitting Bull in his camp at Grand River. Sitting Bull told them that he knew that soldiers were sent there to take his property.

But I have runners coming and going every day and know everything that is going on there and as soon as the soldiers come, I would take my family and ponies and those that would follow me and leave and they will not get me. You see we have abandoned the white man's houses and are living in our native tipis and will not return to the houses nor to the agency.[72]

68. Sitting Bull as quoted in Mary C. Collins, WMCC, IULL, box 6, folder 3, envelope 78.

69. This is a reference to the Crook Commission discussions in 1889 and the partitioning of the Great Sioux Reservation.

70. For Sitting Bull in the press, see Andersson, *The Lakota Ghost Dance of 1890*, pp. 197–98, 227–28.

71. Sitting Bull in *New York Times*, November 26, 1890, pp. 1–2.

72. The fact that so many Lakotas moved away from their houses and started living in tipis during the Ghost Dance period was of great concern to white officials. Living in a house was one of the major indicators of Lakota progress "on the white man's road." For the Lakotas, the traditional camp circle symbolized the unity of the people and, thus, by living in tipis, the Ghost Dancers recreated the Lakota sacred circle.

Old Bull

"Sitting Bull couldn't stop them."

Old Bull was a long-time friend of Sitting Bull. His reflections on the Ghost Dance can be found in the Walter S. Campbell Collection.[73] This and several other interviews in the Campbell collection are very difficult to read as Campbell used mostly shorthand notes. In this short interview, Old Bull notes that he never saw Sitting Bull dance and reiterates that he did not really believe in the Ghost Dance. However, Sitting Bull could not stop the dancing even if he wanted to. Old Bull also sheds light on the difficult situation in which the Indian policemen found themselves. (Campbell's insertions appear in italics.)

Short Bull [and] Kicked [Kicking] Bear came and introduced [the] Ghost Dance to Sitting Bull telling that SB [Sitting Bull's?] people were coming back.[74] *That Sitting Bull must elect police and BTB [Bob Tail Bull] elected wear blue suit.*[75] Sitting Bull's followers told police [that] bullets wouldn't shoot at the dancers—they wouldn't go off. Sitting Bull didn't believe in [the] Ghost Dance. Sitting Bull said: "[It is] impossible for dead man to come back alive." *Jim [James] McLaughlin was his major [agent] and made BTB [Bob Tail Bull] only regular police at that time.*[76]

I used to stop at Lieutenant Bullhead's place, then go to dance to look on and go to Sitting Bull's house and see [the] followers [dance] but not Sitting Bull dance—[some people] claim Sitting Bull dance[d] but I didn't see him. Quite a few members there. Major sent tobacco down and we gave it and Sitting Bull distributed it among old people—mixed [it] with kinni-kinnick. [I] told Sitting Bull not to take part in dancing and he would say he wouldn't.

[They] got tired of me coming. Some asked me not to come anymore—especially Mrs. Spotted Horns. Later—[a] circular informed at agent's office for 42–45 Indian police in res[erve].

73. Old Bull in WSCMC, WHCUOLA, box 105, folder 11. Published by permission of University of Oklahoma Libraries.

74. Old Bull erroneously says that Short Bull introduced the Ghost Dance at Standing Rock. Kicking Bear introduced it to Sitting Bull's people on October 9, 1890.

75. This comment by Campbell seems odd; which police he means Sitting Bull should elect is unclear.

76. Again, Campbell's insertion does not make sense.

I tried to make [the] police and [some] of [the] dancers to break up dance—got [the] following:

1. Old Bull
2. Strike Kettle
3. Black Fox
4. Two Crow

They resign after getting clothes and they believe stronger that arrests will come back and they don't want to be police.[77] Bullhead says: "Let me pick my police. I'll pick men who will stick."—Gets [the] follow[ing] [men] from this district:

1. White Bird
2. One Feather
3. Good Voice Eagle
4. Running Hawk
5. Weasel Bear
6. Iron Thunder
7. Black Pheasant
8. Yells at Daybreak
   Forty-three police in all.

People danced all fall [and] part of winter instead of looking after stock, home, farms, etc. Fall: police camped near the Ghost Dance and two [were] elected to go to Sitting Bull and ask to stop. And Sitting Bull say "yes," but followers wouldn't. Sitting Bull tried, but too many too firm believers. Even Catholic Priest Father Bernard[78] talked to [them] and convinced Sitting Bull the dead couldn't and wouldn't come back. Then Sitting Bull announced he didn't believe etc. and for them to quit.

1. Grover Eagle Boy [and] 2. White Hand Bear caused the trouble, especially 2 [White Hand Bear] who fainted and saw grandfather who told him to keep dancing and 2 [White Hand Bear] convinced [the] rest to come back. [I] didn't see 1 [Grover Eagle Boy] dance but 1 [Grover Eagle Boy] was a good follower and [brought?] others when he followed.

77. Agent James McLaughlin also reported that the Ghost Dance affected some of his policemen. After they returned from a visit to the Ghost Dancers' camp in early October, he reported that they were in a "dazed condition." See James McLaughlin to the Commissioner of Indian Affairs, October 17, 1890. NARA, RG 75, SC 188, M4728, roll 1, 31–43; McLaughlin, *My Friend the Indian*, 184–91.

78. This was most likely Father Bernard Strassmayer form the Catholic Indian Mission at Fort Yates.

People [were] getting stronger believers all [the] time, getting into Sitting Bull's house, and Sitting Bull couldn't stop them.[79]

Grover Eagle Boy

"Touch my thumbs and you will see your dead."

Old Bull accused Grover Eagle Boy of causing trouble, but Grover Eagle Boy himself noted in a short interview with Walter S. Campbell that he was curious about the dance, but lost faith when he did not see his dead relatives.[80] Eagle Boy was one of the policemen asked to guard Sitting Bull just a few nights before he was killed. Eagle Boy described staying in Sitting Bull's cabin, having a relaxing time, and later observing the dance. The text is difficult to read because part of it is clearly a direct citation from Eagle Boy and part is shorthand notes by Campbell (placed in *italics*).

Ghost Dancing [was] introduced by Short Bull upon his return from other tribe or reservation. When introduced, [the] whole tribe didn't believe, but joined gradually in hope of seeing dead relatives. *Ghost part didn't appeal to Grover Eagle Boy.*

I brought dad to home over to TP [tipi?] and intended to go back home and not take part in [the] dance. *The scout arriving tells him he is to guard Sitting Bull as officers [plan?] arrest. He takes 44–40 and goes to Sitting Bull's cabin but nothing [happened] all night so [they] resume dancing and Eagle Boy goes to see how dancing is done.* Wild dance. [The dancers] told [asked] me if I wish to see [my] own dead [relatives]. Ok. I want to see my own grandmother—leader Shave Bear [said]: "Stick hand out, thumbs opposed, touch my thumbs and you will see your dead."[81] Tried it and zero happened. Thumb[s] fell away, [I] lost faith, went home. *Police ask him to go to Bullhead's home to help make arrest.*[82]

79. The text continues with Campbell's notes about the Ghost Dance shirt.

80. Grover Eagle Boy in WSCMC, WHCUOLA, box 105, folder 11. Published by permission of University of Oklahoma Libraries.

81. Eagle Boy drew a picture of two hands with thumbs touching. It is on the left side of the manuscript.

82. The text continues with Campbell's notes about the arrest.

Henry Bullhead

"The number of the backward Indians will be diminished."

The following letter by the captain of the Indian police on the Standing Rock Reservation, Henry Bullhead, to Agent James McLaughlin can be found in the Walter S. Campbell Collection and was first published in Stanley Vestal, *New Sources of Indian History.*[83] In his letter, Henry Bullhead addresses the same problem that Sitting Bull related to John Carignan, namely the issuing of beef on the reservation. Whereas Sitting Bull was concerned about the beef issue and of possibly being arrested if he went to the agency, Bullhead saw the beef issue as an opportunity to convince some of the people who would be at the agency to drop the Ghost Dance. This shows how divided the Standing Rock Lakotas were. Bullhead, like other Indian policemen, clearly opposed the Ghost Dance, referring to the dancers as "bad" and "wild" Indians. Bullhead and Sitting Bull did not get along even before the Ghost Dance. McLaughlin knew well the animosities between the two, but he decided to place Bullhead in charge of Sitting Bull's arrest on December 15. Would the arrest have been conducted in a different way if someone else had been in charge? Most importantly, would the result have been different if someone else had been in charge?[84]

North Dakota, December 12, 1890
Maj. J. McLaughlin:
U.S. Ind. Agt.

Sir: I desire to express my judgement concerning the separate beef issues to both well-behaved and back-ward Indians on *Grand River*[85]

---

83. Henry Bullhead in WSCMC, WHCUOLA, box 114, folder 6. Published by permission of University of Oklahoma Libraries. Published also in Vestal, *New Sources*, 11.

84. Indian accounts relating to the arrest of Sitting Bull and his relationship with Henry Bullhead can be found in the Walter Stanley Campbell Collection and the Walter M. Camp Collection. See Vestal, *Champion of the Sioux*, 277–85; Utley, *Lance and the Shield*, 290–310.

85. Italics original in this text.

respectively; that it would be well, if the plan may be applied to allow those Indians under control of the Ghost outfit to enter *bands* of good *chiefs* to draw their beef on Grand River as may gradually change their mind into good ones and retaining the rest to come after their beef up here [the agency]; for some of the Indians of unsettled mind may be cured to some extent by the application of my judgement, and the number of the backward Indians will be diminished and be won to the right path.

I request to know as to the probability of the application of my suggestion by next ration day.

Very Respectfully

Henry Bullhead

Capt. U.S. Ind. Police

Gray Eagle

"It could do no good and might lead to trouble."

Sitting Bull was married to Gray Eagle's sister and the two men were close. However, a split had already started to occur in the late 1870s as Sitting Bull ordered the punishment of Gray Eagle and his companions for stealing horses while in Canada. Sitting Bull did not want them to break the laws and thus jeopardize their stay in Canada. Although Gray Eagle did not go through the physical punishment ordered for the others, he felt humiliated. On the Standing Rock Reservation, Gray Eagle became a policeman and later a judge. That position again put him at odds with Sitting Bull before the Ghost Dance.[86] Gray Eagle's story of the killing of Sitting Bull can be found in the Walter Mason Camp Collection.[87] This text further illustrates the complicated situation between these two men. Agent James McLaughlin put Gray Eagle in a very awkward position by asking him to guard Sitting Bull. Gray Eagle was certain that Sitting Bull planned to leave the reservation and

86. For Gray Eagle and Sitting Bull, see Vestal, *Champion of the Sioux*; Utley, *Lance and the Shield*.

87. Gray Eagle in WMCC, IULL, box 5, folder 1, envelope 4. Courtesy, The Lilly Library, Indiana University, Bloomington, Ind.

reported that to the agent. Even if most Indian accounts agree that Sitting Bull was not planning to leave without permission, the agent used this as an excuse to order his arrest.[88] Gray Eagle gives a slightly different version of the event on the morning of December 15 than, for example, John Loneman. Gray Eagle says that Sitting Bull was angry and urged his people to attack the policemen. John Loneman (see below), on the other hand, notes that Sitting Bull was quite willing to go at first, but as people gathered around and women started to cry, he refused. But he does not mention a call to attack the policemen.

Several times, while Sitting Bull and his people were dancing, I went down and told him he had better stop it, as it could do no good and might lead to trouble. He said to me, "What do you know about this business? I wish you would stay away from here. I know what I am doing," etc. I therefore became afraid of him and went in and told the agent so and suggested that he should be arrested and taken into the agency where we could talk him out of the dancing.

The agent had me watch him. It appeared that he was getting ready to leave, as he was getting his horses into the corral and feeding them and repairing saddles etc. It was therefore determined to arrest him and take him to the agency. (We were also afraid that Big Foot and others might come up from Pine Ridge [sic; Big Foot was on the Cheyenne River reservation] and encourage him to go away. The day before the arrest I had told Sitting Bull that he would be arrested within a few days and taken to the agency, not having taken my advice and I expressed the hope that he would act discreetly.) I advised sending the policy [police] with a buggy, to get there before daylight when he would be sleeping soundly and to throw him into the wagon and get out in a hurry and meet the soldiers on the road over.

I therefore kept watch and finally learned one night that the police would be along that night. They came down the river and got to my house about 1 am, and I went along with them. We went down and waited to rehearse the plans, but to my surprise they did not adopt the buggy plan. We waited across the river and finally went over to make the arrest. It was agreed that

88. For the discussion about Sitting Bull planning to leave the reservation, see Andersson, *The Lakota Ghost Dance of 1890*, pp. 84–85. Indian accounts denying that Sitting Bull was planning to leave without permission can be found in WMCC, IULL, box 5, folder 1, envelope 41.

Bullhead, Shave Head and Red Tomahawk should go into the house and get Sitting Bull out and that Cook (Yellow Wolf) should go to the other house and see who was there.

As soon as the three went into Sitting Bull's house, I warned the women who were crowding around to stay back and as soon as I got to Sitting Bull's house the police had him outdoors naked and were trying to put a shirt on over his head. He was angry and said he would not go and was calling on his friends to attack the police. Red Tomahawk was holding a pistol to his head and Sitting Bull said: "What are you holding that gun to my head for? Do you think you can scare me into this?" Just then Catch the Bear ran up and fired the first shot, hitting Shave Head. Just at that instant Bullhead, Sitting Bull and Shave Head fell down together. Bullhead never fired a shot, did not shoot Sitting Bull. Red Tomahawk shot Sitting Bull and the firing became general.[89]

Crow Foot was dragged out and killed by the police just to take revenge on the family for the wounded police, as he had done nothing.[90]

Little Eagle (policeman) shot near the barn running away on foot from the place. Before the firing began, as they were leading the old man out of the house, I called out to have his white horse saddled. This [was] a horse Buffalo Bill had given him. He was an old pacing horse. White Bird had led the horse out of the barn when the firing commenced and had not yet got him saddled.[91] Red Tomahawk—Tachankpi Larta [Chaŋȟpí Lúta]. I told him, Sitting Bull he had better go to agency. Little Assiniboine had no gun.

One Bull

"All were told to dance and pray."

Like Old Bull, One Bull was one of Sitting Bull's oldest and most trusted friends and followers. He was the son of Sitting Bull's sister, which created a strong bond between the two. One Bull enlisted as a policeman,

---

89. Gray Eagle made a mistake here. Bullhead did shoot Sitting Bull, wounding him. Red Tomahawk fired the final deadly shot in the head. For a thorough analysis of Sitting Bull's death, see Utley, *Lance and the Shield*, 291–305; Andersson, *The Lakota Ghost Dance of 1890*, pp. 84–88.

90. According to John Loneman, Crow Foot was hit inside the cabin. See below.

91. There were rumors that as the firing started, Sitting Bull's horse started to perform tricks it had learned while being on the tour with Buffalo Bill. See Utley, *Lance and the Shield*, 396; Andersson, *The Lakota Ghost Dance of 1890*, p. 350.

but Agent James McLaughlin still viewed him as one of Sitting Bull's followers. Because of that he forced One Bull to resign from the police force. One Bull's story of the Ghost Dance and the killing of Sitting Bull is found in the Walter Stanley Campbell Collection.[92]

The Ghost Dance was brought by Kicking Bear and it was this way it was started. All those that had died were to be returned by this dance and prayer. All were told to dance and pray. A new world was coming which was baring them. The songs were sung thus:

> We are to journey, to journey
>
> We are to journey, to journey
>
> Coming this way
>
> Coming this way
>
> Those who believe not
>
> will not be men
>
> but beasts, dogs they shall be.

Those that believe must dance. I told this to McLaughlin as it was told to me, and McLaughlin said I was a believer. Afraid of the Bear [Lieutenant Bullhead] also said I was, so I was discharged from the Police Force. Crazy Walking was Captain. Grant Lefthand was Lieutenant. I was a Sergeant. These three were told to go to Sitting Bull, so we went as told to. "This dance must be stopped," said Crazy Walking. "Alright we shall do so, we shall stop," was the reply of Sitting Bull. "What is the foremost thought, is our school. Therefore we shall stop," said he. McLaughlin sent for Sitting Bull so he got on his horse and got there at [Fort] Yates, but McLaughlin was not there. The second time he sent for him, he went again. Afterward we heard from other Indians that he was there, but would not see him. He hid. [District farmer] Mr. [William] Pamplin knew that Sitting Bull was there twice.

---

92. One Bull in WSCMC, WHCUOLA, box 104, folder 11. Published by permission of University of Oklahoma Libraries. The text appears in Lakota and English as well as a more polished version made by Campbell. I have used the Lakota/English version, and compared it to the one written by Campbell. There are only minor differences. For more on One Bull's life, see Vestal, *Sitting Bull*; Utley, *Lance and the Shield*; and LaPointe, *Sitting Bull*.

McLaughlin told me to go on to Heart River on a freighting trip with others. I brought freight to Standing Rock for the large store there. I was told to unload the freight. It was late, so I stayed there that night. Later in the night McLaughlin and Louis Primeau came to me, they said: "If the nation should flee away, I want you and your uncle to not go." This is what they said. From Heart River the soldiers are coming, and from the Slim Buttes and from Ft. Sully on all sides they are coming. Early at dawn I left, [I] was on the way home. One of my horses was lame, could not make it. Near morning, I got home. I slept a while. When dawn came, I heard shooting. I could hear it plain. I went outside and I could hear that it was at Sitting Bull's place. [There] was hard shooting. I heard it. I went that direction. I could see our Indians on the run. As they went by, I was told the Captain was killed. As I went toward my uncle's house the Police raised their guns at me. I heard Eagle Man telling them to stop. He said don't come any further, so I stopped going forward. He told Cross Bear to stop.

"This is our son-in-law One Bull. We have killed each other on both sides," he said. "Have you killed the women too," I asked. "No," he said. "My niece was here a short while ago. Go and get her and return to your house." So I looked for my wife. I found her and the rest, so we returned home.

My wife told this thing to me: "Just before dawn, while it was yet dark, a man peeped into our camp. I spoke and said someone has been peeping in here. Someone said 'feeding cattle, I suppose.' Then again, I heard a noise toward my father-in-law's house, low whispering and talking. So I dressed my feet. I started toward the place. Just then an old woman reached me, Čáŋ Mahé's wife. We reached the corner of the log house. Sitting Bull was being led out of his house. He was without his clothes," so she said. Back of him was Afraid of the Bear [Bullhead], was striking him with a revolver pushing him saying you would not listen, striking him. I heard Sitting Bull's first wife telling his sons that the Police has come after your father. Get his white horse and saddle it up and bring it over to him at once. Just then the white horse was being led up, already saddled. Just then Afraid of the Bear shot Sitting Bull from behind in the back. Just then from the corner of the house Catching Bear rushed forward and shot Afraid of the Bear. Then the Police cried out and much firing of guns started. This much my wife saw. When the firing cooled down Crow Foot was found under the bed. "My father has been killed, do not kill me. I wish to live," he said. But Loneman killed him. Crow Foot was a school boy, fourteen years old.

I stayed home and the second day I went to Standing Rock. The Police came after us, they escorted us back. Sitting Bull's wife, his children, our family, Jumping Bull's wife, children were all taken to [Fort] Yates.

John Loneman

"I had come to advise him to drop the Ghost Dance."

Indian policeman John Loneman gave several accounts of his involvement in the arrest and killing of Sitting Bull. This version can be found in the Walter Mason Camp Collection.[93] While John Loneman mentions the Ghost Dance only briefly, this statement gives valuable insight into his understanding of the Ghost Dance. Loneman's story also reflects on the deteriorated relationships between Sitting Bull and the Indian policemen. Loneman's story of the arrest and killing of Sitting Bull is a valuable eyewitness account of the event.[94]

Killing of Sitting Bull. Story of Loneman.

Several times police had been sent over by McLaughlin to bring Sitting Bull to the agency but they returned each time without him. Finally, I was sent to go and report what I could see or hear from Sitting Bull. I went down and found a house full. They had not treat[ed] me with much courtesy. Sitting Bull said: "I suppose you have come on the same errand as the rest." I said that I had come to advise him to drop the Ghost Dance as it would come to nothing and might deceive the people who were looking to him as a chief. I said that if he wants to dance why not take on[e] of the less attractive dance[s] like a grass dance or scalp dance. Many of the people are old and cannot stand it [the Ghost Dance]. They are my friends. If you have anything to say, say it so that I can report.

In the hostile days, we young men followed you, etc. He replied: "Yes, I depended on you then, but now you have turned with the whites against me. I have nothing to say to you. If these people wish to say anything they may, but I will not. You police have annoyed me. So far as I am concerned you may go home."

I reported and [the] police were called together. An army officer was present and told of trouble at Crow Agency and said this matter would end

93. John Loneman in WMCC, IULL, box 5, folder 1, envelope 41. Courtesy, The Lilly Library, Indiana University, Bloomington, Ind.
94. For thorough analysis of the events leading to the killing of Sitting Bull, see Utley, *Lance and the Shield*, 281–307; Greene, *American Carnage*, 167–90.

up the same way if not stopped. Eight of us made trip to dance in daytime—(?) and went on and got to Bullheads before sundown, and stopped there until midnight, when Red Tomahawk came with dispatches. I was sent from Bullhead to [John] Carrig[nan][95] with a letter. He was living where One Bull now lives. We took Carrig[nan] to Bullhead. When we took Sitting Bull we rushed into [his] house and 5 or 6 took hold of Sitting Bull striking matches in the dark. The old man said "This is a great way to do things, not to give me a chance to put on my clothes in winter time." Someone said: "Go for a horse," and someone went to get it. [We] took Sitting Bull outdoors naked and brought him back in to dress him and tried to do so. Crow Foot came in and said: "What are you going for? They are making a fool of you, you must be crazy." Sitting Bull now said he would not go (said he would die first). Got clothes on and got him outside partly dressed. [His] horse [was] already saddled and at [the] door. Little Assiniboine came along and Bullhead asked him to try to persuade Sitting Bull to go and he (Assiniboine) did so.[96]

Catch [the] Bear came along with gun and said, "Let go of him," and fired the first shot, hitting Bullhead. Bullhead had told me not to fire unless they fired first. Catch [the] Bear tried to fire again and I tried to stop him and failing I shot and killed him and then the fight became general.

We drove hostiles across the river and they charged back. One policeman [was] shot on ice. We charged back and forth. Although I did not see it, I think Bullhead was first man who shot Sitting Bull. We dragged Bullhead into the house and as he lay dying he told us to kill Crow Foot, as he was the cause of all the trouble. I then struck Crow Foot across the forehead with my gun, knocking him down, and as he lay there we fired three shots into his body.[97]

95. John Carignan was the teacher at the Grand River Day School.

96. Little Assiniboine, also known as Kills Plenty and Jumping Bull, was Sitting Bull's adopted brother. Utley, *Lance and the Shield*, 23–25.

97. Other Indian eyewitness accounts of the killing of Sitting Bull can be found, for example, in the Walter Mason Camp Collection, Indiana University Lilly Library, and the Walter Stanley Campbell Collection, University of Oklahoma Libraries and Archives. These accounts, however, do not discuss the Ghost Dance at all and are therefore not reproduced in this study.

John Loneman

"That is just what I had expected all the time—something
unpleasant would be the outcome of this Messiah Craze."

John Loneman gave a lengthier and a more detailed account to Walter S.
Campbell.[98] He further emphasizes that the Ghost Dance was becoming
"a menace to the tribe." Therefore, he believed it had to be stopped,
even if it meant they had to arrest Sitting Bull. Loneman was a former
follower of Sitting Bull, but he had abandoned all "heathenish, hostile
and barbarous ways." This makes Loneman's story very interesting.
For him, the Ghost Dance was causing trouble, "a menace," but he also
rejected it on religious grounds, as a "heathen" practice.

One morning, the 14th day of December, 1890, while I was busily engaged
in mending my police saddle at my home on the Grand River, about 36
miles South of Standing Rock Agency, Policeman Charles Afraid of Hawk
of Wakpala District [on the Standing Rock Reservation] came to me with
the message that all of the members of the entire Reservation Indian Police
had been ordered to report immediately, to Lieutenant Henry Bullhead's
place, about three miles South of Bullhead Sub-Issue-Station. This place
was about 30 miles up the river, West from my home, and about 40 miles
southwest of the Standing Rock Agency. Afraid of Hawk was sent to notify
me in person.

I asked him what was up. "Oh," he said, "I have a hunch that we are
going to be ordered to arrest Sitting Bull and his Ghost Dancers, which I
am very sorry to say." "That is just what I had expected all the time—something unpleasant would be the outcome of this Messiah Craze," I said to
him.

I invited him to dinner—fed his horse—he was on horseback and I
got ready. I had an excellent saddle horse—an iron gray gelding—in the
best condition for service. I had him shod all around on all fours with
"Neverslip" horseshoes. I named him Wačíyaŋpi—Trusty—for he had
proven himself a thoroughly reliable horse. My wife hearing the news

98. John Loneman in WSCMC, WHCUOLA, box 114, folder 7. Published by permission of University of Oklahoma Libraries.

became rather nervous and excited for she seemed to realize that there was a serious trouble coming.

Dinner being over, I bade my wife and children goodbye and we left for Bullhead's place. On the way up we notified several police—Bad Horse, Armstrong, Little Eagle, Wakútemani [Shoots Walking], Brownman, Hawkman and Good Voice Elk and others that, by the time we arrived at Bullhead place there were about 12 of us from our way and the rest of the 37 were all from different districts in the reservation. Of course, we had quite a lot to say on the way among ourselves knowing full well that we were called to take a final action to suppress this Ghost Dance which was becoming a menace to the tribe. I'm simply expressing my viewpoint as one who had reformed, from all heathenish, hostile and barbarous ways, formerly one of the loyal followers of chief Sitting Bull. But ever since I was about ten years of age and was one of the most active members in the band for I had participated in good many buffalo hunts and fought under Sitting Bull against different tribes, but the most important fight I took part was in the Custer Fight. After this fight I still went with Sitting Bull's band to Canada and after being in Wood Mountains two years, I returned with the first bunch of Sitting Bull's followers who were shipped down by steamboat from Fort Keogh to Standing Rock Agency. We were not taken as prisoners of war— we came in at our [own] accord after the Great White Father stripped us of all our ponies, weapons of war and in some cases; valuable belongings such as robes, elk teeth and other relics of our bygone days. Even after Sitting Bull was returned to Standing Rock Reservation, I remained in his camp near the agency, where I tamed down somewhat, received my share of annuities and rations as provided under former treaties and started building a permanent log cabin for [my] family as well as shelter for my oxen and a few ponies.

I also started a little garden where I took particular pains to raise corn and some vegetables. Major McLaughlin, then Indian Agent, took a liking in my efforts trying the new way of living and at once appointed me assistant boss-farmer—position I held for two years. I took a claim where I have been living ever since when the hostile camp[99] broke up and moved out to different parts of Grand River to establish for themselves permanent homes. I was promoted to the position of private Indian police—a work which, they say, I was well-fitted for on account of my past career with the Hunkpapa

99. This is a reference to those who surrendered with Sitting Bull and settled on the Standing Rock Reservation.

band. I merely say this because I was at one time one of the strong supporters of the chief, but did not join him with his Messiah Craze. I had adopted new ways and had discarded all superstitions and other old time customs and practices.

It was about 6 or 7 o'clock in the evening when we reached our destination. White Bird and Red Bear—police privates, were assigned to take care of the saddle horses belonging to the Indian Police. These two were my relatives so [I] felt quite at home with them. Lieutenant Bullhead was likewise a relative to me and needless to say anything of his ever warm reception for me in his home. While we were all assembling, two members of the Force from what is now known as Kenil District arrived. They were Shavehead and High Eagle. Lieutenant Bullhead went out to meet them. There Bullhead and High Eagle were standing with hands clasped and lock-arms. Bullhead said: "So, brother, you are going to be with me again." High Eagle replied, "Wherever you go—I shall always follow you even unto death." Bullhead said: "Good."

It was a well-known fact that these two comrades had been pals from childhood up "sharing each other's sorrow, sharing each other's joy."

After our supper, when all had arrived, Lieutenant Bullhead called a meeting and they all got together on the very spot where Sitting Bull was born many years before. Bullhead said: "Friends and relatives, I am sure you are all overanxious to know why [you] had been called here this evening and am quite positive that everyone knows and expects that sooner or later we would be called to this serious order. I have this communication from Major McLaughlin, which will be read to you by our friend Charles DeRockbraine who is serving as assistant farmer and interpreter in this District." Here Charley, popularly known as Chaske among the Indians, came forward and read the order in Sioux language so that everyone understood what the order was about.[100] I do not think any of the Indian Police, present, could read or write in English or Dakota language. We all felt sad to think that our chief with his followers had disobeyed orders—due to outside influences, and that drastic measures had to be resorted to in order to bring them to discipline. Personally, I expected a big trouble ahead for during the time this

100. McLaughlin's views on planning and executing Sitting Bull's arrest can be found in McLaughlin to Commissioner of Indian Affairs, December 16, 1890, NARA, RG 75, SC 188, M4728, roll 1, 4/96–5/1; McLaughlin to Commissioner of Indian Affairs, December 24, 1890, NARA, RG 75, SC 188, M4728, roll 1, 5/55–77; ARCIA, 1891, Report of Agent James McLaughlin, August 26, 1891, 327–28. Also in McLaughlin, *My Friend the Indian*, 211–22, 406–17.

Ghost Dance was indulged in, several times have the leaders made threats, that if the policemen tried to interfere with the matter, they would get the worst of it for the Ghost Dancers were well-equipped with "ogle wakan" [ógle wakȟáŋ]—medicine shirts [Ghost Dance shirts], which were supposed to be bullet-proof, and for the further fact, several attempts were made by different officers of the Police Force, [who] had attempted to break up the camp in a peaceable way, but failed.

During the month of August, when the Ghost Dance was in full blast, I became curious to know, the thrust of this thing that has set my people "crazy." In company with my brother, White Horse, [I] made a special trip to witness the performance.

Having spent nearly all day, during which I had a chance to have a personal interview with the chief and having satisfied myself of his deepest and sincerest interest with the Ghost Dance, and as I have always been on the best of terms with him and did not care to embarrass him in any way, I refrained from mentioning or asking any questions about the matter. I decided then and there, that if this thing was allowed to continue, some serious trouble would eventually be the outcome of it.

The order being for us to act about daybreak and as the night were rather long, we tried to pass the intervening time in telling war stories.[101] The Indian Police who were on this campaign were a class of Dakotas who had enviable achievements and attainments and who on account of having highest estimation in the minds of government officials, missionaries, traders, as well as possessing good influence in their respective communities.

Daybreak was drawing near and Lieutenant Bullhead asked that we offer up a prayer before starting out and without waiting or calling upon anyone else, led us in prayer. After this order was issued to saddle up our horses. When everyone was ready we took our places by two and at the command "hopo" we started.

We had to go through rough places and the roads are slippery. As we went through the Grand River bottoms it seemed as if the owls were hooting at us and the coyotes were howling all around us that one of the police remarked that the owls and the coyotes were giving us a warning—"so beware," he said.

Before we started, Bullhead assigned Red Bear and White Bird to have the favorite white horse of Sitting Bull's (which was always kept in the shed

101. Some stories claimed that the Indian policemen were drinking during the night. See Miller, *The Ghost Dance*, 190; Utley, *Lance and the Shield*, 310.

or in the corral at nights) caught and saddled up and be in readiness for the chief to ride to the agency upon his arrest. The rest of the force were ordered to station themselves all around Sitting Bull's cabin for the purpose of keeping order while the officers went into the cabin and cause the arrest. Bullhead said to me: "Now, you used to belong to this outfit and was always on the good side of the chief. I wish you would use your influence to keep order among the leaders who are going to become hostile."

We rode in a dogtrot gait till we got about a mile from the camp, then we galloped along and when we were about a quarter of a mile, we rode up as if we attacked the camp. Upon our arrival at Sitting Bull's cabin, we quickly dismounted and while the officers went inside we all scattered round the cabin. I followed the police officers and as per orders, I took my place at the door. It was still dark and everybody was asleep and only dogs which were quite numerous, greeted us upon our arrival and no doubt by their greetings had aroused and awaken the Ghost Dancers.

Bullhead, followed by Red Tomahawk and Shavehead, knocked at the door and the chief answered: *"Hau, thimáhel hiyúwo,"* "All right, come in." The door was opened and Bullhead said "I come after you to take you to the agency. You are under arrest." Sitting Bull said, *"Hau,"* "Let me put on my clothes and go with you." He told one of his wives to get his clothes, which was complied with. After he was dressed, arose to go and ordered his son to saddle up his horse. The police told him that it was already outside waiting for him. When Sitting Bull started to go with the police that, according to the custom of Indian wives and other women relatives, instead of bidding him goodbye, the way it was done by the civilized people, one of Sitting Bull's wives burst into a loud cry which drew attention. No sooner had this started, when several of the leaders were rapidly making their way toward Sitting Bull's cabin making all sorts of complaints about the actions of the Indian Police. Mathó Wawóyuspa, The Bear that Catches [aka Catch the Bear], particularly came up close saying, "Now, here are the *'čheška máza'*—'metal breasts' (meaning police badges) just as we had expected all the time. You think you are going to take him. You shall not do it." Addressing the leaders. "Come on now, let us protect our chief." Just about this time, Crow Foot got up, moved by the wailing of his mother and the complaining remarks of Bear that Catches, said to Sitting Bull: "Well—You always called yourself a brave chief. Now you are allowing yourself to be taken by the *čheška máza.*" Sitting Bull then changed his mind and in response to Crow Foot's remark said, *"Hó čha mníŋ kte šni yeló."* "Then I will not go." By this time the Ghost Dancers were trying to get close to the chief in every possible manner, trying to protect him and the police did their best, begging in their way, not to cause any trouble but they would not listen, instead they said "You shall not take away our Chief."

Lieutenant Bullhead said to the chief: "Come, now, do not listen to anyone." I said to Sitting Bull in an imploring way: "Uncle, nobody is going to harm you. The agent wants to see you and then you are to come back, so please do not let others lead you into any trouble." But the chief's mind was made up not to go so the three head officers laid their hands on him. Lieutenant Bullhead got a hold on the chief's right arm, Shavehead on the left arm and Red Tomahawk back of the Chief—pulling him outside. By this time the whole camp was in commotion—women and children crying while the men gathered all round us—said everything mean imaginable but had not done anything to hurt us. The police tried to keep order but [it] was useless—it was like trying to extinguish a treacherous prairie fire. Bear that Catches in the heat of the excitement, pulled out a gun, from under his blanket, and fired into Lieutenant Bullhead and wounded him. Seeing that one of my dearest relatives and my superior, shot, I ran up toward where they were holding the chief, when Bear that Catches raised his gun—pointed and fired at me, but it snapped. Being so close to him I scuffled with him and without any great effort overcame him, jerked the gun away from his hands and with the butt of the gun, I struck him somewhere and laid him out. It was about this moment that Lieutenant Bullhead fired into Sitting Bull while still holding him and Red Tomahawk followed with another shot, which finished the chief.

The rest of the police now seeing nothing else for them to do but to defend themselves became engaged in a bitter encounter with the Ghost Dancers. It was daybreak and the Ghost Dancers fled to the timber and some already started running away into the breaks South of the Grand River. The police took refuge behind the sheds and corrals adjoining the chief's residence, knocked the chinks out, firing in the direction of the fleeing Ghost Dancers. One of our police was lying on the ground behind a shed when some Ghost Dancer shot him in the head and killed him instantly. This was my brother-in-law John Strong Arms, who came with me from our camp.

Finally, there was no more firing and we proceeded [to] gather up our dead and the wounded.

Hawkman, another relative of mine, a cousin, who hailed from same camp I came from, was sent to carry the news of the fight to the military forces. We brought them to the cabin and cared for them. While we were doing this, my friend, Running Hawk, said to the police: "Say, my friends, it seems there is something moving behind the curtain in the corner of the cabin." The cabin, instead of being plastered, the walls were covered with strips of sheeting, sewed together and tacked on the walls making quite a bright appearance within. All eyes were directed to the corner mentioned and without waiting for any orders I raised the curtain. There stood Crow Foot and as soon as he was exposed to view, he cried out, "My uncles, do not kill me. I do not wish to die." The police asked the officers, what to do. Lieutenant Bullhead, seeing what was up, said, "Do what you like with him. He is one of them that has caused this trouble." I do not remember who really fired the shot that killed Crow Foot—several fired at once.

It was about this time that the soldiers appeared on the top of the high hills toward the agency. According to instructions received, we were expecting them but they did not show up in our critical moment.[102] Maybe it was just as well they did not for they would have made things worse as heretofore they generally did this. Immediately they fired a cannon toward where we were. Being ordered to display a "flag of truce" I tore off the white curtain, tied it on a long pole, ran out where they would see me, thinking they would cease firing but all was of no avail. They continued firing and the cannon balls came very close to where I was that at times I dodged. Finally, they stopped firing and made [a] bee-line toward us. They arrived and upon learning what had happened the officer ranking highest proceeded to where Sitting Bull's corpse was and with a branch took the third coup and said: "Sitting Bull—big chief, you brought this disaster upon yourself and your people."[103] Louis Primeau was interpreting.

The soldiers having dismounted rushed to the camp—ransacking anything worth keeping. Red Tomahawk took charge of the police force and after everything was prepared to take the dead and the wounded Indian police as well as Sitting Bull's corpse, discharged us from this campaign, and having complimented us for doing our duty as we did, ask us to attend the funeral of our comrades, killed in the fight. Strong Arm, Hawkman, Little Eagle and Akíčita were killed. Bullhead, Shavehead and Middle were wounded seriously. Seven Ghost Dancers besides Sitting Bull were killed on the Sitting Bull's side.[104]

---

102. This was an army detachment of the 8th Cavalry led by Captain E. G. Fechét. For military reports, see, ARSW, 1891, Report of Captain E. G. Fechét, December 17, 1890, pp. 197–98; ARSW, 1891, Report of Lieutenant Colonel W. F. Drum, February 27, 1891, pp. 194–97.

103. The taking of the coup is not mentioned in either Fechét's or Drum's reports. Their reports are in ARSW, 1891, Report of Captain E. G. Fechét December 17, 1890, pp. 197–98; Report of Lt. Colonel Drum, February 27, 1891, pp. 194–97.

104. For a list of casualties, see 52nd Congress, 1st sess., Senate Executive Document, No. 84, vol. 6, ser. 2901, pp. i–ii.

About this time, some of the relatives of the police killed arrived and such lamenting over the dead was seldom known in the history of my race. Taking a last look on my dead friends and relatives, I, in company with Charles Afraid of Hawk, started for home. On the way, we past several deserted homes of the Ghost Dancers and felt sorry that such a big mistake was made by listening to outsiders who generally cause us nothing but trouble.

I reached home and before our reunion I asked my wife, brothers, sisters and mother to prepare a sweat bath for me, that I may cleanse myself for participating in a bloody fight with my fellow men. After doing this, new or clean clothes were brought to me and the clothes I wore at the fight were burned up. I then, was reunited with my family. God spared my life for their sake.

The next day I took my family into the agency. I reported to Major McLaughlin. He laid his hand on my shoulders, shook hands with me and said: "He alone is a Man. I feel proud of you for the very brave way you have carried out your part in the fight with the Ghost Dancers." I was not very brave right at that moment. His comment nearly set me a crying.

Brings Plenty

"We kill lots of white people."

Brings Plenty, a Hunkpapa visiting Pine Ridge, wrote this letter to Sitting Bull and it was published in Stanley Vestal's *New Sources of Indian History*.[105] This letter was obviously written before Sitting Bull was killed on December 15. It is a very confusing letter as it discusses fighting that supposedly took place in the Black Hills. That, of course, is not what happened. The Lakotas never attacked any settlements or fought the soldiers outside their reservations. It is difficult to determine why Brings Plenty wrote a letter like this. Perhaps he did not really know what was going on, or perhaps he was talking about events that might occur in the future. There were a lot of rumors circulating at the time, and letters like this, combined with contradictory news reporting,

---

105. Brings Plenty to Sitting Bull, undated, WSCMC, WHCUOLA, box 104, folder 9. Published by permission of University of Oklahoma Libraries. Also in Vestal, *New Sources of Indian History*, 39–41.

certainly added to the confusion. Brings Plenty also says that there would be a big council in the spring of 1891 discussing the possibility of fighting the whites. There was, indeed, much discussion, even among white officials that the Lakotas were planning to renew the Ghost Dances in the spring.[106] Brings Plenty was wounded at Wounded Knee but made a full recovery.[107]

Pine Ridge Agency
Sent through He Bear

Brother I am going to write to you today. I want you to come back, but you didn't. I want you to come this time. There is lots [of] fight[ing] going on at Black Hill[s]. I am in all of them. We kill lots of white people and take away everything they got. We are at Pine Ridge Agency.

The Rosebud Indians are very bad. If anybody comes over the hill, they kill him, so they are very dangerous. The main fight is going to be in [the] spring, so I am telling you this. So keep a gun ready for action. What I said is [the] truth. I have told you [to] come but you didn't while the fight last[s]. I had three war horses but two of them died. The one race[horse] [I] have [is] still alive. Lower Brulé, Crow Creek, Rosebud, Cheyennes and other tribes are coming to Pine Ridge Agency in the spring, and they [are] going have a big council. [My] relations think about this and make some saddle[s] and be ready. We [are] going have a big fight.

I shake hands with you all.

Brings Plenty

He Bear uncle try and come back. I remember my grandmother, try and keep a gun to defend yourself.

Brings Plenty

I am.

106. See, for example, ARCIA, 1891, Report of Captain Charles G. Penney, Acting U.S. Indian Agent, September 1, 1891, 52nd Cong., 1st Sess., H. Ex. Doc., No. 1, pp. 408–10. See also Maddra, *Hostiles?* 177–78. See letter of Louis Primeau, pt. 3.
107. Gage, "Intertribal Communication," 312–13.

Spotted Mountain Sheep

"We thought of fighting them but gave it up until spring."

This letter by Spotted Mountain Sheep to Luke Nážiŋkte (Kills Standing), much like the letter by Brings Plenty, discusses a possible war with the whites.[108] Spotted Mountain Sheep maintains that there were more than 10,000 lodges of Brulés in readiness. That, of course is an exaggeration, as there were no more than 5,700 Brulés on the Rosebud Reservation in 1890.

December 7, 1890
Kills Standing

My Brother-in-law, I wish to write you a letter today. There are 20 companies of soldiers at this place. And we thought of fighting them but gave it up until spring. Then is the time we decided on fighting. There are 10 100 lodges of Brulés. Now my Brother-in-law I wish to ask you for some sweetgrass, so if you can let me have it I wish you would write me a letter. That is all I have to say.

Translation.

I am Spotted Mountain Sheep

or

Hečíŋškayapi Gleŝká

Many Eagles

"It is the truth and will surely come to pass."

This letter by Oglala Many Eagles to his sister can be found in the Walter S. Campbell Collection and was also published in Stanley Vestal,

---

108. Spotted Mountain Sheep to Luke Nážiŋkte, December 7, 1890, WSCMC, WHCUOLA, folder 114, folder 6, p. 119. Published by permission of University of Oklahoma Libraries. Published also in Vestal, *New Sources*, 41–42.

New Sources of Indian History.[109] While Many Eagles does not directly discuss fighting the whites, he urges his sister to be ready and says that the people are attempting to get guns. He also believes that the Ghost Dance "is the truth" and its promises will "come to pass." Clearly, Many Eagles, like many others, still believed in the Ghost Dance in the spring of 1891.[110] These letters by Many Eagles, Spotted Mountain Sheep, and Brings Plenty are interesting in that they discuss either ongoing war or plans for an uprising in the near future. They are good examples of the rumors, uncertainty, and hearsay that were circulating among the Lakotas. Walter S. Campbell (Stanley Vestal) found the letter in 1929 among the papers of Agent James McLaughlin.[111] It is of interest to note that government officials like McLaughlin could have easily used letters like these to support their own accusations against the Ghost Dancers.

Pine Ridge Agency
March 5, 1891

My sister we have always lived in tribulation, still you remembered me even though I have left you. It gives me great pleasure to receive a letter from you as it is just as if I had seen you. In addition to answering your letter I would like to inform you of something. It is in regard to the dance which created a commotion up there. It is the truth and will surely come to pass that is why the whites are so anxious to put it out. The nation are still in expectation. Now you must use every effort to come in possession of some eagle's-down, and have them in readiness. From the time the grass starts you must be on the lookout and when a thunder storm comes up you must attach them to your hair.[112] Take care that you heed what I say. These

109. Many Eagles to his sister, March 5, 1891, WSCMC, WHCUOLA, box 114, folder 6, 151–52. Published by permission of University of Oklahoma Libraries. Also published in Vestal, *New Sources*, 60.
110. For the discussion on survival of the Ghost Dance among the Lakota after Wounded Knee, see Clow, "Lakota Ghost Dance After 1890," 323–333; Warren, *God's Red Son*, 297–324.
111. Gage, "Intertribal Communication," 326.
112. A common thought among the Ghost Dancers was that an eagle feather would lift the believers up in the air for the time of the transformation of the earth.

five camps of Oglalas have enlisted in the U.S. Army.[113] It is a plot amongst the people, for the sole purpose of arming themselves. Try to get arrows, at least. That is all I have to say.

I am Many Eagles.

Gall

"[He] asked the Indians to stop dancing and send their children to school."

The whites considered Gall as one of the leading "progressive" chiefs on Standing Rock Reservation. He and his family belonged to the Episcopalian church. During the Ghost Dance, he tried to assert his influence among the dancers and urged them to stop dancing. The following letter to Agent James McLaughlin was written by someone on Gall's behalf. The letter can be found in the Walter Stanley Campbell Collection and it was also published in Stanley Vestal's *New Sources on Indian History*.[114] Gall seems to be eager to tell the agent that his efforts to bring the Ghost Dancing to a halt had brought some results and that he would try to convince Sitting Bull to give it up too. Indeed, Gall managed to keep most of his own people out of the Ghost Dance.

Grand River November 29th, 1890
Maj. James McLaughlin
Standing Rock Agency, N.D.

Dear Sir:

Gall wishes to report what he has done up to to-day. He says he held a council at the Mouth of Little Oak Creek yesterday and asked the Indians to stop dancing and send their children to school, which they

113. This probably refers to Oglala scouts who served in the U.S. Army after the trouble. Why Many Eagles maintains that is a plot is unclear. There is no evidence to support this argument.
114. Gall to James McLaughlin, November 15, 1890, WSCMC, WHCUOLA, box 114, folder 6. Published by permission of University of Oklahoma Libraries. Published also in Vestal, *New Sources*, 40–41.

all agreed to do. Running Horse in behalf of his band upheld Gall. He says he has employed Hawk Man and a fellow called Uŋkčé Waŋblí to act as spies, with the understanding that they were to be made policemen at once. He says he has told you often about his horses and wagon; meaning that he wants a different outfit; he says that he has not been to [Sitting] Bull's Camp yet, but he says that he will go up today and they are dancing yet up there, he says he brought a wagon load of children to school today.

He says he wants to shake hands with yourself wife and family, and signs himself respectfully

Gall

Gall and John Grass
"Of course we don't want to run off."

Along with Gall, John Grass was considered the major "progressive" chief on the Standing Rock Reservation. Both Grass and Gall were often at odds with Sitting Bull. Like Gall, Grass tried to keep his people away from Sitting Bull's camp.[115] Gall and Grass wrote the following letter to Agent James McLaughlin on December 15, 1890, the day that Sitting Bull was killed.[116] It seems that the chiefs already knew about the events in Sitting Bull's camp because they ask for advice in dealing with possible refugees "run off" from Sitting Bull's camp.

Standing Rock Agency, N.D.
December 15, 1890

Dear Major James McLaughlin, we heard something about the soldiers, but we haven't heard how [what] we [are] going to do about it. We'll camp all together here at Oak Creek, but if any Ghost-Indian[s] come this way for run off, please let us know what we [are]

115. For Gall, John Grass, and the Ghost Dance, see Waggoner, *Witness*, 213–17, 321–22, 423–26.

116. John Grass and Gall to James McLaughlin, December 15, 1890, WSCMC, WHCUOLA, box 114, folder 6, p. 77. Published by permission of University of Oklahoma Libraries. Published also in Vestal, *New Sources*, 56–57.

going to do about it, and if you heard something bad about the Ghost [Dance or Dancers]; please send us about ten guns; of course we don't want to run off: we stay in our places for [to] hold our school boys and girls [with their] teachers. We want [to] heard [hear] them things if any Ghost-Indian come this way what we [are] going to do about it. Please send us 10 guns and send a note and tell us what we [are] going to do. We camp here all together.

Yours respectfully

Chief John Grass

Chief Gall Pizi

Gall

"It better for us to live as we are living."

The following short comment by Gall well illustrates his practical way of thinking about the Ghost Dance. His remark was published in an article entitled "Three Noted Chiefs of the Sioux" in the *Harper's Weekly* magazine on October 20, 1890. The article was written after a conference with Gall, John Grass, and Agent McLaughlin, and the author apparently was present. The article depicts Sitting Bull as an inferior person, whereas Gall and John Grass are described as the most intelligent and capable leaders of all Sioux chiefs.[117]

I think it better for us to live as we are living rather than create trouble, not knowing how it will end.

117. Gall in "Three Noted Chiefs of the Sioux," *Harper's Weekly*, October 20, 1890, p. 995.

American Horse

"The nonprogressive started the Ghost Dance to draw from us."

Oglala chief American Horse wrote a letter through Agent Daniel F. Royer to the acting commissioner of Indian affairs, R. V. Belt, on November 17, 1890. The letter was included in the annual report of the secretary of war in 1891.[118] In this letter, American Horse notes how signing the Sioux Act of 1889 only made their lives worse because one promise after another was broken. American Horse points out how those who believed in the Ghost Dance used it to gradually get away from those who had signed the bill. It is true that many of those who did not sign the bill also became Ghost Dancers. It is important to notice, however, that American Horse was very unpopular among many Lakotas, since he was one of the first signers of the Sioux Act of 1889. Those who did not sign it blamed him and others for the Lakotas' desperate situation. The Ghost Dance brought these tensions to the surface. In that sense, the Ghost Dance was one more issue that aggravated the divisiveness among the Lakotas.[119]

I was speaker for the whole tribe. In a general council I signed the bill (the late Sioux bill) and 580 signed with me; the other members of my band drew out, and ever since these two parties have been divided. The nonprogressive started the Ghost Dance to draw from us. We were made many promises, but have never heard of them since. The Great Father says if we do what he directs it will be to our benefit, but instead of this they are every year cutting down our rations and we do not get enough to keep us from suffering. After we signed the bill, they took our land and cut down our allowances of food. The commissioners made us believe that we would get full sacks if we signed the bill, but instead of that our sacks are empty. Our chickens were all stolen; our cattle, some of them were killed. Our crops were entirely lost by being here with the Sioux Commission, and we have never been benefited one bit by the bill, and, in fact, we are worse off than we were before we signed the bill.

118. American Horse in ARSW, 1891, *American Horse, Report of Major General Nelson A. Miles*, 52nd Cong., 1st Sess., H. Ex. Doc., No. 1, p. 136.
119. See Andersson, *The Lakota Ghost Dance of 1890*, pp. 270–300.

We are told if we do as white men, we will be better off, but we are getting worse off every year. The commissioners promised the Indians living on Black Pipe and Pass Creeks, that if they signed the bill they could remain where they were and draw their rations at this agency, showing them on the map the line, and our people want them here, but they have been ordered to move back to Rosebud Agency. This is one of the broken promises. The Commission promised to survey the boundary line and appropriate funds for the purpose, but it has not been done. When we were at Washington, the President, the Secretary of the Interior, and the Commissioner, all heard the bill appropriating the money passed Congress but we never got the beef. The Commissioner refused to give it to us. American Horse, Fast Thunder, and Spotted Horse, were all promised a spring wagon each, but they have never heard anything of it; this is another broken promise.

American Horse

"I am sorry for those Indians who are crazed with this false idea."

American Horse sent another letter discussing the situation on the Pine Ridge Reservation to his friend John Landy on December 1, 1890.[120] American Horse had befriended Landy and his family a few years earlier. The Landys gave American Horse a large photograph of himself as well as [one of] the Landy family. The picture was destroyed by the Ghost Dancers.[121] As a leader of the non–Ghost Dancing faction, American Horse was in a difficult position, and this letter clearly shows how dangerous the situation had become. The Ghost Dancers threatened his life on several occasions; Jack Red Cloud put a gun against his head on November 11, following an incident just outside the agency office.[122]

120. American Horse to J. Landy, December 1, 1890, AHP, MSS S 903, YCWABL.
121. See Gage, "Intertribal Communication," 69–70, 280.
122. On November 11, the Indian policemen tried to arrest a man called Little. Tensions started to mount and American Horse stepped in to end the trouble. At that point Jack Red Cloud pointed a gun against American Horse's head and loudly blamed him for all the trouble on the reservation. Utley, *The Last Days of the Sioux Nation*, 108–109; Coleman, *Voices of Wounded Knee*, 85–87; Andersson, *The Lakota Ghost Dance of 1890*, pp. 74–75. For an eyewitness account of this incident, see Charles Eastman in part 4.

American Horse laments that as the agent ordered everybody to the agency, the Ghost Dancers were able to destroy their property that was left unguarded.[123] Despite the problems, American Horse assures his friend that he will work hard to keep his people on the right track.

Pine Ridge Agency, S.D.
December 1, 1890
J. Landy, Esq.

My Dear friend,

Yours of the November 17th was gratefully received, but the money you promised has not reached me as yet. I am very much pleased with your advice in regard to the situation at this agency, and I shall follow it out as far as I am able to exert any influence. I have been following it with the idea to lead my people toward civilization, which has made me many enemies, yet I have not been discouraged, although at times the position is a very unpleasant one, among the Indians.

The Ghost Dancers, those who believe in the coming of the new Messiah, and who came from Rosebud Agency to this reservation have destroyed all the properties of my people and appropriated what they did not destroy, even knocked the doors and windows in, so that we are left homeless. These things were done while the agent ordered the Pine Ridge Agency Indians to come in to the agency while the troops are here.

I am sorry for those Indians who are crazed with this false idea. They treated me the same. They entered my house and took everything. I am sorry for one thing, for I fear I shall not have another; that is, they shot my large photo which you made of me. They shot that over the heart and in the forehead. They also took 34 horses of mine and killed all my cattle. These were done while we are here [at the agency]. If these Indians should kill me, remember I shall die for a good cause. I am trying to advance these Indians, but instead they are growing worse and some of them hate me so that they say they would shoot me, if they should have an opportunity.

123. As the people on the Pine Ridge Reservation were ordered to the agency, their farms were left unattended. This caused their crops to fail once again.

My love and kind regards to your family.

I am

Very Respectfully yours,

American Horse.

Oglala Chief

American Horse
"I could not for a thought of taking up arms against the whites."

In a letter dated December 22, 1890, American Horse continued to report to James Landy on the escalating tensions on the Pine Ridge Reservation.[124] By late December, peace efforts were under way, although the Ghost Dancers continued to destroy property. More than 160 Lakotas were sent by General John R. Brooke to the Ghost Dance camp to try to make them move closer to the agency.[125] While American Horse saw this as a positive development, others did not like the idea of pitting Lakotas against Lakotas (for Little Wound's reaction see above).

Pine Ridge Agency, S.D.
December 22, 1890
J. Landy, Esq.

My dear friend:

Your very kind letter of the 12th, and also another of the 15th are before me. I am exceedingly grateful for your kindness in saying that you will make me another picture for the one shot by the Rosebud Indians. I am sorry to tell you that they have afterwards destroyed the entire picture, a group composed of yourself and your children was partially injured but I saved it. I have been hunting for my cattle but found only thirteen, therefore they must have killed one hundred

---

124. American Horse to J. Landy, December 22, 1890, AHP, MSS S 903, YCWABL.
125. Utley, *Last Days of the Sioux Nation*, 134–45; Coleman, *Voices of Wounded Knee*, 115, 158–62; Greene, *American Carnage*, 145–50.

fifty-six (156). Although it is barely possible that I may find one or two more. We found all my ponies except two, that is, we found them at the "hostiles'" camp. It is likely that I shall get them back. And the things destroyed at my house amounted to one hundred and ninety-six dollars.[126] This evening one of the returned "hostiles" told me that almost half the Indians in the Badlands would come way [to the agency] but the other half threaten them so they could not come, but there is a delegation of one hundred and sixty-seven men of the friendly Indians [that] have gone there to persuade them to come in. My own son and thirty of my young men are among the delegation. They are there by this afternoon.

I am thoroughly informed of the state of things immediately surrounding this agency that I could not for a moment thought of taking up arms against the whites. But you must understand what we friendly Indians have to endure, losing all our cattle and thus cutting off all subsistence outside of the rations, which is very meagre enough for any human appetite for food. Among the things taken from my house was my overcoat that you gave me. I am sorry that I did not take this coat with me when I came to the agency.

Now, my dear friend, there is one thing I would like you very much to favor me with, that is, I have a boy at Carlisle School, but at present he is at Dolington, Buck Co., PA, working.[127] He wishes to come home, but I want him to remain there and learn all he can. I wish you to write to him and encourage him as much as you can. Tell him my position in this trouble etc. etc. When this trouble is over and the people are quiet, I would like to remind the government, or rather request the government to make good the losses of the friendly Indians. Can you use your influence in either [in]directly or directly in our behalf? I thought perhaps you may have some friends at Washington who may say a good word for us. This is all I have to say.

I am

Yours faithfully

American Horse

126. American Horse, like many others, asked for compensation afterwards. See Paul, "The Investigation of Special Agent Cooper," 212–35.

127. American Horse's children, Ben American Horse, Samuel American Horse, and Maggie Stands Looking, attended the Carlisle Indian Industrial School in Pennsylvania.

212 / A Whirlwind Passed through Our Country

Young Man Afraid of His Horses

"There was a time when we did not have to assume the character of beggars."

Young Man Afraid of His Horses was at first interested in the Ghost Dance, as he participated in the initial council that decided to send the delegation to the west. He may even have participated in some early dances.[128] He never became an active Ghost Dancer, but he noted on several occasions that the injustices done toward the Lakotas were far too many and caused a great deal of trouble. In this letter sent on July 23, 1890, to the commissioner of Indian affairs, Thomas J. Morgan, he notes that the Lakotas have become like beggars and that is not the way things should be.[129] While this letter does not say anything about the Ghost Dance, together with other similar accounts given by the Lakotas before, during, and after the Ghost Dance trouble, it helps us to understand how and why the Ghost Dance brought hope in the depths of despair.

There was a time when we did not have to assume the character of beggars. When we did not ask favors from anyone. Then we were free to go where we pleased while now we are penned up like so many cattle, not however for slaughter. For if that was the intention, they would furnish us enough to eat to make us fat, so I am forced to think it is for the purpose of starving us that we are confined with the limits of the reserve and forced to subsist on such scanty rations. There was a time when the buffalo covered our plains and furnished us with all the meat we needed. Now they are gone, wantonly destroyed by the white man and we are obliged to beg for something to take their place. Beef is everything to an Indian; you might take away all else, his complaint would not be so great as if his beef was taken from him. We

128. There is not much evidence to show that Young Man Afraid of His Horses would have actually participated in the Ghost Dance ceremony. The only surviving evidence comes through Agent Daniel F. Royer who claimed that he persuaded Young Man Afraid of His Horses to quit dancing in late October 1890. See D. F. Royer to R. V. Belt, October 30, 1890, NARA, RBIA, RG 75, SC 188, M4728, roll 1, p. 71.

129. Young Man Afraid of His Horses to the Commissioner of Indian Affairs Thomas J. Morgan (through Agent Hugh Gallagher), July 23, 1890, NARA, RG 75, LSASPR, M1282, roll 10, 336–38.

Chief Young Man Afraid of His Horses and his tipi, at Pine Ridge Agency, S.D., January 17, 1891. Denver Public Library, Western History Collection, X-31478.

do not blame you for this condition of things. We know you can only give us what is sent here by the Great Father, but we wish you to send our words to Washington that they may know how we feel. Say to them that we want to get our beef the same as we used to get it. That is one beef for thirty (30) persons every fourteen days. We never complained when we got this. We want the million pounds of beef that was taken from us last winter. Three Stars [General Crook] said we would get it. We had the promise of all those highest in authority that we would get it. Then why did it not come? These are the words we wish you to say to the Great Father and we will come and listen to his reply when you receive it.

Young Man Afraid of His Horses

"Unless the soldiers are taken away, we will not be able to hold our young men."

Young Man Afraid of His Horses, like Red Cloud, had to deal with the administration of Dr. Valentine T. McGillycuddy for several years in the 1880s. During McGillycuddy's visit to Pine Ridge in November–December 1890, the two met and Young Man Afraid of His Horses explained his concerns to the former agent.[130] He blames Sitting Bull for stirring up the young men. This is a strong accusation against Sitting Bull, especially since no evidence to support it exists today. What seems to worry Young Man Afraid of His Horses most, though, is the presence of the military and its effect on the young men.

Father, fourteen winters have passed since the Custer massacre [Battle of Little Big Horn]. The children of those days are our warriors now. They do not know the power of the white man as we older people do, and they think that they can hold their own. The troops came here, Sitting Bull in the North at once sent his runners through to us to stir our young men up, and unless the soldiers are taken away, we will not be able to hold our young men.

Young Man Afraid of His Horses

"Why was the whole Sioux nation called to account for dancing a religious dance?"

In February 1891, Young Man Afraid of His Horses gave a talk in Washington, D.C., which was published as a part of an editorial in *Harper's Weekly* magazine under the title "Indian Truth and Eloquence."[131] Man Afraid of His Horses raises several relevant questions that to him were the

130. Young Man Afraid of His Horses in WSCMC, WHCUOLA, box 107, folder 7. Published by permission of University of Oklahoma Libraries. Published also in Vestal, *New Sources of Indian History*, 84.

131. Young Man Afraid of His Horses in "Indian Truth and Eloquence," *Harper's Weekly*, February 21, 1891, p. 131.

real reasons behind all the trouble. "When the red man speaks, it goes in at one ear and out of the other," he notes with evident frustration. Why was Agent Gallagher replaced at a crucial stage with an inexperienced agent, he asks. And, interestingly, even if he did not believe in the Ghost Dance himself, he asks why the army was called to stop "a religious dance."

The troubles spring from seed. The seed was sown long ago by the white man not attending truthfully to his treaties after a majority of our people had voted for them. When the white man speaks, the government and the army see that we obey. When the red man speaks, it goes in at one ear and out of the other. The Indian is for eternity interested in the subject, the white man only when he comes into office for two or three years. I am not an old man, but I have seen many Great Father[s] and his headmen. Why was not the late treaty fixed promptly by the Great Council [U.S. Congress]? Why were our rations cut down a million pounds? Why have not our winter annuities come? Why was the whole Sioux nation called to account for dancing a religious dance? Why are the agents always being changed? Why was Agent Gallagher discharged when he wrote that our crops had failed, and our rations must not be cut down? Why was the army called in by Agent Royer? And if he was right, why was he discharged? And why does not the blame for what followed belong to the white men? Let everything that is said here be written down, so that when we have to speak with other men, it cannot be denied what was said here.

Fast Thunder

"We were growing desperate and might be driven to lawless means to provide for our families."

Like Young Man Afraid of His Horses, Oglala Fast Thunder sent a letter to the commissioner of Indian affairs, Thomas J. Morgan, on July 23, 1890, after a council on Pine Ridge.[132] He notes that people whose wives

---

132. Fast Thunder to the Commissioner of Indian Affairs Thomas J. Morgan (through Agent Hugh Gallagher), July 23, 1890, NARA, RG 75, LSASPR, M1282, roll 10, 337–38.

and children are starving will grow desperate. He says that even white settlers who knew their dire situation were expecting them to "break out."

You may be surprised that we all have the same subject to speak about. But it is the one that affects us the most. The Indian is not like the white man. Our tastes, habits and whole make up are entirely different from the whites. The Great Spirit made us this way and had he not wished us to be different from the whites he would have made us all alike.[133]

Three Stars [General Crook] told us while in Washington that a mistake had been made in our beef by which we were short one million pounds, but that he was going to have it made straight so we would not lose it. The Indians were told this and are wondering why his words have not been made good. We all knew Three Stars to be our friend. His promises to us have always been fulfilled but our friend is dead.[134] Is it possible that with him died the Indian's last friend?

There are over five thousand Indians upon this agency. When they got our beef ration cut down to five million pounds we supposed they intended to allow one million pounds for each one thousand Indians, but last winter more than one thousand were left without beef. I need not say to you that this caused great suffering among our people. You know how many of our children [unfinished sentence]. The white settlers along the reservation line knew of our suffering, expecting us to break out. They fled from their homes knowing we were growing desperate and might be driven to lawless means to provide for our families. You have a family. You know how a man feels when he sees his wife and children starving.

Tell these things to the Great Father. Ask him to take pity on us. You are the only one we can ask to do this for us. We will hear what the Great Father will say to us.

---

133. This is an interesting comment as throughout the Ghost Dance the idea that the Indians and the whites were "not the same" emerges in visions. See part 1.

134. General George Crook died on March 21, 1890.

Rocky Bear

"The white man came and we were driven out."

Rocky Bear, an Oglala leader, weighed in on the Lakotas' situation in an interview with L. W. Colby just after the troubles in early 1891.[135] Colby described him as "one of the finest looking men among the Indian chiefs" and noted that he spoke English and had been to Europe. Like so many others, Rocky Bear gives the famine and broken promises as the fundamental causes of all the trouble.

The cause of the trouble is the same old story. The Great Father sends his agents here to make treaties with us. The white man came and we were driven out. We are promised things, but they never come. The Great Father promises to give us food, money, farming tools, and to educate our children, in exchange for our lands, but he forgets to do it. Treaties are only a lot of lies. The government never kept any treaty it ever made with us. We have always been robbed and lied to. We did not commence the fight. We know that will do no good, but the government takes our lands and puts us here where nothing can be raised, and our wives and children suffer for food; they are cold and hungry. Then they send soldiers to kill us, and the agents lie about us after they rob us. If my people could get what the government agreed to pay us, they would all be fat and there would be no trouble. The Great Father knows this, and the white people know this.

Hollow Horn Bear

"I wish to lead my nation in peace and learn the white man's ways."

Hollow Horn Bear wrote a letter to Commissioner of Indian Affairs Thomas J. Morgan and to the members of the previous year's Sioux Commission on September 13, 1890.[136] His letter emphasizes the major problems facing the Lakotas. The insufficient number of cattle issued

---

135. Rocky Bear in Colby, "The Sioux Indian War of 1890–91," 188.
136. Hollow Horn Bear to President Benjamin Harrison & Commissioner of Indian Affairs Thomas J. Morgan, et al., September 13, 1890, NARA, RBIA, RG 75.4, GRBIA, Letters Received, Letter 29579, box 664.

to them, the question about the boundary line, and finally of special concern were the actions of their agent, J. George Wright. Hollow Horn Bear calls him "the boy agent," who does not know how to run things. This is an interesting complaint, since other Rosebud leaders (see below) say that during his time as agent the Lakotas were prospering.[137] While Hollow Horn Bear does not mention the Ghost Dance, his letter is written right about the time that the dances were becoming more frequent on Pine Ridge, Rosebud, and Cheyenne River Reservations. He notes that the problems on the reservation were making a lot of people "uneasy and mad." This dispute over the boundary sent several hundred Brulés on the move toward Pine Ridge, many of them becoming Ghost Dancers and making depredations on their way. Later Hollow Horn Bear himself became a Ghost Dancer, although it is not known if he fully embraced the dance at any stage.[138]

Valentine, Nebraska
September 14, 1890

Hon. President and Commissioners of Indian Affairs and Charles Foster and William Warren [Warner] of the Sioux Commission

Messrs,

My friends, I this day think of you and I am happy to write to you this letter, on your own account and doings you placed our agent the present Boy J. G. Wright as our agent at Rosebud Agency, S.D. and your recommendations placed him there as agent. Now the agent says all Indians, who are living at or near Black Pipe Creek and who have farms there, must move toward the Missouri River, and if they do not move soon, he will send for the soldiers and drive us, as they would cattle, away from there. He has had called out at our beef issue in public, we are not allowed to visit anywhere. When at our last treaty you promised us that if the treaty was signed, we could

137. For more, see Gage, "Intertribal Communication," 110–12.
138. See Luther Standing Bear, *My People the Sioux*, 221–22; Miller, *Ghost Dance*, 91–93; Andersson, *The Lakota Ghost Dance of 1890*, pp. 81, 170.

go when and where we please—and also he wants the line surveyed between us and Pine Ridge Agency at once, and on these accounts our nation are very uneasy and mad at present, and as I wish to lead my nation in peace and learn the white man's ways, I wish a few words of advice from you. Not to have our line surveyed at present, but when you remove this agent, then send a man to survey it at once, and on my visit to Washington last year on account of the sale of our land, I said there, "in time the treaty would be fulfilled on our part and in peace, when our Boy agent is gone, and the lines can all be run in peace." The Great Father, said, "Yes" to my talk with him. The Great Father said things should be done straight. But our Boy agent is not doing things straight now, and you could know so if you properly enquire into his doings. This letter is for the Great Father and commissioners of last treaty to read. Many years ago the Great Father made a law that our agents should be married men, but now you have given us a boy agent, who has no wife and who is making our people wild instead of pacifying them.[139] Now friends, this is for the Commissioner of Indian Affairs first and he [is] then to send a copy of it to the others and answer me with a registered letter please. Then I will get it, otherwise it will be stopped on the road. Also why do you send us one and two year old cattle for the last two months, and [that] are issued to us [for the] same number of persons as the large cattle was; it is not enough for us, and it is not our authorized rations, our rations are about one half what we used to get before we sold our land to you last summer. Do not laugh at this, but investigate it all. I will prove all to you, so help us all you can, and keep peace amongst us.

Respectfully,

witness to Hollow Horn Bear

Signature wrote by himself of which this is a true copy as dictated of which he claims he is a representative from his nation, and was authorized by them to get wrote [to write].

A. G. Shaw[140]

139. The Lakotas in general felt that unmarried men were not suitable or responsible enough to be their agents. This debate was common throughout the 1880s.

140. Amberson G. Shaw was a white man living in Valentine, Nebraska. He was married to a Lakota woman. He served often as an interpreter or wrote letters on the Indians' behalf. Gage, "Intertribal Communication," 110.

Hollow Horn Bear

"Great Father, we are starving."

Hollow Horn Bear with several others wrote to President Benjamin Harrison on November 6, 1890.[141] In this letter, the Rosebud Lakotas continue their pleas for help. They also repeat their request for a new agent.

Great Father:

This day I will write you a letter with a good heart. When we gave up the Black Hills, you told us in that treaty, that a man would get three pounds of beef a day; the meaning was three pounds for one man. Besides you said: we could get food just like the soldiers. You did not, however, give it to us at this rate.

Great Father, we are starving and beg you therefore to give to us just so [as you have promised]. Thirty men of us get for eighteen days [only] one cow to eat; that is the reason I mention it. And if you do not well understand it, send me [Hollow Horn Bear] travelling money and I will come with five men [to Washington, D.C.].

Great Father, if you do not do so, then please let us have soldier for our Father [agent], when our present Father's term is out.

Great Father, please do us this favor.

Matȟó He Oȟlóǧeča	Wasú Wakíŋyaŋ
Maȟpíya Tȟatȟáŋka	Anúŋkȟasaŋ Waŋblí
Šuŋka Blóka	Waŋblí Wašté
Matȟó Hiyáhaŋ	Wičhása Čaŋtéhahala
Matȟo Oh'áŋkȟo	Hó Wašté
Táku Sápa	Háǧaŋ Lúta
Wak'úkeza Waŋkátuya	

141. Hollow Horn Bear et al. to President Benjamin Harrison, November 6, 1890, NARA, RBIA, RG 75, GRBIA, Letters Received.

Chiefs of the Rosebud Reservation

"Many of our people are crazy and excited over the new religion."

Several leaders of the Rosebud Reservation appealed to President Benjamin Harrison on October 23, 1890.[142] They called for more rations and more work and were worried about the fact that hungry people would get frustrated. At the same time, many believed that the government tried to "starve [us] to death." They also felt that replacing Agent Wright was a terrible mistake. During his time, they had prospered, there was work, and the agent sincerely tried to help them. Now in the midst of the Ghost Dance trouble, the agent was replaced.[143] All this made the young men feel "very bad." Interestingly this letter was signed also by Hollow Horn Bear, who just weeks earlier had complained that Agent Wright was a "Boy agent" and not fit to run the reservation (see above).

Rosebud Agency, S.D.
October 23, 1890

To the Great Father

Sir,

We chiefs and head men of the Sioux tribe here pray you to take
pity upon us, and get for us the rations, which are owed us under the
treaties, and under the [census] count lately made here. Before this
we have got our rations for the year in the month of July. Not a pound
except beef has been sent us, and we are starving, and have no freight
to haul to make money to buy food with. The beef lately given us to
last nine months is not what is due us for that time, but there is owed
us yet about 900 head on the last count for that time. The treaty we

142. Swift Bear et al. to the Commissioner of Indian Affairs Thomas J. Morgan, October 23, 1890, October 23, 1890, NARA, RBIA, RG 75.4, GRBIA, Letters Received, Letter 33608, box 674.
143. See introduction.

made over a year ago seems dead for we have not got anything from it and we were the first to sign and start it here.[144]

Many of our people are crazy and excited over the new religion which has come among us, and on this account and our being hungry, our young men are feeling very bad and think the government is trying to starve us to death. Our rations in the agency issue house are nearly all gone and what is left, only bacon and hardbread, can't last long.

Many of our people have killed their cows and work oxen to eat, and our children cry to us for food. Why was our beef cut down when these last cattle were given us? Have we not been true to our promises and why should we be starved this way? We heard that the man who counted us, and took a long time—months—to do it to make money for himself, said our beef was allowed to rot because he saw in a lodge a lot of dry beef, which was being kept for a few families who lived on the Missouri River, and only come every few months for rations. He lied and everybody here knows it.[145]

Why has our friend the agent been taken from us? Is it because we have known him for 4 years, and that he is honest, and knows how to do business for us? Is a new man to come—who it will take two or three years to learn how to run an agency, and look to our wants. When Agent Wright's father, who was agent, was taken from us, we were doing well and were happy.[146] A new man [Lebbeus Foster Spencer] was sent us who did not care for us and did not try to help us. And we began to go back to our old ways.

This man was with us three years and in that time it seemed like everything was dead and everybody asleep, but the young man Wright when he took charge put life into us and made our hearts strong—and we went to work again and done more farming this year

144. The Sioux Commission of 1889 worked around the Lakota reservations for signatures one reservation at a time. They spent considerable time on each reservation offering feasts and discussions. By promising one thing, and threatening with another, the commission was able to split the Lakotas' unity and eventually acquired enough signatures for the agreement to be valid. See Utley, *Last Days of the Sioux Nation*, 49–54; Ostler, *Plains Sioux*, 228–39.

145. Interestingly, A. T. Lea's report on the census count was read aloud in Congress as part of the discussion regarding the Lakota Ghost Dance in December 1890. His report was used by Senator Henry L Dawes to justify cutting the Lakotas' rations. See Andersson, *The Lakota Ghost Dance 1890*, pp. 261–63.

146. This was James Wright, who served as the agent at Rosebud from 1882 to 1886. He was followed by Lebbeus Foster Spencer.

than we ever done, but there was so little rain that we could not raise anything. The same as our white friends in Nebraska, who could raise nothing. Mr. Wright very often come to our homes to see himself how we were doing, which no other agent had done before and we were trying to do as he wished us to do, but we could not make it rain. When the other agent before young Mr. Wright was here, there was always bad feeling among the men who worked for him [the agent], and it took much of his time to quarrel and make trouble, while since Mr. Wright has been our agent all has been peace[ful] and all the men who worked for him tried to help him, and this helped us. Four schools were shut up and Mr. Wright had them opened and told some of us long ago he would try to get more schools for our children. Last winter and spring many of our people died from a new sickness, which we had not had before, and many of them are sick yet and have never got over that sickness.

Nine hundred cattle were here this month for us, but they were taken away and we were told they were brought here for us, but the man who owned them was told to take them back as we had all we were to get, and these cattle are not far away now, and we ask that they be given us as we have not been given all that are owed us to last us nine months.

Swift Bear	Pretty Eagle
Quick Bear	William Spotted Tail
Hollow Horn Bear	Strange Horse
He Dog	Whirlwind Soldier
Sky Bull	Foolish Elk

Lakota Chiefs

"We danced and prayed that we might live forever."

The following article was published in the *Washington Evening Star* on January 23, 1891, under the title "The Indians' Side."[147] This lengthy article brings together accounts by Lakotas who were considered as hostiles, that is, Ghost Dancers, and by those who opposed the Ghost Dance. In this document Lakota chiefs, one after another, explain in

147. Lakota Leaders in *Washington Evening Star*, January 28, 1891. See Gage, "Intertribal Communication," 324; Warren, *God's Red Son*, 267.

depth their living conditions, problems, and fears. They go to great lengths in their attempt to make the white readers understand what the Ghost Dance really was, why they believed in it, and why it should not have been stopped. In the words of Little Wound, they hoped that "by making a great noise the Great Father would hear of our suffering." Big Road explained that the "dance was the same as going to church. White people pray because they want to go to heaven. Indians want to go to heaven, too, so they prayed, and they also prayed for food enough to keep them out of heaven until it was time to go." Big Road also notes that the Messiah wanted the Indians to keep their children in schools and that they needed to attend the church. Indeed, they could attend both the white man's churches and the Ghost Dance, which were comparable. Interestingly, he denies that the Ghost Dance shirts were considered bulletproof. That, of course, is contradicted by the accounts of Black Elk and other Ghost Dancers (see part 1). This article in the *Washington Evening Star* is one of the most comprehensive Lakota accounts of the crucial period leading to the inauguration of the Ghost Dance among the Lakotas all the way to the tragic end at Wounded Knee. This document also explains the internal divisions among the Lakotas. Crow Dog especially blames other chiefs and several mixed-bloods on the Rosebud Reservation for trying to make him and Two Strike look bad. He actually suggests that several of his antagonists should be removed from the reservation. This document is also important because it shows what the Lakotas expected from the U.S. government just before a delegation of their leaders were supposed to meet with officials in Washington, D.C. (statements made in Washington, D.C., follow this document). The chiefs' account is published in its entirety, with the *Evening Star* correspondent's additions in italics. I have omitted the lengthy background, discussing Indian policy and the trouble among the Lakotas. The text is, by modern standards, quite paternalistic, but attempts to understand the Indian point of view. The author notes that the chiefs understood that giving an interview to the *Washington Evening Star* would enable even the president to hear their words. Still, as the author says,

The task of gathering the statements of these more prominent Indians has not been an easy one, the great barrier being the naturally suspicious nature of the nation's wards. Even when their confidence has been gained they are not inclined to be communicative, and unless they are searchingly cross-examined they will evade the point at issue and ramble off through the green pastures of generalization and disport themselves in the somewhat muddy but pleasant-sounding stream of Native North American oratory.

The Sioux Chiefs Hold a Pow Wow with The Star's Correspondent.

THEIR GRIEVANCES TOLD

Too Little Meat and Too Much Agent—The Big Chiefs Coming to Washington Give The Star Their Stories in Advance— Cigarettes and Beef.

Staff Correspondence of *The Evening Star.*

Pine Ridge, S.D., January 23.

First to secure the floor, by reason of his superiority, was Young-Man-Afraid-of-His-Horses. "The last two agents we have had here," *said he,* "have made many of the Indians' hearts bad.[148] Those agents took away our wagons, our harness, and the things we farmed with, and gave them to other Indians. The Indians who went away with Buffalo Bill to make a little money for their families were not allowed to keep the work cattle and wagons that had been given them some time before they left. The things were given to other families and that caused trouble. Many Indians thought they were not treated right. Another grievance is in [the] matter of ration tickets. If a man had a trouble or dispute with the agent, then the agent would often take his ration ticket away from him, so he would not get food when it was issued. The man's wife and children suffered most. It was they who were punished and not the man. If an Indian is bad he ought to be punished, and when we go to Washington we will talk to the Great Father about that and try to have it so fixed that the man's family shall have something to eat. If an Indian has his ticket taken from him, those who have been good are burdened with his family, although the good people have not enough for themselves to eat.

We get our rations every week, but now they do not last us more than three days, so much have they been cut down, and we must starve nearly

148. Having a "bad heart" is an expression in Lakota—*čhaŋtéšiča*—that could also mean "sad heart" or simply "sad." Translating this expression as "bad heart" might easily be interpreted as being "hostile" or "angry."

all the rest of the week. Oh yes, we have feasts, but our rations could not be used in them, for there is not altogether enough for a feast. Our feasts are of boiled dog, wild turnips and wild cherries. We are not wasteful of the food we get. We keep the rations for our children. Then I want to say that some of the men who work on the agency—the farmers who live in the villages—often behave cruelly to Indians. This the Indian does not like; it makes his heart bad.

Little Wound looked over at the first speaker, and seeing that he was through, said: "I live on Medicine Root Creek, about forty miles from the agency. Once in every month the agent gives me rations, but it is only a little bit. It never lasts more than two weeks. It used to be that our crops helped us very much, but last summer the crops all failed and it is hard to live now. The Great Father does not know how hard it is. I am talking straight now. What beef we get is very poor. The Texas cattle are poor and small. Some of them are but two years old and some of them are very old and very thin. One steer for thirty persons is not enough. Thirty people are too many even when the beef is good. The best beef is the cattle raised in this country. Years ago the Indians got better beef."

"Last summer," *interjected Young-Man-Afraid (as he is locally denominated by people who are in a hurry)*, "the agent gave only one beef to sixty people. That was very hard. It was this and things I have spoken about that made the Indians' hearts bad and brought on the trouble."

"Many Indians left the agency," *said Little Wound*, "because they thought that by making a great noise the Great Father would hear of our suffering. Not very long ago the Indians here gave money to pay for two Indians and one interpreter to go to Washington to tell the Great Father we were hungry. There was enough money to pay for the railroad tickets and for the hotels. Red Cloud and myself were to go, but Big Belly (Agent Gallagher) would not let us go. That was before Three Stars (General Crook) came out here to talk with us and to persuade us to give up the land. Our women and children have suffered much, because there was no food. The Great Father heard not their cries, so many of us made a loud noise and the Great Father heard them, for some of us are going to talk with him soon."

Then Big Road spoke. Said he: "I want to say something about the Ghost Dance. Many people do not understand it because the truth has not been told them. Most of the Indians here belong to the church; we have many church houses. This dance was like religion; it was religion. Those who brought the dance here from the West said that to dance was the same as going to church. White people pray because they want to go to heaven. Indians want to go to heaven, too, so they prayed, and they also prayed for food enough to keep them out of heaven until it was time to go. Heaven must be a nice place or the white men would not want to go there. That was why the Indians would like to go. We danced and prayed that we might live forever; that everything we planted might grow up to give us plenty and happiness. There was no harm in the dance. The Messiah told us to send our children to school, to work on our farms all the time and to do the best we could. He also told us not to drop our church. We and our children could dance and go to church, too; that would be like going to two churches. I never heard that the Messiah had promised that the Indians should be supreme or that the white men should be destroyed. We never prayed for anything but happiness. We did not pray that white people should all be killed. The shirts we wore were made for us to go to heaven. The dance was not a war dance, for none who went in it was allowed to have one scrap of metal on his body. Many lies were told about the dance by interpreters. I never believed that bullets could not go through the shirts. Some foolish people might, for there are foolish Indians just as there are foolish white people, but I never heard any Indian in the dance ever say he thought the shirt would protect him. All the dance trouble here was caused by Agent Royer and his policemen telling stories about us that were not true. God made both the Indian and the white man, and we want the white man to live a great deal more than many white men want us to live.

I get rations every two weeks, but it is only enough for five days. The rest of the time I starve very much. I farmed last year and, like all the other people, I got no crops. I am careful with my food and have learned the white man's ways. I eat a little at morning, at noon and at night. I never waste my rations at a feast or a dance. There is not enough for even a small feast. We eat dog and wild turnips and cherries at our feasts now. Five years ago we had better beef and more of it. We have always since been promised as much to eat and of good beef, but the promise is like wind. Lame and old and big-jawed cattle have been given the Indians. Sometimes when we have a feast we sell a little bead work or a pipe or a pair of moccasins and with the money buy some coffee and some sugar."

"I want to say," *remarked Little Wound*, "that Big Road has talked straight about the dance. The Indians prayed that they might have souls like the white people, so that they could go to heaven. Many lies have been told about some of the Indians who were in the dance. Policemen and other Indians and squawmen lied a great deal. Those Indians wanted to be chiefs and they abused the chiefs and head men who danced; they hoped to get to be chiefs and headmen by making trouble and by talking with the agent."

Mention of the agent opened the mouth of Young-Man-Afraid. "We want a military agent now," *said he.* "Maybe, after a time, we shall want another agent who is not an officer, but we will talk about that when we go to Washington. We do not want any more Indian Police here; they always make trouble. Scouts can do all the work and will not make trouble, because they will be under an army officer. We want to get what the government promised to give us—plenty of beef. We have given up the land the government asked for; now let the government give us what it said it would. Our annuity goods—all our blankets and things—ought to be here when the leaves fall. A woman came in here after her annuities last winter and was frozen to death. If the warm clothes had been here when they were promised the woman would still be alive and many Indians would not have suffered from cold."

"We got our blankets in time twelve years ago," *said Fire Thunder,* "but not since then."

In answer to a question from me, Young-Man-Afraid said: "We want our children all to go to school. It is true that some of those who have been placed at school have run away, but that is not strange. White children often do the same thing, and the Indian children are not better nor do they have better hearts than white children."

"The children at Medicine Root School," *remarked Little Wound,* "are often very hungry and their clothes are poor. Many of them left the school because there was even less there than there was at home. Sometimes they got only a little hard bread and water at the school. I have asked the teacher to send [a letter] to the Great Father for more food and clothes, but there is no more than there has been for a long time."

"My children are at the agency boarding school," *said Fire Thunder.* "They are satisfied."

Then the esthetic side of Little Wound became apparent: "We want," *said he,* "red and white and blue and green blankets. They send us nothing but these black blankets all the time. The Indians like bright colors, and it hurts no one if they do have pretty blankets. The shirts we have now are poor: not as good as they were once. We ought to have a little tobacco with the rest of our supplies. We cannot raise tobacco here and we have not much money to buy it with."

That quietly uttered reference to tobacco was ingenious and there was a lull in the pow-wow while each Indian was made the recipient of a bag of smoking tobacco and a small plug. The Oglalas had nothing more to say, so the Brulé warriors were notified that they would be heard next. The pipe was circulated and new cigarettes were lighted. Then Two Strikes spoke. He comes, as did all the Brulés, from Rosebud Agency, East of here.

"For more than a year," *said he*, "I have not been pleased at the way in which I have been treated at Rosebud. Four of our young men went to Washington last year and they told the Great Father a many good things I did not like. They wanted many changes made and said they would like to have the agency moved to a place twenty-five miles nearer the Missouri river, which was all wrong. The agency was in a good place and the new place had less timber and less water than the place where the agency is now. There was nothing to be gained by moving the agency, but the agent wanted it and these four young men would like to be head chiefs. Some half-breeds and the police were helping them. It was because of these things that he [I] left Rosebud. If these disturbers were only sent away somewhere, the Rosebud Indians would get along better. We want to stay there, but we cannot get along. Rosebud was a big agency when Spotted Tail lived, but it is small now and the Indians there are very poor."

Crow Dog grunted concurrence and then said: "We used to have plows and wagons and harness and many things to work with, but bad Indians talked to the agent and he took these things away from us older men and gave them to his friends. While we had these things we did our best to work. Twice in every three years our crops would almost surely fail. Our rations are given us every week, but there is not enough for more than two and a half days. Then we are very hungry. Our rations have been far too small for nine years. Before that time there was enough all the year. Now there is no good game in the hills, so we are very poor indeed. What little beef we get is not always good. Some of the steers are too young, some are very old and tough. We have been given many of those big-jawed steers to eat and some old bulls. White people would not have these, but any-thing was good enough for the Indian. At Rosebud we have twelve school houses and many children, although they do not get enough to eat. We would rather have not so many schools and more good beef. Better have a satisfied stomach and know little of school learning than to starve half the time and be very wise. I have often told the superintendent of the schools that the children should be given clothes to keep them warm and plenty to eat, but it was not done. Indians cannot learn to be happy and good when they are very cold and very hungry. Many children left the schools because there was more liberty and almost as much to eat in the tipis.

Now, about our farming. We were given two work cattle, one cow, one mare, a plow, a wagon and other things. The agency farmers often take them away and give them to their friends—Indians who try to make trouble and talk much—not because we did not care properly for the things, but because we were not liked by the farmers. Sometimes the mare or one of the oxen would get hurt by no fault of the man, but the agent would put the man in the guard house. We do not like that; white men are not done with that way. We have tried to complain of these things to the agent, but he will not hear us; his policemen keep us out of the agency. That and all these other things made us leave Rosebud and come here to Pine Ridge. This was the only place we could go to.

Big Road told the truth about the dance. We do not want to fight the whites. The police at Rosebud lied about the dance; Big Road talked straight. When "Three Stars" (General Crook) and two other men were here to talk about our giving up more land I did not want to talk with them. I wanted to talk with the Great Father himself. Thirteen years ago I was in Washington and the Great Father told me to come to see him when we wanted to talk about a treaty.

Many things are not right at Rosebud. The annuities are always late. We used to be paid in money for hauling goods to the agency, but now the agent gives us orders on the store and the post trader gets too much, the Indian not enough. There was an agent once who gave us a great deal—one beef for every ten people. That was years ago. Now there is only one beef for thirty people, and it is not so good to eat. Texas steers are small and poor; we don't want them anymore. Major Lee (Capt. Jesse M. Lee, ninth United States infantry) was the best agent we ever had. He took good care of us. We are glad to see him here at Pine Ridge. He is a good and a just man. Whatever he told us was true. We would like to have him at Rosebud again. We know him, and if he is agent there again, we will gladly return and be with him. I did not want to fight the whites; that is why we came away. Had we stayed at Rosebud there would have been fighting there, for some of us were very mad, especially our young men. It has been said that we destroyed houses and furniture at Rosebud. That is not true. The half-breeds and bad white men did that and said it was we who did it.

The men who have caused all this trouble are Louis Yellow-Eye, Tom and Billy, half-breeds. Then there is a white man, brother-in-law of Maj. Lee's interpreter. Bob Dyer is another; he is the boss herder. He drinks whisky all the time and abuses the Indians he does not like. Louis Richaud and Louis Burdo, both half-breeds, are responsible for many lies about us. Several Brulé Indians are very bad and they try all the time to get myself and Two Strike in trouble. Their names are He Dog, Bullhead, Good Eagle, Bare Head and Hollow Horn Bear. If the Great Father would send them away we would get along nicely. Crazy Elk, Thunder Hawk and Good Shield are also very bad indeed. Some of the employees ought to be changed and good ones put in their places. The employees were all good when Maj. [Jesse M.] Lee was agent."

"Maj. Lee always gave us plenty of beef," *wailed Two Strike.*

Long Bull, a Minneconjou Sioux who escaped from the battle of Wounded Knee, told how the Big Foot band came to leave Cheyenne River. He said: "We did not like the way we were treated at Cheyenne River. Our rations were poor and many hearts were bad. Red Cloud had sent to us to say that if we were not well treated we might come to Pine Ridge and live. We were at our homes when a white man came to us—I do not know his white name, but his Indian name is Red Beard[149]—and he said the soldiers were coming to fight, so we had better get out. Then we came to Wounded Knee and had that fight. We did not want to fight. The soldiers said we must give up our guns and some of us did. I had no gun. Then the soldiers went into the tipis and kicked the beds about and upset everything a great deal. Some Indians had guns under their blankets, hiding them, for an Indian thinks much of his gun. The soldiers used the Indians very roughly and made them mad, until by and by Sits Straight (the medicine man) gave the signal to shoot.[150] Big Foot did not want to fight; he was sick. We were prisoners all the night before and in our tipis we talked peace. Among ourselves we said we would give up all the guns, for we did not expect to fight. Indians [are] much like white men. They get mad when a man hurts them and tears their clothes and pulls their guns away. That made us fight."

The big Cheyenne River chief, Hump, did not care to talk before the others, so I interviewed him apart from the crowd.

"Big Foot," *said he,* "left Cheyenne River because he wanted to dance. Red Cloud and others had been writing to him to come here, and Big Foot thought it meant that there would be fighting at Pine Ridge. There was a great deal of discontent among the Indians at Cheyenne River Agency. Rations were issued once a month and they were very small. There was a little flour and beef every month. Sometimes there was a piece of bacon as big as my hand, but that was not regular. Sometimes there was baking powder and sometimes there was not. Annuity goods were not as much as promised and they never came until late in the winter. They ought to come in the fall. The agents kept on promising more and giving less all the time. The agent says, 'Work hard and you get more.' Indians work hard and get

149. Red Beard was John Dunn, a white rancher. See Andersson, *The Lakota Ghost Dance of 1890*, pp. 89, 153. John Dunn's report of his meeting with Big Foot can be found as part of ARSW, 1891, 52nd Cong., 1st Sess., H. Ex. Doc., No. 1, pp. 235–36.

150. The medicine man's name was Yellow Bird and during the disarmament he started to sing Ghost Dance songs and was raising his arms in prayer. This has often been interpreted as either a harangue or a signal to start a fight.

not so much. Only about one crop in every three is any good. I think Big Foot was coming to Pine Ridge to get better than he was getting at Cheyenne River or to fight.[151] I don't like the government to change good agents. When we begin to know a good man he is taken away and some man who is not good is put in his place. I would rather have a soldier officer for agent, because soldiers when they are not fighting the Indians they always treat them well. Indians are willing to work many ways, but the agent says they must farm whether they know how or not. The agent only lets his favorites among the Indians to freight goods in from the railroad, and that does not give as many Indians a chance to work as would like to. We want more rations, more wagons, more tools and more ways to work. All white men are not farmers, even where the lands is good and grows much. Our land is not good. We must have something to eat while we are working and waiting for the crops that so often do not come. There is no hunting. Many of us would like to enlist as soldiers. There are one or two hundred Indians at Cheyenne River who want to be government soldiers."[152]

Lakota Chiefs

"The soldiers trespassed in our country."

The following conversations between the Secretary of the Interior John W. Noble and Lakota leaders Young Man Afraid of His Horses, Two Strike, High Hawk, American Horse, and Hollow Horn Bear took place during the chiefs' visit to Washington, D.C., in February 1891. The proceedings of this meeting were recorded by Thomas A. Bland in "The Late Military Invasion of the home of the Sioux" in 1891, published by the National Indian Defense Association.[153] In this meeting the Lakota chiefs again place the Ghost Dance in the larger context of reservation

151. This is an interesting comment, since all other Lakota accounts deny that Big Foot had any hostile intentions. He was invited to come to Pine Ridge, and he hoped to get there to settle all the trouble peacefully. See, for example, Joseph Horn Cloud and Dewey Beard in Jensen, *Voices of the American West*, 1:391–208, 208–26; Gage, "Intertribal Communication," 318.

152. There was a lot of discussion about the possibility of recruiting Indians as regular cavalry. General Nelson A. Miles, for example, was in favor of such a plan.

153. Lakota Chiefs in Bland, "A Brief History of the Late Military Invasion of the Home of the Sioux," 12–14.

Lakota delegation that traveled to Washington, D.C., January–February 1891.
Top row: Zaphier, Hump, High Pipe, Fast Thunder, Reverend Charles Cook,
P. T. Johnson; *Middle row:* He Dog, F. D. Lewis, Spotted Horse, American
Horse, Major George Sword, Louis Shangreau, Baptiste Pourier; *Bottom row:*
High Hawk, Fire Lightning, Little Wound, Two Strike, Young Man Afraid of
His Horses, Spotted Elk, Big Road. Denver Public Library, Western History
Collection, X-31799.

problems. They unanimously maintain that the trouble was caused by
the agents, lack of food, broken promises, and finally the unjustifiable
call for the military. They call the Ghost Dance a "whirlwind that passed
through" their country. It is noteworthy that both those who were Ghost
Dancers and those who opposed it were now in unison in condemning
the government for the trouble.

American Horse: We representatives have come on a mission of peace,
and place ourselves in your hands. The recent trouble has already been
referred to. We have landed in Washington where it originated. There is no
other place but Washington where treaties are made, promises given and

not kept—Washington only. Our people are growing anxious to walk in the right road marked out for us, and when we had one foot in that road we were put back, and so far back that it will take fifteen years to put us forward again. We have been under the impression that you were trying to civilize us. I and my people have tried to help you, and today I am ashamed that I have been included as a hostile.

We are called a lazy set. It is not true.

We want to work. The government has the power to employ people and only the whites get the privileges and they drive us out.

Let us have some of the high positions, so as to help ourselves. If you thus help us to rise and give these positions to those of Indian blood, and let us earn money from these positions, that is the way to civilize us. I also request this: We can judge as to a man's fitness to fill a position. If we know a man whom we know is fit to act as agent, we want you to help us and give us the privilege of recommending people for that office. You cannot grant us a better blessing or help us more. If you have the choice only in your hands and we have no voice in the matter, the agent you send brings his brothers, sisters, cousins and aunts—and we are left in the cold. Let this be abolished and give us a chance. We know some are given certain positions by politicians, who in a measure get pay. We beg you to give us justice that we may have a voice in the selection of agent and clerk.

I am anxious to be enlightened on one subject, and that is the squawmen and half-breeds. Are they whites, Indians or animals? Occupying this non-descript positions, theirs is a hard lot—like football between two partiers. Let their position be defined so that we may know how they stand. Many half-breeds and squawmen have been heavy losers in the recent troubles, and I pray that these losses be repaid to them, as they need it very much. I will refer to schools in the East. When our children come east they change climate and it causes trouble. I made a plea the last time I was here that the Carlisle school be removed bodily to a nice place on our reservation, between the Rosebud and Pine Ridge agencies. I don't want to talk against Captain [Richard Henry] Pratt, but I ask that he and his whole forces be removed to the west.

The children come east as a matter of contract. You promised us and this promise is on my heart. You said you would give these children positions at the agency, but it has not been done. Why not? I now refer to two who are present, Robert American Horse and Clarence Three Stars. They were pupils of Carlisle school and were promised positions on their return, but they were not given them. Robert is a missionary in the Episcopal Church and doing good work. Clarence Three Stars is a clerk in the traders' store and doing fairly well. A source of discouragement to boys coming from the East is that if ever a position is given them it is the smallest one—one that is hardly worth while for a white man, and our boys become discouraged. We are slowly but steadily growing, and we want our children so educated that they may read all our papers and do our work.

Our great desire today, *continued American Horse*, is that we come to a proper understanding of all the promises made and their fulfilment.

Young Man Whose Foe is Afraid of His Horse [Young Man Afraid of His Horses] *spoke next, he said:* "I always listened to the words of the Secretary and Commissioner. That has been my way at all times on the agency. In any trouble that may arise I am always ready to make peace in the time of war. When General Crook was in command of the soldiers I brought in Crazy Horse, in 1876.[154] The Commissioners come out and make us plenty of promises.[155] Four in all came, each one making better promises than the other, but what does it amount to? We had a little trouble recently. I told them to stop [the Ghost Dances]. In the meantime I went on a visit and hunting trip to the Crow Agency. I got news from the army officers that General Miles wanted me. At once I got on the railroad and came to his assistance. The Indians were all on the Sioux Reservations. General Miles asked me to go out to them, which I did, and I have listened to the Secretary, to the Commissioner and to General Miles. I went out to those who were called hostiles and brought them in and had them surrender their arms.[156] They are now for peace and will remain so. That trouble I hope, has all passed like a whirlwind, never to be heard of again.

154. Young Man Afraid of His Horses, like George Sword, served as mediator during the 1876–77 troubles following the Little Big Horn battle.

155. The U.S. government had already begun its pressure on the Lakotas in 1882 when a commission headed by Newton Edmunds tried to make the Lakotas give away much of their reservation lands. That commission was followed by another in 1888, this time headed by Richard Henry Pratt. These commissions, however, did not succeed in getting enough Lakota signatures to break up the Great Sioux Reservation. The final commission in 1889 was led by Governor Charles Foster, but it became known as the "Crook Commission," since General George Crook was in effect in charge of the negotiations. This commission was able to secure enough signatures, which led to the Sioux Act of 1889. See introduction.

156. Young Man Afraid of His Horses had been visiting the Crow Agency for two months and returned to Pine Ridge on January 8, 1891. He was one of the delegates sent by General Miles to the Ghost Dancers' camp after the Wounded Knee massacre. For his speech in the Ghost Dance camp, see Black Elk's account in part 1. See also Utley, *The Last Days of the Sioux Nation*, 258–59; Ostler, *Plains Sioux*, 360.

A good deal of property has been destroyed belonging to various Indians and half-breeds, and I hope these depredations will be paid for. I hope that all our children will hereafter be educated on the agency. You have always told us to become civilized and rich, and the best way to do it is to give our children work and not the whites."

Two Strike: American Horse has expressed my sentiments. A whirlwind passed through our country and did much damage, we let that pass.

High Hawk: I am a peacemaker. I have followed the treaty of 1868. The late trouble was caused by the Army.

Hollow Horn Bear: I was here last winter and made some suggestions about our agency, which have not been put in operation, and I want to say them again. I want to talk about the agency where the lightning struck. It was not at our agency where the trouble was. I want our agency to go on and be a good agency. The trouble was caused by the civilian agent [Daniel F. Royer] who called on the military. It does not discourage me. I will go right and do right. The soldiers trespassed in our country and gave my people a bad whipping. We have one rule at all agencies. Your intentions are to punish any who do not do the right thing. At the time of the Big Foot fight the trouble was caused by one man. It was wrong to serve us in this way. As far as I am concerned I have done right. The white man was the cause of the trouble. On one occasion a man, woman and child came to my house late at night all shot up. They came a distance of 160 miles. That was enough to discourage anyone, but I did all I could to alleviate their pains and have them cared for, but it made my heart bad. After the military have done their bloody work they want to throw everything on our shoulders, and I want to prove differently. I have much to say which may be unpleasant for the ladies to hear. If they will step out I will say it."

Secretary [John W.] Noble: I will see you Monday about that. We know all about the fight.

Hollow Horn Bear: "We will put that off till Monday. We have not received everything in the General Crook treaty. Our horses were not paid for. Do not forget that General Crook's treaty agreed to pay for all depredations in an Indian war. Much has been destroyed. The interest of the $3,000,000 should be given half to the schools and half to the people. We want to keep it in sight at all times. The cows promised were not given. We try farming, but with no success. We can raise nothing. The ground is not good. Last winter I spoke of beef that was retained from us, and we have not had it yet. I watched for it, but it did not come. Why did it not come? If you cannot furnish that, furnish something in its place. Buy us American mares from which we will get some good. If it is put into our appropriation we get no good from it. I depend on you and the Commissioner, to do the best for our good and interest. We have had no issues of cows on our agency as promised.

I want to say another thing. In order to facilitate matters let us arrange so that we need not spend too much time in going for our rations. Some go fifty or sixty miles. Let us have issue houses in our camp so that we can [have] more time to work."

Lakota Chiefs

"Many of these people were related to us by blood."

The following statements by Turning Hawk, George Sword, Spotted Horse, and American Horse were directed to the commissioner of Indian affairs on February 11, 1891, following their discussion with the secretary of the interior, John W. Noble. The proceedings of the meeting were published in the annual report of the commissioner of Indian affairs.[157] Turning Bear interestingly says that he and his companions decided to take the hostile attitude toward the Ghost Dance as they knew that the authorities would not like it. He also notes that the Ghost Dancers did not know if there was anything "absolutely bad, nor did they know if there was anything absolutely good in connection with the movement." He also says plainly that the appearance of the soldiers on their reservations scared people, causing them to run away and ending up in the Badlands. In these statements we can get a firsthand look into the peace efforts launched by General John R. Brooke, but carried out by non–Ghost Dancers. As Turning Hawk says, the Ghost Dancers were "related to us by blood." Here we can also see how devastating the Wounded Knee massacre was to those Lakotas who were considered "progressive" and took the government's side in the conflict. As Turning Hawk says, they

157. Turning Hawk et al. in ARCIA, 1891, 52nd Cong., 1st Sess., H. Ex. Doc., No. 1, pp. 180–81. See Grua, *Surviving Wounded Knee*, 84–88. See letter of Louis Primeau, pt. 3.

"suffered much distress and are very much hurt at heart." American Horse was very disappointed and carried with him the burden of guilt. He came to Washington, D.C., with "a very great blame on my heart."

Turning Hawk, Pine Ridge (Mr. Cook, interpreter).[158] Mr. Commissioner, my purpose today is to tell you what I know of the condition of affairs at the agency where I live. A certain falsehood came to our agency from the West, which had the effect of a fire upon the Indians, and when this certain fire came upon our people those who had certain far-sightedness and could see into the matter, made up their minds to stand up against it and fight it. The reason we took this hostile attitude to this fire was because we believed that you yourself would not be in favor of this particular mischief-making thing; but just as we expected, the people in authority did not like this thing and we were quietly told that we must give [it] up or have nothing to do with this certain movement. Though this is the advice from our good friends in the East, there were, of course, many silly young men who were longing to become identified with the movement, although they knew that there was nothing absolutely bad, nor did they know there was anything absolutely good in connection with the movement.

In the course of time we heard that the soldiers were moving toward the scene of trouble. After a while some of the soldiers finally reached our place and we heard that a number of them also reached our friends at Rosebud. Of course, when a large body of soldiers is moving toward a certain direction they inspire a more or less amount of awe, and it is very natural that the women and children, who see this large moving mass are made afraid of it and be put in a condition to make them run away. At first we thought that perhaps Pine Ridge and Rosebud were the only two agencies where soldiers were sent, but finally we heard that the other agencies fared likewise. We heard and saw that about half of our friends at Rosebud Agency, from fear at seeing the soldiers, began the move of running away from their agency toward ours (Pine Ridge) and when they had gotten inside of our reservation, they there learned that right ahead of them at our agency was another large crowd of soldiers, and while the soldiers were [there], there was constantly a great deal of false rumor[s] flying back and forth. The special rumor I have in mind is the threat that the soldiers had come there to

158. Reverend Charles Smith Cook, Pine Ridge Episcopal Church.

disarm the Indians entirely and to take away all their horses from them. That was the oft-repeated story.

So constantly repeated was the story that our friends from Rosebud, instead of going to Pine Ridge, the place of their destination, veered off and went in some other direction, toward the Badlands. We did not know definitely how many, but understood there were 300 lodges of them, about 1,700 people.[159] Eagle Pipe, Turning Bear, High Hawk, Short Bull, Lance, No Flesh, Pine Bird, Crow Dog, Two Strike, and White Horse were the leaders.

Well, the people after veering off in this way, many of them who believe in peace and order at our own agency, were very anxious that some influence should be brought upon these people. In addition to our love of peace we remembered that many of these people were related to us by blood. So we sent out peace commissioners to the people, who were thus running away from their agency. I understood at the time that they were simply going away from fear because of so many soldiers. So constant was the word of these good men from Pine Ridge Agency that finally they succeeded in getting away half of the party from Rosebud, from the place where they took refuge, and finally were brought to the agency at Pine Ridge, Young Man Afraid of His Horses, Little Wound, Fast Thunder, Louis Shangrau, John Grass, Jack Red Cloud, and myself were some of these peacemakers.

The remnant of the party from Rosebud not taken to the agency finally reached the wilds of the Badlands. Seeing that we had succeeded so well, once more we went to the same party in the Badlands and succeeded in bringing these very Indians out of the depths of the Badlands and were being brought toward the agency. When we were about a day's journey from our agency we heard that a certain party of Indians (Big Foot's band) from the Cheyenne River Agency was coming toward Pine Ridge in flight.

Captain [George] Sword: Those who actually went off of the Cheyenne River Agency probably number 303, and there were a few from the Standing Rock Reserve with them, but as to their number I do not know. There were a number of Oglalas, old men and several school boys, coming back with that very same party, and one of the very seriously wounded boys was a member of the Oglala boarding school at Pine Ridge Agency. He was not on the war-path, but was simply returning home to his agency and to his school after a summer visit to relatives on the Cheyenne River.

159. The number 1,700 seems quite accurate. The Rosebud agent estimated the figure to be 1,800. See introduction.

Turning Hawk: When we heard that these people were coming toward our agency we also heard this. These people were coming toward Pine Ridge Agency, and when they were almost on the agency they were met by the soldiers and surrounded and finally taken to the Wounded Knee Creek, and there at a given time their guns were demanded. When they had delivered them up the men were separated from their families, from their tipis, and taken to a certain spot. When the guns were thus taken and the men thus separated there was a crazy man, a young man of very bad influence and in fact a nobody, among that bunch of Indians fired his gun, and of course the firing of a gun must have been the breaking of a military rule of some sort, because immediately the soldiers returned fire and indiscriminate killing followed.

Spotted Horse: This man shot an officer in the Army; the first shot killed this officer.[160] I was a voluntary scout at that encounter and I saw exactly what was done and that was what I noticed; that the first shot killed an officer. As soon as this shot was fired, the Indians immediately began drawing their knives and they were exhorted from all sides to desist, but this was not obeyed. Consequently, the firing began immediately on the part of the soldiers.[161]

Turning Hawk: All the men who were in a bunch were killed right there, and those who escaped that first fire got into the ravine and as they went along up the ravine for a long distance they were pursued on both sides by the soldiers and shot down, as the dead bodies showed afterwards. The women were standing off at a different place from where the men were stationed, and when the firing began those of the men who escaped the first onslaught went in one direction up the ravine, and then the women who were bunched together at another place went entirely in a different direction through an open field, and the women fared the same fate as the men who went up the deep ravine.

American Horse: The men were separated as has already been said from the women, and they were surrounded by the soldiers. Then came next the village of the Indians and that was entirely surrounded by the soldiers also. When the firing began, of course the people who were standing

160. This was most likely Captain George D. Wallace, although he probably was not the first casualty.

161. For a recent scholarly analysis of the events at Wounded Knee Creek see Greene, *American Carnage*, 215–46.

immediately around the young man who fired the first shot were killed right together, and then they turned their guns, Hotchkiss guns, etc., upon the women who were in the lodges standing there under a flag of truce, and of course as soon as they were fired upon they fled, the men fleeing in one direction and the women running in two different directions. So that there were three general directions in which they took flight.

There was a woman with an infant in her arms, who was killed as she almost touched the flag of truce, and the women and children of course were strewn all along the circular village until they were dispatched. Right near the flag of truce a mother was shot down with her infant; the child not knowing that its mother was dead was still nursing, and that was especially a very sad sight. The women as they were fleeing with their babies on their backs were killed together, shot right through, and the women who were very heavy with child were also killed. All the Indians fled in these three directions, and after most all of them had been killed, a cry was made that all those, who were not killed or wounded should come forth and they would be safe. Little boys, who were not wounded came out of their places of refuge, and as soon as they came in sight a number of soldiers surrounded them and butchered them there.

Of course we all feel very sad about this affair. I stood very loyal to the government all through those troublesome days, and believing so much in the government and being so loyal to it, my disappointment was very strong, and I have come to Washington with a very great blame on my heart. Of course it would have been all right, if only the men were killed; we would feel almost grateful for it. But the fact of the killing of the women, and more especially the killing of the young boys and girls, who are to go to make up the future strength of the Indian people, is the saddest part of the whole affair and we feel it very sorely.

I was not there at the time before the burial of the bodies, but I did go there with some of the police and the Indian doctor [Charles Eastman] and a great many of the people, men from the agency, and we went through the battle field and saw where the bodies were from the truck of the blood.

Turning Hawk: I had just reached the point where I said that the women were killed. We heard, besides the killing of the men, of the onslaught also made upon the women and children and they were treated as roughly and indiscriminately as the men and boys were.

Of course this affair brought a great deal of distress upon all the people, but especially upon the minds of those who stood loyal to the government and who did all that they were able to do in the matter of bringing about peace. They especially have suffered much distress and are very much hurt at heart. These peacemakers continued on in their good work, but there were a great many fickle young men, who were ready to be moved by any change in the events there, and consequently, in spite of the great fire that was brought upon all, they were ready to assume a hostile attitude. These young men got themselves in readiness and went in the direction of the scene of battle so that they might be of service there. They got there and finally exchanged shots with the soldiers. This party of young men was made up from Rosebud, Oglala (Pine Ridge), and members of any other agencies that happened to be there at the time.[162] While this was going on in the neighborhood of Wounded Knee—the Indians and soldiers exchanging shots—the agency, our home, was also fired into by the Indians. Matters went on in this strain until the evening came on, and then the Indians went off down by White Clay Creek. When the agency was fired upon by the Indians from the hillside, of course the shots were returned by the Indian police who were guarding the agency buildings.[163]

Although fighting seemed to have been in the air, yet those who believed in peace were still constant at their work. Young Man Afraid of His Horses, who had been on a visit to some other agency in the North or Northwest [the Crow Agency, Montana], returned, and immediately went out to the people living about White Clay Creek, on the border of the Badlands, and brought his people out. He succeeded in obtaining the consent of the people to come out of their place of refuge and return to the agency. Thus the remaining portion of the Indians, who started from Rosebud were brought back into the agency.

Mr. Commissioner, during the days of the great whirlwind out there, these good men tried to hold up a counteracting power, and that was "Peace." We have now come to realize that peace has prevailed and won the day. While we were engaged in bringing about peace our property was left behind, of course, and most of us have lost everything; even down to the matter of guns with which to kill ducks, rabbits, etc., shotguns, and guns of that order. When Young Man Afraid brought the people in and their guns were asked for, both men who were called hostiles and men who stood loyal to the government delivered up their guns.

162. See Black Elk's account in part 1.
163. Some of the Indian policemen fired a few shots, but by orders of General John R. Brooke, they stopped and the military did not return fire. See parts 1 and 2.

PART 3

"They see their relatives who died long before."

This part presents documents describing the Ghost Dance by Lakotas and Dakotas who were not Ghost Dancers themselves, but who were in a unique position to follow the developments on the Lakota reservations very closely. This part also includes the opinions of several mixed-bloods and men married to Lakota women. The first four documents describe the journey of the delegates, the teachings, and the ceremony of the Ghost Dance. It is worth noting that these accounts differ remarkably in certain aspects from the stories told by Short Bull, Kicking Bear, and other Ghost Dancers, reflecting the authors' or narrators' personal views and, perhaps, their dislike of the Ghost Dance, Ghost Dance shirts, or Ghost Dancers. These stories, then, deepen our understanding of the factionalism among the Lakotas.

George Sword (Mílawakȟáŋ Yuhá, Míwakȟáŋ, ca. 1847–1910), who was the captain of the Indian police force on the Pine Ridge Reservation, was able to follow the spread of the religion very closely. George Sword was a prominent medicine man, warrior, and a shirt wearer in the 1870s.[1] On the reservation he decided to "walk the white man's road" and was confirmed in the Episcopalian faith in 1880. As the captain of the Indian police he hoped to direct his people in their attempt to adapt to a new way of life.[2] The English version of Sword's account published by Emma Sickels, and later by James Mooney, states that the Ghost Dance shirts were "made for war," an expression that became a standard interpretation of the meaning of the Ghost Dance shirt for almost one hundred years. However, one needs to realize that when Good Thunder was arrested in the spring of 1890, the Ghost Dance shirts were not yet part of the religion. So Sword clearly later added his own opinions of the shirt, as well as other things, to the story.[3] As the captain of the police force he was responsible for arresting Good Thunder when he returned from his trip to the west. Sword interviewed Good Thunder while he was being arrested and then based his own account on these interviews. Furthermore, the translation used by Sickels and other

1. Becoming a shirt wearer (*wičháša yatápika*) was one of the great honors for Lakota men. A shirt wearer was a protector of the people and a leader who was supposed to behave properly and bravely in all circumstances and to work for the good of the people. See Walker, *Lakota Society*.

2. For George Sword's life, see Walker, *Lakota Belief and Ritual*, introduction, 74–75; Red Shirt, *George Sword's Warrior Narratives*, 50–77.

3. For more on how George Sword's story has become the standard interpretation of the Ghost Dance among the Lakotas, see Raymond J. DeMallie in Mooney, *The Ghost-Dance Religion*, Introduction, xxiii; Maddra, *Hostiles?* 31–32; Andersson, *The Lakota Ghost Dance of 1890*, pp. 33–40; Warren, *God's Red Son*, 349–51.

scholars following her contains errors and mistranslations. Thus, the new translation corrects some of them and offers new interpretations of others. Another short account by Sword reflects upon daily life on the reservation and also briefly touches upon the Ghost Dance by noting that he did not believe in it.

William T. Selwyn (Ohán, 1858–1905), a Yankton Dakota, was working as the postmaster on the Pine Ridge Reservation in 1890. He was educated in the East and came to Pine Ridge Reservation as a schoolmaster a few years earlier. He sided with the agents in several crucial incidents, working as a translator for the Sioux Commission of 1889 and as a census taker on Standing Rock in 1881. He gives another outsider's account of the Ghost Dance. His account is critical, even hostile, toward the Ghost Dance. It is likely that he sought personal gain from reporting negatively about the Ghost Dance to Agent Hugh D. Gallagher. The historian Louis Warren notes that Selwyn was known for seeking personal advantages in most of his ventures and often sought the acquaintance of powerful white officials.[4] The other account by Selwyn is an interview with Khuwápi, a Rosebud Ghost Dancer, who was arrested by Selwyn.

These documents are significant because they have affected the way that scholars have portrayed the Ghost Dance ever since the time James Mooney used them in his work. James Mooney arrived at Lakota reservations soon after the Wounded Knee massacre in 1891. However, the Lakota Ghost Dancers refused to talk to him, so he had to rely on other sources when creating his narrative of the Lakota Ghost Dance. Thus, the words of Sword and Selwyn became his major sources on the Lakota Ghost Dance "doctrine." For many scholars following Mooney, these accounts have been the primary source. Only recently have scholars started to question the information presented in these accounts and its reliability.[5]

Robert P. Higheagle (Waŋblí Waŋkátuya, ca. 1873–1938), a Hunkpapa, witnessed a Ghost Dance ceremony in Sitting Bull's camp on the Standing Rock Reservation. He was still a young boy and was attending a reservation school but was intrigued by the dance. He never became a dancer himself. Later he attended the Hampton Normal and Agricultural School in Virginia. After returning home, he served as an interpreter and representative for his people in meetings held in Washington, D.C., and as an informant for

---

4. For more on Selwyn, see Maddra, *Hostiles?* 32–33; Warren, *God's Red Son*, 232–23, 272–75, 350–51, 385–86.

5. See Maddra, *Hostiles?* 31–44; Andersson, *The Lakota Ghost Dance of 1890*, 33–40; Warren, *God's Red Son*, 349–51.

researchers like Frances Densmore. He also served as judge on the Standing Rock Court of Indian Offenses.

Dewey Beard (Wasú Máza, also known as Iron Hail and Dewey Horn Cloud, 1858–1955), was a survivor of the Little Big Horn battle and the Wounded Knee massacre. He gave several accounts of the Wounded Knee massacre in his lifetime, but as they do not discuss the Ghost Dance, I have left them out of this study. However, he gave one statement to Dr. James R. Walker in which he also discusses the Ghost Dance and his attempts to understand the new religion. This account, including his description of the Wounded Knee massacre, is included here.[6]

Minneconjou Alice Ghost Horse (also known as Alice Kills the Enemy and Alice War Bonnet, 1878–1950), who was thirteen in 1890, was a survivor of the Wounded Knee massacre. Like Dewey Beard, she was never a Ghost Dancer, but lived among Big Foot's people, most of whom were Ghost Dancers. She gave a lengthy description of her experiences to her son John War Bonnet. Her statement was eventually presented in a congressional hearing in 1991.

The accounts of Dewey Beard and Alice Ghost Horse, who were indeed caught between the U.S. Army and the Ghost Dance, could also have been placed in part 2, but they were both looking at the Ghost Dance from the outside; Alice Ghost Horse says that she was too young to participate and Dewey Beard simply did not believe in it. This, I believe, makes their stories fit into part 3.

By 1890 many white men had settled on Lakota reservations and married Lakota women. They were called "squawmen" and their children were often referred to as "half-breeds." Despite these somewhat derogatory terms, these people were often full members of Lakota society and served as interpreters and guides to the Lakotas. As many of them were literate, they helped illiterate Lakotas convey their thoughts and hopes to the authorities through letters and statements.[7] During the Ghost Dance, many of them worked as scouts or mediators between the Ghost Dancers and the officials. They also read newspaper accounts to the Ghost Dancers, who at times laughed at the sensation they caused in the press. The mixed-bloods

6. For Beard's life, see Philip Burnham, *Song of Dewey Beard: Last Survivor of the Little Big Horn* (Lincoln: University of Nebraska Press, 2014).

7. In a recent study, Dr. Justin R. Gage shows that intertribal communication, visitation, and letter writing was a very common practice among the Indians throughout the 1880s. In his study, Gage for the first time explores these networks in depth and imparts new information on the spread of the Ghost Dance. See Gage, "Intertribal Communication."

and men married to Lakota women were in an advantageous position to follow developments in the Lakota camps because they knew the language and had access to the meetings. This makes their opinions on the Ghost Dance very valuable.

Interestingly, most accounts by men married to Lakota women and by mixed-bloods cited here agree that the Ghost Dancers had no intention of waging war. The Ghost Dancers feared the possibility of an armed conflict, for example, in case the officials decided to force them to give up their arms. They often had a very practical approach to the Ghost Dance. The first document is by Aleck Mousseau (ca. 1856–?).[8] He was married to the Oglala Medicine Woman and by 1890 he was employed as a scout at Fort Robinson, Nebraska. Mousseau lived on Pine Ridge Reservation where he later became a rancher. His statement is followed by an interview of Baptiste (Big Bat) Pourier (1843–1928). Baptiste Pourier was a longtime friend of Red Cloud. He was married to the daughter of Louis Richard and a Lakota woman, and by 1890 he had lived among the Oglalas for more than thirty years.

Louis Primeau (1853–1903), the son of a French-Canadian trader and an Omaha woman, worked as a clerk, guide, interpreter, and scout at Fort Yates on the Standing Rock Reservation. He accompanied the reservation's Indian police on their mission to arrest Sitting Bull. Philip Wells (1851–1947) is perhaps the most well-known of the mixed-blood men, or men married to Lakota women. He was the son of a white man and a mixed-blood Santee woman. During his career, he served as an interpreter, scout, and farmer, and he was an official interpreter for the 1889 Sioux Commission. He was acting as a scout during the Wounded Knee massacre and his nose was cut nearly off by a Lakota. He gave several lengthy statements regarding the Wounded Knee massacre.[9] Louis Shangrau (Shangraux, Shangreau, 1848–1896), was also of mixed French-Canadian-Lakota descent. Together with his brother John Shangrau (1854–1926), he worked as an army scout for many years in the 1870s. In November–December 1890 he was the chief of the scouts working for General John R. Brooke. His account of the "Sioux war" of 1890 was published in the *Illustrated American* in January

8. U.S. census records give his name as Alex, not Aleck. He is still listed in the 1932 Indian census.

9. For Philip Wells's account of the Wounded Knee massacre, see Jensen, *Voices of the American West*, 1:126–63. His life story is found in Philip Wells, "Ninety-Six Years among the Indians of the Northwest," *North Dakota History* 15, no. 2 (March 1948): 85–143; no. 3 (July 1948): 169–215; no. 4 (October 1948): 265–312.

1891. John Shangrau was present at Wounded Knee and was among the soldiers who were sent to search the Lakota camp for weapons. He had been employed by Buffalo Bill's Wild West show as an interpreter in the early 1880s and again joined the tour with his family after Wounded Knee.

George Sword

"This is what they say happens in the Ghost Dance."

George Sword, the captain of the Indian police on Pine Ridge Reservation, gave an account in Lakota to schoolteacher Emma C. Sickels on December 7, 1891. The original manuscript, entitled "Wanagi Wacipi toranpi owicakiyakapi kin lee," is deposited in the Smithsonian Institution National Anthropological Archives, Manuscript 936. An English translation was published in the *Folk-Lorist* as "The Story of The Ghost Dance. Written in the Indian Tongue by Major George Sword, an Ogallala Sioux, Captain of Indian Police."[10] George Sword's narrative was most likely translated to Emma Sickels by a Lakota named Pȟeží Iyénakeča. When comparing the translation by Sickels to the original Lakota language manuscript, it becomes evident that there are major differences in the texts. Sickels has omitted several sentences, combined paragraphs, and added sentences that do not appear in the original text. Therefore, a new translation was necessary. In translating this text I have kept in mind that it is an oral narrative, and therefore I have not made a polished English version. It needs to reflect the words of George Sword.[11] To add to the difficulties in translating this text, some of the words in the original manuscript have been stricken through and replaced by other, sometimes clearly incorrect, words. These notes were made by the ethnologist James Mooney. He also added quotation marks in places where he felt they were necessary. Unfortunately, they are not always in correct places, making the text more confusing and difficult to read. George Sword's narrative starts with the first rumors of the Ghost Dance arriving on Pine Ridge and the subsequent decision to send a delegation

10. George Sword, "Wanagi Wacipi toranpi owicakiyakapi kin lee," Smithsonian Institution National Anthropological Archives, Manuscript 936, Pine Ridge Agency, S.D., December 7, 1891. Courtesy National Anthropological Archives, Smithsonian Institution. For comparison, see George Sword in Emma C. Sickels, "The Story of the Ghost Dance," 28–36.

11. For further analysis on translating Lakota narratives, especially other George Sword stories, see Red Shirt, *George Sword's Warrior Narratives.*

west to meet with the Son of God, as he called Wovoka. George Sword mentions two Lakota delegations to the west, but recent research has shown that this was highly unlikely.[12] George Sword received much of his information from Good Thunder, and for the most part, Sword's account reflects the statements made by the Ghost Dancers. For example, he notes that the Son of God showed the believers a new world, but it was not yet the time for it to take place (for comparison, see Young Skunk in part 1). And according to Sword, Good Thunder taught that the Ghost Dancers should become farmers and send their children to school. However, Sword's version differs in a couple of critical points. First, the English translation published by Sickels states that "the Ghost Shirts are made for war," and second, that the dancers carried guns during the ceremony. It is, of course, a matter of interpretation, and translation from Lakota to English, how Sword's account should be understood. Did he mean, as most scholars following Sickels and Mooney have suggested, that the invulnerable shirts were a clear sign of warlike intentions by the Ghost Dancers? Or did he mean that the shirts made people invulnerable and were thus useful in case fighting would come about? I believe that a much better translation of that particular sentence is "They wear them whenever they dance and they wear them whenever they fight."[13] And in the new translation the text continues, with Sword explaining:

Whenever they shoot bullets at the sacred shirts, sacred dresses and sacred leggings, the bullets will not pierce them; that is why each man wears them and whoever they have as enemies and point their guns to shoot is not able to do it, and also if they shoot at those, the bullets cannot pierce the sacred shirts.

Sword clearly acknowledges that the shirts and dresses were used for protection, not "made for war." Similarly, he notes that guns were carried only when "trouble sprung up." In any case, Sword's story remained for decades the major Native source that was used to confirm that the Lakota

12. For this discussion, see part 1.
13. See Andersson, *The Lakota Ghost Dance of 1890*, p. 74.

Ghost Dance was a "warlike" ceremony. Because of all the problems in the earlier English version, I believe that my new translation helps us to understand George Sword's story in a more insightful way.

In the year 1889 the Oglala People said [heard] that the Son of God (Wakȟáŋ Tȟaŋka Číŋča) lived over there toward the west.[14] The Shoshones and Arapahos were the first to learn about it. And so in 1889 the Oglalas, Good Thunder, and about four or five others went there, but they went there without permission; they went in secret.[15] And it was so that the Son of God was there, but he was there entirely for the Lakotas [Indians], thus the Lakotas all rejoiced and were attracted to it.[16]

In the year 1890 the Brulés Good Thunder, Cloud Horse, Yellow Knife, and Short Bull went there again and when they returned they told about the good things they saw there.

This is what they said: They [we] went to the northwest from the Shoshone/Arapaho reservation, they [we] traveled on train for five nights and then arrived to a wide country that lies below a large mountain [the Rocky Mountains], so they [we] arrived there. There were many people [tribes] there, because they live there, they now see the Son of God, thus they saw him. They would clear a place in the woods and, behold, he would arrive in the center, they said. And so now he is coming, they said. The people themselves who live there are the ones who know about it and who said this.[17]

And then as if stretching out mist came from the clouds and arrived there in the center of the place in the woods they had cleared and then it [the mist] went away. And then a young man about forty years old sat there. And then he was the Son of God, they said.

"Well," he said, "my grandchildren," he said, "you have arrived from far away to see your relatives, so my heart is glad. Behold, your people are the ones who will live," he said. "Those who have died live and [will] return here," he said. "Look here," he said, and we looked toward him. And then across the ocean a land grew up again and through it so many people

14. Sickels uses the word "Messiah" to describe Wovoka.

15. Indians needed to have a permission from their agent to visit other reservations. Throughout the 1880s Indians around the United States filed hundreds of letters to get permission to visit other tribes, relatives, etc. See Gage, "Intertribal Communication."

16. Sickels version translates as "he was there to keep the Indians, and not the whites." The words "not the whites," however, do not appear in the original manuscript. Sickels, *The Story of the Ghost Dance*, 28–36.

17. The last sentence does not appear in Sickels's translation.

moving camp [were] arriving [home], but the Son of God looked [at them], he said: "It will be so, but it will not take place yet, so go back." And he is the Son of God and so he gave them these.[18]

And so the people all turned around, and so he made the land across the ocean for those who were coming, and he made it for them, but he did not permit it [yet] and so he took it away, and then he said: "My grandchildren, behold these and return home!" "And grandchildren, when you arrive home, go to farming and make children attend school," he said. "And when you all are on your way home, if you shoot a buffalo, if you cut off his head, four feet and the tail and leave them right there, in a little while it will come back alive again," he said. "And then the white grandfather's [the president's] soldiers will arrest me, but I will stretch my arm and wipe them all out and that makes them helpless or if not that, they will go right there into the earth and all those [white people] will follow," he said.

"Well, the Father commanded me to come to the Lakotas [Indians] on purpose. At first I came to the white men, but they were lost, and they killed me and so these are the wounds," he said, and then he showed the wounds in his back [side], hands, and feet and he said: "All of you Lakotas will live the old life with the Father, who will keep you."[19]

"And you have come to see your relatives, but you will not take me [them] with you yet. When you arrive home tell your relatives that they will [should] follow my ways. In time whoever has no ears and does not listen, and helps the white man, when there will be something [a new world] from above that will cover the old world, the whites and those Lakotas who consider themselves as whites will be under the earth among the dead," he said. "In time, all the people will make use of this red paint and white clay and these medicines.[20] And then in the springtime when the green grass comes up, then my people, the spirit people, will be moving camp coming home, and then at last, you will see your own people," he said. "Behold, I will tell you these and give you these because you have come [when I called for you].

And so, we went and made a feast to one another with the spirits from the past camp. And Chasing Hawk who died recently [was there] and so his

---

18. Here Sickels writes: "The Messiah then gave to Good Thunder some paints, Indian paint, a white paint, a green grass." See Sickels, *The Story of the Ghost Dance,* 28–36. The items given do not appear in the original text, but it is well known that Wovoka gave the delegates red paint and other sacred items.

19. Here Sickels has made two paragraphs into one, omitting several sentences in the process. Sickels, *The Story of the Ghost Dance,* 28–36.

20. Sickels has "grass," but it should be "clay."

wife who died in war long time ago took him back there, and they live in a big ordinary buffalo hide tipi and they made a feast and he wished that all my relatives live there and he said: "Tell them to return here," he said. And they made a feast [for them] in return.[21]

Good Thunder also talked to his son who died in a battle a long time ago and so he was the one who gave a feast to all of them and so they all saw their own [dead relatives], they said. Then they took Good Thunder and several others, and those they went to a place where there were many buffalo standing, and they chased them and they shot one and they cut it all up, and they left the head, the four feet and the tail lying right there, and they packed the meat of the body, and they went on their way and turned around and stood, and the dead buffalo they shot really recovered as they were standing there looking, and the buffalo stood up and went running back home in the direction of the tracks they had gone to the past world.[22]

And these are the words of the Son of God, so it is, and he said this: "The country is far [away] and you do not want to suffer [on your way], so call upon me, I will shorten the [journey to the] country, it is so," he said. So it was, they started from one country [place] to go and be at home, but they went facing forward on their way home but they did not want to suffer. That is why they called out to the Son of God and they said: "Behold, Father, thus you spoke; we are mentally tired of the [journey to the] country," [and] saying this they prayed to him. And then they went running [traveling], and then the daylight went away and it became dark and they spent the night at that place, and it being so, in the dawn light came upon them in a country ahead.[23]

21. Sickels does not mention the feast at all.
22. An alternative translation could be "it went running back in the direction of home."
23. These two paragraphs are very confusing. Sickels translates: "When coming we came to a herd of buffaloes; we killed one, and took everything except the four feet, head and tail, and when we came a little ways from it, there was the buffalo came to life again, and went off. This was one of the Messiah's word came to truth. The Messiah said: 'I will short your journey when you feel tire(d) of the long ways, if you call upon me.' This we did when we were tired. The night came upon us; we stopped at a place, and we called upon the Messiah to help us, because we were tired of long journey. We went to sleep, and in the morning, we found ourselves at a great distance from where we stopped." See, Sickels, *The Story of the Ghost Dance*, 28–36. I believe that her translation, although not a literal translation, does convey the basic idea quite well. However, I think that these two paragraphs may refer to a vision experience. There is no way to determine if the killing of the buffalo, etc., took place while they were on their way back or when they were still in Nevada where they had a vision about these events. The

And then they arrived to their people, and those who ignore the grand-father's [president's] words and also those who live by it, gathered together for a meeting at Wounded Knee Creek and they camped there, but the father [the agent] sent his soldiers [Indian police] and they arrived there and took Good Thunder and two others [to the agency] and imprisoned them.[24] These were the ones who saw the Son of God. Sword and the agent asked Good Thunder to conceal it all [not to speak about it], and so he said he would not [stop speaking about it]. They held them in prison for only two days and again ordered them not to speak [about it], and [then] they said they would not [speak about it].

And so they let them go and they returned to the gathered people and they told their story [about the imprisonment] and they did not [hold a] council and broke up the gathering and they determined for themselves that they would call another meeting for the middle of the summer at White Clay Creek.[25]

And then in the springtime a Minneconjou called Kicking Bear went right there where the Arapahos live and the Arapaho people danced the Spirit Dance [Ghost Dance] and [as they danced], they became unconscious

---

problem is that the word *k'uŋ* appears in several places where it can refer to the past as if something happened in the "past world" or "past country." That could be a reference to the world in the vision that Wovoka was giving them, but then took away. Or, more likely, it could be a reference to the "old world" that was going to be replaced by the "new world." If that is the case, then the reference to going to "the past world" or "past country," i.e., home, would be metaphoric or symbolic. Young Skunk refers to the "old world" as the "old camp" (see part 1). However, the word *k'uŋ* can also mean simply "the" or "aforesaid" or it can be used as a strong statement or assertion meaning "as I said before." So this paragraph leaves a lot of room for speculation. In any case, it is an important paragraph, as James Mooney took it up in his work as an example of how "crazy" the Ghost Dancers were for believing that their journey had been made shorter by Wovoka. He says, "They [the delegates] were simply labouring under some strange psychological influence as not yet unexplained." See Mooney, *The Ghost-Dance Religion*, 822. Yet, if it is a vision experience, it reminds us of the Ghost Dance vision experiences presented in part 1.

24. Here Sword implies that the initial meeting concerning the Ghost Dance was attended by both "progressives" and "nonprogressives," to use the stereotypical label-ing. This is further proof that the religious message of the Ghost Dance was under-standable and appealing across this line.

25. The translation in Sickels is "In the following spring, the people at Pine Ridge Agency began to gather at the White Clay Creek for councils." See, Sickels, *The Story of the Ghost Dance*, 28–36. This translation is incorrect and the time frame is off. The arrest of Good Thunder took place in April 1890 and therefore the idea of organizing another meeting in the middle of the summer of 1890 makes more sense.

Indian police on drill, Pine Ridge Agency, S.D., 1890. George Sword, captain of the Pine Ridge Indian police, in left foreground. Photo: C. G. Morledge. Denver Public Library, Western History Collection, X-31356.

and they saw the Son of God and they said they saw something sacred, and those who were unconscious lay there as if dead, but they returned to life and so many know about these things, they said, and those who are unconscious and dead, they will know about those who were killed [a long time ago]; that is why they dance.

They brought an old man into the center of the circle carrying him and he became unconscious [and said]: "An eagle came to me and the Son of God took me home, there I thus talked with him." They all danced holding each other by the hand, and a man and a woman stood alternately [in a circle], and they danced going around and around, indeed they went around and around for a really long time sweating profusely, and they became exhausted and they became glossy-eyed and got foam in the mouth, and whoever stood there in the dust cried, and then they threw brownish dirt all over their faces and they put Indian red paint all over their faces, so it was. And they made many sacred shirts and the women made many sacred dresses and they were painted thus: In the middle the cloth was white, they did not use a sewing machine, but they sewed with an ordinary big needle[26] and across the shirt neck there were blue clay lines and then they drew a

26. Sickels does not mention the sewing machines. I think it is an interesting point as it emphasizes that these sacred shirts and dresses were made in a traditional way using only needles. Sewing machines were given to the Lakotas as part of government annuities and thus they reflect the world of the whites.

single line going forward and then they painted yellow dot markings behind the other and then it was cut off with dots painted with Indian red paint and the skirts, from top down, were painted exactly so, and in the back they painted an entire eagle body and on the shoulder and sleeves toward the end [hands] and then from the bottom of the skirts they tied, with a needle, single eagle wings and single wing feathers here and there, and they wear them whenever they dance and they wear them whenever they fight, they say.[27]

Whenever they shoot bullets at the sacred shirts, sacred dresses and sacred leggings, the bullets will not pierce them; that is why each man wears them and whoever they have as enemies and point their guns to shoot is not able to do it, and also if they shoot at those, the bullets cannot pierce the sacred shirts, they say. And all the men thus wear an eagle feather in the hair, and they are sacred, and a man holding eagle wing feathers paints himself sacredly and someone holding an eagle wing feather fans it in front of their faces making them insanely excited, they say.[28] And so the men do this way and dance until the dark and women become insanely excited and they carry them out behind the camp and place them there, yet not every woman do so, they do so one by one, and they ruled that nobody should wear any metal in the dance, but when trouble sprung up again, they danced carrying their guns.[29]

And those who died [were unconscious], they returned to life and they brought back home pemmican, they say, and the Son of God gave it to them, they say, and they brought brave fire, brave wind and brave water home and so the whites and those Lakotas who help the whites and the president, those will be killed, they say. And those [things] they brought home and they made a sweat lodge, and from the center of the lodge, water will pour out and inside he [the Son of God] will make a hole in the ground by hands

27. Sickels translates this as "the Ghost Shirts are made for war." Sickels, *The Story of the Ghost Dance*, 28–36. It is, however, significantly different to say that "they wear them whenever they dance and they wear them whenever they fight" than to claim that they were made for war. Even George Sword notes in the following paragraph that the shirts were used only for protection if an enemy points a gun and shoots.

28. Mooney noted that hypnotism might have been used in the dance. The *Illustrated American* also mentioned hypnotism in an article in January 1891, but it was not a common feature among the Lakotas. See *Illustrated American*, January 17, 1891, p. 330; Mooney, *The Ghost-Dance Religion*, 922–26; Andersson, *The Lakota Ghost Dance of 1890*, p. 61.

29. This is an interesting comment. According to Sword, when trouble sprang up, the Ghost Dancers started to wear guns in the dance. However, as seen in part 1, all Ghost Dancers deny that arms were carried during the ceremony.

and takes the water and the world will go under it and so one prays and those who are proved to be liars [nonbelievers], he will put into the water, they say.

Well, that is unspeakable, but then.[30]

Pheží Iyénakeča[31]
Signed George Sword,
December 7, 1891

George Sword

"I think [it] is not right way to worship."

George Sword wrote the following letter to Commissioner of Indian Affairs Thomas J. Morgan in November 1890, right at the height of the Ghost Dance on the Pine Ridge Reservation.[32] He reflects briefly upon the Ghost Dance, noting that it is not the right way to worship. Sword's letter demonstrates that the Ghost Dance was not the only cause of concern for the Lakotas. In October and November the newspapers and the agents by and large portrayed life on the Lakota reservations as totally chaotic and the Indians as being out of control. Yet Sword gives a glimpse into "normal" reservation life. He relates his deeds for the army and the government and hopes that he would be given a house and a piece of land as a reward for his services. Finally he notes that the Ghost Dancers do not listen to him (and other non–Ghost Dancers), and that he was "getting tired of it."

30. The original manuscript ends here. It may be George Sword's comment that the whole story seems unspeakable to him, but the sentence seems to stop abruptly. Sickels has an additional paragraph: "Before they begin to dance, they all raise their hands toward the Northwest and cry in supplication to the Messiah, and then begin the dance with the song, 'Ate Nusun-Kala,' etc., etc." See Sickels, *The Story of the Ghost Dance,* 34–36. It is not related to the previous sentence, and I do not know where she got that additional sentence and why it is not in the original text.

31. Pheží Iyénakeča was probably the person who translated the text for Sickels. See Mooney, *The Ghost- Dance Religion,* 797.

32. George Sword to the Commissioner of Indian Affairs Thomas J. Morgan, undated, received November 22, 1890, NARA, RBIA, RG 75.4, GRBIA, Letters Received, Letter 36111, box 680.

Pine Ridge Agency
Commission[er] of Indian Affair[s]

Dear Sir:

I am going to say a few lines to you this pleasant morning. I would
like to get my land and please I want you to help me and make me
a nice frame house, when I went to visit at Santees, and I saw nice
frame houses and out here [there are] no frame houses except chief
Red Cloud has [the] only one at this agency, but I think [it is] very old
now. I want you to help me all you can; when I visit[ed] at the Santee,
I saw with two eyes. Would you please give us a Judge of the Court,
if you can please? Our Great Father, I am stand[ing] by your rules
and do what is right and give me them rules. The Indian[s] are against
us, so I ask you [to give] them rules, some of the head chief[s] allow
them to Ghost Dance, but I think [it] is not right way to worship.

General Custer [was killed in 1876] by Indians and General
Crook kill[ed] all Cheyenne, most of them anyhow.[33] In that year and
in that winter some military were sent me to [make a] treaty with
Crazy Horse and I bring them at the agency[34] and since then war was
ended, I join in [the] military [for] two years and after two year[s]
I [was] relive [relieved], then I join the police force; since I join the
police I am Captain of police for 12 years now. When I ask you [for]
something, I would like you to approve [it] when you think it is right;
at the agency some of our people are wild yet, they make up a Ghost
Dance pretty wild yet, what we told them do they never listen to us,
then I am getting tired of it.

Respectfully yours,

George Sword

Captain U.S. Indian Police

Pine Ridge Indian Agency, S.D.

Answer soon

33. This is a reference to the Cheyennes who escaped from Fort Robinson in 1877
and were hunted down by the U.S. Army.

34. Sword refers to an incident during the fighting of 1876–77 when he went to
Crazy Horse's camp as a negotiator and finally made them surrender to the U.S. Army.
See DeMallie, "These Have No Ears," 528–32.

William T. Selwyn

"Did not the Rosebud people prepare to attack the white people this summer?"

This letter by William T. Selwyn to Colonel E. W. Foster, the agent of the Yankton Agency, South Dakota, on November 22, 1890, presents his interview with Khuwápi, a Ghost Dancer from Rosebud.[35] This text is basically Khuwápi's description of the Ghost Dance and could have been placed in part 1 as well. However, since Selwyn clearly pressed Khuwápi for answers regarding the Ghost Dance and possible plans to attack the whites, this letter also relates Selwyn's views. Khuwápi explained the message of the Ghost Dance, the destruction of the white race in a whirlwind and the emerging Indian paradise. He explained why people believed in the message. He believed in the Ghost Dance because he had eaten buffalo meat brought back, perhaps, by one of the Ghost Dance leaders who acquired it in a vision. Yet, when repeatedly asked about a possible outbreak, Khuwápi replies that a certain portion of the Rosebud Indians might be planning an attack. Khuwápi also shares the common Lakota understanding that the Messiah was the Son of God or the Son of the Great Spirit.

November 22, 1890
Col L. W. Foster, U.S. Indian Agent
Yankton Agency, S.D.

Dear Sir:

It has been reported here a few days ago that there was an Indian visitor up at White Swan from Rosebud Agency who has been telling or teaching the doctrines of the new Messiah, and has made some agitation among the people up there. According to the request of Captain [Casper] Conrad, United States Army, of Fort Randall,

35. William Selwyn to Agent E. W. Foster, November 22, 1890, NARA, RBIA, RG 75, SC 188, box 199. Published also in Mooney, *Ghost-Dance Religion*, 799–801. See Maddra, *Hostiles?* 32–33.

South Dakota, and by your order of the 21st instant, I went up to the White Swan [Yankton Agency] and have arrested the wanted man (Khuwápi, or One They Chased After). On my way to the agency with the prisoner I have made [a] little interview with him on the subject of the new Messiah. The following are the facts which he corroborated concerning the new Messiah, his laws and doctrines to the Indians of this continent:

Q: Do you believe in the new Messiah?

A: I somewhat believe it.

Q: What made you believe it?

A: Because I ate some of the buffalo meat that he (the new Messiah) sent to the Rosebud Indians through Short Bull.[36]

Q: Did Short Bull say that he saw the living herd of roaming buffaloes while he was with the son of the Great Spirit?

A: Short Bull told the Indians at Rosebud that the buffalo and other wild game will be restored to the Indians at the same time when the general resurrection in favor of the Indians takes place.

Q: You said a "general resurrection in favor of the Indians takes place"; when or how soon will this be?

A: The Father sends word to us that he will have all these caused to be so in the spring, when the grass is knee high.

Q: You said "Father;" who is this Father?

A: It is the new Messiah. He has ordered his children (Indians) to call him "Father."

Q: You said the Father is not going to send the buffalo until the resurrection takes place. Would he be able to send a few buffaloes over this way for a sort of a sample, so as to have his children (Indians) to have a taste of the meat?

A: The Father wishes to do things all at once even in destroying the white race.

Q: You said something about the destroying of the white race. Do you mean to say that all mankind except the Indians will be killed?

A: Yes.

Q: How and who is going to kill the white people?

36. It was common in the Lakota Ghost Dance that meat (sometimes even buffalo meat) was brought back from the spirit world. See part 1.

A: The Father is going to cause a big cyclone or whirlwind, by which he will have all the white people to perish.

Q: If it should be a cyclone or a whirlwind, what are we going to do to protect ourselves?

A: The Father will make some kind of provisions by which we will be saved.

Q: You said something about the coming destruction on the white people by your Father. Supposing your Father is sick, tired out, forget, or some other accidental cause by which he should not be able to accomplish his purpose, what would be the case about the destroying of the white people?

A: There is no doubt about these things, as the miracle performer or the Father is going to do just as what he said he would do.

Q: What other object could you come to by which you are led to believe that there is such a new Messiah on earth at present?

A: The Ghost Dancers are fainted whenever the dance goes on.

Q: Do you believe that they are really fainted?

A: Yes.

Q: What makes you believe that the dancers have really fainted?

A: Because when they wake or come back to their senses they sometimes bring back some news from the unknown world, and some little trinkets, such as buffalo tail, buffalo meat, etc.

Q: What did the fainted ones see when they get fainted?

A: They visited the happy hunting ground, the camps, multitudes of people, and great many strange people.

Q: What did the ghost or the strange people tell the fainted one or ones?

A: When the fainted one goes to the camp, he is welcomed by the relatives of the visitor (the fainted one), and he is also invited to several feasts.[37]

Q: Were the people at Rosebud Agency anxiously waiting or expecting to see all their dead relatives who have died several years ago?

A: Yes.

37. Khuwápi explains here that the word "visitor" or "traveler" refers to the person experiencing the vision. See part 1.

Q: We will have a great many older folks when all the dead people come back, would we not?

A: The visitors all say that there is not a single old man or woman in the other world—all changed to young.

Q: Are we going to die when the dead ones come back?

A: No; we will be just the same as we are today.

Q: Did the visitors say that there is any white men in the other world?

A: No; no white people.

Q: If there is no white people in the other world, where did they get their provisions and clothing?

A: In the other world, the messenger tells us that they depended all together for their food on the flesh of buffalo and other wild game; also, they were all clad in skins of wild animals.

Q: Did the Rosebud Agency Indians believe the new Messiah, or the Son of the Great Spirit?

A: Yes.

Q: How do they show that they have a belief in the new Messiah?

A: They showed themselves by praying to the Father by looking up to heaven, and call him "Father," just the same as you would in the church.

Q: Have you ever been in a church?

A: No.

Q: Do you faithfully believe in the new Messiah?

A: I did not in the first place, but as I became more acquainted with the doctrines of the new Messiah that I really believe in him.

Q: How many people at Rosebud, in your opinion, believe this new Messiah?

A: Nearly everyone.[38]

Q: Did not the Rosebud people prepare to attack the white people this summer? While I was at Pine Ridge Agency this summer the Oglala Sioux Indians say they will resist against the government, if the latter should try to put a stop to the Messiah question. Did your folks at Rosebud say the same thing?

38. This is an inaccurate estimate. Most likely only 30 percent of the Lakota population on Rosebud became Ghost Dancers. See Andersson, *The Lakota Ghost Dance of 1890*, pp. 76–77.

A: Yes.

Q: Are they still preparing and thinking to attack the white people should the government send our soldiers with orders to put a stop to your new business of the Messiah?

A: I do not know, but I think that the Wojaji [Wažáže] band at Rosebud Agency will do some harm at any time.

Q: You do not mean to say that the Rosebud Indians will try and cause an outbreak?

A: That seems to be the case.

Q: You said something about the "Son of the Great Spirit," or "the Father." What do you mean by the Son of the Great Spirit?

A: This Father, as he is called, said himself that he is the Son of the Great Spirit.

Q: Have you talked to or with any Indian at White Swan about the new Messiah, his laws and doctrines, or have you referred this to anyone while there?

A: I have told a few of them. I did not voluntarily express my wish for them to know and follow the doctrines of the new Messiah.

Q: Yes, but you have explained the matter to the Indians, did you not?

A: Yes, I have.

Q: Do the Yankton Indians at White Swan believe in your teaching on the new Messiah?

A: I did not intend to teach them, but as I have been questioned on the subject, that I have said something about it.

Q: Did any of them believe in you?

A: Some have already believed it, and some of them did not believe it.

Q: Those that have believed in you must be better men than the others, are they not?

A: I do not know.

Q: Do you intend to introduce the doctrines of the new Messiah from Rosebud to this agency as a missionary of the gospel?

A: No, I did not.

Q: What brings you here, then?

A: I have some relatives here that I wanted to see, and this was the reason why I came here.

Q: Where does this new Messiah question originate? I mean from the first start of it.

A: This has originated in White Mountains.

Q: Where is this White Mountain?

A: Close to the big Rocky Mountains, near that country that belong to the Mexicans.

Q: Do you think that there will be a trouble in the west by next spring?

A: Yes.

Q: What makes you think so?

A: Because that is what I have heard people talk of.

That is all that I have questioned Khuwápi on the subject of the new Messiah.

Respectfully, your obedient servant,

William T. Selwyn

William T. Selwyn

"There will be a general Indian war in the spring."

In another letter on November 25, 1890, to Colonel E. W. Foster, Indian agent of the Yankton Agency, S.D., William Selwyn explains his own views on the Ghost Dance.[39] According to him the Messiah claimed to be the Son of God who had now come back to earth to "kill all the whites" and take "revenge" for the Indians. That is in stark contrast with Wovoka's message and also the teachings of Lakota Ghost Dance leaders like Short Bull. Selwyn claims that Red Cloud was a true believer in the Ghost Dance, which contradicts most other sources. Selwyn also speculates that the Mormons were behind the Ghost Dance and believed that Wovoka was actually a Mormon himself.[40] Selwyn concludes by

39. William T. Selwyn to E. W. Foster, November 25, 1890, NARA, RBIA, RG 75, SC 188, M4728, roll 1, 2/97–372.
40. For this discussion, see Mooney *The Ghost-Dance Religion*, 766, 792–93; Hittman, *Wovoka*, 84–86.

asserting that based on his knowledge of the Ghost Dance through letters and other communication, he was certain that there would be an uprising by the Lakotas in the near future.

November 25, 1890
Colonel E. W. Foster, U.S. Indian Agent
Yankton Agency, S.D.

Dear Sir,

According to your request of the 24th instant I take pleasure in giving [a] brief statement concerning the new Messiah. In 1889 there has been some talk on the different agencies in Utah, Wyoming, Montana, Dakota and Indian Territory about the advent of this new Messiah. The way I came to find out all these is through the reading of some letters for the Sioux and Cheyenne at Pine Ridge from several agencies.[41] I was post-master at that place then, and parties who could not read letters generally brings their letters to me to read for them.[42]

There were some talk in the fall of 1888 by the Utes, Shoshones, Crows and Arapahos who have visited Pine Ridge about the New Messiah but not so much as what has been prevailing in 1889 and 1890.

In the fall of 1889 in a private council Chiefs Red Cloud, Young Man Afraid of His Horses, Little Wound, American Horse, Big Road, Fire Thunder and a few more others appointed a delegation to visit the western agencies in order to find out more about the new Messiah. The young men who were appointed to go out on [a] journey from Pine Ridge were Good Thunder, Yellow Bull [Breast], Broken Arm and another one; from Rosebud Agency were Short Bull and another one; from Cheyenne River Agency Kicking Bear, also Flat Arm from Pine Ridge. All these have been writing from Wyoming, Utah and some distant agencies that the Messiah has now come to the world and that there is no mistake about the advent of the new Messiah.[43]

41. See Gage, "Intertribal Communication."
42. By November 1890 Selwyn had moved to the Yankton Agency and later worked hard to get the Yanktons to sell their lands. Warren, *God's Red Son*, 231–35.
43. It is noteworthy that the council that decided on sending the delegation included

When the parties came home in the spring of 1890 there was quite an excitement over the arrival of the visitors from the west. As soon as they had arrived I had an interview with them all on the subject. All have said that there was a man in the plains at the fort of the Rocky Mountains, near the White Mountains, close to Mexico, who has clothed himself in wonderful garment, [has] scar in the palms of [his] hands, feet and also on one side, and scars on the forehead, claiming that he was the Son of the Great Spirit who has been killed by civilized people once and now he has come down to kill all the white people and will cause a general resurrection in favor of the Indians of this continent, he will alas bring all the buffalo and other wild game back for the Indians and kill all the whites. He has performed some wonderful act[s], he can make two horses talk, two birds to talk to each other. He makes one object visible as two or things that no man can do in this world (sleight-of-hand-performers and ventriloquist). How as he is the Indians' God that they must pray to him and call him Father and he will hear their prayers. He has alas come down to the world to revenge for the Indians. That is to wipe the white race from the face of the earth because they have treated the Indians very bad all way through. And that he is also going to exterminate the whites by some phenomena in the spring of 1891. That all the Indians must prepare for this event. Upon my questioning if their Father advises them to cause trouble on the whites by next spring. That was the orders they had from their Father, but will be kept secret.

In April 1890—the apostles (they might be called) held a council to organize the new religion and upon discovering the business I have reported this matter to Colonel H. D. Gallagher, the U.S. Indian Agent at Pine Ridge, who immediately took up the case and have arrested all the visitors and put them all in jail. This jailing of the arrival of [the] visitors made a kind of cool-down for a while.

Red Cloud himself believed it and told me faithfully that he will stand by his Father (the new Messiah) and will have his people to do just as they were commanded by the Father.

---

chiefs like Young Man Afraid of His Horses and Red Cloud. None of the letters sent by the delegation have been located nor do Short Bull, Kicking Bear, or Good Thunder mention sending letters back home. However, Josephine Waggoner (part 4) says that she read letters to Hunkpapas that Kicking Bear sent from Nevada.

I see the way they have been corresponding from one agency to another is doing some harm, the Cheyennes and Arapahos at Darlington, Indian Territory, are wild with this excitement. This I came to find out by the reading of some letters while at Pine Ridge.

In my opinion this whole business is started or originated by the spies or missionaries of the Mormons, because some of the visitors told me themselves that this new Messiah has told them that the plural wives is not sin; from this I think that this man or Messiah is a Mormon with practice of sleight-of-hand performers and ventriloquist.

In my opinion there will be a general Indian war in the spring according to what letters I have read for the Sioux and Cheyenne Indians. Also the secret plans that they have been getting up for the last one year or so.

Respectfully Your obedient servant,

William J. Selwyn

Keeps the Battle

"This strange person was to set right the wrongs of my people."

This account by Keeps the Battle (Kičhízapi Tȟáwa) was published in Warren K. Moorehead's article, "Ghost Dances in the West: Origin and Development of the Messiah Craze and the Ghost Dance." in *The Illustrated American* on January 17, 1891.[44] It is unclear which Ute village Keeps the Battle visited and who the "minister" he mentions was. Did Keeps the Battle meet the Paiutes, not the Utes? Whether he met Wovoka or someone else repeating Wovoka's teachings, is uncertain. Keeps the Battle does not say whether he became a Ghost Dancer, but he says that the Ghost Dance weighed heavily on a number of his people, perhaps signifying that he was not a believer. Kicking Bear and other Lakota delegates also describe meeting people who acted as priests or ministers of the new religion.

44. Keeps the Battle in Moorehead, "Ghost Dances in the West," 327. Published also in Boyd, *Recent Indian Wars*, 177–78.

Scarcely had my people reached the Ute village when we heard a white preacher whom the Utes held in the highest esteem, who told a beautiful dream or vision of the coming of a great and good red man. This strange person was to set right the wrongs of my people; he could restore to us our game hunting grounds, [he] was so powerful that every wish or word he gave utterance to then came fulfilled. His teachings had a strange effect upon the Utes, and, in obedience to the commands of this man, they began the Messiah dance. My people did not pay much attention to this dance at first, and it was not until [close] to our departure that the matter began to weigh heavily upon the minds of a number in the party. As we left the Ute camp the minister stood with uplifted hands and invoked the blessing of the Great Spirit upon us. He told us to look for the coming of the Savior, and assured us that he would soon and unexpectedly arrive. He further cautioned us to be watching and ready to accompany him to the bright and happy hunting grounds, to be sorry for our sins, to institute the Messiah dance among our people at Pine Ridge, and to keep up the dance until the Lord himself should appear.

Robert P. Higheagle

"It meant the buffalos were coming back. That is what they were praying for."

Robert P. Higheagle witnessed a Ghost Dance in Sitting Bull's camp. His account was first published by Stanley Vestal as "I saw the Ghost Dance at Standing Rock" in *New Sources of Indian History*. The original is in the Walter Stanley Campbell Collection.[45] Higheagle's account is a rare glimpse into an experience of a young person, a schoolboy. He describes how one day a boy with a Ghost Dance shirt arrives and tells about the new religion. Higheagle got curious about the shirt and the Ghost Dance, so much so that he wanted to see it for himself. However, he also describes how other schoolboys ridiculed the boy wearing the Ghost Dance shirt. It is worth noting that he says that this event took place in

45. Robert P. Higheagle in WSCMC, WHCUOLA, box 104, folder 22. Published by permission of University of Oklahoma Libraries. Published also in Vestal, *New Sources of Indian History*, 42–44.

the summer of 1890. The bulletproof shirts, however, did not become part of the dance until later in the fall, perhaps in October.[46] And there were no dances on Standing Rock before October when Kicking Bear taught the dance to Sitting Bull's people. Higheagle's account shows how interesting the Ghost Dance was for many Lakotas, even those attending the white man's schools.

I was home from school and Loneman, my relative, had some business with Sitting Bull and had to see him.[47] I went up with him. He was one of the Indian Police.

I had heard of this Ghost Dance while I was away at school.[48] One of the school boys had run away. They were very strict about keeping the children in school, but this boy was gone about a month, at the end of which time he was brought back. When he came back everybody crowded around him. He was telling some interesting stories and singing Ghost Dance songs. He also wore a bullet-proof shirt. This was in the summer, 1890. He got the crowd of boys around and they began to sing these songs. I asked him one day about this and he told me they had started this Ghost Dance and showed me the bullet-proof shirt. It was buckskin with a picture of a crescent on the front and a picture of a buffalo on the back. It meant the buffalos were coming back. That is what they were praying for. The moon meant that every time there was a new moon that was the time to pray the most.[49]

I asked him if he thought the shirt was bullet-proof. He said he hadn't tried it. Well, we had a game among the boys called Throwing Mud. We put a piece of mud on the end of a long willow. We would throw this mud and have fights with it. Sometimes when we ran out of mud we could use our sticks to strike the opposing players.

It happened that the Blackfeet Sioux boys and Yanktonais were going to have a match. They said it was not fair to have the boy with bullet-proof shirt on one side. Then they said, "Now, we are going to see if this shirt *is* bullet-proof."[50] This bullet-proof shirt boy didn't run away at first, but

46. Ostler, *Plains Sioux*, 279–88; Andersson, *The Lakota Ghost Dance of 1890*, pp. 63–71.

47. For Loneman's story, see part 2.

48. Robert P. Higheagle attended the reservation boarding school and later the Hampton Institute in Virginia.

49. Wovoka gave instructions to dance every five weeks.

50. Emphasis in the original.

we ran after him and one big boy jumped on him and downed him. They kicked him, took off his bullet-proof shirt, etc. They made fun of it.

Later I was curious about this Ghost Dance, so I went to see. We were camping near Sitting Bull's place on Grand River and there was a dance going on in the middle of the circle. There were guards all around the camp. Anybody not wearing Indian clothes was not allowed in the camp. We took out our saddle blankets to wear, but they wouldn't let us in unless we also took off our store clothes. So we stayed back. They were dancing, holding hands. After a while one fell down and they all stopped to see what he would say. He would then tell his vision. Then they would continue dancing until some more fell down and were given a chance to tell what they had seen.

I had an uncle who was one of the main administrators of this ceremony. He came over and asked me if I wanted to join it. "Don't you want to be saved? All those who wear white men's clothes are going to die." He gave me a feather to wear and wouldn't let me in unless I would discard my civilian clothes. Loneman had a policeman's uniform. He called Sitting Bull over and interviewed him in his log house. He had some orders from the agent, I think.

This was the only chance I had to see the Ghost Dance. I kept this feather and every now and then they told me to throw it away. Later I went away to school and left this feather at home and my brother got to believing in the Ghost Dance and sent me the feather, telling me to wear it when the time came for the Messiah to return.

Sitting Bull was all painted up when I saw him. He was dressed in his ordinary Indian way, but he wore no feather on his head. It didn't appear to me that he was the leader. He was merely a sort of advisor. He didn't wear a Ghost [Dance] shirt when I saw him, but wore a blanket. He was very nice and invited Loneman and me to supper. We went into a tent alongside of his log house. He had some cattle and horses there, especially the white circus horse he had got from Buffalo Bill. He had a deep bass voice. He was very kind that day, as was his general custom. He was a little bit shorter than Black Prairie Dog, but heavier set, about the size of Gray Whirlwind. He welcomed children to his home at any time but did not give them any presents or anything like that. He was always very kind. He dressed very much like other Indians, but had to live up to his office of chief by painting his face, etc. and had to be kind to everybody.

Robert P. Higheagle

"This shirt that they got . . . has the power to resist a bullet or arrows or anything."

In this document, Robert P. Higheagle explains to Walter S. Campbell the reasoning behind the Ghost Dance and the Ghost Dance shirt.[51] Higheagle repeats the story of the schoolboy, who had a Ghost Dance shirt. He further explains the meaning of some of the symbols in the shirt. Higheagle notes that the only thing the Ghost Dancers "could combat with" was "to have something about them that was bulletproof." This clearly illustrates the protective nature of the shirts and gives support to the argument that there was a social call for these garments. The shirts helped the Ghost Dancers to stay united even as the threat posed by the U.S. Army was growing. Higheagle again says he saw the shirt in June, but it is highly unlikely that the shirts would have been used that early. After his discussion of the Ghost Dance shirt, Higheagle relates the story of Sitting Bull's arrest and death. His story has some inaccuracies, but mostly follows the conventional storyline.

There were medicine men among the Indians who could talk with the dead. There was a great deal of that in the Ghost Dance.

At the time when they were using the Ghost [Dance] shirts I didn't get close enough to the Ghost Dancers to notice the designs, but this one that the school boy brought back was the only one that I saw. It was a buckskin shirt. On the back it had the design of a buffalo head just like the buffalo was looking at you and right on the breast it had a crescent and a star. Then I saw some little marks here and there, but I didn't notice what they signified. These were the main objects that showed plainly. According to the information I received, the buffalo signified that the Indians are going to be blessed with the return of the buffalos. That is one of the things they knew this Messiah had told them. The crescent, the star signifies the world. I didn't see any design on the shirt that indicated the world because in explaining, he said that there was going to be another big flood and those who wear the

51. Robert P. Higheagle in WSCMC, WHCUOLA, box 108, folder 14. Published by permission of University of Oklahoma Libraries.

eagle down are the only ones to be saved. They know that in the past the white man was always provided with plenty of ammunition. The only thing they could combat with would be the medicine man, who claimed to have something about them that was bulletproof.

This shirt that they got according to the way it is gotten up it has the power to resist a bullet or arrows or anything. All was brought to Sitting Bull by Kicking Bear. Then again some of them heard from Short Bull of Pine Ridge, who advocated this new religion. When I saw the shirt, it was the early part of the Ghost Dance, about June. It was at Fort Yates. School was out in July. Sometimes they even kept us during vacation. They were afraid we would go back and put blankets on.

They had some tents outside and there were several tents nearby belonging to some of his immediate friends. They had already sent White Bird and Red Bear to saddle Sitting Bull's white horse. They helped each other. He was willing to go and was dressing when Crow Foot called him a coward, that he had always said he was brave and now he was going to go with the police. So he changed his mind. Up until that time he was willing to go. After he said he wasn't going the police took him by the arm. There were not anything like 150 of Sitting Bull's followers. It was getting cold and some of the people had gone home. The Ghost Dancers came out when they brought Sitting Bull out. His followers had been awaiting a chance in case he should need their help. He didn't call on them for help. It was his followers who stirred up trouble. They said, "You are Indian Police, and now you are here." While they were talking like this, Loneman and others tried to stop them. Catch-the-Bear tried to fire into Loneman, so the latter jerked the gun from his hand and killed him with the butt of the gun. Never heard that Bullhead fired the first shot. He was the first policeman that fired after Sitting Bull was already shot. Six policemen [were] killed. Never heard that the women attacked the police. Loneman described how certain policemen got killed: Little Eagle and Armstrong. Grand River was on the south. The timber was between the river and cabin. The Ghost Dancers ran away through the timber. Right on the bluff behind the trees some of the Ghost Dancers were still firing, so the policemen went into some nearby sheds and into the house. From the house and from the sheds they were firing at the Ghost Dancers after Sitting Bull was killed. It was getting daylight by that time. It seems that several policemen were lying down on the ground firing. One of the Ghost Dancers fired and hit either Armstrong or Little Eagle and killed him. So these policemen, Shave Head (died in hospital), Catch-the-Bear, Bullhead (died in hospital), were killed in a short space of time before daybreak. The Ghost Dancers ran away toward the river.

Anonymous Woman

"Why do the innocent suffer while the guilty go unpunished?"

The *Illustrated American* correspondent Warren G. Moorehead wrote in a very sympathetic way about the Lakotas' destitution, even though his tone often was quite paternalistic.[52] The following lament, by a "chief's wife," as Moorehead writes, was published in January 1891.[53] By the time of this interview, most likely in December 1890, those who did not join the Ghost Dancers, that is, "friendlies," were ordered to the Pine Ridge Agency. They had to leave their homes and live in canvas tipis, which often were of poor quality. The fact that they were absent from their homes enabled the Ghost Dancers to plunder their homes (see, for example, statements by American Horse and others in part 2). The article ends with a good example of Moorehead's writing style and attitudes. He writes: "And here the poor woman broke down, sobbing. Her lord looked on in silence, bearing, with all the impassiveness of his race, the troubles brought down upon his home by the action of the dancers."[54]

Why are we detained here? My husband, my brother, my cousin are not going to join the dancers in the Badlands. There is not a family in this large camp (of one hundred and ninety-five tipis) that does not watch over at least one sick child. The coughing and crying of poor distressed babies keeps us all awake at night. It is two miles from here to the government buildings, and, should a great blizzard swoop down upon us, many women and children would perish before the men could get us into the Great Father's warm houses.

Look about you, young man! You see a much-patched lodge. There are holes in every strip of canvas on the poles, through which the chilly blast penetrates. Our little fire is not large enough to keep the children warm, and, were it made greater, the smoke would be so dense we could scarcely remain inside. We cannot haul much wood in our wagons, for the distance

52. Bearor, "The *Illustrated American* and the Lakota Ghost Dance," 143–63.
53. Anonymous Woman in *Illustrated American*, January 24, 1891, p. 393.
54. Moorehead, *Illustrated American*, January 24, 1891, p. 393.

to the bluffs where the pines grow is eight miles, and our horses are not strong.

Oh! Why are we kept here? The hostiles should be made to suffer, not us. They caused all this trouble. Why do the innocent suffer while the guilty go unpunished?

Dewey Beard

"The spirit would not come to me."

Dewey Beard gave the following account to James R. Walker and it was published fully in *Lakota Society*. The original manuscript is held at the History Colorado Archives.[55] During his life Beard gave several accounts of the Wounded Knee massacre.[56] Most of his accounts are directly related to Wounded Knee and outside the scope of this study. The following text, however, also describes the Ghost Dance religion and the events in Big Foot's camp before they left toward Pine Ridge. Beard describes him and his family's sincere efforts to gain more knowledge of the Ghost Dance. They first went to see a dance at White Clay Creek but did not receive a vision. Then they traveled to Big Foot's camp on the Cheyenne River Reservation in order to learn more. From then on he describes how the misunderstandings between Big Foot and the soldiers started to escalate, leading to the "escape" of Big Foot and Big Foot's

55. Beard in JRWC, HCSHL, MSS 653. I have used the transcribed copy held at the American Indian Studies Research Institute, Indiana University, with their permission. Published also in *Lakota Society*, ed. Raymond J. DeMallie (Lincoln: University of Nebraska Press, 1992), 157–68. For more on James R. Walker and his work among the Lakotas, see Raymond J. DeMallie, preface, in *Lakota Society*, ix–xiv.

56. The most complete account of the Wounded Knee massacre by Beard was given to Judge Eli S. Ricker in 1907. In that statement, he, however, mentions the Ghost Dance only in passing. For that reason, I have used his statement given to James R. Walker. For comparison, see Beard in ESRC, tablet 30. It is also published in Jensen, *Voices of the American West*, 1:209–26. For discussion of other accounts by Beard, see Jensen, *Voices of the American West*, 1:208; Burnham, *Song of Dewey Beard*, 213 (endnote 61). For an analysis of Dewey Beard's and the Wounded Knee Survivor's Association's attempt to change the traditional narrative of Wounded Knee, see Grua, *Surviving Wounded Knee*.

people and their eventual capture.[57] Dewey Beard also relates how the medicine man Yellow Bird was asked to perform Ghost Dance prayers and songs right about the time the disarmament started on December 29. Beard's father told the medicine man in a somewhat sarcastic tone that if the Messiah was true, now was the time for him to help. Subsequently the medicine man did as asked, which was interpreted by many as a signal to open fire, which it clearly was not.[58] Beard's story then continues with a description of the massacre.

The buffalo were gone and old Indians were hungry. I sat with my father in his tipi when a messenger came and told us that a Savior for the Indians had appeared to an Indian in the far land of the setting sun, and promised to come and bring again the buffalo and antelope and send the white man from all the land where the Indians hunted in the old times.

This messenger was holy and told us that if we would dance and pray to the Savior, he would appear and show us things that were sacred. My father said: "My sons, we will go and see this thing." We went and saw the Indians dancing the Ghost Dance on the White Clay Creek and I and my father and all my brothers danced.[59]

When we danced some Indians acted as if they died and some acted as if they were holy. When they did this, they told that they saw mysterious things and some said they saw the Savior of the Indians and that he promised them to come and bring the good old times again. But I observed that it was bad Indians and Indians that no one used to pay any attention [to] and the medicine men who saw these things.

---

57. For thorough analysis of the events in Big Foot's camp before they decided to leave for Pine Ridge, see Andersson, *The Lakota Ghost Dance of 1890*, pp. 88–90; Greene, *American Carnage*, 196–214. See Indian testimonies in vol. 1 of Jensen, *Voices of the American West*.

58. For many years the standard interpretation of Yellow Bird's actions was that he was giving some kind of a signal for the men to start a fight. Most likely he was praying, as both Dewey Beard and Alice Ghost Horse say. He was also singing a Ghost Dance song and wearing a Ghost Dance shirt. The throwing of dust in the air was also common in Lakota traditions to display pity and grief, and it was a typical gesture in the Ghost Dance. Andersson, *The Lakota Ghost Dance of 1890*, pp. 92–93. For a different view, see statement by Philip Wells above.

59. Dewey Beard's father's name was Horn Cloud. Beard had six brothers and one sister. See Burnham, *Song of Dewey Beard*, 4–6.

The spirit would not come to me nor to my father nor to my brothers and my father said: "My sons, I hear that they danced the Ghost Dance better away from here. We will go to the camps of the Indians in the Cheyenne [River] Agency and we may see the Holy One there." Kicking Bear also went with us, and my father [and] all his sons went to the camp of Big Foot [that] was on the Cheyenne [River] Reservation. The Indians were dancing the Ghost Dance there every day, but it was the same, nothing mysterious would come to any of my father's family.

One day, soon after we came to Big Foot's camp, some soldiers came and camped close by, there were about 500 of them. Big Foot went and counseled with the officer[60] and said to him: "My friend, why do you come and camp so close to me?" The officer said: "You were dancing the Ghost Dance. I am afraid you will do something wrong." Big Foot said: "If my people have guns and do nothing wrong, what harm is it to you or to anybody?" The officer said: "You must not dance the Ghost Dance." Big Foot said: "I go, and will take my people with me, and I do not want you to come after me. We will dance to the Holy Spirit and we will do no harm to anyone." The officer said: "If you go from the reservation you must have a pass for 10 days." Then my father said to the officer: "My friend, do you get a paper from the Great Father at Washington when you pray to the white man's God? I think maybe the Great Spirit does not know you."

When the sun went down, Big Foot called us all together and told us to get ready in secret, and that night we all moved to Cherry Creek and close together in a circle. The next day the soldiers came and camped near us again. Then the officer came to our camp and said to Big Foot: "You had better move back to your camp." Big Foot said: "I and my people are not cattle to be put in a pen. We do not want to go back now." The soldiers moved away. After they were gone Sitting Bull's old people and squaws and children came by riding bareback and we knew there was trouble gathering in Sitting Bull's camp. Big Foot said: "We will go back to our camp so the Great Father will know we do not belong to the bad Indians."

We moved back toward the Cheyenne [River], and many more soldiers came and camped near us. In the nighttime they came, so that when we got up in the morning they had a cannon pointing at our camp and the soldiers stood in a line with the guns in their hands. We came out of our tipi and

60. This officer was Lt. Colonel Edwin V. Sumner, also known as Three Fingers to the Lakotas.

looked at them and while we were looking a half-breed came to us and said the officer wanted to talk with Big Foot.[61]

Big Foot said: "He's welcome to our camp to talk, but why does he point his guns at us? I do not like that."

Then the officer came and said he wanted us to surrender. Big Foot told him that we were not hostiles and asked the officer to give him and his people something to eat and let him have a day to think over this. The officer and some of the headmen talked till afternoon. Big Foot promised the officer he would not go away before morning and that in the morning he would tell him what he would do.

The soldiers stayed nearby all night and in the morning they came in line again. The cannon was pointing at the camp, close by, and the officers sent word to Big Foot [that] he would give him only a very little time to surrender, and that if he did not surrender before the sun was as high as his hand, the soldiers would fire the cannon and shoot the women and the children. Big Foot said to his people: "We will go with this man." We all went with the soldiers. The next day some of the soldiers marched before the Indians and some of them marched behind and some marched alongside of the Indian wagons. Big Foot rode on a pony near the front and said nothing, and all the Indians watched him. In the afternoon he said to one of the braves, "Get ready." The brave rode back by all the Indians, and the squaws threw out the tipi poles one by one and threw away every heavy thing and scattered them for a long way.

The officer said to Big Foot, "Why are your people throwing away their things?" And Big Foot said, "The ponies are weak." When the sun was two fingers high, Big Foot said to the officer, "The ponies can go no farther. We will camp near here where there is good water." All the Indians turned out from among the soldiers and the soldiers looked foolish. By the time the soldiers had all gotten together, the Indians were all together and going up a creek and the soldiers came after them. Then Big Foot said, "We will camp here but do not let one pony get loose." The Indians all unhitched the ponies and built fires and began cooking, and the soldiers came near and stopped, for it was dark.

Then Big Foot told all the Indians who were riding on ponies to put blankets about them so they look like women, and to build small fires. He told

61. The mixed-blood person who came to Big Foot may have been interpreter Felix Benoit. His account can be found in ARSW, 1891, 52nd Cong., 1st Sess., H. Ex. Doc., No. 1, 237–38.

the people in the wagon farthest from the soldiers to move on, and when it was gone a little time he told the next wagon to move on, and so with every wagon until the last. When the last two wagons moved, an under-officer came and asked where the wagons were, and Big Foot told him they had gone to the other side of the camp. He came again and Big Foot told him he would show him the wagons. Big Foot and all the Indians who stayed to build fires went with the under-officer and when he saw them all gather together he ran back shouting that the Indians were attacking.

Then Big Foot told us to ride fast and when we came to the wagons he told them to drive fast, and he went ahead. We drove very fast all that night and were in the Badlands the next day.

A half-breed had told us that the General was at Pine Ridge Agency, and Big Foot said he would go to Red Cloud's camp at the Pine Ridge Agency.[62] We all traveled together. One morning we came to a pass through the wall of the Badlands through which we could go down to the valley of White River, but when we got there we saw soldiers marching in the valley of the White River. We lay in the Badlands all day and watched them, and they camped that night at Cane Creek, north of White River. When they had passed the place where we lay, we went down in the valley and crossed the White River and camped on its banks the same night that the soldiers camped at Cane Creek. These soldiers were looking for us, and we were watching them.

The next morning Big Foot was sick and bleeding at the nose, but we moved on to what is now called Big Foot Springs. The next day we moved to Red Water Creek. Big Foot was so sick he could go no farther, and we stayed there two days and two nights. All the time the young men were watching the soldiers, and saw them come up on the north side of the White River and get farther away from us, and we felt safe from them.

Then Big Foot said, "We will try to get to Red Cloud's camp before I die," and at sundown we broke camp and moved all night and camped on American Horse Creek opposite where [Day] School No. 17 is now, and stayed there all day. The next day we moved up Yellow Thunder Creek and when we came opposite to Porcupine Butte we crossed over to Porcupine Creek and stopped for dinner, when we saw four Indian scouts. We called for them to come to us but they ran away as fast as their horses could go.

62. General John R. Brooke was at Pine Ridge, but General Nelson A. Miles arrived after Wounded Knee.

After noon we hitched up and started toward Porcupine Butte, and when near there, to the northeast of the butte, we saw soldiers coming to the northwest of the butte, and they had pack mules. Big Foot said, "Go and meet the soldiers." The soldiers formed in a line and set a cannon pointing at us, and it looked as if they were about to shoot at us. Then Big Foot said he would go ahead and meet the soldiers and tell them we only wanted to go to Red Cloud's camp at the agency.

Big Foot was so sick that he could not ride on a horse and he had been lying in a wagon ever since we left the Red Water. He had the wagon driven toward the soldiers, and the officer came to meet the wagon. I rode by the wagon with Big Foot and when the officer came near I said, "Do not shoot. We don't want to fight. We want to go to the agency."

The officer said, "Which is Big Foot?" An Indian said, "He is [in] that wagon. He is sick." The officer asked, "Is he able to talk?" The officer ran up to the wagon and pulled the blanket off of Big Foot's head and said, "Can you talk?" Big Foot said, "Yes." The officer said, "Where are you going?" Big Foot said, "We are going to our friends and relations at the Pine Ridge Agency." The officer said, "You will have to lay down your arms, Big Foot."

Big Foot said, "Yes. I am friendly and I will give up my arms. But I am afraid something will happen to me after I do this. Will you not wait until we get to the agency? I will go with you to the agency and my people will give you all their guns when we get to the agency. When we get there we will have a council with the General and we will understand everything. But now I do not understand, and I am afraid something will happen to my people if they give up their guns now. I am sick, and I do not want to have any trouble."

The officer said, "Oh, I am glad to hear this. I have a good wagon here with four mules to draw it and I will put you in it." Big Foot said, "Yes, I will go in your wagon and you may do with me as you wish, but I put my people in your hands, and I wish you would see that no trouble comes on them."[63]

The soldiers brought a sick wagon (ambulance), and four soldiers put Big Foot on two gray blankets like the soldiers have and they carried him and put him in the sick wagon. I was then afraid for Big Foot, for the officers laughed when they put Big Foot in the wagon. Then the soldiers moved

63. For other descriptions of the journey from the Cheyenne River Reservation to Pine Ridge, see Alice Ghost Horse below and Andrew Good Thunder in WSCMC, IULL, box 6, folder 14, envelope 90. See also Greene, *American Carnage*, 191–214.

back toward Wounded Knee Creek with a guard around Big Foot and all the Indians followed.

I said to the medicine man, "My friend, you would better stop and dance the Ghost Dance for I am afraid there will trouble come to Big Foot."

One Indian wanted to shoot the officer but my father told him that that would do no good as the soldiers would only shoot at all the Indians and kill the women and children. Besides, it would only be worse for Big Foot.

I rode close to the soldiers with an Indian who could understand English, for I was troubled at the way the soldiers acted and I wanted to know what they said. We came to Wounded Knee Creek and the soldiers camped. They put Big Foot in a tent and kept him there with guards around him and all the Indians came up and put their tipis close to the camps of the soldiers. When the Indians put up their tipis an under-officer came with soldiers and put them as guards around the Indians.

My father said, "Why do you put guards around us? We would not have followed you if we had wished to run away." But the soldiers only laughed at us. Then my father called me and my brothers and said, "My sons, I am thinking some trouble will come to us. Whatever the soldiers tell you to do, I want you to do it, and do not do anything that will give the soldiers an excuse to do you any harm."

Then some of the Indians wanted to come on to the agency, but the guards turned them back. This made all the Indians very uneasy so that they could not sleep. The guards were changed very often and a fast-shooting cannon was put on a hill nearby and pointed at the camp with the Indians in it. The soldiers were working about this gun and we were afraid they were getting ready to fire on us.

In the night many more soldiers came and with the soldiers were some Indian scouts, but the soldiers would not let the scouts come to us and this made us very much afraid. About midnight, some of the Indians tried to get way to go to the General at the agency, but they found that a great many more guards were placed around us and they could not slip away. When we were told this, we felt that we were prisoners. Some of the soldiers told an Indian who could understand that we were to be disarmed and taken to the railroad and sent far away to the south where the ocean would be all around us.

Nobody in the Indian camp slept much that night except the children, for we were going from tipi to tipi talking about our situation. All agreed to give up their guns if they were asked to do so, but I intended to hide my gun and come and get it again. Some of the young men who had good guns, magazine guns that they had bought, would not say they would or they would not give them up.

Then my father asked the medicine man what he could do and told him that if his Messiah was of any account, now was the time to get his help. But the medicine man was sullen and would only say he would bring help when the time came for it.

When it was coming light the bugles sounded and we all came out and stood watching what the soldiers would do. Then the bugles sounded again and the soldiers surrounded the Indian camp. Some soldiers were on foot and they were nearest the Indians, and some were on horses and they were further away, out around the others. A half-breed named Philip Wells interpreted for the officer and said, "All the Indians get in a ring and there will be a council."[64] Then all the Indians sat in a ring except four men and the women and the children and Big Foot, who was still in the tent under guard.

Then the soldiers came up close around the Indians on three sides and the soldiers on the horses were farther away across a deep ditch. Some of the soldiers were about the cannon on the hill nearby and some were in a line by the camp of the soldiers. Then the interpreter said that the officer wanted the Indians to give up all their arms. An Indian asked what Big Foot said about this and the interpreter said that Big Foot said for the Indians to give up their guns to the officer.

Then the Indians all went into their tipis. I dug a hole in the ground and buried my gun, and when I came out a great many guns were piled nearby where the Indians were sitting. When I sat down there were soldiers behind me and soldiers on both sides of me. I was looking toward the hill at the cannon so I did not feel afraid. Then the officer said, "You have twenty-five more guns and I want you to bring them out. I know that you have more guns for we counted them yesterday. You have plenty of cartridges and knives and I want you to give them all up." But the Indians had piled nearly all their guns in the pile and not more than four or five had hidden their guns.

My father asked the officer, if the Great Father would feed the Indians after he took all the guns away from them. The officer said, "I don't know anything about that. All I know is that I am going to get all the guns, and they are not all in that pile." But the Indians would not bring any more guns.

64. For the statement of Philip Wells, see Jensen, *Voices of the American West*, 1:126–60. See also part 3.

Then one of the four Indians who would not come into the circle at first came and sat down with the rest. The other three were the medicine man and two young men named Black Fox and Yellow Turtle. Black Fox and Yellow Turtle said they would not give up their guns and they held them in their hands. They told the officer they would give up all their cartridges and would carry their guns empty. But the officer said they must give up their guns and that he would go into the tipis and get all the rest of the guns. He went into a tipi and came out and went into another. While he was doing this an under-officer and four soldiers went toward Black Fox and Yellow Turtle who were standing by the tipis. There were soldiers behind them, and they began to walk away from the tipis toward the creek. The medicine man came and stood between the tipis and the Indians and my father said to him, "Give up your gun. Your Ghost [Dance] shirt will be all you need." The medicine man said, "My friend, I am afraid."

Then Philip Wells came and said, "When the soldiers have all your guns, you Indians will all march past them and they will hold out their guns toward you." He meant they would hold their guns in front of them, but the Indians thought they would point their guns and take aim at them. My brother said, "When they point their guns at us they will shoot us." Then my father said to the medicine man, "You told us your Messiah could protect us from the white man's bullets. They will aim their guns at us. Now is the time for your Messiah to help us. See now if he can protect us. You stand there like an old woman."

The officer was talking very excitedly to the soldiers and the medicine man began to sing a prayer to the Great Spirit. Then an under-officer and two soldiers started toward Black Fox and Yellow Turtle. Yellow Turtle said to the soldiers, "My friends, do not come to me in that way for I do not want to hurt you." Then he said to Black Fox, "Now you will see if I am brave. Do not give up your gun." Black Fox said to the soldiers, "Keep away from me. I will die before I will let you have my gun, and if I die I will take some of you with me."

Then some of the Indians said, "They are going to shoot us. Let us get our guns and get to that ditch and get away." Then I looked away from the two young men and an old Indian said, "No, do not do that. It is the interpreter who is making all this trouble. If he brings trouble, I will kill him with my knife."

My father said to the medicine man, "Now is the time for help. Now do your best." Then the medicine man stopped singing and began to cry to the Great Spirit, and gathered up a handful of dust and threw it toward the sky and waved his blanket under the dust, as they did in the Ghost Dance when they call for the Messiah.[65] Just then the officer came out of a tipi with a gun in his hand, and I was looking at it for I thought it was my gun, and I heard a soldier cry out, "Look out! Look out! Run back!" And someone cried out in Indian [Lakota], "Stop! Don't shoot!"

I turned and looked toward Black Fox and Yellow Turtle. They were holding their guns in their hands as if ready to raise them to shoot and were laughing at the under-officer and the two soldiers who were walking away from them very fast and looking back at them as if they were afraid. I was looking down the ditch toward the creek. I heard a gun fire behind me and up the ditch from where the two young men were, and the two soldiers and the under-officer were walking away from the ditch, and not toward where the gun was fired. Immediately, both Black Fox and Yellow Turtle turned and raised their guns and fired toward where I heard the first gunfire.

Then all the Indians jumped up. Some cried that we would all be killed and some cried "Get your guns and get away!" Several shots were fired by the soldiers on both sides of us, and both Black Fox and Yellow Turtle fell. Yellow Turtle began to sing his death song and, raised on his elbow, shot at the soldiers. It appeared to me that all the soldiers began to shoot and I saw Indians falling all around me. I was not expecting anything like this. It was like when a wagon wheel breaks in the road.

An Indian shouted in my ear, "Get your gun!" I was very much frightened and started to run. I saw some soldiers running, and I ran that way. I ran into smoke so thick that I could not see anything. While I was running I took my knife out. The first thing I saw in the smoke was the brass buttons on a soldier's coat. A gun was thrust toward me and fired, and it was so close that it burnt my hair. I grabbed the gun and stabbed at the soldier with my knife. I stabbed him three times and he let go the gun. I tripped and fell and when I got up I found that I was among the soldiers, and I started to run back toward the ditch. I saw some soldiers aiming at me and I felt something hit me in the shoulder and I fell down.

I raised my head and saw a soldier aiming at me, but he missed me. I aimed at him with the gun I had taken from the soldier and snapped it, but I had forgotten to load it, so I quickly began to load it, and the soldier ran away. I began to breathe very hard and every breath hurt me very much. I got up and tried to run but could not, so I walked. I was strangling with something warm in my throat and mouth. I spit it out and looked at it, and it was blood, so I knew that I was shot.

---

65. For comparison, see Alice Ghost Horse below and Black Elk in part 1.

Before I got to the ditch I saw some soldiers coming toward me and I charged toward them, for I thought I was dead anyway. They ran back into the smoke. I went on toward the ditch and came to a dead soldier and I stopped and cut off his belt of cartridges, for the cartridges I had would not fit the gun I had taken from the soldier. I tried to take his gun also, but I was too weak to carry it.

When I started for the ditch again I thought I stepped into a prairie dog hole for I fell, but when I tried to get up I could not do so, and I found that I was shot through the leg. So I sat there and loaded and fired toward the soldiers as fast as I could. When my cartridges were nearly all gone I broke a cartridge in the gun and could not use it any more. I then began to hop toward the ditch, and I could see nothing but dead women and children and dead soldiers among them.

I got into the ditch and an Indian gave me a carbine he had taken from a dead soldier. Then the fast-firing cannon (Hotchkiss) began to fire and I began to crawl up the ditch. I met White Face, my wife, coming down the ditch. She was shot, the ball passing through her chin and shoulder. She said to me, "Let me go, you go on. We will die soon. I will get my mother. That is her body at the top of the bank." She went up to her mother's body and took it under the arms to lift it up when she fell dead, shot again. I came up on the bank for I thought I would as well die quickly.

Just as I got to the top of the bank, an Indian pulled me back, and as I fell back he was shot through the head. I took his cartridges, as they suited the carbine I had, and I started up the ditch again. I saw a woman coming toward me with a revolver in her hand. It looked like [a] soldier's revolver and I think she took if from a soldier, for she was very bloody. I started toward her and I saw some soldiers peep over the bank and shoot her. I shot at them and they ran back. I crawled up the ditch as fast as I could and I came to White Lance, my brother. He was sitting against the bank and another brother, Pursued, was lying by him. They were both wounded and Pursued was almost dead. He said, "My brothers, we will all be dead soon. But you must kill as many as you can before you die." They had three belts of cartridges taken from soldiers. When we saw that Pursued was dead, we went behind a little knoll where the ditch turns and where we could see the soldiers, and we fired at the soldiers. I looked and saw the Hotchkiss aiming at us. White Lance and I lay down close behind the knoll and the dirt and gravel scattered over us, thrown up by the Hotchkiss cannon. I got very sick and weak and thirsty and could shoot no more.

I could hear the soldiers coming close by me, and I saw a soldier peep over the bank. I fired at him, but I was too weak to take aim. The soldiers ran back and they fired the Hotchkiss again, and a shot from it cut Hawk Feather almost in two. Some soldiers were on a hill not far from the cannon, and they shot at me also. One of their bullets struck so near me that it threw the gravel in my face and I thought I was shot again. I lay very still and after a little while all quit shooting at me.

White Lance had gone on up the ditch and after a while I crawled on up the ditch to look for him. While I was crawling an Indian scout shot at me, and then ran away. I felt very sick and wanted to die as I crawled on top of the bank and shot at some soldiers, but I was too weak to stand up. They fired the Hotchkiss gun at me again and the balls passed very close to me so that I could almost feel the wind from the balls lift me from the ground. But I was too sick to stand up, so I lay very still. After a long time all the firing stopped. I crawled over the top of the hill and my brother, Yell At Them, and Jack LaPlant came to me with a horse, but I could not ride so they put their arms around me and took me away. But I was so sick I told my brother to go and leave me, but he said, "We have started for the agency and we will go there together or we will die together."

Then some of the Oglala Sioux came to us and they told us that all the Indians had gone from the agency to the hostiles' camp with Short Bull. So I went to Short Bull's camp, but when I got there I found that the Indians were not all there. But I was so badly wounded I could be taken no farther then. I learned while there that my father, whose name was Horn Cloud, my mother, whose name was Yellow Leaf, my wife, whose name was White Face, my child, whose name was White Foot, my brother, whose name was Pursued, and my sister, whose name was Her Horses had all been killed in the fight, and that my two brothers, White Lance and Enemy, were wounded.

When Big Foot was in the Badlands we were very much closer to the camp of the hostile Indians than we were to the agency, and I sometimes think that if we had all gone and joined the hostiles instead of trying to go to the agency, my people would not have been shot down like wolves. But I remembered my father's words, and as soon as I could be hauled without danger to my life I was taken from Short Bull's camp and finally came to the agency.

Alice Ghost Horse

"The Ghost Dance was like Sun Dance."

Alice Ghost Horse dictated her story of the Ghost Dance and the Wounded Knee massacre in the Lakota language to her son, John War Bonnet. Alice Ghost Horse was thirteen years old at the time of the Wounded Knee Massacre, escaping with her mother and a younger brother. Her father and another younger brother were killed. This account was kept in the family until 1979, when a relative gave it to the Lakota language instructor Stanley Keith to be translated into English. Alice Ghost Horse's story was included in the congressional hearings for the possible establishment of a Wounded Knee national park and memorial.[66] This story is a valuable source for understanding how Big Foot and his people ended up at Wounded Knee and how some of the survivors made their way into safety afterwards. It is also rare as the events are told from the point of view of a young girl.

We were camped at the mouth of Cherry Creek, last part of December 1890. I was 13 years old at the time. There was my father (Ghost Horse) and my mother (Alice Her Shawl) and two younger brothers. The *wičháša itháŋčhaŋ* (leader) was Spotted Elk (Big Foot).[67] Up the creek was Hump and his followers. Our people were scattered all up and down the Cheyenne River toward Bridger, S.D., a place called Takini (barely surviving). They lived farthest away but they were all Hohwojus, just as we are all Minneconjous (Hohwoju).[68]

Rest of the Lakotas were already assimilated with the whites out toward east end and were already under military rule. They were being trained to be farmers and were given land to plant things.

At this time, my people were Ghost Dancing above Plum Creek, straight

---

66. *Hearing Before the Select Committee on Indian Affairs*, U.S. Senate, 102nd Cong., 1st Sess., April 30, 1991 (Testimony of Alice Ghost Horse), (Washington, D.C.: Government Printing Office, 1991), 58–69.

67. Big Foot (Sí Tȟáŋka) was also known as Spotted Elk.

68. Hoȟwóžu is a term sometimes used for the Mnikȟówožu or Minneconjou Lakotas.

east of Cherry Creek across the river. We went up there when they have the dances but children were not allowed in, so my brothers and I play near the wagons.[69] The dances usually last for four days and quite a few camp up there during that time. We usually go [went] back to Cherry Creek when they get [got] through.

The agent at Fort Bennet (Cheyenne Agency) was a military officer and he would send Lakota scouts to the camp to ask questions about the Ghost Dance.[70]

The Ghost Dance was like Sun Dance, which was held once a year about August. In the Ghost Dance they form a circle, holding hands and they dance stationary, not like the Sun Dance, but they sing and dance. [The dance] usually starts at almost sundown and lasts for [a] couple hours. They do this till someone falls or several fall, they wait till they tell what they saw or hear during their trance. The purpose of the dance was to see their dead relatives and converse with them, and they continue.

One day some people came from Standing Rock and told Big Foot that Sitting Bull was shot and killed by Indian Police, provoked by the agent.

Big Foot decided they should flee to Pine Ridge. They thought that Sitting Bull was killed because of the Ghost Dance; on short notice, it was decided to move out the very next day so they all staked out their horses close by and all went to bed.[71]

Next day, we packed up in a hurry that morning and we were ready to move out. I was on my horse and my two brothers rode in the wagon. My mother rode in the back with the youngest brother and the other one rode up front with my father. We had an extra horse tied to the team. This one can be rode or used as one of the team.

69. This contradicts what Short Bull says about children being allowed to participate. According to Short Bull, even children received visions. But both Robert P. Higheagle and Alice Ghost Horse maintain that children were not allowed to participate. Perhaps it was a question of age, smaller children not being allowed in the dance circle, but even so, one would imagine that a girl of thirteen would have been old enough to dance.

70. By late December, Captain J. J. Hurst was in effect in charge of Fort Bennett and the Cheyenne River Agency. He sent Lieutenant Harry E. Hale, accompanied by Hump (who had recently abandoned the Ghost Dance) and Indian policeman White Thunder, to discuss the situation with Big Foot and assure him that there was no danger. Utley, *Last Days of the Sioux Nation*, 176.

71. For more on Big Foot and his decision to go to Pine Ridge, see Joseph Horn Cloud, Dewey Beard, ESRMC, NSHS, box 4, tablet 12, box 5, tablet 30, also published in Richard A. Jensen, *Voices of the American West* (Lincoln: University of Nebraska

We crossed Cherry Creek at the mouth where it empties in the river. We were to follow the wagon trails that went west all along the river, on the north side. The old wagon trails lead to Takini.

We ran all the way, bottom of the river and stopped half way to water the horses and cook something to eat. My mother had some pemmican, which we all shared before we continue[d] on toward Takini.

Late afternoon, we pulled into Takini amid clusters of lean-tos and tents. Most of them were getting ready for winter, by looking at the wood piles. Some had stacks of wood piled high; after we put up our tents my mother started her cooking, she had good soup and kabubu bread and hot government coffee. After a hearty meal my mother and my father went to a meeting at Big Foot's tent so my brothers and I went down to the river and played for a while and came to bed.

The next morning, I heard my father hitching up the horses, so I got up and saddled my own horse and was ready to go. I plan[ned] to ride all the way to Pine Ridge.

First wagon to leave was Big Foot's wagon, followed by all his relatives. All the horsebacks and some were walking for a time up the hill. We fell in, about the middle of the wagon train and were headed up a long hill last side of the river. I looked back and I could see more wagons joining in and coming and many children were on horseback, too. It was a sight to see. It was also exciting because we were running from the military.

We ran like this all morning without stopping. Sometimes, some riders would fall back to check on us at the request of Big Foot. By noon, we stopped to rest but we were not allowed to start a fire so we ate what little mother had for us. In a short while, we were again on our way with Big Foot

---

Press, 2006), 1:191–226. According to Dewey Beard, Big Foot decided to go to Pine Ridge after receiving a letter from Red Cloud, No Water, and Big Road. The letter said: "My Dear Friend Chief Big Foot. Whenever you receive this letter I want you to come at once. Whenever you come to our reservation a fire is going to be started and I want you to come and help us to put it out and make peace. Whenever you come among us to make a peace we will give you 100 head of horses." Dewey Beard, ESRMC, NHS, box 5, tablet 30; Jensen, *Voices of the American West*, 1:209. See also Dewey Beard's account above. According to Philip Wells, Red Cloud and other chiefs later denied inviting Big Foot. See Wells, "Ninety-Six Years among the Indians of the Northwest," 293. Studies that reconstruct the events in Big Foot's camp and their subsequent escape are, for example, Utley, *Last Days of the Sioux Nation*, 173–99; Andersson, *Lakota Ghost Dance of 1890*, 88–92; Greene, *American Carnage*, 196–201.

and his wagons still leading the way. We were trotting all the way, southerly direction, keeping to the low areas, valleys and creek beds.

My younger brother sat in the back with my mother who kept an eye on me. The other brother rode up front as before. The extra horse was still tied to the side of the team.

By mid-afternoon, the going was tough, but we went below Porcupine Butte still keeping in the draws and gullies. Sometimes there was no trail so the going was really rough in the wagons.

Sometime later, the head wagons stopped on top of a hill and they were all looking down at something. My father went to see, and my mother came over and started to tighten my cinch and said, there were some cavalry camped below on Wounded Knee Creek. She told me, we might have to make a run for it and she asked me to stay close to the wagon.

My father returned and said Big Foot was very sick and laying in the back of the buggy all bundled up. My father said they picked some men to go down and talk to the officers.

I saw four riders riding down toward the center of the camp where they have big guns on wheels. One of the riders had a white flag, a white material tied to a stick riding in front of the other three riders. Soon as they cross the Creek, all the soldiers laid down and aim their rifles at them but they kept on going and arrived at the big gun on wheels, where there were some soldiers and officers standing. They dismounted and they had a short talk.

A lone rider galloped up the hill to Big Foot's wagon and they told him that the officers wanted to talk to him but his relatives said "no," that he was very sick, so the rider went back to tell them.

Sometime later, a buggy was sent up with a doctor to examine the old man. The doctor said he had pneumonia. He gave him some medicine and they loaded him in the special wagon and took him down.

They talked a long time and finally a lone rider came back and told them [us] to camp along the creek on the west side of the creek.

Everyone pitched their tents as ordered and pretty soon an army wagon was coming along the camp, issued bacon, flour, coffee beans, army beans and hard tacks.

By sundown, we were completely surrounded by foot soldiers, all with rifles. My mother and I went down to the creek to pick up some wood and to go to the bathroom, but two soldiers followed us, so we hurried back with some sticks.

Everyone went to bed as they were all tired from the hectic trip. Some of the young men stayed up all night to watch the soldiers. Some of the soldiers were drunk, saying bad things about the Lakota women.[72] Early next morning, a bugle woke us up. I went outside and noticed all the soldiers were gone but there was [a] lot of activity at the military camp.

We ate in a hurry because most of the Lakotas were loading their wagons and my father had the horses and he was saddling my horse.

At this time, a crier was making his way around the Lakota camp, telling the men folks to go to the center for more talks, so they dropped everything and left but the women folks continued to pack their belongings in the wagon. I was on my horse just standing there. In a little while, there seem[ed] to be an argument at the confrontation which developed into a shouting match. Pretty soon, some cavalry men rode in from the center at a fast gallop and they started to search the wagons for axes, knife, guns, bow and arrows, and awls. They were really rude about it, they scattered the belongings all over the ground.

The soldiers picked up everything they could find and tied them up in a blanket and took them. They also searched the Lakotas in the center. They emptied contents on the ground in the center, in front of the officers and continued to argue with the Lakotas but the Lakotas did not give in.

During the heated discussion, a medicine man by the name of Yellow Bird appeared from nowhere and stood facing the east, right by the fire pit which was now covered with fresh dirt. He was praying and crying. He was saying to the eagles that he wanted to die instead of his people. He must sense that something was going to happen. He picked up some dirt from the fire place and threw it up in the air and said this is the way he wanted to go back . . . to dust.[73]

At this time there were cavalry men all on bay horses all lined up on top of the hill on the north side. One officer rode down toward the center at a full gallop. He made a fast halt and shouted something to his commanding officers and retreated back up on the hill and they all drew their rifles and long knife (swords) and you can hear them load it with bullets.

<hr />

72. There has been extensive discussion about the possible misuse of alcohol by the officers and perhaps the regular soldiers alike. See, for example, Utley, *Last Days of the Sioux Nation*, 199; Greene, *American Carnage*, 218–19. Indian accounts maintain that the soldiers were drunk the night before the massacre. Several Indian accounts can be found in James H. McGregor, *The Wounded Knee Massacre: From the Point of View of the Sioux* (Rapid City: Fensek Printing 1997).

73. See the account of Dewey Beard above.

In the meantime, some more cavalrymen lined up on the south side. A big gun was also aimed down toward the center and toward where we were. I heard the first shot coming from the center followed by rifles going off all over; occasionally a big boom came from the big guns on wheels.[74] The Lakotas were all disarmed so all they could do was scatter in all directions.

The two cavalry groups came charging down, shooting at everyone who is running and is a Lakota.

My father made it back to our wagon and my horse was trying to bolt, so he told me to jump so I got off and the horse ran for all its worth toward the creek. We fled to the ravine, where there was lots of plum bushes and dove into the thicket. The gunfire was pretty heavy and people were hollering for their children. With children crying everywhere, my dad said he was going to go out to help the others; my mother objected but he left anyway. Pretty soon, my father came crawling back in and he was wounded below his left knee and he was bleeding. He took my youngest brother who was 6 years old and he said he was taking him further down the river.

Soon, he came crawling back in and said, "*Huŋhuŋhé, mičhíŋkši kté peló*."[75] He had tears in his eyes so we cried a little bit because there was no time to think. My father said we should crawl further down but my mother said it's better we die here together, and she told me to stand up so I did, but my father pulled me down.

With a little effort, we were able to crawl to a bigger hiding place. Bullets were whistling all around us but my father went out again to help. He never came back for a long time.

Some people crawled in. They were all wounded. I recognized Phillip Black Moon and his mother. They were okay. More women and children came crawling in. The young ones were whimpering, groups at intervals came in. Four of the wounded died right there but there was nothing anyone can do.

A man named Breast Plate (Wawóslal Wanáp'iŋ) came in and told us that my father was killed instantly. We all cried but for a short while lest we would be heard.

Charge in Kill and Ništúšte (Black Hip) came in later but they left again. They were brave. It seemed like eternity but actually it didn't last that

---

74. These were four Hotchkiss guns that had been placed on the hill overlooking the camp.

75. *Huŋhuŋhé* is an expression that can be used in a mixed way to show emotions. *Mičhíŋkši kté peló* translates to "My son is dead!"

long. It was getting late; toward sundown more people staggered in. It got dark, and the shooting stopped all of a sudden and we heard a wagon moving around, probably to pick up their dead, killed in the crossfire. None of the Lakotas had guns so they were engaged in a hand to hand combat. At a given signal we all got up, those who could, and walked or limped to the north, tip-toeing our way through creek beds and ravines. Occasionally, we stumbled over dark objects which turn[ed] out to be dead animals or sometimes dead Lakotas. We heard a child crying for water someplace in the dark, cold night; many more wounded were crying for help.

We walked in the creek bed a ways north, it must have been Wounded Knee Creek, where we separated into four groups, each to take different routes, to [have a] better chance of escaping. By morning, our group reached a hill. From there can see long ways. We stopped there, being careful to find whatever cover there was, by trees. We had traveled mostly a northwesterly direction all night, for the sun up showed the plains and more level landscape to the east. The higher buttes and pine-covered hills to the west. The sky showed polka-dotted white puffs with blue background, changing patterns by the wind strong enough to make eyes water. We had two boys to go stay up the hill to watch for soldiers in all directions. "A rider is following our trails," the boys hollered down, and like cottontails we dove deeper into the ravine among the brushes and trees. But it turn[ed] out some moments later it was a Lakota wearing a woman's scarf. It was Ništúšte (Black Hips) whom we met earlier. After we shook hands with him, we all cried. He told us that after the shooting he escaped to Pine Ridge and found all the Oglalas had run away toward the hills. He had stayed up on the hills while scouting the Pine Ridge encampment. He then walked back to Wounded Knee where he found his horse, luckily catching it. He then started tracking our trails northward hoping to meet up with somebody. He insisted that our group go with him back toward Pine Ridge.

Before our group could decide which way to go, some more riders appeared so [we] took off for the creek to hide. But this one man stayed behind, and they rode in yelling "We are Lakotas, do not run." They dismounted at the sight of the four Lakota people, all got up there and shook hands with them. One woman and three men, we all cried. We hadn't eaten anything since we left Wounded Knee a day and [a] half earlier. They had some pemmican which they shared with us. One of the men said there were cattle foraging over the hill, that he was going after one; the other two men who had rode in with him went with him. Soon they brought in a quarter of beef; one lady did the cooking from a pail and dishes she had gotten from a deserted log house not far from there. We really ate for once, thanks to the men and the nice lady. Ništúšte (Black Hips) and the three men rode back toward Wounded Knee, but the woman stayed with us. That left us with 13 people, mostly women and children. I was with my mother and brother, a lady who had her braids cut off—she was slightly wounded, a lady that always carried a little one on her back, and there was Alex High Hawk, Blue Hair, and five members of the Many Aprons family, were all there that night.

Next morning, we got ready to leave and found Dog Chasing with two women had come in sometime during the night. The men who rode out must have sent them in. With them upping our number to 16. We left bright and early, the men walking ahead a little way. Very good fortune it was, for I was again riding a horse with my little brother, and my mother on foot, was leading the horse.

Along the way, I must have dozed off and on, half asleep, half awake. I didn't know anything for a while. When I became clear headed again, we were heading down a hill. Down at the bottom of the valley stood a log house with even a wooden floor and a fireplace which they fired up and we rested and got warmed up. Some daylight left, we started off again covering some miles before dark. It started to cloud up, clouds rolling in from the west and the north, cloud waves seeming to roll over the hills and valleys like water, from misty fine drops somewhere closer to a drizzle. It started then, the wind came. Some minutes later it turned into a blizzard, but one of the men had steered us toward a cabin, which he had spotted from a butte some miles back. This blessed haven we reached along a creek, so we stayed warm sitting out the storm. We had plenty of meat from the last butchering to keep us fed. Later in the night, their voices woke me up, loud voices, high pitched women arguments to scatter or stay together, the calmer voices of the male, sometimes whispering as we listened. I sat up in a hurry when a new meaning came to my senses. I got scared for the first time. My heart was beating faster, my breathing becoming shorter and harder. Quickly moving closer to my mother and squirming closer to my mother's body was to me natural as a cottontail jumping from danger into its lair. The noise the women thought they heard was maybe a rumbling of horse running or of buffalo stampeding, maybe even cavalrymen. But it turned out that they may have heard something they imagined their fears into loud noises. For some time we just sat there, staring at the darkness, only the occasional, flickering firelight and dying embers to see by. During the night, riders went some place and later they came back and they said in a low voice, "It is time to go." No one complained, all acted on instinct to survive. It was still cloudy and dark when we left the cabin. The men loaned us their horses so some of us rode double. Sometimes the snow would blow, but we kept on moving into a deep draw, where the wind wasn't blowing that much. So, we kept to the low lands.

Finally, we stumbled into a camp of Oglalas who ran away from Pine Ridge during the shooting. They were camped in a nice place among the pine trees. At the end of the camp we came across Short Bull's tent. All of the people came to welcome us in, and the rest of the group were all taken into different tents and were all fed good. We stayed at this camp for three months, and the sun kept coming out higher and higher. Soon the snow was melting and all knew it was spring.[76]

One day a rider came into the camp and said there was going to be a meeting (treaty) at Pine Ridge. Next day, early as usual, we headed for Pine Ridge again. It must be quite a ways because we camped in a deep gully.

When we started out again the next day, it was a long caravan of buggys, travois, horseback and on foot. The chiefs were walking in front, followed by young warriors on horseback.

Over the last hill we could see many tents and cavalry all over the place, dust was flying, horses were tied to hitching posts face to face.

We made camp near the post. Čháŋ Ȟakáka [perhaps Čhaŋȟáhake] (Plenty Limbs) and Iron Thunder came to the camp and said they came after all the Hoȟwóžus, Cheyenne River people, who were wounded or deceased, that they belonged to our band.

In Pine Ridge, my mother reluctantly signed our names as survivors, along with the rest of the family.

They pitched up 3 big tipis in the center where they told us to go. I remember there was Black Moon and his mother and brothers. Iron Horn and Wood Pile was there. There were many Hoȟwóžus that showed up at the tipi. Even some we thought had been killed. Ashes was a young girl then, she was there, too. I noticed other people, were Blue Hair, Axe, Brown Eagle, and Čáŋ Ȟakáka (Plenty Limbs).

We left for Hoȟwóžu country toward Cherry Creek. We were traveling in five wagons, one wagon was loaded with oats and hay, another one of rations, one wagon full of soldiers was leading the way as escorts, out of

76. Although this sentence implies that Alice Ghost Horse and the rest of the people stayed camped in this particular place for three months, she most likely means that they stayed with these people in their camp for three months even though they all came to the Pine Ridge Agency to surrender on January 15, 1891. The other possibility is that she meant three weeks instead of three months, but that would still make the time frame inaccurate.

Pine Ridge in a different direction so we won't have to go through Wounded Knee.

Despite all these nice things being done for us, I can't forget what happened at Wounded Knee. Some nights I cried thinking about it, many months afterwards. I have never touched a white man during my lifetime. I just can't trust any white man and never will because they killed my father and brother for no reason at all.

Aleck Mousseau

"They join hands in a circle and dance until they drop."

Aleck Mousseau gave a lengthy explanation about the origin of the Ghost Dance to the *Omaha Daily Bee* on November 21, 1890. The article was written by *Bee* correspondent Charles Cressey and was entitled "Aleck and the Messiah: how the craze was introduced to Pine Ridge Agency."[77] Mousseau reflects upon how the Ghost Dance came to Pine Ridge and what the ceremony meant. His story is similar to those of the Ghost Dance believers, like Short Bull or Pretty Eagle, but his description of a substance that was to be thrown down on the ground to cause various natural phenomena has not been mentioned elsewhere. The "red substance" he mentions was most likely red paint that was considered sacred in the Ghost Dance, but other accounts do not mention its power to affect natural phenomena.

Aleck: "Three months ago two men returned to Pine Ridge Agency from the Messiah. They belonged to the agency. The name of one is Brave Bear and the name of the other I don't remember. They met the Messiah way up in the mountains and told me about him, Brave Bear did not believe in the Messiah, but the other man did. Brave Bear said he thought the Messiah work[ed] with sleight of hand.[78]

---

77. Aleck Mousseau in *Omaha Daily Bee*, November 21, 1890, p. 1.
78. Despite Brave Bear's claim that he did not believe in the Messiah, he was among the Lakota delegation that met Wovoka and also one of the leaders in the White Clay Creek Ghost Dance camp mentioned by Young Skunk and Pretty Eagle (see part 1).

Question: "What did the Messiah do when he was called upon?"

Aleck: "He immediately told them that he had come to deliver them. He showed them his hands and pointed out marks on them. He then showed them where he had been cut on the feet, he then gave them something red, and he took a piece of it and marked a cross upon their foreheads between their eyes. He then gave them something else: I don't know what it is, but it was to show them or to help them to show their friends that his preaching was true. When they would reach home they were to tell their people that they had seen the Messiah and that he had come to save them. If their people did not believe them, they were to throw the second substance he had given them on the ground. The substance when thrown on the ground because [would cause] whatever disturbance they wanted in the elements. They could thus cause rain, hail, wind or fire, and this were to convince their people that the Messiah's powerful.

There was another thing. The red substance which he gave them could not to be destroyed. The more it was used the more they secured of it. Brave Bear said this was a trick and he wouldn't believe in it.

The Messiah was dressed in buckskin and Brave Bear couldn't tell whether he was an Indian or a half-breed, he said, as he talked Indian just as well as he did. Brave Bear told me that when he saw the Messiah he and his friend fell right down. Brave Bear has lost his sister, beautiful daughter, and when he fell down the Messiah said he had gone to heaven and he would there see both of them.

Question: "Did Brave Bear tell you he had seen them?"

Aleck: "Yes he said he'd be in this way only for a minute just as they were passing. Brave Bear admitted [that he] still held that it was some sleight of hand work. And he and his companion went back to Pine Ridge and told all the people what they saw. Since then they have been dance [dancing]. They dance during the day and night. They join hands in a circle and dance until they drop. Then the medicine man says they have gone to heaven. They let them remain there until they get up themselves and then they tell all what they have seen. They see their friends, wives and everything. Some time they never get up because they are dead. They die because they kill themselves dancing.[79] They dance because they are told there is to be a slide of

79. There are actually no reliable sources that would corroborate that people really died during the ceremony.

the earth and that slide is to cover up the white man, and to keep themselves on top of the crust they must keep dancing.

Question: "Who direct[s] the dance?"

Aleck: The medicine man, the one who went with Brave Bear to see the Messiah. He believes in it, and just before they begin to dance he makes a cross on the forehead of every man who dances.

Question: "Do you believe in the Messiah?"

Aleck: "Oh, no!"

Baptiste Pourier

"The Indians have been dancing but that does not signify that they want to murder white settlers or fight soldiers."

Baptiste Pourier was known as "Big Bat" by the Lakotas. Big Bat gave an interview to the *Omaha Daily Bee* on November 25, 1890.[80] Pourier has a very practical approach to the Ghost Dance. He does not expect any kind of outbreak or depredation, and the Indians know that there is no place for them to go if fighting were to begin. What might cause trouble, predicts Pourier, would be an attempt to disarm the Indians.

"The Indians have been dancing but that does not signify that they want to murder white settlers or fight soldiers."

Being asked if the Indians would peacefully stop the dance and surrender their arms, he said they undoubtedly would if it was demanded of them.

"I don't think they care much about giving up the dance, but they would kick some on giving up their guns. They would not fight for their guns, though."

Question: "Are many of them armed?"

"Yes, about two thirds of the males, but they do not want to fight. I attended a council of the dancers night before last when they discussed all these matters, and the leaders' speeches to the young bucks were all to the effect that, while they could easily wipe out the troops now on hand, if they

80. Baptiste Pourier in *Omaha Daily Bee*, November 25, 1890, p. 1. The same article was published in the *New York Times*, November 26, 1890, p. 1.

did so there would be 10 soldiers there next day where there was only one the day before, and it would only be a question of days until the last Indian would die. 'Besides,' they said, 'where would we go. We are surrendered on all sides by soldiers and settlers, we have no provisions for a campaign and would surely starve, and our squaws and papooses would perish before our eyes.' The whole council united in advising and agreeing to submit peacefully to whatever the government demanded."

Philip Wells

"There is no telling what will grow out of it in the near future."

Philip Wells's letter of October 19, 1890, to Agent James McLaughlin is in the Walter Stanley Campbell Collection and was initially published in Stanley Vestal, *New Sources of Indian History.*[81] Wells essentially warns McLaughlin of the dangers the Ghost Dance presents. He also warns him of Kicking Bear, but his warning came too late. Kicking Bear had arrived at Standing Rock on October 9, and by the time Well's letter reached McLaughlin, the dances were already started in Sitting Bull's camp, and the agent had taken steps to stop the dancing. Philip Wells was clearly of the opinion that the Ghost Dance was dangerous as even some of the "best Indians are nearly crazy over it."

United States Indian Service
Pine Ridge Agency, South Dakota
October 19, 1890
James McLaughlin, U.S. Indian Agent
Standing Rock Agency, North Dakota

Dear Major: Pardon me for the privilege I take in asking you some questions in regard to your Indians taking part in the new religious craze the Ghost Dance, or what is known as the coming of [the] Messiah next spring. Are your Indians practicing it to such an extent

---

81. Philip F. Wells to James McLaughlin, October 19, 1890, WSCMC, WHCUOLA, box 114, folder 6, 40. Published by permission of University of Oklahoma Libraries. Published also in Vestal, *New Sources,* 5–7. On the back of the letter the date is October 10.

that you anticipate any difficulty in suppressing it, or what in your opinion would be the best means of stopping it? The reason I ask, is our Indians are getting so crazy over it that it is certainly getting serious, as they are defying the police force, and from what I can learn the Rosebud Indians are worse than ours, and there is no telling what will grow out of it in the near future. Some time ago Colonel [Hugh D.] Gallagher, myself and a lot of police went to the place of dancing to stop it but they had stopped before we got there, but the Indians were laying in ambush for us, all armed and striped for fighting, and as we rode up they drew their guns on us, but the Colonel told the police to stand back in readiness and walked into their midst and ordered them to lay down their guns; a few of the leaders who were in sight did so, we found out before we left there that the woods was full of armed Indians.[82]

I am telling you this that you can see the magnitude the craze has taken, if it will be any service to you to know. Dr. D. F. Royer our new agent took charge this week, but I think he has got an elephant on his hands, as the craze had taken such a hold on the Indians before he took charge. As yet I have all hopes he will be able to stop it without any serious trouble. If you will kindly give me your valuable opinion on the subject, you will confer a great favor on me and it will be confidently kept by me, so far as getting any information from you, if you so desire it. I will at any time cheerfully give you any information on the subject you desire.

As yet we have not been paid for last quarter. Now there is no likelihood of it before the last of this month and so far as I know there are no appointments made yet, as yet there is no certainty about my being kept on, but I think I am solid. Tom Reey is hanging on a balance now and is undecided which way to fall, whether he will quit the Indian service or not as we have all been kept in uncertainty since July 1st.

The Colonel will move to Chadron, Nebraska next week to remain there for the winter.

Frank Young got married last Sunday to a very nice half-breed girl of this place.

82. This incident took place on Pine Ridge Reservation on September 22. See introduction and Philip Wells's statement below.

Both Tom's & my family are all well.

Give my warmest regards to Mrs. McLaughlin & children and except the same yourself.

Yours sincerely

P. F. Wells

P.S. While on my way to mail this to you, I met Amos Ross a half-breed missionary who was just from Stand-rock [Standing Rock] convocation. He came through Cheyenne Agency and he learned there that Matȟó Wanáȟtake [Kicking Bear] the Indian who is the origination of all this trouble is going amongst your Indians to start it there; if you can nab him before he can get them started, you will save yourself no end to trouble. I say this because you or anyone else can have no idea how bad it takes hold of the Indians as some of our best Indians are nearly crazy over it.

Yours etc.

P. F. Wells

Philip Wells

"This rank, religious delusion gained its foothold among the Indians."

Eli S. Ricker interviewed Philip Wells on October 6, 1906. Wells turned out to be a good source of information for various topics of Lakota history, including the Ghost Dance and Wounded Knee. The following is Wells's statement about the Ghost Dance.[83] Wells was well informed about the origins of the Ghost Dance and his description of the ceremony is quite similar to other eyewitness accounts.

---

83. Philip F. Wells in ERMC, NSHS, tablets 4–5. Published in Jensen, *Voices of the American West*, 1:126–63. I have decided to leave Wells's account of the Wounded Knee Massacre out, as it is separate from his discussion of the Ghost Dance, which is more relevant for this study. As noted in part 1, the Ricker collection is very difficult to use because Ricker at times used shorthand notes, then polished the text later. Thus, it is at times difficult to say if it is Ricker who "speaks" or the interviewee. I have therefore used the transcribed copies held at the American Indian Studies Research Institute with

This rank, religious delusion gained its foothold among the Indians early in the year 1890. In the previous year Short Bull, of the Brulé band of the Sioux, a Rosebud Indian, and Kicking Bear, formerly of the Minneconjou band of the Sioux of the Cheyenne River Reservation, a renegade and a vagrant Indian and a Pine Ridge Indian bearing the nickname of "Sells-the-Pistol" (Red Star, Dr. Walker has it) hearing of the so-called Messiah who was said to be living near Walker Lake, Utah [Nevada] went there for the purpose of seeing him and bringing back word to the people of his remarkable revelations and powers.[84]

They returned early in 1890. (In 1896 when the Little Wound delegation was elected to visit Washington, Short Bull had some ambition to be chosen as one of the delegates, and in the council a speaker taunted him by telling him that he was the man who once went away and returned with news which had brought direful results. Short Bull replied by saying, "Why speak to me of that? Didn't we talk of that secretly, and you chose me to go? Whatever has come of it, you are as much to blame as I." Mr. Wells was in the council and heard this and he says no refutation of Short Bull's statement was offered. It is therefore admitted by the council that these three men went with the secret approval of the Indians.)[85]

On the return of these men in March Short Bull went to the Rosebud Reservation and set about organizing the Ghost Dance among the Indians there, and Kicking Bear and "Sells-the-Pistol" began the same work on Pine Ridge Reservation.

They brought back word that the Messiah spoke miraculously the languages of all Indians who come to him. They had to approach him with certain elaborate ceremonies. He fed all his visitors. Many different versions

---

their permission and compared those to the texts published in vol. 1 of Jensen, *Voices of the American West*. There are no major differences. For readability, I have left out the sentences that Ricker struck through, but included the text he put in parentheses. Philip Wells gave a testimony of Wounded Knee for the army investigation of the Wounded Knee battle for the so-called Kent-Baldwin Report. See "Report of Investigations into the Battle at Wounded Knee Creek, South Dakota, Fought December 29, 1890," NARA, RG 94, AIWKSC, M983, roll 1, vol. 2, 651–1134.

84. Sells the Pistol was not a member of the delegation, at least not according to Short Bull. See part 1.

85. It is noteworthy that the council also included "progressive" chiefs like Young Man Afraid of His Horses. As Short Bull notes, he was selected by all the chiefs to go. For comparison, see Short Bull in part 1.

of his teachings were given, but the one most generally circulated was that a heavy cloud would appear in the west and pass to the east, and all white men would be destroyed by it, and all Indians who did not believe and participate in the Ghost Dance would be destroyed along with the whites. But all Indians who believed and wore the Ghost [Dance] shirt and took part in the Ghost Dance would rise above the cloud and escape destruction. Following this cloud there would be a new earth, with all their dead relatives restored to life, and the buffalo and the game would also return.

The Messiah had exhibited to all who went to see him, the nail-prints in his hands and feet and the spear wound in his side, of the crucified Savior, inflicted by the white man; and because the white men had crucified the Savior they would be destroyed and because the Indians had had no part in the crucifixion they would be shown mercy and be saved. The Messiah prescribed the pattern of a shirt which was called Ghost [Dance] shirt, which all believers should wear in the dance; and he also prescribed a song which was to be sung in the dance.

The converts assembled and went into camp. Prior to the dance each one performed the act of purification necessary to make himself fit for the sacred performance by passing through the sweat bath.[86] The first step in the dance was to clasp hands and circle to the left, each jerking one another's hands forward and backward, and singing and dancing, with eyes averted to the skies. The dance would proceed for hours—five or six hours—until nearly all had fallen in trance. They would begin falling; within [before] half an hour had elapsed the ground would be strewn with the prostrate forms of dancers. This was kept up until the few who were not conquered by their frantic exertions would give up from sheer exhaustion. During the performance the dancers became wrought up to a high pitch of excitement and went through various indescribable contortions, singing meanwhile the song prescribed by the Messiah, and when going into trance uttered unearthly moans and groans and all manner of utterance and noise, the most inconceivable discord and tumult smiting the ear, while they clawed the air and flung froth from their mouths, the numerous performers in the stygian concert keeping the regular cadence of step and motion to the music, the trancers only breaking into these accents which baffle description.

Such as succumbed would lie apparently unconscious from ten minutes to three-quarters of an hour when they would rise without help. After the dance was over the leaders would call the trancers together and hold a sort

---

86. See Short Bull, Pretty Eagle, and Young Skunk in part 1 for "old camp men" smelling bad, thus requiring purification.

of class-meeting when each would describe his vision. Some realized nothing. Others would relate how they had seen departed relatives, or buffaloes, and various game animals, or had heard or seen buffaloes or other animals passing in the air, or a buffalo or a grizzly bear had conversed with them—in short each trancer had a vision distinctly his own and unlike any others. Men, women and children engaged in the dance, and were affected without disparity on account of age or sex.[87]

Philip Wells

"We have to arouse the white people or they will pay no attention to our petitions."

Philip Wells also discussed the Ghost Dance and Wounded Knee in his memoir that was published in the *North Dakota History* as "Ninety-Six Years among the Indians of the Northwest."[88] In his memoir, Wells starts by explaining the causes of the Ghost Dance war, as he calls it. His list of causes of the trouble are very similar to those presented by Lakota chiefs in part 2. Wells gives a detailed description of the problems regarding the new borderline between the Pine Ridge and Rosebud Reservations and the subsequent "trek" by Brulés to Pine Ridge, ending up in the Badlands.[89] Wells notes that the whites living near the Lakota reservation thought that it would be "the Indians, instead of the Messiah [who] would destroy the whites," clearly stating as his opinion that the Ghost Dancers had no warlike intentions. Wells discusses Big Foot's journey to Wounded Knee and offers a detailed description of Wounded Knee. I have included it here because it offers a somewhat different point of view than the statements by, for example, Dewey Beard and Alice Ghost Horse.[90] In Wells's statement, a crucial role in the start of the fighting is

---

87. See introduction and parts 1 and 2 for further discussion.
88. Philip F. Wells in Philip Faribault Wells Papers, h75.134, South Dakota Historical Society Archives, Pierre, South Dakota. Courtesy of the South Dakota Historical Society Archives. Based on this manuscript, Wells wrote his memoirs that were published as Philip F. Wells, "Ninety-Six Years among the Indians of the Northwest."
89. See introduction and parts 1 and 2 for further discussion.

played by the holy man Yellow Bird. According to Wells, Yellow Bird was urging the Lakotas to resist and was giving signals to open fire. This interpretation appeared also in the army investigation known as the Kent-Baldwin Report and made its way to history books.[91] However, in his memoir, Wells has a subchapter entitled "The War in Retrospect." In that part of his reminiscences, the meaning of the medicine man's performance was explained differently. Wells says that Yellow Bird was "walking around in a circle extolling the virtues of the Ghost Shirt and throwing up dust, not in signal to fight, but to illustrate the harmlessness of the soldiers' bullets."[92] Obviously Wells had changed his opinion over the years, the latter interpretation being much closer to those of Dewey Beard and others. Following Wells's description of the fighting, his memoir continues with a conversation about the Ghost Dance that he had with several Lakota chiefs during the fall of 1890. This subchapter was entitled "What the Indians Gained" from the Ghost Dance. According to Wells, the chiefs said that they encouraged the Ghost Dance because it was the only way they could make the government listen to their problems. Much like Turning Hawk (part 2), they said: "We have to arouse the white people or they will pay no attention to our petitions asking for better treatment." When asked if they were intending to fight the whites, they, according to Wells, said that if they had to, they would. Wells concludes by saying that they actually got what they wanted: they made noise, had a fight, and then their rations were increased.

Previous to the Ghost Dance War of 1890–1891 I had resided for some years on the Pine Ridge Reservation. During the war I was chief-of-scouts under Lieutenant Charles W. Taylor, of the Ninth United States Cavalry. I also

90. For other descriptions of the battle by Wells, see Philip Wells, in Jensen, *Voices of the American West,* 1:155–60. See also "Report of Investigations into the Battle at Wounded Knee Creek."

91. For this discussion, see statement of Dewey Beard above.

92. Wells, "Ninety-Six Years among the Indians of the Northwest," 303.

acted as interpreter at times for General James W. Forsyth and other officers. My experience included the causes, conflicts, and results of the war.

There were four main causes of the war. The Indians began to realize as
early as 1888 that the Black Hills had been taken from them by means of
white cupidity. The Fort Laramie treaty had specified that no land should
be acquired from the Indians without the signatures of three-fourths of
the adult males over eighteen years of age. This called for at least 6,000
to 8,000 signatures, whereas only 240 odd signatures were secured for the
Black Hills Treaty of 1877.[93] Although much disturbed over the loss of their
land, the Indians had no thought of hostilities before 1888.

General George A. Crook, head of a government commission, visited
the Indians in 1889 and negotiated for the purchase of 11,000,000 acres of
land in the Great Sioux Reservation. The commission promised the Indians that no reductions would be made in their rations and other supplies.
Almost as soon as the senate ratified the treaty and the president signed it,
the government reduced the rations 500,000 pounds and other supplies in
like proportions.

Still angry and excited over the deception, the Indians sent a delegation from the Rosebud and Pine Ridge reservations on a secret mission
to Walker Lake, Nevada, to investigate the merits of a new religion. The
delegation returned with an enticing message from a purported Messiah,
who promised destruction of the whites and resurrection of Indians who
had died in the past. He also promised that the buffaloes and other game
animals would be restored and that things too numerous to mention would
occur. The white settlers in South Dakota and Nebraska heard of the purported message. They construed it to mean that the Indians, instead of the
Messiah would destroy the whites. They became gravely alarmed and clam-
ored for protection. The government responded with federal troops, while
South Dakota and Nebraska mobilized their militias and sent them to the
seat of the trouble.

The treaty made by the Crook Commission changed the boundary line
between the Rosebud and the Pine Ridge reservations from Pass Creek to
Blackpipe Creek, shifting it a distance of fifteen miles. Chief Lip, a leader

93. The Sioux Act of 1877 was put into effect in the aftermath of the Battle of the
Little Big Horn. The Fort Laramie Treaty of 1868 required that two-thirds of adult male
Lakotas sign any new treaty for it to become valid. In 1871, the U.S. government quit
making treaties with Indian tribes and started instead passing acts, which allowed them
to work around the requirements set by the 1868 treaty. For the Black Hills case, see
Ostler, *Black Hills*.

of the Rosebud Indians, had previously moved his band to the east of Pass Creek where his people had built good homes and cultivated productive fields. The new boundary excluded him from the jurisdiction of the Rosebud Agency. Lip objected to leaving his home and moving into the Rosebud Reservation. He demanded that he be placed under the jurisdiction of the Pine Ridge Agency, as he had been promised in the Crook Treaty. He suspected, after the treaty was ratified that he might have to leave his home and move to the Rosebud Reservation. When he and his band heard that General Nelson A. Miles with an army was coming to Pine Ridge, they assembled their belongings, including livestock, and prepared to move to Pine Ridge Agency, intending to appeal to Miles for a transfer to the Pine Ridge Reservation.

As soon as they began to prepare for the "trek," rumors were circulated among the Rosebud Indians that Lip and his people would move into the Badlands, where they intended to fortify themselves for a stand against the whites. The Rosebud Indians made [a] quick dash and overtook Lip and his people before they reached the agency and tried to force them into the Badlands, but they escaped and made their way to Pine Ridge Agency.

The hostiles went on to the Badlands, where the Pine Ridge Indians were preparing to undergo a siege by throwing up breastworks and assembling hundreds of cattle from the reservation.

When Lip arrived at Pine Ridge Agency, he found General John R. Brooke, instead of Miles, in immediate command of the troops. Brooke sent "friendly" Indian couriers to the hostiles in the Badlands to persuade them to attend a peace conference, which they refused to do.

At this stage the Reverend John J. Jutz, a Catholic missionary, asked permission to visit the hostiles with overtures of peace. The Indians had the utmost confidence in Jutz, and Brooke gave his assent. Accompanied by Jack Red Cloud, a son of the noted Chief, Jutz visited the hostiles, who agreed to surrender under certain conditions. Returning to the agency, Jutz reported the conditions to Brooke, who approved them. After making a second trip to the Badlands Jutz returned with the hostiles, who camped two or three miles from Pine Ridge Agency.[94]

Meantime Lieutenant-Colonel E. V. Sumner had been ordered to proceed with a troop of cavalry to Big Foot's camp on the Cheyenne River, where he was to take the band into custody and prevent it from joining the hostiles in the Badlands. Big Foot agreed to submit and move his band to a site to be

94. See parts 1 and 2 for further discussion.

designated by Sumner. Giving illness as a reason, he asked permission to remain where he was until the following morning. Sumner fell for the ruse and went ahead to locate a camp site. Waiting until about noon the following day, he dispatched scouts to meet Big Foot and guide his band to the new camp site. The scouts failed to meet Big Foot en route, but proceeded to the old camp site, which they found deserted.

Big Foot's escape was reported to Brooke at Pine Ridge with the suggestion that the fugitives might have fled to the Badlands. Brooke ordered Major Samuel M. Whitside to take a detachment of the Seventh Cavalry and intercept Big Foot's band and prevent it from joining the hostiles. Whitside reported on the evening of December 28, 1890, that he had captured Big Foot and his band and was in camp at Wounded Knee Creek. Brooke ordered the remainder of the Seventh Cavalry, together with a detachment of Indian scouts, out to Wounded Knee Creek that night. The battle, which occurred the following day, is described in subsequent chapters.

Battle of Wounded Knee

I was interpreting for General Forsyth just before the battle of Wounded Knee, December 29, 1890. The captured Indians had been ordered to give up their arms, but Big Foot replied that his people had no arms. Forsyth said to me, "Tell Big Foot he says the Indians have no arms, yet yesterday they were well armed when they surrendered. He is deceiving me. Tell him he need have no fear in giving up his arms, as I wish to treat him kindly." Continuing, Forsyth said, "Have I not done enough to convince you that I intend nothing but kindness? Did I not put you into an ambulance and have my doctors care for you? Did I not put you in a good tent with a stove to keep you warm and comfortable? I have sent for provisions, which I expect soon, so I can feed your people."

Big Foot replied, "They have no guns, except such as you have found. I collected all my guns at the Cheyenne River Agency and turned them in. They were all burned."

They had about a dozen old-fashioned guns, tied together with strings— not a decent one in the lot.

Forsyth answered, "You are lying to me in return for my kindness."

While the soldiers were searching for arms, Big Foot gave substantially the same answer as before.

During this time a medicine man [Yellow Bird], gaudily dressed and fantastically painted, executed the maneuvers of the Ghost Dance, raising and throwing dust into the air. He exclaimed, "Ha! Ha!" as he did so, meaning he was about to do something terrible, and said, "I have lived long enough," meaning he would fight until he died.[95]

Turning to the young warriors, who were squatted together, he said, "Do not fear, but let your hearts be strong. Many soldiers are about us and have many bullets, but I am assured their bullets cannot penetrate us. The prairie is large, and their bullets will fly over the prairies and will not come toward us. If they do come toward us, they will float away like dust in the air."

Then the young warriors exclaimed, "Hau!" with great earnestness, meaning they would back the medicine man.

I turned to Major Whitside and said, "That man is making mischief," and repeated what he had said.

Whitside replied, "Go direct to Colonel Forsyth and tell him about it," which I did.

Forsyth and I went to the circle of warriors, where he told me to tell the medicine man, who was engaged in silent maneuvers and incantations, to sit down and keep quiet, but he paid no attention to the order. Forsyth repeated the order. After I had translated it into the Indian [Lakota] language, Big Foot's brother-in-law answered, "He will sit down when he gets around the circle."

When the medicine man came to the end of the circle he squatted down.

Big Foot's brother-in-law asked at the end of the conversation that the Indians be permitted to take Big Foot, who he said was dying, and continue the journey begun before the troops intercepted them.

Forsyth replied, "I can take better care of him here than you can elsewhere, as I will have my doctors attend him."

Forsyth then went to one side to give instructions elsewhere. A cavalry sergeant exclaimed, "There goes an Indian with a gun under his blanket!" Forsyth ordered him to take the gun from the Indian, which he did.

Whitside then said to me, "Tell the Indians it is necessary that they be searched one at a time."

The old Indians assented willingly by answering, "Hau!" and the search began.

The young warriors paid no attention to what I told them, but the old men—five or six of them—sitting next to us, passed through the lines and submitted to search. All this time I kept watching the medicine man, who

95. This interpretation of Yellow Bird's performance contradicts the statements of Alice Ghost Horse and Dewey Beard, for example. For their statements, see above.

was doing the Ghost Dance, for fear he might cause trouble. While turning my eyes momentarily away, I heard someone on my left exclaim, "Look out! Look out!" Turning my head and bringing my arms to "port," I saw five or six young warriors cast off their blankets and pull guns out from under them and brandish them in the air. One of the warriors shot into the soldiers, who were ordered to fire into the Indians.[96] The older Indians sitting between the younger ones immediately rose up so that the farther end of the circle, forty or fifty feet away was hidden from my view. I heard a shot from the midst of the Indians. As I started to cock my rifle, I looked in the direction of the medicine man. He or some other medicine man approached to within three or four feet of me with a long cheese knife, ground to a sharp point and raised to stab me. The fight between us prevented my seeing anything else at the time. He stabbed me during the melee and nearly cut off my nose. I held him off until I could swing my rifle to hit him, which I did. I shot and killed him in self-defense and as an act of war as soon as I could gain room to aim my rifle and fire.

By this time a general fight was raging between the soldiers and the Indians. Troop "K" was drawn up between the tents of the women and children and the main body of the Indians, who had been summoned to deliver their arms. The Indians began firing into Troop "K" to gain the canyon of Wounded Knee Creek. In doing so they exposed their women and children to their own fire. Captain Wallace was killed at this time while standing in front of his troops. A bullet, striking him in the forehead, plowed away the top of his head. I started to pull off my nose, which hung by the skin, but Lieutenant Guy Preston shouted, "My God, Man! Don't do that! That can be saved!" He then led me away from the scene of the trouble.[97]

After the heavy fighting ended, I went back to where the dead and wounded lay and called out, "The white people came to save you, but you have brought death on yourselves. White people are merciful to a wounded enemy if he is harmless. So, if any of you are alive, raise your heads. I am a man of your own blood."

At this a dozen heads were raised from among the seemingly dead. One

96. Philip Wells's testimony regarding the start of the fight differs from other Indian accounts. See Dewey Beard and Alice Ghost Horse above and Black Elk in part 1.

97. A good description of the troop movements and placement before and during the fight can be found in Greene, *American Carnage*, 216–44.

man, resting on his elbow, said, "Are you the man they call Fox," which is my Indian name. I answered that I was.

"I want you to favor me by coming to me," he said.

But suspecting foul play, I raised my gun as I approached him.

He asked, "Who is that man lying over there?"

He referred to an Indian who had run into a scout's tent and killed three or four soldiers. But a shot from a Hotchkiss gun plowed through the tent, set it and the hay in it on fire and burned the Indian [Yellow Bird]. Assuming the Indian was a medicine man, I answered the question accordingly.

The Indian who had asked the question raised up a little higher and, shooting out his fingers—a deadly insult among the Indians—toward the dead man said, "I could stab you and be satisfied in doing so. I am sorry I could no more."

Trembling with emotion and using words I could not understand, he said, speaking to the dead man, "If I could be taken to you, I would stab you." Then turning toward me, he exclaimed, "He is our murderer. He incited our young men, else we would all be alive and happy."

An old woman, whom I conducted to a safe place, volunteered the information, "The treacherous ones are of Big Foot's band. The medicine men tried constantly to incite the others since we of Hump's band have been with them. Some of us really meant peace when we raised the white flag, but trouble occurred anyhow."[98]

Some of the wounded women said about the same thing.

Before this, while the soldiers were still firing, I heard Forsyth order in a loud voice, "Quit shooting at them," in an effort to save the women and children. Then the soldiers ceased firing.

After the firing ceased, I heard a soldier say, "That fellow," alluded to a wounded warrior among the women, "is raising his gun to shoot."

An instant before I heard Forsyth's order, I heard a similar order, given by someone else, but Forsyth's order was the more distinct. What the soldier said was apparently an excuse for his disregarding the first order.

98. Big Foot had raised a pole with a white flag above his wagon just before they surrendered to the soldiers. Utley, *Last Days of the Sioux Nation*, 195.

What the Indians Gained

I talked with many Indian leaders during the Ghost Dance craze. I asked each chief, "Do you believe the story about the Messiah's coming to earth?"

A number of them said, "No, I do not believe it any more than you do."

"Then," asked I, "why do you encourage it?"

The most frequent answer given was, "We have to arouse the white people or they will pay no attention to our petitions asking for better treatment. The white people have lied to us."

There were other leaders, however, who believed in the craze.

The commissions sent out by the government had promised the Indians that their supplies would remain unchanged if they would sign the Crook Treaty. But the government, when the Senate ratified the treaty, reduced the beef supply one-half and other supplies accordingly. The reduction affected the Pine Ridge, Rosebud, and other reservation Indians.

I said to the Indian leaders, "You would arouse the white people," and asked, "Will not that cause a war with them?"

They answered, "We prefer not to have war, but if we have to, we will."

I added, "And risk the danger of many getting killed?"

"Yes," they replied, "we will take the chance rather than endure the things we put up with now."

I asked them, "Do you expect to defeat the whites in a war?"

"No," they answered, "we do not expect to win a war with them, but there are other ways in which we stand to gain."

I asked them, "In what other ways do you stand to gain?"

They answered, "All white people are not bad. Many conscientious people in the East will work for us and help us win our point."

They answered correctly, for after the war the government increased their rations and other supplies. Although some Indian leaders did not believe in the Ghost Dance craze, they encouraged it for the effect it would have in winning concessions from the white government. It might be said that they lost the war but won the peace. They got what they wanted, as they did in the Red Cloud War.[99]

99. This refers to the war of 1866–1868 that ended in the Fort Laramie Treaty of 1868. The U.S. government essentially gave in to what the Lakotas demanded. As Red Cloud was one of the leading Lakota chiefs at the time, the war is sometimes referred to as "Red Cloud's War." See, for example, John McDermott, *Red Cloud's War: The Bozeman Trail, 1866–1868* (Norman: Arthur H. Clark, 2010).

Louis Shangrau

"People were so excited they trembled all over."

Following Father John Jutz's peace effort, the Ghost Dancers arrived at the Pine Ridge Agency on December 6 for negotiations with General John R. Brooke.[100] After the talks Louis Shangrau with approximately thirty others followed the Ghost Dancers back to their camp in the Badlands. It is not exactly certain, if Shangrau acted as an official emissary for General Brooke, or if he went on his own accord.[101] Shangrau stayed in the camp for several days. Upon his return on December 13, Warren G. Moorehead interviewed Shangrau and his story was published in the January 1891 issue of the *Illustrated American* under the title *"Sioux on the Warpath: Adventures of Louis Shangraux, the Scout, in His Effort to Persuade the Hostiles to Return."*[102] Shangrau gives quite a dramatic description of his visit to the Ghost Dance camp. He describes the ceremony and, perhaps more importantly, gives a glimpse into the tensions that were growing among the Ghost Dancers. Shangrau tells how Short Bull urged people to stay in the Badlands, while other prominent chiefs like Crow Dog and Two Strike eventually suggested that it might be wise to surrender. In his own account of the event, Short Bull gave a somewhat different description saying that he was the one covering his head with a blanket, not Crow Dog as stated here (see Short Bull in part 1). It is, however, important to notice that even in Shangrau's rendition of Short Bull's speech, the peaceful message comes through. According to Shangrau, Short Bull says that the Father wants him to "send my children to school, to make large farms, and not to fight

100. See part 1.

101. Utley, *Last Days of the Sioux Nation*, 140–42; Ostler, *Plains Sioux*, 318–20.

102. Louis Shangrau, *Illustrated American*, January 10, 1891, pp. 263–69. I have kept some of Moorehead's text here in italics to keep the structure of the text coherent. A summary of Louis Shangrau's story was published in Boyd, *Recent Indian Wars*, 205–10. Shangrau also gave a brief statement to Thomas A. Bland. See Bland, "Late Military Invasion," 9.

anymore. Do not fight, my children, unless the soldiers first fire upon you." In a few days after the meeting, a great number of Ghost Dancers started the slow journey toward the Pine Ridge Agency.

One week ago (the 8th) the General [Brooke] called me (Shangraux) into his office, and told me he was very desirous of bringing in the hostiles without bloodshed. He said that the mission of Father Jutz had resulted in great good, that the government scouts sent out had failed to reach the campsite of Short Bull and Kicking Bear, and that all information regarding the strength of the hostiles was entirely unreliable. *Louis was given the power to select his party and accordingly chose some good, true men who he knew could be depended upon in case of trouble. No white men went with them, for it was believed the hostiles would kill anyone not an Indian who should venture near the camp. From subsequent events this was found to be true. Bright and early the "friendlies" set out, with several days' provisions and plenty of ammunition. They rode at a good pace and reached a high point of land about five miles from the hostiles at sundown—there went into camp near a small stream. The fire which they started to prepare coffee was seen by the hostiles, and at sunrise twenty Sioux, armed to the teeth, rode into the friendlies' camping ground and demanded:* "What do you want here? Have you come to spy on us? Speak quick or we will shoot you." *Louis Shangraux was escorted to the Ghost Dance camp by the Indians.*

When we entered there were about two hundred and sixty-two lodges present. One hundred and forty-five returned with us to the agency. The squaws and men came forward to greet us, and all seemed very friendly. They supposed at first that we had come to join them, but when they learned our true mission they seemed very suspicious, and refused for some time to have anything to do with us. Just before we began the council, which lasted the greater part of four days, the high-priest and his helpers came forward and announced that there would be a Ghost Dance. They formed a circle about the sacred tree and began their chant. Of all the wild dancing I saw on Wounded Knee, this beat the "shooting-match." People went into trances by the dozen, and the priests were kept busy relating the experiences of the fainters. Several remained in trances as long as twelve hours, and gave evidences of utter exhaustion when the directors roused them. Short Bull said:

> I see the Messiah coming from the west. He is riding in a plain-wagon drawn by two mules, and looks very much like a black man. If he is our Messiah, we are greatly fooled. Now I see him again, and he is an Indian. Ah! Wait: I see him the third time, and he is a white man. He

tells me to send my children to school, to make large farms, and not to fight anymore. Do not fight, my children, unless the soldiers first fire upon you.

People were so excited they trembled all over, their eyes rolled, and the muscles of their faces twitched. They were the most crazy Indians I ever beheld.

The dancing continued for nearly thirty hours; then there was an intermission of several hours, during which a council was held in order to give audience to the peace commission. Short Bull and Two Strike aided by Crow Dog, championed the cause of the hostiles while No Neck and Louis Shangraux spoke on behalf of the friendlies. Louis does not remember what he said in the first council, but the substance of his remarks could be put in one sentence: "The agent will forgive you if you will return now, give you more rations, but not permit you to dance." Short Bull's reply was so forcible as to remain in Louis's memory in the exact words of the speaker. The speech of Tathanka Ptecelan [Tȟatȟáŋka Ptéčela, Short Bull] ran as follows:

I have risen today to tell you something of importance. You have heard the words of the brothers from the agency camps, and if you have done as myself, you have weighed them carefully. If the Great Father would permit us to continue the dance, would give more rations, and quit taking away portions of the reservation, I would be in favor of returning. But even if you (*turning to Louis*) say that he will, how can we discern whether you are telling the truth? We have been lied to so many times that we will not believe any words that your agent sends to us. If we return he will take away our guns and ponies, put some of us in jail for stealing cattle and plundering houses. We prefer to stay here and die, if necessary, to loss of liberty. We are free now and have plenty of beef, can dance all the time in obedience to the command of great Wakȟáŋ Tȟáŋka. We tell you to return to your agent and say to him that the Dakotas [Lakotas] in the Badlands are not going to come in.

No Neck rejoined: Think, my people, how foolish is this action! Do come in, and all will be well; remain out here, and you will be killed.

Short Bull added: It is better to die here as brave men, and in obedience to the commands of the Good Spirit, than to live like cowards at the agency on scanty rations, disarmed, without horses and guns. No, we will not return. If we dance, our Good Spirit will protect us, and when all dancers are sincere, the bullets of the soldiers will harmlessly fall to the ground without power to hurt.[103] There is no army so powerful that it can contend with Wakȟáŋ Tȟáŋka; therefore we are not afraid to remain here.

The gathering broke up, and nearly everyone continued in the Ghost Dance. For two days the hostiles would not have further words with the friendly scouts. Friday and Saturday, the 12th and 13th, the last council was held. The scenes accompanying the closing of this gathering, Saturday afternoon, were very thrilling, and for a space of two hours it seemed as if a general battle would ensue between those who desired to return to the agency and the hostiles.

About noon, Saturday, Two Strike—who had been one of the leaders in the dance—arose and announced his intention to return to the agency with the scouts, accompanied by about one hundred and forty-five lodges. Crow Dog (Kangi Sunka, the Indian who killed Spotted Tail about ten years ago) also announced his intention of returning. At this declaration from two such prominent men, Short Bull sprang to his feet and cried out, angrily:

> At such a time as this, we should all stick together like brothers. Do not leave; remain with us. These men from the agency are not telling us the truth; they will conduct you back to the agency and they will place you in jail there. Louis is at the bottom of this affair. I know he is a traitor; kill him, kill him!

And, running to the place where the guns were stacked, Short Bull grasped his gun and, followed by many of his young men, surrounded Shangraux. Louis's situation was desperate. He knew these furious men might kill him at the slightest resistance, so he laughed as good-naturedly as possible under the circumstances and told them to put up their guns, as he was their friend instead of their enemy.

"No, do not let the friendlies return," cried the young men; "kill them, or compel them to remain with us. They will tell the agent all they have seen and the soldiers will know how to enter our camp."

With clubbed guns many of the desperate youths rushed upon the friendlies, and scouts, others cocked their Winchesters, and for a few moments it looked as if poor Louis and No Neck, Two Strike and Crow Dog, would lose their lives. Crow Dog sat upon the ground and drew his blanket over his head. He told your correspondent afterward that he expected to be struck

---

103. See also Short Bull's speech on October 30 in part 1. According to Shangrau, Short Bull again says that bullets would fail to harm the Ghost Dancers. He does not mention the bulletproof shirts.

and killed any moment, and that he did not wish to know the person who should commit the dastardly act—murdering a brother Dakota.

The wiser heads prevailed, however, and after a great hubbub, in which several young men were knocked down, order was restored. One of the horses and several of the dogs of the friendlies were shot during the melée. When the one hundred and forty-five lodges started from the camp another difficulty arose. It was during this trouble that Crow Dog made his famous short speech:

I am going back to White Clay (the location of the agency); you can kill me if you want to, now, and prevent my starting. The agent's words are true, and it is better to return than to stay here. I am not afraid to die.[104]

William Vlandry

"The Indians do not want war."

William Vlandry, a mixed-blood scout, was interviewed by L. W. Colby in January 1891.[105] Vlandry bluntly states that the Indians did nothing wrong; they were robbed of all necessities of life and when they resisted by dancing the Ghost Dance, they were killed.

The Indians had no intention of fighting until they were forced to it, in what they thought was self-defense. They made no attacks upon the settlements or settlers; they were guilty of no raids or depredations. At Wounded Knee Big Foot was very sick with pneumonia and was shot in his tipi. His band thought they were going to be disarmed, imprisoned and sent to Florida or Alabama and kept there as prisoners. They had done nothing whatever, but had been robbed of their rations and were suffering for the necessities of life, and so they resisted and were killed, with their wives and children. The government has not carried out its treaties with the Indians. It has made promises, but never performed them. Last year was a very hard year. The Indians who tried to farm raised nothing. The dry weather killed the crops. Then they did not get only half their usual ration of beef. This was their cause of complaint. If the government had issued them full rations, and

---

104. Moorehead's text continues with a description of how the Ghost Dancers started to move toward the Pine Ridge Agency and how the death of Sitting Bull further escalated tensions at the agency. Moorehead, *Illustrated American*, January 10, 1891, 269–70.

105. William Vlandry in Colby, "The Sioux Indian War," 189–190.

send no soldiers, there would have been no trouble. Agent Royer got scared, and then the trouble began. The Indians do not want war.

Louis Primeau

"There is danger of trouble between the two factions of Indians at Pine Ridge and Rosebud Agencies."

Louis Primeau's letter of March 3, 1891, to T. W. Blackburn is an important document, as it discusses the situation among the Lakotas after Wounded Knee.[106] There was a lot of discussion in the press and among white officials during the spring of 1891 about the Lakotas resuming Ghost Dancing. That, for many, indicated a possible outbreak. The letter also discusses the factionalism among the Lakotas in great detail. The Ghost Dance had aggravated the situation to the point where possible fighting between the factions, which Primeau labels as "friendlies" and "hostiles," might occur.

Standing Rock Agency
March 3, 1891
T. W. Blackburn, Esqr
Washington, D.C.

Dear Sir,

In reply to your letter dated February 20 requesting me to state the facts, which brought about the interview contained in the clipping which you enclosed and if I thought the Indians would fight in the spring, in which all the Indians would participate.[107] I had a talk with a reporter in which I told him that the friendly Indians felt as if they had been well treated by the Department, but that the hostiles

---

106. Louis Primeau to T. W. Blackburn, March 3, 1891, NARA, RBIA, RG 75.4, GRBIA, Letters Received, Letter 10173, box 714.
107. I have not been able to locate the interview in question.

had been treated in every manner just as well as they were, which impressed the friendlies that the hostiles would feel elated over their victory as they might call it. The friendlies counseled together and selected Louis Richard and myself to go and speak to the Hon. Commissioner [of Indian Affairs] in regard to the way they felt and that they thought it their duty to notify the Commissioner as to the two factions that he might put the question direct to each one, whether they intended to continue the Ghost Dance or not. As Big Road's speech looked very much like as if they intended to revive it in the spring. But I could not get to speak to Genl. [Commissioner] Morgan the evening before I came away, and the Indians then requested me to write, which I did from Carlisle, PA.[108]

Now this had a very bad impression on the friendlies and they apprehend trouble in the spring unless some reconciliation be brought about. This applies to Pine Ridge and Rosebud Agencies only. As I told the reporter, the Standing Rock, Cheyenne River, Lower Brulé and Crow Creek Agencies would not take part in any trouble at those agencies, the Indians of the Northern Sioux Agencies being all friendlies, the slight disaffection having been effectually eradicated.

American Horse in his speech said he would no longer stand between the government and Indians. He knew well that the factions are equally divided and unless the authorities reprimanded the hostiles they could not live and remain together.

At Philadelphia we took pains in introducing our Indians to make mention of the friendlies and a synopsis of their good qualities but when Rosebud was introduced, Louis Richard took particular pains to tell that Two Strike was an obstinate and misleading Indian and a man, who never listened to the Great Father and at that, the audience just fairly shook the house by clapping hands and stamping the floor.

How all this was noticed by the Indians and commented on by them; the friendlies feeling hurt at the marked applause given the announcement of Two Strike's name and the hostiles elated, and with

108. The Lakota delegation that came to Washington, D.C., on January 29, 1891, consisted of approximately forty men, including interpreters Louis Richards and John Shangrau. Louis Primeau obviously was among the delegation, although he does not appear in any of the photographs or the official list. For a good discussion regarding the meetings in Washington, D.C., see Grua, *Surviving Wounded Knee*, 84–88. See also the statements of Lakota chiefs in part 2.

this state of feeling existing, I cannot but believe that there is danger of trouble between the two factions of Indians at Pine Ridge and Rosebud Agencies and so expressed myself to the reporter.

I am, very respectfully

your obedient servant,

Louis Primeau

PART 4

"Messíya Itóŋšni"—"The Lie of the Messiah"

Part 4 presents documents by Christian and Western-educated Lakotas and Dakotas who opposed the Ghost Dance for practical, political, and religious reasons. Many of them had attended schools either in the East or on reservations. A few had become catechists or ministers themselves. For them, the Ghost Dance signified a return to "the old ways" and "barbarism." They use phrases such as "delusion," the "lie of the Messiah," and "Messiah craze" in their accounts of the Ghost Dance. At the same time, they were concerned about possible trouble brewing on the Lakota reservations.

This part begins with letters sent by Thomas P. Ashley (1863–ca. 1932),[1] Laurence Industrious (Blihéča, ca. 1867–ca. 1939),[2] George Means (1871–ca. 1937),[3] and E. G. Bettelyoun (1872–1948). They represent young Lakotas who had received a Western education. Ashley and Industrious attended the Hampton Normal and Agricultural Institute in Virginia, whereas Bettelyoun received his education at the Lincoln Institute in Philadelphia. Bettelyoun returned home to Pine Ridge in 1889 and worked at a store. George Means attended the Carlisle Indian Industrial School in Pennsylvania. At the time of the Ghost Dance he was working as a clerk at the Pine Ridge Agency and went to help the wounded after the Wounded Knee massacre.

The voices of these young Lakotas are followed by letters of Henry Eagle Horse (Tȟašúŋke Waŋblí, ca. 1857–1917), Good Voice (Hó Wašté, ca. 1830–1907), and Sky Bull (Maȟpíya Tȟatȟáŋka, ca.1835–ca. 1907),[4] representing Brulé leaders who had decided to "walk the white man's road" several years earlier. Good Voice, for example, had been working as a scout and was among the first Brulés to start wearing "white man's clothing." At the time of the Ghost Dance he was living at Oak Creek, where most of his followers had built log cabins and were cultivating land.

These letters, and those presented in parts 2 and 3, are extremely valuable as they are the voices of less well-known Lakotas, which are seldom heard. These letters provide a rare look at daily life on the reservations, the divergent approaches to the Ghost Dance, and also reveal some of the internal factions among the Lakotas.

1. The last census for Thomas P. Ashley is 1932.
2. U.S. census records give his name as both Laurence and Lawrence. His birth date is reported as 1867 or 1870, and he still appears in the 1939 census.
3. The U.S. federal census for Means gives conflicting information about his ancestry. The 1910 census reports that his father was from Maine. He also self-reported his native tongue as English. In the 1920 census, however, the language is "Indian," and both parents are listed as born in South Dakota. In the 1930 census, his father is mixed-blood and his mother Crow. The last Indian census for Means is 1937.
4. The last available census for Sky Bull is 1907.

This part then presents several documents published in the Dakota-language newspaper *Iapi Oaye*, which was published during 1871–1939 in Greenwood, South Dakota, by Presbyterian missionaries. An English version of the newspaper was called the *Word Carrier*.[5]

The first *Iapi Oaye* document regarding the Ghost Dance was written by Samuel White Bird (ca. 1865–1940) from the Lower Brulé Reservation. Just before the Ghost Dance he was actively trying to improve living conditions on the reservation by seeking help in the fight over reservation lands from attorneys in Washington, D.C.[6] His account was published in the November 1890 issue of *Iapi Oaye*. Sisseton Dakota Louis Mazawakiyanna (Mázawakíŋyaŋ, ca. 1836–?) and Samuel Spaniard (ca. 1862–?), both Presbyterians, also wrote descriptions of the Ghost Dance from the Cheyenne River and Rosebud Reservations. Their comments are followed by statements from Dakotas Elias Gilbert (1844–1921), Clarence Ward, (Ȟó Híŋ Ȟóta, Roan Bear, ca. 1851–ca. 1932), Robert White (Blokášiča), and Albert Frazier (Tȟaóya Tȟatȟáŋka, 1850–ca. 1932).[7] Many of these Dakotas, who had converted to Christianity, worked on Lakota reservations. Elias Gilbert, for example, was a missionary on the Standing Rock Reservation at the Grand River No. 2 Station. Mazawakiyanna, who had participated in the 1862 Minnesota War, converted soon afterward and became one of the most famous Native ministers of the time. Ward was a licensed minister for the Episcopal Church. In 1892 he led a sixty-nine-member congregation on the Cheyenne River Reservation. Owen Lovejoy (ca.1855–1934), a Santee who worked as a teacher on the Standing Rock Reservation, accompanied the Reverend George W. Reed to Sitting Bull's camp where they witnessed the Ghost Dance. Lovejoy called the Ghost Dance a "delusion" and hoped that God would "change" the Ghost Dancers' minds.

Part 4 concludes with accounts by Josephine Waggoner, Charles Eastman, and Luther Standing Bear, who were all Western-educated but at the time of the Ghost Dance were working closely with the Lakotas on the Standing Rock, Pine Ridge, and Rosebud Reservations, respectively.

---

5. For a good analysis of the *Iapi Oaye* and *Word Carrier* reporting on the Ghost Dance, see Todd Kerstetter, *God's Country, Uncle Sam's Land: Faith and Conflict in the American West* (Urbana: University of Illinois Press, 2006), 81–124; Todd Kerstetter, "Spin Doctors at Santee: Missionaries and the Dakota-Language Reporting of the Ghost Dance and Wounded Knee," *Western Historical Quarterly* 28 (Spring 1997): 45–67. Kerstetter provides translations of some *Iapi Oaye* texts, mostly sentences and paragraphs. The translations differ from mine, but they mostly convey the same ideas.

6. Gage, "Intertribal Communication," 99–100.

7. Ward still appears in the 1932 census.

Hunkpapa Josephine Waggoner (Josiewiŋ, 1871–1943) was a daughter of Charles A. McCarthy, an Irishman, and Wind Woman, a Hunkpapa Lakota. Josephine Waggoner's life is remarkable in many ways. She attended the Standing Rock Day School from the age of five, then spent six years at the Hampton Normal and Agricultural Institute in Virginia. After returning to Standing Rock in 1889, she married John Franklin Waggoner. She worked as an interpreter for the Episcopal Church for a while and as a nurse for the Congregationalist mission. She witnessed the Ghost Dance on Standing Rock firsthand and she acted as an interpreter to Sitting Bull. She was also one of the first to see Sitting Bull's body after the disastrous attempt to arrest him on December 15, 1890. Later, Josephine Waggoner spent her life recording and writing the story of her people. Her manuscript ended up, after many twists and turns, at the Museum of the Fur Trade in Chadron, Nebraska. In 2013 Emily Levine edited Waggoner's texts, published as *Witness: A Húŋkpapĥa Historian's Strong-Heart Song of the Lakotas*.[8] Josephine Waggoner was one of the few women who left accounts of the Ghost Dance, which is why I decided to include her statements here despite the fact that they have been so recently published in Levine's work.[9]

Similarly, Charles A. Eastman (Ohíyesa, 1858–1939), a Western-educated Santee Dakota who served as a physician on the Pine Ridge Reservation, describes the developments on that reservation in his memoirs, which were published as *From the Deep Woods to Civilization: Chapters in the Autobiography of an Indian*.[10] Luther Standing Bear (Matĥó Nážiŋ, 1868–1939), a prominent Brulé leader on Rosebud Reservation, never took up the Ghost Dance, but he provides an interesting account of the dance on that reservation and describes how tense the situation was after the Wounded Knee Massacre. Luther Standing Bear was one of the first Lakota children

---

8. For a biography of Josephine Waggoner, see Waggoner, *Witness*, edited by Levine, editor's introduction, xxv–xlii, and for the story of the manuscripts, 493–515.

9. I came across Josephine Waggoner's manuscripts in the year 2000 when I was writing my doctoral dissertation. I used the transcribed copies (only a part of the entire collection) held at the American Indian Studies Research Institute, Indiana University, for that purpose first and later for my book *The Lakota Ghost Dance of 1890*. I was astonished by the richness of material in the collection. For the current book, I continued to work with the transcribed copies until the publication of *Witness*. After that I decided to rely on Emily Levine's work.

10. See Charles Eastman, *From the Deep Woods to Civilization: Chapters in the Autobiography of an Indian* (Boston: Little, Brown, 1916). For a good biography of Charles Eastman, see Raymond Wilson, *Ohiyesa: Charles Eastman Santee Sioux* (Champaign: University of Illinois Press, 1999).

to be sent to the Carlisle Indian Industrial School in Pennsylvania in 1879. Luther Standing Bear's account of his experiences in the school along with his statement on the Ghost Dance were later published in his book *My People the Sioux*.[11]

It is important to understand, as the historian Louis Warren has pointed out, that "the school graduates were living in a highly charged political context during and after 1890. While all of them seem to have taken up the challenge of representing their people to the American public, this placed heavy burdens on them." For many of them, the idea of supporting or practicing the Ghost Dance could have proven disastrous since they were often economically dependent on their white eastern friends. To endorse the Ghost Dance, or even to defend it, would be to risk being labeled as "hostile" or "nonprogressive." Each of the accounts in this part is in this way potentially political and should also be understood in this context.[12]

11. For the life of Luther Standing Bear, see Luther Standing Bear, *My People the Sioux*, and the introduction by Richard N. Ellis to the 1975 University of Nebraska edition.

12. Quotation from Louis Warren, personal correspondence with author, February 2017.

Thomas P. Ashley

"Oh Father help me through this trouble."

Thomas P. Ashley, a Catholic Lakota, wrote the following letter to Agent James McLaughlin on November 19, 1890.[13] While he does not directly discuss the Ghost Dance, it is clear that he refers to it by noting that people are not using their education, that is, they are falling back to savagery through the Ghost Dance. Even his wife has gone "back the old way" and has started to wear Indian clothing again, Ashley complains.

Dear Maj. McLaughlin

I will drop you a few lines to let you know that we have been [a]part nearly [a] month ago, my wife dress Indian, she is go [has gone] back [to] old way, we must show there is a way a good many times better than the old way. I am sorry to say some of us do not use all our education. Oh Father help me through this trouble, so that I may live happy in this dark world and work for my Father, which is in heaven. May God give you more strength to do good for all nations, and especially for my good people. Oh Father, let me die with sorryfull [sorrowfully].

Yours true son

Thomas P. Ashley

Maj. James McLaughlin

U. S. Indian Agent

13. Thomas P. Ashley to James McLaughlin, November 11, 1890, NDHS, James McLaughlin Papers—Roll 2. Published by permission of North Dakota Historical Society Archives.

Ring Thunder

"If I would join them, I would never have any more pain or
sorrow."

Lebbeus Foster Spencer served as the agent on the Rosebud Reservation
until 1889. Even after his time as the agent he continued to communicate
regularly with several Brulés. Ring Thunder, an elderly Brulé leader,
wrote a letter to Spencer on December 5, 1890.[14] Ring Thunder clearly
was caught between the Ghost Dancing faction and the non–Ghost
Dancers. His attempts to keep all of his people away from the dance
did not succeed; some joined the Ghost Dancers on their way to Pine
Ridge. It is also evident that the tensions were running high, as the Ghost
Dancers did not listen to him and called him a fool for not joining them.
Perhaps some discussion about fighting the whites took place because
Ring Thunder says that once he was one of "their bravest warriors, but
now that time is past," and "if the Dakotas [Lakotas] fight, they fight."
Ring Thunder concludes that the white man's road is difficult to follow,
but if only the Lakotas would be given more food, all would be well.

Rosebud Agency
December 5, 1890

Kȟolá Mithá Atéyaŋpí.

My dear friend.—It made my heart very good to get your letter and
that you remembered me. It made me glad that you thought I had not
gone with the wild Indians. The agent sent me over to Black Pipe
[Creek] three times to counsel with the dancers, but they had no
ears, called me a fool, and would not listen. I did all I could to keep
my people from joining the Ghost Dancers, but some of them would
not listen to me, and went off to Pine Ridge.[15] I expect to stay in my
camp, with my people, and if the Dakotas fight, they fight. My heart
is not with them.

14. Ring Thunder to L. F. Spencer, December 5, 1890, LFSP, HCSHL, MSS 596.
Published by permission of History Colorado.
15. See parts 1 and 2.

The Ghost Dancers told me if I would join them, I would never have any more pain or sorrow, but if I followed after the ways of the white man, my path would be hard and full of trouble. I told them a long time ago, I was one of their bravest warriors, but now that time is past. I have no more desire to fight. The ways of the white man seem hard at times, but if they will give us back our beef and rations, all will be well with us. I shake your hand with my heart.

Your friend,

Ring Thunder

E. G. Bettelyoun

"I think it will be settled peaceably."

The following letter by E. G. Bettelyoun dated December 6, 1890 was forwarded to the commissioner of Indian affairs by Mary McHenry Cox of the Lincoln Institution in Philadelphia.[16] In his letter, Bettelyoun reflects on the situation on the Pine Ridge Reservation right about the time when negotiations between the Ghost Dancers and the U.S. Army were taking place. Things seemed to be quieting down and the Ghost Dancers were gradually thinking of coming to the agency. The only trouble was caused by the Rosebud Brulés. Bettelyoun notes that the press was making things worse than they actually were.[17]

United States Indian Service
Pine Ridge Agency, S.D. Agency
December 6, 18[90]

Miss Cox

Your letter of the 25th ult. was received. I answered it as soon as I could. All the Indians of the agency have quieted down. It is the Indians of Rosebud Reservation that are making all the trouble now.

---

16. E.G. Bettelyoun to Mary McHenry-Cox, December 6, 1890, forwarded to the Commissioner of Indian Affairs Thomas J. Morgan December 10, 1890, December 6, 1890, NARA, RBIA, RG 75, SC 188, box 199.

17. For the developments in early December, see introduction and part 1.

They have been making good many depredations and are afraid
to come to the agency for fear the troops will make them prisoners.
I think it will be settled peaceably if they come in. It is some of the
Indians that have been wanting to get transferred from Rosebud
Agency to this agency. I don't like [it] too much because some of it
might not be so. I think all the papers are making it worse than it is.
Remember me to all school mates.

Respectfully,

E. G. Bettelyoun

Good Voice

"I am not going to be foolish and join the dance."

Good Voice, living on Big Oak Creek on the Rosebud Reservation,
wrote a letter to Agent Lebbeus Foster Spencer on December 15, 1890.[18]
He is replying to a letter from Spencer, who evidently asked about his
possible participation in the Ghost Dance. Good Voice implies that he
would be foolish to join the dance. He has tried to live as the whites
hoped and would continue to do so. He, too, complains about the meager
rations and failing crops.

Big Oak Creek
December 15, 1890

My Friend

It's made my heart glad to receive a letter from you. I am glad that
you think of one. I think of [you] as my friend. In your letter you
said you did not think I had been foolish and went with the Ghost
Dancers. My friend I have not—I have always been a friend of the
whites and try to do as they tell one, and I believe the good people of
the Church and the good book that tell there is only one God, and that
God don't like bad people. My friend, when I was young I fought my
own people and helped the white people and would do so again, if I
was young. I have tried to live as white people, and I sent my children

---

18. Good Voice to Lebbeus Foster Spencer, December 12, 1890, LFSP, HCSHL,
MSS 596. Published by permission of History Colorado.

to school to be taught what white people teach, and I want them to live as white people and now in my old days I am not going to be foolish and join the dance. My children would not believe what I told them, if I done that. My friend, I came to Oak Creek when the Great Father at Washington told us to take our land and I built a house and I plowed some land and try to raise corn and potatoes, and some years we have some, but last year we had no rain and we had no crop so we have nothing to eat, only what the Great Father at Washington gives us, and we do not get much and we are hungry sometimes.

I hope you will come back sometime to us.

Good Voice

Blackfeet Lakotas

"We will never join the Ghost Dance nor believe what they are doing."

This letter, signed by sixty-one Blackfeet Lakotas of the Cheyenne River Reservation, was written to Agent Perain P. Palmer on December 15, 1890.[19] The authors want to tell Palmer that they will not join the Ghost Dancers led by Big Foot on Cheyenne River. They emphasize that they have become farmers, go to church, and want another boarding school in their camp. They hope that the letter makes certain that they would not be confused with the "wild Indians" in case of trouble.

Mouth of the Moreau River
December 15, 1890
Hon. P. P. Palmer, U.S. Indian Agent
Cheyenne River Agency, South Dakota

Dear friend:

We the undersigned of the Blackfeet camp at Mouth of the Moreau River, we wish to tell you these things. We are [have] always obeyed your order[s] and also the Great Father. Therefore we wish to tell you

19. Blackfeet to the Commissioner of Indian Affairs Thomas J. Morgan, December 15, 1890, NARA, RBIA, RG 75, GRBIA, Letters Received, Letter 40165, box 690.

that we will never join the Ghost Dance nor believe what they are doing.

We know that we are all farmers and furthermore we are all members of the True Church and we know what we are doing, so we will never join the wild Indians on Cheyenne River—we wish to tell you this in order to make you glad.

We always look out for ourselves and always think about what will [be] good for us in the future, especially for our children, therefore we wish a boarding school for our children at our camp—we also hoped that you would be able to establish the agency building at Charger's Camp.

Please consider these things and tell our Great Father with your approval.

We shake hand with a glad heart—we are your friends.

Signed by 61 people

Sky Bull

"The Indians think that Great Father has sent his soldiers to starve us."

Sky Bull, an elderly Brulé, also voiced his concerns to former agent Lebbeus Foster Spencer on December 26.[20] While Sky Bull is concerned about the crops and famine, he also worries about how their young men have become "foolish," referring to their belief in the Ghost Dance. He accuses Short Bull and others for taking the young men away. The soldiers being on the reservation was also of great concern to him. "They spoil our girls," he says, perhaps referring to inappropriate behavior or even rape. Here again we can see an interesting contradiction as Sky Bull was one of the signers of the letter in part 2 that complained about Agent Spencer, noting that his term as the agent sent the Lakotas backward. In this letter, however, Sky Bull praises Spencer as the one agent who

20. Sky Bull to Lebbeus Foster Spencer, December 26, 1890, LFSP, HCSHL, MSS 596. Published by permission of History Colorado. See also Gage, "Intertribal Communication," 318–19.

provided enough food and equipment for the Lakotas, and because of that the Brulés adopted him.

Rosebud Agency
December 26, 1890

Colonel L. Spencer,

My Friend—we have much trouble since you threw us away. You were very near the Great Father and got your children more plows, oxen wagons and horses than any other agent from the Great Father's house. We always had ears for what you told us and looked to the ground for our rations, but last year we put our corn and potatoes in the ground and they staid there; we did not get any back and we have had time for many mourns. Short Bull, Two Strike and Crow Dog have made much of our young men foolish and taken them away. The soldiers are now here and they spoil our girls. Wont you tell the Great Father about it. Many of the Indians think that Great Father has sent his soldiers to starve us. I do not believe that for we now get the rations General Harney [probably General Crook] promised us.[21] I am an old man and will soon sleep with my fathers the Dakotas. You gave us a steer every twelve days. Now we have been getting a cow in eighteen days and don't get anything from the ground. We have been very hungry since you left us. You are the agent we adopted and we want you to come back to us. I shake your hand with a good heart.

Your Friend,

Sky Bull

Pretty Eagle

"We don't want to have any trouble here in this country."

Pretty Eagle, whose Ghost Dance vision experiences are presented in part 1, dictated a letter to Joseph Stephan Lance for former agent

---

21. Sky Bull refers to General William S. Harney who made a treaty proposal to the Lakotas following his campaign in 1855–56. However, I see no reason for Sky Bull to refer to Harney's campaign some thirty-five years earlier. I think that he actually meant General George Crook and his promises made the previous year. See also Gage, "Intertribal Communication," 319.

You are the agent we adopted and
we want you to come back to us. I
shake your hand with a good heart
        Your Friend Sky Bull

                Rosebud Agency
                  Dec 26th 1890

Col L F Spencer

My Friend — we have much
trouble since you threw us away.
You were very near the Great Father
and got your children more plows
oxen wagons and horses than
any other agent from the Great
Fathers house. We always had
ears for what you told us and
looked to the ground for our rations
but last year we put our corn and
potatoes in the ground and they
staid there we did not get
any back and we have had

Sky Bull, a Brulé, wrote to former agent Lebbeus Foster Spencer on December
26, 1890, voicing his concerns about crop failure, famine—and the Ghost Dance.
Lebbeus Foster Spencer Papers, History Colorado, Stephen H. Hart Library and
Research Center.

time for many moons. Short
Bull Two Strike and Crow Dog have
made many of our young men
foolish and taken them away.
The soldiers are now here and they
spoil our girls. Wont you tell
the Great Father about it Many
of the Indians think the Great Father
has sent his soldiers to starve us. I do
not believe that for we now get the
rations Genl Harney promised us. I
am an old man and will soon
sleep with my fathers the Dakotas.
You gave us a steer every twelve
days. now we have been getting a
cow in eighteen days and dont get
anything from the ground we have
been very hungry since you left us

Lebbeus Foster Spencer in December 28, 1890, just one day before the Wounded Knee massacre.[22] In the letter he basically denies his interest and participation in the Ghost Dance and accuses Short Bull of forcing people to join the Ghost Dancers. It is impossible to know when Pretty Eagle came to the agency, but it is very likely that he was among the Brulés led by Two Strike who arrived at the Pine Ridge Agency in mid-December. This letter, however, is sent from the St. Francis Mission on the Rosebud Reservation, so clearly he had made his way back to Rosebud at some point during December 1890.

St. Frances Mission
Rosebud Agency
December 28, 1890

To My Friend, L. F. Spencer,

I will tell you something, you knew us how the people here at Rosebud [are], we don't want to have any trouble here in this country. The Great Father says he will make us alright. You had told me [to] mind your word so I do so, my friend will you help us? We jump over two months account from the Great Father.[23] I said that the children [are] getting [growing] happy and [on] the reservation; I mean that the same of the children understood the Great Father's way. So I wish you would help them children. By this time I am doing alright, as what the Great Father said to me, so I wish you would help also if anything can help it. I got the ration less [get fewer rations] by this time and then when you had [were] to the agent here. Short Bull makes run off half of my people, this [is] the reason I want to hear some word from the Great Father about it, so will you help me? I wish you would help me all you can; you would help something [could you manage to get some help] from the government manage. I am very glad, I shake hand with my [friend] Spencer.

Your Friend Pretty Eagle

22. Pretty Eagle (John Stephan Lance) to Lebbeus Foster Spencer, December 28, 1890, LFSP, HCSHL, MSS 596. Published by permission of History Colorado. See also Gage, "Intertribal Communication," 318–19.

23. This probably means that they were missing rations for two months.

We [want] to see the Great Father (He Dog and Sky Bull, Pretty Eagle one of my school boy [the rest is illegible]).

Dear friend,

I didn't received any [illegible] yet. I am very sorry for that you had left here. This is I [who] write for Pretty Eagle.

Yours truly,

John Stephan Lance

Henry Eagle Horse

"I don't go to that dances at all."

Henry Eagle Horse wrote to Agent Lebbeus Foster Spencer on January 9, 1891.[24] The letter is somewhat difficult to interpret because Eagle Horse made some obvious mistakes about dates and numbers regarding the fighting at Wounded Knee. Most interestingly, he says that although he does not go to the Ghost Dances "at all," he is curious about it and "looked into it." This is yet another example of how the Ghost Dance affected people across the artificial "progressive"–"nonprogressive line."

Rosebud Agency, S.D.
January 9, 1891

Dear Friend, L. F. Spencer,

Your welcome letter is on hand now, and you told me something. I was very glad to know that you are still think[ing] of me. So I am going to tell you how I am getting along out here. I am well and in good health. And then there was a thing growing and [it] makes everybody crazy on this agency [Rosebud] and now there was about half of the Indians [who] went away toward the Badlands [on] account of that Ghost Dance, but I know that was not worthy to go to.

24. Henry Eagle Horse to Lebbeus Foster Spencer, January 9, 1891, LFSP, HCSHL, MSS 596. Published by permission of History Colorado.

So I don't go to that dances at all, but the Great Father and the agents we always have on this agency wanted us [to] live in the world. So that is all I looked into it; about the land and the other things we have heard from the Great Father and then there was only a few horses went off with the Ghost Dancers, and all the rest of them were [had] come to camp at the Little White River with me; that is all about that part and then I am going to tell you about [how] they have had a fighting at Pine Ridge Agency.

They had the fight on the 28th [29th] day of December at Wounded Knee Creek right at the big crossing and 25 soldiers were killed and many of them were wounded and they fight again on the 29th [30th] right at the Pine Ridge Agency only one soldier killed and four wounded.[25] So there was 26 of them were killed altogether and many wounded but some of them died now, and then some [of] the Indians killed too, Turning Bear, Ed White Horse, Little Chief's brother-in-law, Brave Bear's son and two of the Short Bull's brothers were killed too, and [illegible] uncle were wounded. That is all news from the war just now.

Please let me know all the news from the Great Father and all the other places too. That is all for present.

Good bye

from your friend

Henry Eagle Horse

George W. Means

"As far as I know there have been killed about two hundred Indians in all."

These two letters were written by George W. Means, a graduate of the Carlisle Indian Industrial School, to the principal of the school, Richard

---

25. Altogether thirty members of the U.S. Army, including Indian scout High Backbone, were killed at Wounded Knee, and thirty-six were wounded, including Indian scout Philip F. Wells. In the Drexel Mission fight of December 30, one soldier was killed and seven wounded. Greene, *American Carnage*, 398. The number of Lakota casualties is still under debate. For relatively reliable numbers, see Richard A. Jensen, "Big Foot's Followers at Wounded Knee," *Nebraska History* 71 (Fall 1990): 194–212; Greene, *American Carnage*, 402–16.

H. Pratt, on January 23 and 24, 1891. The letters were published in the *Indian Helper* newspaper on January 1891.[26] Pratt had been sending Means letters to inquire about the former Carlisle students, especially about their involvement in the Ghost Dance. He was very concerned to learn if any Carlisle students had gone back to the "old ways."[27] George Means refutes the news printed in the previous *Indian Helper* about former Carlisle students being killed at Wounded Knee. He also reports on the skirmishes after Wounded Knee and notes that he and a few other former Carlisle students carried arms for two days following the battle.[28]

Pine Ridge Agency, S.D.
January 23, 1891
Capt. R. H. Pratt

Dear Sir:

In this letter, I send you a picture of the battle that occurred at Wounded Knee last month. I went to the battlefield, after it was over to pick up the bodies into a wagon to bring to the agency—that is, the wounded ones. I see in the *Helper* that Mack Khútepi, Paul Eagle Star, and some other Carlisle students were killed in the fight. Whoever wrote that letter must have been scared at the time he wrote that letter. Mack Khútepi, Paul Eagle Star, and the others are here, none of them killed as the *Helper* stated. That is [what] I want to tell you.

   The photographs sent by Moses [Red Kettle], were views of Wounded Knee Battlefield, taken shortly after the fight, the bodies of those killed still on the field.

26. George W. Means to Richard Henry Pratt, January 24, 1891, in *The Indian Helper*, January 30, 1891.

27. Richard H. Pratt to George W. Means, December 4, 1890, RHPP, YCWABL, MSS S-1174, Outgoing Letters, box 10. See Gage, "Intertribal Communication," 365–67.

28. For more discussion on former Carlisle Indian School students and their participation in the Ghost Dance see Gage, "Intertribal Communication," 370–91.

January 24, 1891
Pine Ridge Agency, S.D.
Captain R. H. Pratt
Carlisle, PA.

Respected Sir:

It is with pleasure I write this letter to inform you of the excitement at this point. As far as I know there have been killed about two hundred Indians in all, and about forty or fifty wounded. There may be more, but I don't know of any more. In regard to the soldiers, I don't know how many were killed or wounded. The police and agency force were attacked by a few hostiles. In this attack three of the hostiles were killed and two wounded.[29] A great many head of cattle were killed, houses ruined, and horses stolen by the hostiles. They have been giving in their arms for the last week or over. They have come to their right senses and have come in and made peace with the military, but how long they will remain so, is hard to tell.

Óta Chief Eagle, Charlie Bird, Alex Yellow Wolf, Moses Red Kettle, several returned pupils and myself carried a rifle for two days. In last week's *Helper* I read that Paul Eagle Star, Mack Khútepi, Clayton Brave, were killed. Paul Eagle Star came here from Rosebud, but did not take part in the fight. He was one of the friendly ones. Clayton got wounded, and Mack is still living. Eleven of the returned Carlisle boys are working in the agency and one in one of the trader's stores.

The Rosebud Indians will probably be sent back to their agency.

I have told about all I know, so I will close. Hoping to hear from you again.

I remain, as ever, your friend,

George W. Means

29. See parts 1 and 2.

Laurence Industrious

"The present condition of the Indians is very hard."

Laurence Industrious wrote the following letter to his cousin One Bull on the Standing Rock Reservation.[30] Laurence Industrious relates how the Ghost Dancers had destroyed their own property, leaving them in dire straits during the harsh winter months. Despite his dislike of the Ghost Dance, he notes that it felt good to see the Indians camping in the old way, referring to the recreation of the sacred camp circle by the Ghost Dancers. He urges his cousin to keep an eye out for a possible renewal of the Ghost Dance in the spring of 1891.

Pine Ridge Agency, S.D.
March 4, 1891

I received your letter yesterday in which you asked me two
questions. I am able to answer one. Kicking Bear and Short Bull each
accompanied by ten followers were taken east by [General Nelson A.]
Miles to remain there six years; the object of taking them east is to
show the Ghost Dance and its effect if any.[31] I understand they have
danced, and the general opinion of the whites is that the dance was
harmless and would not have any bad effect and that a great many
lives had been lost for nothing, and these people will be returned to
their agencies early next spring. Tákutaiŋšni is the only name I know
outside of the two leaders [Short Bull and Kicking Bear]. You asked
me how the people here are. I must say that the present condition
of the Indians is very hard. You see they never expected to return
to the agencies but again as they had made up their minds to fight
the whites as long as they lasted and consequently burned up their
former homes, killed all their cattle and burned all the hay they had,
and now that peace has been restored they are suffering very much—
to add to the misery the snow is very deep—to see the Indian[s]
camped as in early life does one good.[32] They are camped in the

30. Lawrence Industrious to One Bull, March 4, 1891, WSCMC, WHCUOLA, box 114, folder 6, 149–50. Published by permission of University of Oklahoma Libraries. Published also in Vestal, *New Sources*, 59.

31. For their experiences, see Maddra, *Hostiles?*

32. Industrious refers to the recreation of the camp circle and living in tipis.

Badlands.[33] It would make you feel good to see them. It is possible that they will give Kicking Bear his dance back to him again. Bear this in mind keep your ears open this way. I say this to you on the quiet. My heart shakes hands with you cousin.

It is me,

Laurence Industrious, Blíheča

Anonymous Lakota Girls

"We are trying very hard not to be led away to believe in false ones."

Two Episcopalian Lakota girls wrote letters to Episcopalian Bishop William H. Hare. The letters are in the Walter S. Campbell Collection as part of a statement by William H. Hare.[34] Unfortunately, the names of the girls are not given, but they both attended the Episcopal St. John's School. The first letter was written by a former student and the second by a girl attending the school at the time.

Girl 1

I think you have heard of very strange stories of what is going on in Dakota at this time. But, dear Bishop, do not worry about us, for we are trying very hard not to be led away to believe in false ones. When I hear an Indian talk of this strange story, I tell them of the Saviour who came to save all the world.

I was thankful that my father put me in school and I have been told of the true Christ. The Indians are going to have a Christmas tree in this camp, and also have a dinner for everybody. I am going to make all the pies, so I am very happy about it, for I like to help with such things. We hope that

33. This is an interesting comment, since by March, when Industrious wrote his letter, the Ghost Dancers had been out of the Badlands for nearly two months.
34. Anonymous Lakota girls to Bishop William H. Hare as quoted in a statement by Bishop Hare in WSCMC, WHCUOLA, box 110, folder 2, 18–19. Published by permission of University of Oklahoma Libraries. Originally published in *Sioux Falls Press*, December 16, 1890.

our good friends in the East will offer prayers for us in this time of great trouble.

Girl 2

I suppose you have heard about the Indians having "Ghost Dances"? I think none of the Church Indians have anything to do with the matter, but the Indians that live on Cherry Creek[35] don't know any better, and are very wild. I hope they won't go too far or make any trouble.

Sam White Bird

"Messiah lies and false prophets will spring up."

Sam White Bird voiced his concerns about the Ghost Dance in the November issue of the *Iapi Oaye*.[36] He basically claims that the Messiah is a false prophet and those who believe in him will be deceived and disappointed. To back his argument he quotes the Bible's warning against believing in false prophets.

Many people believe in something sacred, therefore I wish us to remember our [Christian] prayers. Recently [some news] was received from Lower Brulé Reservation to Rosebud Agency and people went and took part in a prayer [Ghost Dance] and then a man told them about spirits. And then they considered it to be true and really worshipped. And then I took the Bible and read it, and then my heart was sad:

Beware that no one leads you astray. For many will come in my name, saying, "I am the Messiah!" and they will lead many astray. And you will hear of wars and rumors of wars; see that you are not alarmed; for this must take place, but the end is not yet. For nation will rise against nation, and kingdom against kingdom, and there will be famines and earthquakes in various places: all this is but the beginning of the birth pains. [Matthew 24:3]

---

35. People belonging to Big Foot's camp.

36. Sam White Bird in *Iapi Oaye*, November 1890, p. 38, quotation from the Holy Bible, Matt. 24:3. In the original text he quotes Matthew 24:3–24, but I decided to retain the most relevant part only. The text was translated by Rani-Henrik Andersson, December 2013.

IAPI OAYE.

SANTEE AGENCY, NEBRASKA.　　　　TAKU WAŜTE OKIYA, TAKU ŜICA KIPAJIN.　　　　A. L. RIGGS, PUBLISHER.

VOLUME XIX. NUMBER 11.　　　　NOVEMBER, 1890.　　　　WOKAJUJU KAŜPAPI ŜAKPE.

ANPETU OYAKAPI.

October 8. Mohook Lake ekta tona Dakota kodawioŋyapi etaŋhan wicaŝta qa winoĥiŋca ko opawiŋge sanpa wikcemna topa hen uŋicityapi qa anpetu yamni en yukaŋpi. Albert Smiley hen owote tipi waŋ yuha qa iye hena owasiŋ wicakico. Taku owasiŋ oŋ Ikcewicaŝta kiŋ iyooptapi kte ciŋ hena iwohdakapi. Uŋkiyepi etaŋhan Rev. Thomas L. Riggs hen opa.

October 20. Washington ekta A. B. Mullett ĵeĥte. Wicaŝta kiŋ de Tuŋkaŋŝidaŋ tieaĥkiya itaŋcaŋ kiŋ hee. He tohan tokiya Tuŋkaŋŝidaŋyaŋpi oŋ tipi waŋji kaĝapi, wowapi ojuju tipi qaiŝ womnaye tipi, hehaŋ wicaŝta kiŋ de iwaŋyaka ece. Tawaciŋ hnuni ecen heeoŋ naceca.

October 24. Dakota makoce Miniŝoŝe ohna nakaha wiyopeyapi kiŋ he etaŋhaŋ oŋŝpa Nebraska makoce en iyayeyapi. Qa he anpetu kiŋ de yuhiŋkiapi qa waŋna waŝicuŋ kiŋ ohna yukaŋpi. He itokaŋ Paŋka oyate ataya makoce wicaquŋpi, tona deciya tipi kic. Hena waŋna owasiŋ Nebraska makoce ohna yukaŋpi.

October 26. Mobile otonwe, Alabama, he ekta ide woĥitika waŋ taŋkaya tipi ihaŋhaŋga. Mazaska woyawa taŋka waŋji iyawapi kuŋ, Wita waŋ waŋji qa ĵeta wata yamni hen ide. Qa cotton wopiye kektopawiŋge wikcemna ĥullaŋga.

October 13. Wicaŝta waŋna nonpa anpetu kiŋ de en tapi. Waŋji iŝ Wayacu Wakaŋtu Itaŋcaŋ waŋ, Justice Miller, he hee. Omaka 1860 heciŋ Presideŋt Lincoln he Judge Miller wayute ĵaĝa. Waŋna waŋiyetu 74 hehaŋ ja. Wicaŝta uŋma kiŋ he General W. W. Belknap hee. Tohan General Grant Tuŋkaŋŝidaŋyaŋpi hehaŋ General Belknap Tuŋkaŋŝidaŋ Okiĥe waŋji ee, Secretary of War hee.

November 4. Makoce owaŋcaya wowapi iyohpeyapi qa wicaŝta ota iyokiŝniwicayapi. Republican oŋŝe kiŋ Tukteŋkteŋ kĵepidaŋ, qa Democrat qaiŝ Independent oŋŝe kiŋ ohiyapi. Heceŋ tokata Tuŋkaŋŝidaŋ Tomniĵye Tipi hukuŋ̇ya, House of Representatives, he en Democrat qa Independent wicotapi kta. Tuka Senate he en Republican waŝkapi kte.

Prohibition, miniwakaŋ awaŋtapi kiŋ he Nebraska en ohiye ŝni. Tuka tokata tohan ohiye kta.

South Dakota waŋna otonwe itaŋcaŋ waŋji ĥdaĥuiĝa, qa Pierre hee. Huroŋ hee kta niŋa ciŋ qa oŋ mazaŝka ota yusota. Eya Pierre ahiye kta. Wicaŝta ota opetoŋpi wowapi iyoĥpeyapi. Deoŋ Pierre qa Huron napin waŝpaŋyaŋiciyapi, qa wicaŝta wioŋyuŝicapi.

November 5. Henry M. Stanley tawicu kici United States makoce kiŋ en tipi. Mr. Stanley he Africa cokaya etaŋhaŋ uŝkatudan hdi. Oiciuaŋ kiŋ he en wohdake kta, otonwe tankinkinyan kiŋ en.

November 9. Santee Normal Training School ea tipi waŋji uŋŝpa ide. Hoĥpidaŋ cikistinna ohna yukaŋpi kiŋ hee. Akewaŋji waŋna iwaŋkapi qa uŋnapi owasiŋ waŝecekiye ipi. Tateyaŋpa uŋkaŋŝ tipi ocowasiŋ ide kta, tuka awicakehaŋ amdakedaŋ hecen kaŝniŝpi. Tuwedaŋ kluŋniye ŝni. Tiwaŋna piyapi qa katinyan ohna yukaŋpi.

Dakota oyate ehna huŋkakepi yauŋpi niciŋcapi teyaĥiŋdapi nawahoŋ. He wicayakapi qaiŝ wicayakapi ŝni ito oŋkiyukcaŋpi kte. Tuwe ciŋca awicakehaŋ teĥinda ehantanhaŋś he tokeŋ ciŋca tokata ekta wadake kte qa taku owaŋŝi en taŋyaŋ uŋ kta awaciŋ kte qa akite kta. Hokŝidaŋ waŋ ŝkate kta ciŋ qa tiyata uŋ kta ciŋ. Atkuku kiŋ hokŝidaŋ caŋtekiye qa taku ciŋ kiŋ owaŋjiŋ iyowiŋkiye. Tuka hokŝidaŋ de tokiya wayawa i uŋkaŋś tohaŋ icaŋge kiŋhaŋ wicaŝta wadake kte, woŋŝpe kiŋ eciyaŋhaŋ ; qa wayawa i ŝni kiŋhaŋ waŝduŋye ŝni oŋ etaŋhaŋ wicaŝta oŋŝika kte. Hecen hokŝidaŋ tiyata uŋ kiŋhaŋ tohaŋ wicaŝta icaŋga teĥiya uŋ kte. Heoŋ etanhan tuwe wayawa tipi ekte yeŝ ŝni kiŋhaŋ he hokŝidaŋ kiŋ iyececa ocakioŋn. Qa wayawa tipi waŝte, qa tukteŋ woonŝpe waŋkaŋtu kuwapi kiŋ ekta yeŝ kta iyecetu, hokŝidaŋ ciŋ ŝni ciŋ. Hecen tuwe ciŋca awicakehaŋ teĥinda ŝni, taku oyo kiŋ he wicakte ŝni. Wicaŝta he ciŋca awicakehaŋ teĥinda ŝni. Hokŝidaŋ qa wiciŋyaŋpidaŋ owasiŋ wayawa uŋpi kta iyececa, qa woonŝpe waŋkaŋtu ekta ewaciŋpi kta.

FRED B. RIGGS.

MESSIYA ITONŜNI.

Tona taku wakaŋ waciŋyayapi kiŋ mitakuyepi wocekiye oŋ uŋyekuyapi waciŋ ye lo. Eya Iecaĥa Kutawicaŝta Oyaŋke kiŋ ietanhaŋ Rosebud Agency ekta wowacin oŋ oyate kiŋ okiŝeya ŝi. Yunkaŋ wocekiye opakiŋ ota ekta oyaŋpi. Yunkaŋ heci wicaŝta waŋ waŋaĵi to oyaŋke. Yunkaŋ wicake lapi, ohoŋpi ŝica. Yunkaŋ eya Wowapi wakaŋ kiŋ iwacu na blawa, yunkaŋ cante maŝice en Matthew 24: 3 eun : Uŋkaŋ Oliwe Paha kiŋ akaŋ iyotaŋkehaŋ yaŋka he haŋ waonpewicakiye ciŋ iŋaŋna en hipi qa heciyapi ; Lena tohaŋ ecetu kta qa niye yaŋhi kte qa maka ihaŋke kta taku oŋ slonyaŋpi kta, he ito uŋkokiyaka miye. Oegle topa : Uŋkaŋ Jesus wayupte qa howicakiya ; Iĥnuĥaŋ tuwe niĥnayaŋpi kiŋhaŋ. Wicota inica je oŋ upi kta qa, Messiya he miye ce, eyapi kta qa wicaŝta ota wicaĥnayaŋpi kta. Oegle nŋe waŋji : Qa waŋna wokeaŋ itonŝni ota icaĝapi kta qa wicota wicaĥnayaŋpi kta. Oegle ake nonpa : Hehaŋ wicoĥaŋ ŝica ota icaĝe kta heoŋ oŋ wicota waŝtelake ciŋoŋ he sni aye kta. Oegle ake yamni : Tuka tuwe owihaŋke hehaŋyaŋ najiŋ kiŋ he ni kta. Oegle wikcemna nonpa nŋpa yamni. Hehaŋ tuwe Messiya den uŋ ce qa kakiya uŋ ce eniciyapi eŝa wicadapi ŝni po. Jesus maka akaŋ hi kiŋ he ehaŋna gni kte ciŋ he ehaŋ taokiye akenonpa pi hena tokata maka ihaŋke kta qa woekiceŋ ita taku oŋ sloŋuŋyaŋpi kta he eya iyuŋĝapi. Yunkaŋ Jesus wayupte, wowakta kiŋ he uŋqupkye lo. Ho heoŋ mitakolapi he wowapi wakaŋ kiŋ he ia wacin po. Tona taku wakaŋ-wicauŋlapi hena owasiŋ ptayela kiciyus owihanke kiŋ hehaŋyaŋ najiŋpi iyececa ye lo. Waŋĵigji waŋaĵi toie oyakapi kiŋ ie ekta. wicauŋlapi kiŋhaŋ he Wakaŋ kiŋ toŋkicoŋze ŝi makiyuŋpi kte ciŋ he teĥike lo. Mitakolapi qa ayahlcapi wacin. Wocekiye opa kiŋ ota wauĝi toie oyakapi kiŋ he wicalapi keyapi. Eya Wowapi wakaŋ nakuŋ heye lo: Messiya itonŝni na wicaŝta wokcaŋ itonŝni kiŋ heca icaĝapi kta qa wowauyakiŋ

ke tanks wicoĥaŋ tanka ko ecoŋpi kta, hecen okiĥipica uŋkaŋś wicaĥluiĝapi kiŋ hena eopi kaeŝ wicahŋayaŋpi kta. Tuka Je taku kapi na on etaŋ hepe ciŋ le Wowapi wakaŋ he wicakapi keye lo, ca oŋ wicayakapi kiŋ he hecetu, kta heeetu kte ciŋ he le ŝica ea itokaŋ Wowapi wakaŋ uŋkoklayakapi. Mitakuyepi eya miŝ wocekiye owaŋpa uŋkaŋ he Taku wakaŋ oŋe kiŋ wicawaka; na wahtani śo tka Jesus maka akaŋ hi uŋkaŋ he uŋipi kta oŋ hi, wicaŝta waĥtani śo kiŋ heoŋ iyopeuakiŋyapi kta oŋ hi uŋ heoŋ maŝiea tka wocekiye el owapa ; uŋkaŋ he iyotaŋ waŝte oŋ wocekiye opa oyasiŋ iyuŝkiŋyaŋ wowapi cicaĝape lo.

SAM WHITE BIRD.
Lower Brule Agency, S. D.,
October 17, 1890.

CHRISTMAS WOTKEYAPI.

Waŋna ake waŋiyetu oŋkaya ikiyedaŋ uŋyaŋpi. Heoŋ wicaŝta en ihaŋ ohiŋni Christmas wotkeyapi ekta etoŋwaŋ uŋpi wadake. Heuŋcecapi kta iyececa. He wicoĥaŋ tanka nakaeŝ. Hnuyetu kiŋ he cinca awicake-haŋ teĥinda śni. Hokŝidaŋ qa wiciŋyaŋpidaŋ owasiŋ wayawa uŋpi kta heceŋ. Qa tona okliĥipi haŋ wakieicupi ecee, tankapi qa ŝieeca ko, taku ŝiceeapi kiŋ iyotaŋ wicoĥaŋ ke tawapi seeeca. Tuka taku kapi kiŋ he (1) Jesus Messiya yuoniĥaŋpi. (2) Wocekiye wicoĥaŋ hekapi. Heoŋ tohaŋ he ecoŋoŋpi oŋ ohiŋni yuoniĥaŋyaŋ cekiya econqoŋpi kta hecetu.

Dakota ehna wicoĥaŋ de waŋna uŋhapi uŋkaŋ token wokeunyaŋpi waŋ-jigji ito iwanunyakapi kta. Waŋjigji omakiyakapi qa oŋĝe sdonwaya. Waŋ ji napaohotonuŋa een ŝpaŋ waŋ otkeya. Qa waŋji ŝ napaohotonuŋa na waŋ otke-ya. Waŋji iŝ yaĥiĝapidaŋ ŝukaŋa waŋjidaŋ qa waŋji caŋhaŋpidaŋ ŝukaŋa waŋji wowaŝpi opemni otkeya. Tuka kiŋhaŋ he-haŋ piya uŋkamdeeapi kta. Wicaŝta kaŝpapi eyaŋ wanyakapi qeĥaŋ itokaŋ makaŝta eĥpeicĝyapi qa ohodapi. Uŋkaŋ wopiye hduhdokapi qa taku qupi, mazaŝkaŋi, pejihuta waŝteuŋna kaya. Hecen tokata kiŋ owaŋ cistiŋna eŝta wowapi qupi.

PETER HUNTER.

Mitchell (Caŋkaĝipe) ikiyedaŋ woju wicaŝta waŋ aŋpaohotonuŋa tawanuŋ-heza ota icaĥye. Qa ĥemani oiŋaĵiŋ ekta caŋpahmiŋna ohnaka wikcemna ŝahdoĝaŋ waŋ topa al, qa Boston ekta yeye kta.

Thankton waŋ Huŋte Okodakiciye de-haŋ tipi wakaŋ teca kaĝapi. Armour (Heyata Otonwe)hetaŋhaŋ caŋmdaŝka toksŋpi. Okodakiciye iye tokikŝupi, caŋpahmiyaŋ ake-waŋjiĝi. Charles Ironheart, Alleŋ Walter, Tom Benton, Guy Williamson oŋ ŝkaŋpi, qa eeŋdaŋ yuŝtaŋpi kte.

Dehaŋ Santee Koŝka Okodakiciye waoekiyapi ea Gideon Walker caŋdowaŋkiya ece.

Ehnamani Minitaŋka ohnayaŋ mdo ŝkoeka qa i qa ojutoŋpi toŋ ahdi. Waĥeinca Wakpa ekta ake waŝicuŋ wakaŋ waŋ yuhapi, Rev. E. J. Lindsey, John tojaŋku hiĥnaku hee. Qa waŋna heciya anpetu wakaŋ iyohi Wowapi Wakaŋ yawapi ece.

Waŋna Maĥpiyaduta Oyaŋke en pejihuta wicaŝta yuhapi kiŋ Dakota wicaŝta heca. He John Eastman en-nakuŋ, Chas. A. Eastman eciyapi. Waŋiyetu ota hutaŋ wayawa uŋ, qa koŝka kaŝpa qa wuiĥeca.

KOŜKA WAN TINWIQAKTE.

Koŝka waŋ William Carmichael eciyapi waŋiyetu akeŝahdoĝaŋ John Bockhouse kte. Wicaŝta kiŋ de ĥtaniwicaŝta heca. Uŋkaŋ William Bockhouse tl kiŋ ekta l, qa William taŝuŋktaŋka kida. Uŋkaŋ Bockhouse iŝ heya: Tohaŋ miyecicajuju kiŋhaŋ hehaŋ iyacu kte do. Uŋkaŋ William heeeĥaŋ kibde uŋkaŋ tiyata ki. Hehaŋ taukŝitku mazawakaŋ kida. William heya: Taliuca nakuwa mde kte. Uŋkaŋ mazawakaŋ qupi hehaŋ iyaye. Itohaŋ iyaye hehaŋ John Bockhouse ti kiŋ ekta l, uŋkaŋ tipi kiŋ en tuwe-daŋ en uŋ ŝni. Hehaŋ coŋkaŝke tiyo-pa yulidoke qa ŝuŋktaŋka waŋji yu-ze. Hehaŋ qu qa iyotaŋka naĵiŋ. Uŋkaŋ itehaŋ iyaye kiŋhaŋ wicaŝta waŋ u. Hehaŋ kici caŋpahmiĥma opa qa iyayapi.

Tuka John Bockhouse iŝ waŋna ti kiŋ ki. Hehaŋ coŋkaŝke maĥen waŋyake uŋkaŋ ŝuŋktaŋka waŋji ee qa ŝni. Hehaŋ William token iyaye ce heciya okuwa iyaye. Uŋkaŋ itoĥaŋ hehaŋ waŋwicayake uŋkaŋ heciya, Iŋĵiŋ po. Hehaŋ iŋaĵiŋpi. Uŋkaŋ ŝuŋktaŋka waŋna iyuze kte he ŝkaŋ, Tuka wowapi de atayo oyake, koŝka kiŋ de tokeŋkeoŋ oyake, uŋkaŋ waŋya-kapi heceĥnana yuzapi qa qape yaŋpi. Hehaŋ wakeŋ waŝuŋyakapi heeĥaŋ yuzapi ŝni, ceiŋ itokaŋ naŋoŋpi ŝni. Tuka wowapi de atayo oyake, koŝka kiŋ de toketkeon oyake, uŋkaŋ wanyakapi heeĥnana yuzapi qa qape yaŋpi ŝihu ko. Tuka William iŝ naĵice uŋkaŋ toki-yaye taŋiŋ ŝni. Okiŋni waŋna aŋpe-tu wakaŋ nonpa naceeŋ. Uŋkaŋ de-haŋ Coal Harbor en Hassŋpa ti okiŋni makŋ iyutapi yaŋmi koŝka de en tito-kaŋ ki. Tuka uŋkiŝ waŋna maza uŋkahdiĥpeyapi qa Hassŋpa tipi kiŋ en wowapi uŋpi. Hehaŋ wowapi waŋya-kapi icuŋhaŋ William opeya wanyake yaŋke. Eya dena koŝka nonpa slonyapi ŝni, cein itokaŋ naŋonpi ŝni. Tuka wowapi de atayo oyake, koŝka kiŋ de toketkeoŋ oyake, uŋkaŋ wanya-kapi heeehnana yuzapi qa qape yaŋpi qa siha ko. Tuka William iŝ naĵice uŋkaŋ toki-yaye taŋiŋ ŝni. Anpetu wakaŋ hektam October 26, he eŋaŋ yuzapi qa den ahi-yi, Waŝhburn wokaŝke tipi timŝhen. Okiŋni eeadaŋ Bismarck ekta aŋpi kte nacecŋ.

Miŝ waŋna de mazaĥdeĥnayapi eŋ waŝkaŋ. Washburn, N. D., October 23, 1890.
E. C. HOPKINS.

WOWAPI MAQUPI.
FORT BENNETT, S. D.,
October 16, 1890.

Mitakola : Aŋpetu kiŋ dee iyokipiya wowapi waŋji cica kte. Eya token wau-uŋ kiŋ nayaŋoŋ kta wacin. Eya wi noŋpa Cĥeyŋno River ekta wauŋ. Heciya aŋpetu wakaŋ iyohi waĥokon-wicawakiya qa token owakiĥi nina waŝkaŋ. Qa nakun aŋpetu itoŋa kiŋ hee nakuŋ waĥokonpi uŋhapi. Qa wi noŋpa amduŝtaŋ. Icin Mr. T. L. Riggs wi noŋpa he econmaŝi cea waŋna wi noŋpa qa amduŝtaŋ. Qa October wi kiŋ dee Fort Bennett en waun qa, ohinni taŋyaŋ waun. Eya ohinni ta-waciŋ wacinyaŋ wauŋ, qa ohinni mitawacin awaŋmiĥdakŋ, qa token tauyaŋ kte ciŋ ohinni awakita. Wico-waŋji iyomakipi, tukadehaŋ owaŋji waun qa eya tukteŋ Wakaŋtaŋka ecie oyakapi waŋji en omdake kta mduha heca. Eya S. N. T. S. wicoĥaŋ mduha hena aŋpia epiŋ kte. Micaŝte oŋ napi cŋyze do.

EDWIN W. POTTER.

My friends, I want you to be clear-minded. Many take part in the prayers and they say that they believe in the spirit words, it is said. But the sacred book also said this: Messiah lies and false prophets will spring up and they will show big sights and do great deeds; in that way the ones that will choose them will be deceived. This is what it means and therefore I wish to say that the Bible speaks the truth, so it is that they believe in something, but it is so that this one is indeed bad, so the Bible tells us. My relatives, I myself joined the prayers [the Christian church] and then I believe in the sacred words, and I did wrong regularly, but Jesus came on top of the world so that we would live. Those men who do wrong regularly will scold us and because of that he came.

Louis Mazawakiyanna and Samuel Spaniard

"The people dance very much and in the springtime all the spirits will arrive, they say."

Louis Mazawakiyanna and Samuel Spaniard reported on the situation on the Pine Ridge and Rosebud Reservations in the November issue of the *Iapi Oaye*.[37] Both men briefly introduce the basic beliefs of the Ghost Dance and note that many people are sad, but by dancing they believe they will live forever.

Louis Mazawakiyanna writes this from Pine Ridge: I came here in the winter [November–December 1890] [and] no one goes to church.[38]

37. Louis Mazawakiyanna and Samuel Spaniard in *Iapi Oaye*, November 1890, p. 38. Translated by Rani-Henrik Andersson with the assistance of Timo Oksanen, fall 2015.

38. This was not quite true. Fathers Emil Perrig and Florentine Digman, for example, noted in their diaries that although church attendance dropped during the Ghost Dance, a lot of people still attended mass at Pine Ridge. Only after the agent ordered people to come to the agency and after Wounded Knee did people stop coming to churches, but that was due to the chaotic situation, not so much to the Ghost Dance. See Father Emil Perrig Diary, MUA, BCIM, HRMC; September 30, Father Florentine Digman Diary, MUA, BCIM, History of St. Francis Mission, 1886–1922, SFMC.

The people dance very much and in the springtime all the spirits will arrive, they say, and the people's hearts are withered.[39] They all do not want any kind of school and they thought Wakȟáŋ Tȟáŋka is weak.[40] But presently people will believe [in the Ghost Dance].

And Samuel Spaniard relates this from the Rosebud Reservation: "Today I always remember what they tell us in the Bible. Before the end of the world men will do, one by one, mysterious things. And it is said there will be something wrong with all the people.[41]

"And then over here, among all the people, it will come true. In that way I will be alive here, then those [whites] who I know will not at all [be alive here], I think. And then in the present day all spirits will arrive, it is so, they say. And they will see God's son, it is said. And all those who do in that way are told to pray and the people really dance. And all in the camp dance. So in the dance they died, but returned to life again. They do a lot of hand waving [praying, faces turned upward and hands pointing or waving toward the west] and more than 2, 3, 4, 5, 10, 15, 20 dancers gather and they also die and again they come back to life. And many of those who dance want feathers, they say, and red grass, they say.[42] And there is a lot of bad speaking, and because of that, I am sad," he [the Spaniard] relates.

Elias Gilbert

"Then I heard them cry and therefore my heart was very sad."

Elias Gilbert visited Sitting Bull's camp in December at the same time as Mary Collins and Owen Lovejoy. He reported about his visit in the *Iapi Oaye* issue of January 1891.[43] He, too, condemns the Ghost Dance

---

39. The implication here is that as the people's hearts are "withered," they turn to the Ghost Dance and its promise of the return of the spirits in the spring.

40. In this context, Wakȟáŋ Tȟáŋka refers to the Christian God.

41. This sentence is unclear. It seems to suggest that people are stripped of their possessions, which makes them wrong, or sad. Yet it could also refer to the idea that people "smell" or that the "world is worn out," both common themes in the Ghost Dance (see part 1). I am, however, unable to provide an exact translation of the end of the sentence.

42. Red grass refers to a specific kind of grass, *saŋtúhu*. I have not seen the grass used in the Ghost Dance specified elsewhere.

43. Elias Gilbert in *Iapi Oaye*, January 1891, p. 1. Translated by Rani-Henrik Andersson with the assistance of Timo Oksanen, fall 2015.

and, much like Mary Collins, blames Sitting Bull for it. Gilbert describes seeing Sitting Bull leading a Ghost Dance from his sacred tipi. Despite Gilbert's dislike of the Ghost Dance he was moved when he heard people pray and cry. He wondered why people who knew the teachings of the Bible would continue the Ghost Dance. Clearly, some Christian converts were participating in the dance at Sitting Bull's camp. Finally, Gilbert notes in a sorrowful tone that "we killed our own," referring to the arrest and death of Sitting Bull and several others, all Lakotas.

Also at Standing Rock today [by now] they call[44] for many spirits; because of that they all dance. Sitting Bull is the one who leads the dance. He said that he makes many sacred shirts and he himself paints all the faces. On Sacred day [Sunday] during the time we pray, we arrived up there, and in the meanwhile they set up Sitting Bull's sacred tipi and there he sat together with Miss M. C. Collins, [his] face painted when I arrived. "They told us to stop but there is nothing [important] in it; it is for all those who are related to each other," he [Sitting Bull] said only.[45]

Then he said no more. Then right away he took off his dirty clothes and in a plain skirt, or petticoat, he went and he joined those sitting and they sang a song: "Father said this! Father said this!" The people sang this and then a hundred [people] danced close by, but they all stood together their faces turned upward and they all were really able to cry.[46] Then I heard them cry and therefore my heart was very sad. They know the Bible so why then nobody is able to do [behave] sophistically, I thought standing there. At that time they told us that in Sitting Bull's tipi the chief was praying, but nobody came there; one by one they called for them, but only Hiȟdóka[47] and Tȟáčadeskawiŋ, those two came. By now many more move around [danced]. Their father [the agent] really loves them, but by now they do not listen to anything; therefore the father [the agent] makes 20 new policemen.

44. The literal translation would be "growl," but I believe the word "call" is more appropriate.

45. The second part of this sentence is unclear. I assume there is a typo in the original text and I base this translation on that assumption.

46. The literal translation would be "opening upward," but "their faces turned upward" makes more sense in this context.

47. The Lakota spelling used here is derived from the original text, but I am unable to verify it through other sources.

Gradually they change, sooner or later many more will move around hard and they will indeed endure greatly. Now they all clearly do not attend school. So you hear that Sitting Bull's name is great, but now he made himself unimportant; that is why many hearts are sad. Nothing good will become from those things, I think. On December 15, S[itting] B[ull] was killed. It was eight who were killed.[48] Qz caught seven were killed.[49] Little Eagle was killed. We pray for this good man. We killed our own.

Elias Gilbert

Clarence Ward

"This day my heart is sad."

Clarence Ward reported from Cheyenne River in January 1891.[50] While this text was published as late as January 1891, Ward's description of the Ghost Dance ceremony clearly dates back to November–December of 1890. He believes that the Ghost Dance will take the Lakotas back to their old customs, that is, "savagery." That made his "heart sad."

From Cheyenne River

The people at this place where I live are the ones who did something. From the west came the Son of God, they said, and [they] danced and when one becomes dizzy and goes [around] becoming confused, he is knocked down. And whenever he wakes up in the west,[51] the Son of God was there when he arrived, he said, and their relatives, those who died in the past came to life; they warned them of various things and the people were rejoicing.

In the dance whoever is blind and whoever does not speak and whoever does not hear and whoever is sick, many of those will participate in the dance and they will speak and hear things, and those who are sick will recover, they say. Thus I sit there at this place with the people and there are indeed many. Thus [some] people live on top and [some] people live in the

---

48. In addition to Sitting Bull, thirteen people were killed, five of them, including Little Eagle, policemen. See Greene, *American Carnage*, 186.

49. This sentence is unintelligible; the meaning of "Qz" remains unclear.

50. Clarence Ward in *Iapi Oaye*, January 1891, p. 3. Translated by Rani-Henrik Andersson with the assistance of Timo Oksanen, spring 2016.

51. This is a reference to the vision and the journey to the spirit world. When people "woke up" or "rose up" in the spirit world, they saw their dead relatives.

bottom in the world; they assemble there at the Cheyenne Creek community and anything they do is measured in five, six, eight, tens that far in each case in anything one they do.[52] Those who are sick, one by one they bring them and on a flat prairie they stick a tall tree in the ground and to the top of the tree they tie a cloth as offering and they all hold hands around it and dance.[53] There, by the tree, one man, blind many winters, he stood there that day really holding the tree, and thus he did; he stood toward the west and cried. Yet what he could not see was the world; it stood invisible.[54] Thus they pray to God and all Lakotas get dressed up, and all wear the red shirts and they paint [their] faces. So thus they do, and because of that, we will work hard to bring the Gospel [to them]. They cannot refuse it. Two Sundays I rang the [church] bell, but no one came. This dance will bring Lakota customs back downhill [back to savagery]; this day my heart is sad.

Robert White

"Because of the Ghost Dance, God must have something in return."

Robert White wrote a letter from Pine Ridge, dated January 22, 1891, and it was published in the *Iapi Oaye* on February 2, 1891.[55] White fiercely condemns the Ghost Dance, saying that because of it, God took the lives of those killed at Wounded Knee.

January 22, 1891
I give you a letter from Pine Ridge Agency.

My Friend,

I will tell you about something that happened at the Oglala [Pine Ridge] Reservation. They gave up God, because of the Ghost Dance. That is why more than two hundred Lakotas died. They did not

---

52. This sentence is unclear. I am unable to provide an exact meaning to this sentence.

53. For a discussion on the sacred tree, see introduction and part 1.

54. This probably means that he could not receive a vision; thus, the spirit world, and the real world too, remained invisible to him.

55. Robert White in *Iapi Oaye*, February 2, 1891, p. 5. Translated by Rani-Henrik Andersson, March 2017.

permit them [to dance], but they did not listen. Thus they died and thirty-three soldiers also died! Therefore, those who fought, died! Now, on January 21, we stopped [doing something] and all guns were laid down.

Robert White, Blokášiča

Albert Frazier

"In Lakota customs and ceremonies they pray to God in a different way."

Albert Frazier wrote about the killing of Sitting Bull and the fate of one of the Indian policemen, Little Eagle, in the February issue of *Iapi Oaye*.[56] Little Eagle was one of the policemen who was killed during the arrest, and evidently Frazier felt that he was misunderstood because he fought his own people. He emphasizes that Little Eagle did not want to cause trouble for the Ghost Dancers but felt it was his duty as a policeman to follow the agent's orders. Frazier also notes that the Ghost Dance was a reaction to the disruption in the customary religious ceremonies of the Lakotas.

Little Eagle was killed.[57] This man was a shepherd [in the church]. He was that kind of a man. Thus they [the Indian police] arrived to arrest Sitting Bull and he joined them. And there was a fight and he was killed. Because this man faced his own people, I think it is proper for the *Iapi Oaye* to straighten some things out. He lived where Miss [Mary] Collins lives at Grand River. He was a very reliable man. He joined the church society there, the young men's society, and oversaw their money. He was that kind of a man. And again, he was killed on the second sacred day.[58] They had made him *huŋká* relative in the society.[59] He was the kind of man who reached for God. In Lakota customs and ceremonies they pray to God in a different way, and

56. Albert Frazier in *Iapi Oaye*, February 2, 1891, p. 5. Translated by Rani-Henrik Andersson, March 2017.
57. For Little Eagle, see statements by Loneman, Gray Eagle, and Higheagle.
58. This refers to Sunday, and maybe specifically to the second Sunday in Advent. However, December 15, 1890, was a Monday.
59. *Huŋká* is a traditional Lakota ceremony of adoption or making relatives.

now those [traditional] customs stop. Because many do that, the old customs come to stir. And so, on account of the Ghost Dance, he wanted them very much to stop, and he went to them only to cherish them.[60] And our father [agent] commanded them [the Indian police] to arrest Sitting Bull, and he joined them. And he [the agent] wanted them to go that sacred day and they [the policemen] asked him [Little Eagle] to pray the last time when he came, and he said the words in this manner: "God, our Father, have pity on us sinners, and whenever we die one by one, we will live up there in the heaven with our relatives. We want to be part of something."[61] Well, he spoke the words in this manner; thus he talked and now he lives there in heaven, we think.[62]

Paul Crow Eagle

"It is said that because of the Spirit Dance there is fighting."

Paul Crow Eagle wrote a letter from Fort Pierre, S.D., to the *Iapi Oaye* and it was published in March 1891.[63] Crow Eagle's letter is somewhat obscure as it jumps from one thought to another. He, however, blames the old chiefs for keeping the Lakotas from making progress. At the same time, he notes that the Lakotas and the whites will not be the same—they both have their customs, "they are a certain way," he says. That idea was also common among the Ghost Dancers (see part 1, Young Skunk, Pretty Eagle, and Short Bull). He fears that the Ghost Dance, or Spirit Dance, will bring about fighting. The letter is, of course, written after Wounded Knee, right about the time of the final skirmishes between the U.S. Army and the Ghost Dancers.

60. The idea is that he embraced the Ghost Dancers who were perhaps his relatives. He was not there to cause trouble.
61. Other accounts do not mention Little Eagle's prayer. Instead, Bullhead prayed before the policemen left his house.
62. The text continues with a description of Little Eagle's family after his death.
63. Paul Crow Eagle in *Iapi Oaye*, March 1891, p. 10. Translated by Rani-Henrik Andersson with the assistance of Timo Oksanen, spring 2016.

Fort Pierre, S.D.
January 13, 1891

My friend: Today I will give you a letter about what bothers me. I want to say something concerning the Lakota people. The Lakota people are a certain kind, in the same way the whites will be in a certain way. As it is so, they [the whites] taught them, but because of that they obstruct, I think. Men sixty winters [old] and also fifty winters [old], those are the ones that make it so that the white man's customs do not pass with the Lakotas, I think. They stand for the [old] Lakota generation; those ones are [the] symbols of that.

One man was really sick coughing, his breast was really badly thick, so it is incurable. They were not able to be like medicine men.[64]

Up to this day fighting was coming up, but because of that, it is time for men to reason, I think. Those [who] will regularly [want to] prove that they are men, the leaders of the people want fighting to come up from there, I think. By means of wisdom then, such fighting is not to be, I think. Thus my friend, I think it is so: No matter what the white men [do], any Lakotas will remain the same way. It being so, they follow [look for] the grandfather's help,[65] but because now there is no buffalo, it is proper for all men to watch over their children in the future. It is said that because of the Spirit Dance [Ghost Dance] there is fighting, they say. So I have heard, but it is not at all so. God made the world; from it he made one man, he named him Adam. But the Spirit Dance is not in accordance with that. Indeed I fear that something will happen: The fighting will take the Dakota assembly [people] down, it is so, they say.

Paul Crow Eagle

64. This sentence means that the Ghost Dance leaders, that is, those who acted as medicine men, could not cure the man.

65. In traditional Lakota culture, the term "grandfather" symbolized the powers of the universe, i.e., Wakȟáŋ Tȟáŋka.

Owen Lovejoy

"The people here are now held in a strange delusion."

Owen Lovejoy accompanied the Reverend George W. Reed to Sitting Bull's camp twice in November 1890. He wrote a letter to the Christian Endeavor Society on November 13, which was published in the *Word Carrier* under the title "In Sitting Bull's Camp."[66] Owen Lovejoy describes his meeting with Sitting Bull in a frustrated tone because Sitting Bull chose not to speak to Lovejoy and Reed. Still, Owen Lovejoy decided to keep on trying to change "those men."

Friends: Two weeks ago I came to Standing Rock Agency and there I stayed over Sunday. Mr. [George] Reed asked me to take charge of the morning service, which I was glad to do. Quite a good many were present, although not so many, they say, as there have been at other times. The people here are now held in a strange delusion. On this account I took as my subject the story of Simon the Sorcerer and Philip in the eighth chapter of Acts. After the Sabbath I went the last forty-four miles of my journey with Mr. Reed to Sitting Bull's camp. We talked to him and I told him that I wanted to teach there this winter, but he didn't say anything. Then Mr. Reed spoke, but again he didn't answer. So we came away, but today we went again and still he is not willing. So it seems very hard. But I want to keep on trying. If I go there, and then go again, and again, God is able after a while to change those men. This I know, and I believe He will do it. So I ask you to remember me always when you pray.

66. Owen Lovejoy in the *Word Carrier*, November 1890, p. 31.

Josephine Waggoner

"These fanatical beliefs preyed on the minds of the poor distracted Indians."

This text is Josephine Waggoner's reflection on the Ghost Dance. The original handwritten text is in the Josephine Waggoner Collection, Museum of the Fur Trade, in Chadron, Nebraska. The text was recently published in *Witness: A Húŋkpapȟa Historian's Strong-Heart Song of the Lakotas*, edited by Emily Levine.[67] Waggoner is very critical of the Ghost Dance, but she says that it coincided with the Bible, since the Indians were eagerly waiting for the Second Coming of the Messiah, or Christ. She reflects upon a meeting between herself and the Ghost Dancers. During the meeting, which took place in January 1890, she read letters sent by Kicking Bear. At that time, Kicking Bear was in Nevada to meet with Wovoka. Waggoner's account seems to verify that the Lakota delegates did indeed send letters home while in Nevada (see Selwyn, part 3). Unfortunately, none of these letters have survived. Waggoner notes that she argued with the Indians about the Ghost Dance for an hour and a half after which some decided to drop it.

The last time I saw the chief [Sitting Bull] it was at Thunder Hawk's house when I read letters for them from Pine Ridge, when they asked my opinion and I spoke to them, until I saw his dead body at the agency hall with the dead policemen. He was refused a place of burial at the agency; his body was turned over to the military. My husband, being a carpenter in the post, made his rough pine box. All the Ghost Dancers fled for the Badlands after Sitting Bull was killed.

Before this trouble, in nearly every log cabin on the reservation there was a Bible. All the Indians were eager to hear the stories of the Bible read by

---

67. Josephine Waggoner in JWP, MFT. Published also in Waggoner, *Witness*, edited by Levine, 175–76, 218–24. Reproduced from Josephine Waggoner, *Witness: A Húŋk-papȟa Historian's Strong-Heart Song of the Lakotas*, edited by Emily Levine, by permission of the University of Nebraska Press. Copyright 2013 by the Board of Regents of the University of Nebraska. I have also used the copies of the original Waggoner papers held at the American Indian Studies Research Institute, Indiana University, but followed Emily Levine's edition.

their young men who had learned to read their own language. In the New Testament, the promise of the Second Coming of the Messiah was hopefully listened to. That the kingdom of God was right at hand was firmly believed. All the promises that those who believed would not die but enter into everlasting life inspired them to hold on to their faith. It was like the proverbial last straw for a captive to believe. They urged each other to have more faith and not give up. Most of those Ghost Dancers were people who had retreated into Canada and stayed in exile for four years after Custer's battle. They had suffered untold misery from want and the cold winters in Canada.[68]

The new religion came to them from Walker Lake, Nevada. Jack Wilson, a half-blood of the Fish Eaters, first began to preach in 1887. He claimed he went into a trance and had revelations from God. He was told to spread the new gospel. I read many letters that came from Pine Ridge, where the worship and dance was practiced. I read some of the letters that came from Walker Lake. I did not see anything very objectionable in Wilson's ideas. He spoke of a new heaven and a new earth that was to come. It was metaphysical illustration, but the Indians took these sayings as material facts, misconstrued the ideas. They believed God would help them get back the vast dominion of hunting grounds and herds of wild game that the government had taken from them. Jack Wilson's new religion coincided with the teachings from the Bible.

One night, January 10, 1889 [1890], I was recalled to a meeting at Thunder Hawk's house near Kenel, S.D. There I read more letters that had come from Kicking Bear, who said that he had heard from Nevada.[69] He wanted all the people to stand firm, to keep praying and dancing, for the Messiah would soon be here. Now, all these fanatical beliefs preyed on the minds of the poor distracted Indians. I told them that I thought their new belief was all a mistake. It was not true. I said the Great Spirit never planned for all the white people to be extinguished. One Indian who was more radical said to me, "If you don't believe, you will die." I talked and argued for an hour and a half. I believe I convinced some of them that night: Thunder Hawk, Bear Face, Iron Horn, Crow Feather, and their bands. Indians are thinking and reasoning human beings, who are intelligent and good observers with good

68. For their life in Canada, see Howard, *Canadian Sioux.*
69. The date here should be 1890. Kicking Bear and the rest only left for Utah in the fall of 1889. In a short statement Waggoner gave to Walter S. Campbell, she also claims that the Ghost Dance trouble took place in 1889. See, Waggoner in WSCMC, WHCU-OLA, box 104, folder 14.

judgment and wisdom. But the highest and wisest can be deceived as well as the lowest.

———

The last Sitting Bull battle was fought on the morning of the 15th of December, 1890, on Grand River, about four miles northwest of Little Eagle and about ten or twelve miles below Bullhead. Out of the forty-three policemen who were sent to arrest Sitting Bull, four were killed by the Ghost Dancers. These were Armstrong, Little Eagle, Warriors Fear Him, and Hawk Man. Shave Head and Bullhead were wounded and died in a few days. The bodies of the police were gathered, placed in a wagon by the order of Captain [Edmund G.] Fechét, and hauled to Fort Yates. Colonel [William F.] Drum was the commander and was with the troops. There were but a very few men left in the garrison. G Troop under Fechét, F Troop under De Rudio, and four companies of infantry, H, E, I, and G companies of the 12th, all left Fort Yates the afternoon of the 14th of December.

The dead of the hostiles who were left at Sitting Bull's camp were Crow Foot, Sitting Bull's young son; Wakíŋyaŋ Ohítika, Brave Thunder—a chief; Tȟatȟáŋka Hégleška, another chief; Matȟó Wawóyušpa, Catching Bear; Tȟatȟáŋka Šíča [?]; Ziŋtkála Sápa; Wanápȟa Wakhúwa; and Sitting Bull made eight. There were some wounded who did not die.[70] The two troops of cavalry reached Sitting Bull's camp after the battle was over and the four companies of infantry were still at Oak Creek near McLaughlin when the troops were getting back to Fort Yates. In the meantime, the Ghost Dancers fled through the woods and brakes as the police chased them and kept up a continual fire at women and children as well as the men. Intelligence had been brought in to Fort Yates that the Ghost Dancers were preparing to leave the reservation without permission to go to a convention in the Badlands south of White River near Wounded Knee Creek. This report was sent in by Mr. John M. Carignan, who was a teacher at the Sitting Bull camp.[71] No sooner had the intentions of the Ghost Dancers been discovered, wires were being flashed all over the northwest between military camps. The Ghost Dancers were surrounded, although they were not aware of it. So sure were the Indians of the Second Coming of Christ to save them from starvation and destruction that nothing but death would have stopped their flight, as was the case. Some of the families, about fifteen or twenty, went

70. For a full list of casualties, see Greene, *American Carnage*, 186.
71. See part 2.

south to White Horse from Standing Rock. This place is on the Moreau River. All these families were arrested and taken to Fort Sully.

The largest number of the Ghost Dancers started direct west up the Grand River—a few in wagons, most of them on horseback, and a large number were on foot with packs of provisions and bedding on their backs; some were carrying children on their backs. The men stopped every now and then to demand ammunition from any of those they found at home along the river. The policemen's wives, who were at home, had to give up gun and ammunition. Mrs. Weasel Bear was at home with her children near Firesteel—her husband being a policeman and on duty—she was compelled to give up three or four rounds of ammunition, his winter's allowance. She told me afterwards each horseback rider going by would stop to demand bullets, food, and blankets till she had to lock her door and leave her home. Later her home was ransacked of everything that was needful to the hostiles.

The journey led them westward up the river toward the Slim Butte country. When they reached Firesteel River, a rider reported that soldiers had been sent out toward the headwaters of Grand River to head off all travelers. This report changed their course; the Firesteel River was followed, camping under bluffs and thickets where discovery would almost be impossible, till they passed over the level prairies where Isabel is now situated on the Milwaukee Railroad. Following the brakes and sloping country that led toward the Little Moreau, they reached Cherry Creek—a stream that flows into the Cheyenne River. In a most pitiful condition, starved, footsore, and ragged, these half-demented, religion-crazed human beings reached Spotted Elk or Big Foot's camp on Cherry Creek. Big Foot was a believer in the new Messiah and took immediate steps to go to Pine Ridge, where the Messiah was reported to be in a few days.[72] Hasty preparations were made. Wagons and horses were furnished by his band so that from there on, no one would have to walk.[73]

There were a few families who were behind in their journey and reached Cheyenne River a day or two later. These were intercepted by soldiers and taken to Fort Sully. Hump, who has been mentioned before, was a scout, a very intelligent man and a nonbeliever.[74] He advised Big Foot to give

72. I have not seen this statement elsewhere.
73. See statements of Dewey Beard and Alice Ghost Horse in part 3.
74. Hump was a Ghost Dancer but decided to give it up after consulting his old friend Captain Ezra P. Ewers. Andersson, *The Lakota Ghost Dance of 1890*, pp. 88, 146.

himself up. He told Big Foot that the coming of the new Messiah was a great mistake. Big Foot was convinced. After wandering around in the Badlands not being able to find the Stronghold where all the believers had gathered together to dance and pray till the new Messiah should come, he decided to go in to the military camp and give himself up under the escort of Hump. He was sick with the pneumonia. It was just as well to go forward and meet the soldiers as to go home and contend with the Indian police.[75]

The police had the law back of them and although there were some very good men among them, there were others that were mean and treacherous, who were always reporting stories to the authorities—some of which were utterly untrue—especially against the unfavored factors in the case. A great deal of injustice was practiced under the blanket of law. Old feuds still rankled in some of their hearts. A great many reports that went into the agent's office of petty, trivial happenings were just prompted by jealousy from old grievances that still rose up to do injury to their old-time enemies in a hateful and revengeful spirit. Of these things the Indian agent knew nothing; being in the dark about their past, he gave credence and listened and was influenced by many distorted lies. Yet these poor, deluded Ghost Dancers were disobeying orders from the Indian agents. They had no right nor no freedom to worship in any form of religion—only as the white man dictated. They forgot that they were wards of the government.

Jack Wilson may have had a revelation and may have had a good message for the Indians but, as it was not written, the message was changed by the time it reached the Sioux. It had been only eight years since these people surrendered and gave themselves up to the U.S. government.[76] Even their age-old customs had to be given up. There was no more liberty. They felt like prisoners, living on foods not adaptable to them. Their spirits were broken and dead. When they broke away from the reservation, half-crazed and hungry, they killed anybody's cattle.[77] On the reservation they had cattle, but they were not allowed to kill them, so they just left them. Little did these people know that their new religion was causing such a great commotion and disturbance among the white people. In the surrounding settlements, the white people were always afraid that Sitting Bull might get desperate and break out. They were afraid of losing their lives.

75. Waggoner's account is not accurate. Big Foot was not on his way to the Stronghold and he was not escorted by Hump when he surrendered.

76. This applies to Sitting Bull's people who surrendered in 1881.

77. The Ghost Dancers never broke away from the reservation or killed cattle owned by whites off the reservation.

The Ghost Dancing of a distracted nation was causing a panic in some of the nearby towns. Mass meetings were held, resolutions were adopted calling for arms and ammunition.[78] All sorts of stories were told that easily found credence. General Miles of Chicago and General [Thomas H.] Ruger of St. Paul were watchful; they were in communication by wire at all times. Orders were issued for the troops at Fort Yates and Fort Lincoln to be in readiness at short notice. At Cheyenne, Wyoming, the post there received the same orders. So did those at Fort Robinson at Nebraska. Along the middle of November, four companies had arrived at Pine Ridge from Omaha. Troops also arrived from Fort Robinson, Fort McKinny, and Fort Niobrara. General Brooke from Omaha arrived at Pine Ridge until there was said to be six thousand soldiers; half of these were mounted; about six soldiers for every Ghost Dancer.

At Pine Ridge, where the dancing was continually kept up, great chiefs like White Thunder, No Neck, White Bull, Afraid of His Horses, Short Bull, and Turning Bear were all swept into the new belief. The Rosebud Brulés were not exempt: chiefs like Iron Shell, Two Strike, Big Turkey, High Pipe, Big Bad Horse, Bull Dog, Crow Dog, Kicking Bear, High Hawk, and Pine Eagle—so great was their belief in their prophets and their blessings that Chief Porcupine gave himself up to be shot at, believing that material bullets could not penetrate a blessed Ghost Shirt.[79] He was placed at a little distance and the Ghost Dancers opened fire on him. At the first discharge, Porcupine, the Oglala chief, was shot through the thigh. The Indians tried to say that he was not hurt, but he could not walk for quite a while.

The Indian agent, Royer, of Pine Ridge and Special Agent Cooper sent five hundred agency Indians out to induce the Ghost Dancers to come in. Father Jutz, a Catholic priest, was with them. He promised perfect peace if they would come in to have a conference with General Brooke, the army officer stationed at Pine Ridge. Father Jutz succeeded in bringing in the principal men, the leaders in the Messiah craze: Two Strike, Little Wound, Turning Bear, Short Bull, Bad Horse, Bull Dog, High Horse, Big Turkey, and High Pine, with their bands. General Brooke talked with them, told them to give up their rebellious attitude, to stop making raids on private property. He asked them to come in and tell their grievances so that the mis-

---

78. For discussion about settlers' reactions, see Andersson, *The Lakota Ghost Dance of 1890*, pp. 45, 119–20; Greene, *American Carnage*, 93–96; Gage, "Intertribal Communication," 250–55.

79. Waggoner's list of Ghost Dancers is not quite accurate. Short Bull, for example, was from Rosebud, and Kicking Bear from Cheyenne River.

understandings and reports carried on by the irresponsible persons could all be remedied and explained away. He told them that the United States government did not want them; they should all come in and live peaceably. He promised that they should have an increase of rations. After this conference, the hostiles were given a liberal allowance of rations.

The hostiles began fighting among themselves after this. Turning Bear and Short Bull went back to their retreat in the Badlands. This conference took place about the sixth of December. From that time on, many people went out to try to make peace but to no avail. They persistently remained in their retreat preparing to sell their lives dearly. There were many reports reached them of being sent to Florida or Oklahoma, to which places they swore they would never go.[80]

There were many councils held by the peaceable agency Indians to urge their tribesmen to come in. Little Wound and Big Road did a great deal of work among them. Red Cloud sent word to his tribesmen to come in. Afraid of His Horses talked quite sensibly to General Miles.[81] Chief White Eagle, Standing Soldier, Standing Bear, and American Horse were doing their level best to win the confidence of the Ghost Dancers. Lieutenant Taylor of the 9th Cavalry, who commanded the scouts, was working hard. And among the scouts were Chief Standing Soldier, American Horse, Standing Bear, Fast Thunder, Spotted Horse, White Bird, and Bad Wound. And among the Brulé scouts were High Pipe, Iron Bull, and Eagle Pipe, and others. There were many more scouts that I could not find out.

As Big Foot made his way slowly, intending to give himself up to the army, he was met by Captain [Major] Whitside. Big Foot was so sick he was lying in the wagon in the back, his wife doing the driving. This was on the 28th of December, 1890. Big Foot immediately gave himself up. Whitside was the captain of the 7th Cavalry. Colonel [James W.] Forsyth came to reinforce Whitside; the whole procession moved on into Wounded Knee Creek. Forsyth threw his army around the Indian camp. The Hotchkiss guns were directed toward the Indian camps in preparation to disarm the Indians. The command was given to the Indians to come forward from the tents, the women and children remaining in the tents. At eight o'clock the orders were given to the Indians to come forward by twenties to give up their guns. Captain Whitside was irritated because in this first number only two guns were

80. See statements in part 2.
81. General Miles was not at Pine Ridge in early December; he arrived only after Wounded Knee.

brought forward. He demanded that the Indians be searched for arms. The search was made through the tipis in no gentle manner, which angered the Indians. A half-crazy Indian, who was considered simple, shot his gun off, which started the awful turmoil. The Indians knew they were outnumbered and were not very well armed. At the same time, they thought the soldiers wanted to disarm them so as to make them defenseless and either to kill them easily or to be sent down to Florida.

When an Indian sings a song of grief, sorrow, and regret, it is because he thinks of his former days of freedom, plenty, and happiness in comparison with the present times when he is reduced to want, hunger, and poverty. As soon as the white people hear these songs, they take alarm: they think the old Indians are singing a war song and are just about to raise the tomahawk or use the scalping knife. Now, there is no such thing as a war song. If an Indian was going to make an attack, he certainly would not sing about it. Someone was singing one of these grief songs at the Wounded Knee battle and the soldiers, naturally, interpreted it as a war song. It was an easy matter to conquer this friendly band of disarmed Indians. Those of them that fell in that battlefield were men and were heroes. They fought even after they were riddled to pieces, lying on the ground while their women and children were shot in the back as they ran to try to save themselves. What if they were in the wrong and suffering under a false illusion because they had a wrong idea about the Messiah? Should such a massacre take place?

Josephine Waggoner

"Christ (of red race) would return and rule [the] world good."

Josephine Waggoner gave a shorter statement to Walter S. Campbell.[82] Here, she also refers to the letter she read to the gathered Ghost Dancers. The document is written in Campbell's shorthand notes and difficult to read, but the essence of the text is that Waggoner did not believe in the Ghost Dance, but others were clearly excited about the coming of the new world.

82. Josephine Waggoner in WSCMC, WHCUOLA, box 105, folder 41. Published by permission of University of Oklahoma Libraries.

Thunder Hawk and brother One Feather [held a] Ghost Dance in [a] long room indoors.[83]

[They] wanted me to read [a] letter from [the] spirit world. [It was in] poor soo [Sioux] writing. [The] new world [is] coming soon, be prepared, good and obedient. All white people [will be] swept off [the] Earth. [The] world [will be] as before and Christ (of red race) would return and rule [the] world good and save it. There would be plenty as before. People must not squander food and be careful what they used. Everyone must be good (true principle *good* by three months (?) [in] hearing, seeing and speaking).[84]

Christ [is] coming to save [the] Indians and Indians only.

Indians thought Christ [is] coming in [as a] material being.

Messiah of Utes [was] like any other. [He kept his] head down when [he] speak [spoke], [he] spread arms out and shook them, [his] voice [was] like [a] medium. [He] said [it is the] voice of Christ. He said to be *good.* But they wouldn't listen.[85]

[The] letter came from Pine Ridge (reservation near Badlands). [It was] repeated several times to exceedingly quiet Indians.

[They] got [the] letter at Thunder Hawk's house on Missouri River in South Dakota—corner of Vanderbilt and Pollock.

Belief was rank so Mrs. Waggoner didn't care to express [her] opinion.[86] *Iron Horn's brother asked her. She wouldn't believe it till she saw it! Thunder Hawk said:* "Don't you know new world [is] coming," etc., "that you will lose life if not to believe in it?" *She said:* "No. I am [illegible], didn't believe in it and didn't want it."[87]

83. There is no other account that mentions dancing indoors.

84. The word "good" underlined in the original. While this sentence, added by Campbell, is ambiguous, the three months perhaps refer to the expected arrival of the Messiah.

85. Waggoner suggests that the Ghost Dancers did not listen, as they broke the rules of the reservation. For comparison, see Waggoner's statement above.

86. For comparison, see the text above.

87. The text continues with shorthand notes by Campbell.

Charles A. Eastman

"The 'Messiah craze' in itself was scarcely a source of danger."

The following statement regarding the Ghost Dance on Pine Ridge appeared in Charles Eastman's autobiography, *From the Deep Woods to Civilization: Chapters in the Autobiography of an Indian*, in 1916 in the chapter titled "The Ghost Dance War."[88] Eastman's statement gives an insight into the daily events around Pine Ridge Agency in November–December 1890. Eastman, who spoke Dakota, befriended Red Cloud and other notable leaders, which enables him to tell the story from the vantage point of those staying at the agency throughout the trouble. He condemns the Ghost Dance but sees it in the wider context of the problems of reservation life.

A religious craze such as that of 1890–91 was a thing foreign to the Indian philosophy.[89] I recalled that a hundred years before, on the overthrow of the Algonquin nations, a somewhat similar faith was evolved by the astute Delaware prophet, brother to Tecumseh.[90] It meant that the last hope of race entity had departed, and my people were groping blindly after spiritual relief in their bewilderment and misery. I believe that the first prophets of the "Red Christ" were innocent enough and that the people generally were sincere, but there were doubtless some who went into it for self-advertisement, and who introduced new and fantastic features to attract the crowd.

The Ghost Dancers had gradually concentrated on the Medicine Root Creek and the edge of the Badlands, and they were still further isolated by a new order from the agent, calling in all those who had not adhered to the new religion. Several thousand of these "friendlies" were soon encamped on the White Clay Creek, close by the agency. It was near the middle of

---

88. Charles Eastman in *From Deep Woods to Civilization*, 92–115.

89. This is not exactly true. As recent scholarship has shown, the Ghost Dance had many features common to Native American belief systems in general. See, for example, Andersson, *The Lakota Ghost Dance of 1890;* Warren, *God's Red Son.*

90. For more about Tecumseh and other revitalization movements, see Andersson, *The Lakota Ghost Dance of 1890.*

December, with weather unusually mild for that season. The dancers held that there would be no snow so long as their rites continued.[91]

An Indian called Little had been guilty of some minor offense on the reservation and had hitherto evaded arrest. Suddenly he appeared at the agency on an issue day, for the express purpose, as it seemed, of defying the authorities. The assembly room of the Indian Police, used also as a council room, opened out of my dispensary, and on this particular morning a council was in progress. I heard some loud talking, but was too busy to pay particular attention, though my assistant had gone in to listen to the speeches. Suddenly the place was in an uproar, and George burst into the inner office, crying excitedly "Look out for yourself, friend! They are going to fight!"

I went around to see what was going on. A crowd had gathered just outside the council room, and the police were surrounded by wild Indians with guns and drawn knives in their hands. "Hurry up with them!" one shouted, while another held his stone war club over a policeman's head. The attempt to arrest Little had met with a stubborn resistance.

At this critical moment, a fine-looking Indian in citizens' clothes faced the excited throng, and spoke in a clear, steady, almost sarcastic voice.

"Stop! Think! What are you going to do? Kill these men of our own race? Then what? Kill all these helpless white men, women, and children? And what then? What will these brave words, brave deeds lead to in the end? How long can you hold out? Your country is surrounded with a network of railroads; thousands of white soldiers will be here within three days. What ammunition have you? What provisions? What will become of your families? Think, think, my brothers! This is a child's madness."

It was the "friendly" chief, American Horse, and it seems to me as I recall the incident that this man's voice had almost magic power. It is likely that he saved us all from massacre, for the murder of the police, who represented the authority of the government, would surely have been followed by a general massacre. It is a fact that those Indians, who upheld the agent were in quite as much danger from their wilder brethren as were the white; indeed it was said that the feeling against them was even stronger. Jack Red Cloud, son of the chief, thrust the muzzle of a cocked revolver almost into the face of American Horse. "It is you and your kind," he shouted, "who

91. The idea that snow would not fall if dancing continued was not common among the Ghost Dancers. However, according to some witnesses, Sitting Bull prophesized that the winter would be mild and thus suitable for dancing. See Andersson, *Lakota Ghost Dance of 1890*, p. 66.

have brought us to this pass!"[92] That brave man never flinched. Ignoring his rash accuser, he quietly reentered the office, the door closed behind him, the mob dispersed, and for the moment the danger seemed over.

That evening I was surprised by a late call from American Horse, the hero of the day. His wife entered close behind him. Scarcely were they seated when my door again opened softly, and Captain [George] Sword came in, followed by Lieutenant Thunder Bear and most of the Indian Police. My little room was crowded. I handed them some tobacco, which I had always at hand for my guests, although I did not smoke myself. After a silence, the chief got up and shook hands with me ceremoniously. In a short speech, he asked my advice in the difficult situation that confronted them between the Ghost Dancers, men of their own blood, and the government to which they had pledged their loyalty.

Thanks to Indian etiquette, I could allow myself two or three minutes to weigh my words before replying. I finally said, in substance, "There is only one thing for us to do and be just to both sides. We must use every means for a peaceful settlement of this difficulty. Let us be patient; let us continue to reason with the wilder element, even though some hotheads may threaten our lives. If the worst happens, however, it is our solemn duty to serve the United States government. Let no man ever say that we were disloyal! Following such a policy, dead or alive, we shall have no apology to make."

After the others had withdrawn, Sword informed me confidentially that certain young men had threatened to kill American Horse while [he was] asleep in his tent, and that his friends had prevailed upon him and his wife to ask my hospitality for a few days. I showed Mrs. American Horse to a small room that I had vacant, and soon afterward came three strokes of the office bell—the signal for me to report at the agent's office.

I found there the agent, his chief clerk, and a visiting inspector, all of whom obviously regarded the situation as serious. "You see, doctor," said the agent, "the occurrence of today was planned with remarkable accuracy, so that even our alert police were taken entirely by surprise and readily

92. The incident on November 11, while not directly linked to the Ghost Dance, shows how the tensions between the Ghost Dancers and non-Ghost Dancers had escalated. Yet it is too simplistic to say that it was specifically the Ghost Dancers who were trying to free Little. In reality, many, but not all, of them were Ghost Dancers. More importantly, it shows, in the words of Jack Red Cloud, the deep split that had grown between those who signed the previous year's Sioux Act and those who did not. For American Horse's comments, see part 2.

overpowered. What will be the sequel we cannot tell, but we must be prepared for anything. I shall be glad to have your views," he added.

I told him that I still did not believe there was any widespread plot, or deliberate intention to make war upon the whites. In my own mind, I felt sure that the arrival of troops would be construed by the Ghost Dancers as a threat or a challenge, and would put them at once on the defensive. I was not in favor of that step; neither was Mr. [Reverend Charles S.] Cook, who was also called into conference; but the officials evidently feared a general uprising, and argued that it was their duty to safeguard the lives of the employees and others by calling for the soldiers without more delay. Sword, Thunder Bear, and American Horse were sent for and their opinions appeared to be fully in accord with those of the agent and inspector, so the matter was given out as settled. As a matter of fact, the agent had telegraphed to Fort Robinson for troops before he made a pretense of consulting us Indians, and they were already on their way to Pine Ridge.[93]

I scarcely knew at the time, but gradually learned afterward, that the Sioux had many grievances and causes for profound discontent, which lay back of and were more or less closely related to the Ghost Dance craze and the prevailing restlessness and excitement. Rations had been cut from time to time; the people were insufficiently fed, and their protests and appeals were disregarded. Never was more ruthless fraud and graft practiced upon a defenseless people than upon these poor natives by their politicians! Never were there more worthless "scraps of paper" anywhere in the world than many of the Indian treaties and government documents! Sickness was prevalent and the death rate alarming, especially among the children. Trouble from all these causes had for some time been developing, but might have been checked by humane and conciliatory measure. The "Messiah craze" in itself was scarcely a source of danger, and one might almost as well call upon the army to suppress Billy Sunday and his hysterical followers. Other tribes than the Sioux who adopted the new religion were let alone, and the craze died a natural death in the course of a few months.

Among the leaders of the malcontents at this time were Jack Red Cloud, No Water, He Dog, Four Bears, Yellow Bear, and Kicking Bear. Friendly

93. The dates are not quite accurate here. Agent Daniel F. Royer did send telegrams to call for troops, but President Benjamin Harrison gave the orders to send troops on November 13. So the troops were not on the move on November 11, as claimed by Eastman. See President Benjamin Harrison to Secretary of War Redfield Proctor, November 13, 1890, NARA, RG 94, AIWKSC, M983, roll 1, vol. 1, pp. 19–20.

leaders included American Horse, Young Man Afraid of His Horses, Bad Wound, Three Stars. There was still another set whose attitude was not clearly defined, and among these men was Red Cloud, the greatest of them all. He who had led his people so brilliantly and with such remarkable results, both in battle and diplomacy, was now an old man of over seventy years, living in a frame house which had been built for him a half mile from the agency. He would come to council, but said little or nothing. No one knew exactly where he stood, but it seemed that he was broken in spirit as in body and convinced of the hopelessness of his people's cause.

It was Red Cloud who asked the historic question, at a great council held in the Black Hills region with a government commission, and after good Bishop [Henry B.] Whipple had finished the invocation, "Which God is our brother praying to now? Is it the same God whom they have twice deceived, when they made treaties with us which they afterward broke?"[94]

Early in the morning after the attempted arrest of Little, George rushed into my quarters and awakened me. "Come quick!" he shouted. "The soldiers are here!" I looked along the White Clay Creek toward the little railroad town of Rushville, Nebraska, twenty-five miles away, and just as the sun rose above the knife-edged ridges black with stunted pine, I perceived a moving cloud dust that marked the trail of the Ninth Cavalry.[95] There was instant commotion among the camps of friendly Indians. Many women and children were coming in to the agency for refuge, evidently fearing that the dreaded soldiers might attack their villages by mistake. Some who had not heard of their impending arrival hurried to the offices to ask what it meant. I assured those who appealed to me that the troops were here only to preserve order, but their suspicions were not easily allayed.

As the cavalry came nearer, we saw that they were colored troopers, wearing buffalo overcoats and muskrat caps; the Indians with their quick wit called them "buffalo soldiers."[96] They halted, and established their temporary camp in the open space before the agency enclosure. The news had already gone out through the length and breadth of the reservation, and the wildest rumors were in circulation. Indian scouts might be seen upon every hill top, closely watching the military encampment.

94. The reference is to the negotiations in the aftermath of the 1876–1877 war, resulting in the Sioux Act of 1877 and the loss of the Black Hills.

95. Eastman's dates are not quite accurate here either, as the troops arrived on November 20 and the attempted arrest of Little took place on November 11.

96. The Ninth and Tenth Cavalry consisted of black soldiers, but their officers were white.

At this juncture came the startling news from Fort Yates, some two hundred and fifty miles to the north of us, that Sitting Bull had been killed by Indian police while resisting arrest, and a number of his men with him, as well as several of the police.[97] We next heard that the remnant of his band had fled in our direction, and soon afterward, that they had been joined by Big Foot's band from the western part of Cheyenne River Agency, which lay directly in their road. United States troops continued to gather at strategic points, and of course the press seized upon the opportunity to enlarge upon the strained situation and predict an "Indian uprising." The reporters were among us, and managed to secure much "news" that no one else ever heard of.[98] Border towns were fortified and cowboys and militia gathered in readiness to protect them against the "red devils." Certain classes of the frontier population industriously fomented the excitement for what there was in it for them, since much money is apt to be spent at such times. As for the poor Indians, they were quite as badly scared as the whites and perhaps with more reason.

General Brooke undertook negotiations with the Ghost Dancers, and finally induced them to come within reach. They camped on a flat about a mile north of us and in full view, while the more tractable bands were still gathered in the south and west. The large boarding school had locked its doors and succeeded in holding its hundreds of Indian children, partly for their own sakes, and partly as hostages for the good behavior of their fathers. At the agency were now gathered all the government employees and their families, except such as had taken flight, together with traders, missionaries, and ranchmen, army officers, and newspaper men. It was a conglomerate population.

During this time of grave anxiety and nervous tension, the cooler heads among us went about our business, and still refused to believe in the tragic possibility of an Indian war. It may be imagined that I was more than busy, though I had not such long distances to cover, for since many Indians accustomed to comfortable log houses were compelled to pass the winter in tents,

97. Here, too, Eastman's story is not accurate. He indicates that Sitting Bull was killed immediately following the troops' arrival. However, he was killed on December 15.

98. For the news reporting, see Elmo Scott Watson, "The Last Indian War, 1890–1891: A Study of Newspaper Jingoism," *Journalism Quarterly* 20, no. 1 (1943): 205–19; George R. Kolbenschlag, *Whirlwind Passes: News Correspondents and the Sioux Indian Disturbances of 1890–1891* (Vermillion: University of South Dakota Press, 1990); Andersson, *The Lakota Ghost Dance of 1890*, pp. 192–250.

there was even more sickness than usual. I had access and welcome to the camps of all the various groups and factions, a privilege shared by my good friend Father Jutz, the Catholic missionary, who was completely trusted by his people.

The Christmas season was fast approaching, and this is perhaps the brightest spot in the mission year. The children of the Sunday Schools, and indeed all the people, look eagerly forward to the joyous feast; barrels and boxes are received and opened, candy bags made and filled, carols practiced, and churches decorated with ropes of spicy evergreen.

Anxious to relieve the tension in every way within his power, Mr. Cook and his helpers went on with their preparations upon even a larger scale than usual. Since all of the branch stations had been closed and the people called in, it was planned to keep the Christmas tree standing in the chapel for a week, and to distribute gifts to a separate congregation each evening. I found myself pressed into the service, and passed some happy hours in the rectory. For me, at that critical time, there was inward struggle as well as the threat of outward conflict, and I could not but recall what my "white mother" had said jokingly one day, referring to my pleasant friendships with many charming Boston girls, "I know one Sioux who has not been conquered, and I shall not rest till I hear of his capture!"

I had planned to enter upon my life work unhampered by any other ties, and declared that all my love should be vested in my people and my profession. At last, however, I had met a woman whose sincerity was convincing and whose ideals seemed very like my own. Her childhood had been spent almost as much out of doors as mine, on a lonely estate up in the Berkshire hills; her ancestry Puritan on one side, proud Tories on the other. She had been moved by the appeals of that wonderful man, General Armstrong, and had gone to Hampton as a young girl to teach the Indians there. After three years, she undertook pioneer work in the West as teacher of a new camp school among the wilder Sioux, and after much travel and study of their peculiar problems had been offered the appointment she now held. She spoke the Sioux language fluently and went among the people with the utmost freedom and confidence. Her methods of work were very simple and direct. I do not know what unseen hand had guided me to her side, but on Christmas day of 1890, Elaine Goodale and I announced our engagement.[99]

Three days later, we learned that Big Foot's band of Ghost Dancers from the Cheyenne River Reservation north of us was approaching the agency,

99. See Graber, ed., *Sister to the Sioux.*

and that Major [Samuel M.] Whitside was in command of troops with orders to intercept them.

Late that afternoon, the Seventh Cavalry under Colonel [James W.] Forsythe was called to the saddle and rode off toward Wounded Knee Creek, eighteen miles away. Father [Francis M.] Craft, a Catholic priest with some Indian blood, who knew Sitting Bull and his people, followed an hour or so later, and I was much inclined to go too, but my fiancée pointed out that my duty lay rather at home with our Indians, and I stayed.[100]

The morning of December 29th was sunny and pleasant. We were all straining our ears toward Wounded Knee, and about the middle of the forenoon we distinctly heard the reports of the Hotchkiss guns. Two hours later, a rider was seen approaching at full speed, and in a few minutes he had dismounted from his exhausted horse and handed his message to General Brooke's orderly. The Indians were watching their own messenger, who ran on foot along the northern ridges and carried the news to the so-called hostile camp. It was said that he delivered his message at almost the same time as the mounted officer.

The resulting confusion and excitement was unmistakable. The white tipis disappeared as if by magic and soon the caravans were in motion, going toward the natural fortress of the Badlands. In the "friendly" camp there was almost as much turmoil, and crowds of frightened women and children poured into the agency. Big Foot's band had been wiped out by the troops, and reprisals were naturally looked for. The enclosure was not barricaded in any way and we had but a small detachment of troops for our protection. Sentinels were placed, and machine guns trained on the various approaches.

A few hot-headed young braves fired on the sentinels and wounded two of them. The Indian police began to answer by shooting at several braves who were apparently about to set fire to some of the outlying buildings. Every married employee was seeking a place of safety for his family, the interpreter among them. Just then General Brooke ran out into the open, shouting at the top of his voice to the police: "Stop, stop! Doctor, tell them they must not fire until ordered!" I did so, as the bullets whistled by us, and the General's coolness perhaps saved all our lives, for we were in no position to repel a large attacking force. Since we did not reply, the scattered shots soon ceased, but the situation remained critical for several days and nights.

100. For more on Father Craft, see Foley, *At Standing Rock and Wounded Knee.*

My office was full of refugees. I called one of my good friends aside and asked him to saddle my two horses and stay by them. "When general fighting begins, take them to Miss Goodale and see her to the railroad if you can," I told him. Then I went over to the rectory. Mrs. Cook refused to go without her husband, and Miss Goodale would not leave while there was a chance of being of service. The house was crowded with terrified people, most of them Christian Indians, whom our friends were doing their best to pacify.

At dusk, the Seventh Cavalry returned with their twenty-five dead and I believe thirty-four wounded, most of them by their own comrades, who had encircled the Indians, while few of the latter had guns. A majority of the thirty or more Indian wounded were women and children, including babies in arms. As there were not tents enough for all, Mr. Cook offered us the mission chapel, in which the Christmas tree still stood, for a temporary hospital. We tore out the pews and covered the floor with hay and quilts. There we laid the poor creatures side by side in rows, and the night was devoted to caring for them as best we could. Many were frightfully torn by pieces of shells, and the suffering was terrible. General Brooke placed me in charge and I had to do nearly all the work, for although the army surgeons were more than ready to help as soon as their own men had been cared for, the tortured Indians would scarcely allow a man in uniform to touch them. Mrs. Cook, Miss Goodale, and several of Mr. Cook's Indian helpers acted as volunteer nurses. In spite of all our efforts, we lost the greater part of them, but a few recovered, including several children who had lost all their relatives and who were adopted into kind Christian families.

On the day following the Wounded Knee massacre there was a blizzard, in the midst of which I was ordered out with several Indian police, to look for a policeman, who was reported to have been wounded and left some two miles from the agency. We did not find him. This was the only time during the whole affair that I carried a weapon; a friend lent me a revolver, which I put in my overcoat pocket, and it was lost on the ride. On the third day it cleared, and the ground was covered with an inch or two of fresh snow. We had feared that some of the Indian wounded might have been left on the field, and a number of us volunteered to go and see. I was placed in charge of the expedition of about a hundred civilians, ten or fifteen of whom were white men. We were supplied with wagons in which to convey any whom we might find still alive. Of course a photographer and several reporters were of the party.

Fully three miles from the scene of the massacre we found the body of a woman completely covered with a blanket of snow, and from this point on we found them scattered along as they had been relentlessly hunted down and slaughtered while fleeing for their lives. Some of our people discovered relatives or friends among the dead, and there was much wailing and mourning. When we reached the spot where the Indian camp had stood, among the fragments of burned tents and other belongings we saw the frozen bodies lying close together or piled one upon another. I counted eighty bodies of men who had been in the council and who were almost as helpless as the women and babies when the deadly fire began, for nearly all their guns had been taken from them. A reckless and desperate young Indian fired the first shot when the search for weapons was well underway, and immediately the troops opened fire from all sides, killing not only unarmed men, women, and children, but their own comrades who stood opposite them, for the camp was entirely surrounded.[101]

It took all of my nerve to keep my composure in the face of this spectacle, and of the excitement and grief of my Indian companions, nearly every one of whom was crying aloud or singing his death song. The white men became very nervous, but I set them to examining and uncovering every body to see if one were living. Although they had been lying untended in the snow and cold for two days and nights, a number had survived. Among them I found a baby of about a year old warmly wrapped and entirely unhurt. I brought her in, and she was afterward adopted and educated by an army officer.[102] One man who was severely wounded begged me to fill his pipe. When we brought him into the chapel he was welcomed by his wife and daughters with cries of joy, but he died a day or two later.

Under a wagon I discovered an old woman, totally blind and entirely helpless. A few had managed to crawl away to some place of shelter, and we found in a log store nearby several who were badly hurt and others who had died after reaching there. After we had dispatched several wagonloads to the agency, we observed groups of warriors watching us from adjacent buttes; probably friends of the victims, who had come there for the same purpose as ourselves. A majority of our party, fearing an attack, insisted that someone ride back to the agency for an escort of soldiers, and as mine was the best horse, it fell to me to go. I covered the eighteen miles in quick

101. An army investigation was conducted by Major Jacob Ford Kent and Captain Frank Baldwin that would also determine whether the troops were incorrectly positioned so that they accidently fired upon each other. For the Kent-Baldwin Report, see Report of Investigations into the Battle at Wounded Knee Creek, South Dakota, Fought December 29, 1890, NARA, RG 94, AIWKSC, M983, roll 1, vol. 2, pp. 651–1134.

102. This little girl became known as Lost Bird. She was adopted by Colonel Leonard W. Colby. Renée Sansom Flood, *Lost Bird of Wounded Knee: Spirit of the Lakota* (New York: Scribner, 2014).

time and was not interfered with in any way, although if the Indians had meant mischief they could easily have picked me off from any of the ravines and gulches.

All this was a severe ordeal for one who had so lately put all his faith in the Christian love and lofty ideals of the white man. Yet I passed no hasty judgment, and was thankful that I might be of some service and relieve even a small part of the suffering. An appeal published in a Boston paper brought us liberal supplies of much needed clothing, and linen for dressings. We worked on. Bishop [William H.] Hare of South Dakota visited us, and was overcome by faintness when he entered his mission chapel, thus transformed into a rude hospital.

After some days of extreme tension, and weeks of anxiety, the hostiles, so called, were at last induced to come in and submit to a general disarmament. Father Jutz, the Catholic missionary, had gone bravely among them and used all his influence toward a peaceful settlement.[103] The troops were all recalled and took part in a grand review before General Miles, no doubt intended to impress the Indians with their superior force.

In March, all being quiet, Miss Goodale decided to send in her resignation and go east to visit her relatives, and our wedding day was set for the following June.

Luther Standing Bear

"Like all religious beliefs there were those who believed and there were sceptics as well."

Luther Standing Bear was a Brulé Lakota, who decided on his own to attend the Carlisle Indian Industrial School in Pennsylvania. After receiving his education, he returned to live on the Rosebud Reservation. His account of the Ghost Dance is part of his memoir *My People the Sioux*, originally published in 1928.[104] Standing Bear's story begins with

103. Father Jutz visited the Ghost Dance camp earlier in December, not after Wounded Knee. See part 2.

104. Luther Standing Bear, *My People the Sioux* (New York: Houghton & Mifflin, 1928), 217–30. The original text accessed at https://babel.hathitrust.org/cgi/pt?id=ucl.$ b306020;view=1up;seq=15. For more on Luther Standing Bear's life, see, for example, Richard N. Ellis, introduction to *My People the Sioux*, the 1975 University of Nebraska Press edition.

a reference to the recent allotment of Lakota lands and the signing of the Sioux Act of 1889. Interestingly, Standing Bear was present when Agent J. George Wright questioned Short Bull about the Ghost Dance and was thus able to hear his story firsthand.

The Ghost Dance Troubles

It was agreed by the government that the man of the house was to receive six hundred and forty acres of land for farming.[105] Here my father again spoke. He said the Indians knew nothing about farming, but that they could take the land for grazing. This was satisfactory.

From the day my father signed the treaty, we all began to realize that we were to have something given us which was to be our own—and the thought of ownership gives anyone a higher appreciation of life, regardless of how little that ownership may be; so we all began looking around at various sections of the reservation to see where we would care to live.

My father knew all of our country, but when he realized that he was going to have some land for himself, he commenced looking around to see where the best land was. He went over to visit at Pine Ridge Agency, and when he saw the land over there, he liked it so much better than that at Rosebud that he decided to move his family over to Pine Ridge.

But I remained at Rosebud.[106] I had my position as school teacher there. George Wright was still our agent, and he was a very nice young man. My house was close to my work, and my little family was a happy one. My cordwood was all ready for winter; the cattle, pigs, and horses were all well fed, and with the approach of the holiday season, everyone seemed to be feeling happy.

And then suddenly great excitement came into our midst. It broke so suddenly over us that a great many of the Indians did not know which way to turn. It was the craze of a new religion called the Ghost Dance. This was in 1890. At that time very few of the Indians had any education, but they were very superstitious and their feelings were easily aroused and played upon.

105. In 1887, the General Allotment Act (or Dawes Act) was passed. It stated that every head of a household would get 160 acres of land as an allotment. The rest of the reservation lands were to be sold as surplus lands.

106. Luther Standing Bear and his brother later took up allotments on Pine Ridge. See Ellis, introduction, in *My People the Sioux*.

One day I was called into the agent's office. There I saw an Indian called Short Bull and a young man known as Breaks-the-Pot-on-Him. The agent started to question them in front of me, and I shall never forget what Short Bull said. The agent asked him to tell about the new religion which they were all getting so excited about, and why he believed in it. Said Short Bull:

"We heard there was a wonderful man in the Far West. He was a Messiah, so several tribes gathered together to go and see him. We went to the place where the sun sets, and there we saw this man. He told us we were to have a new earth; that the old earth would be covered up, and while it was being covered we were to keep dancing so that we could remain on top of the dirt. This man told us that all the white people would be covered up, because they did not believe; even the Indians who did not believe would also be covered. He showed us visions of the olden times when the buffalo were plenty; when the big camps were on the plains. All our people were dancing and having a big feast. This man hit the ground and he made fire. He spoke to all of us at once, and all the different tribes understood him. He said that all the white people would be destroyed. He taught us a song to sing during this dance. He showed us where the sun dropped down into the ocean, and it boiled up and became hot."

At this point I spoke up and said to Short Bull, "That is not so; the ocean does not boil up with the setting of the sun."

Short Bull looked straight at me, but he had nothing further to say about the sun.

The agent spoke to both these men politely, and asked them not to stir up the Indians at Rosebud Agency. They both promised, and then left for home.

The first thing we knew, the majority of the Rosebud Indians had joined the Ghost Dancers.[107] We could see the dust flying skyward from the dancing, and hear the beat of the tom-toms.[108] They would keep up dancing until they fell from exhaustion.

The Ghost Dance was being held about eight miles west of the agency on a flat, on the west side of the Little White River. We could plainly locate the

107. On Rosebud, perhaps only 30 percent (1,556) of the total population of 5,187 became Ghost Dancers. For these estimates, see Andersson, *The Lakota Ghost Dance of 1890*, pp. 75–77.

108. This is an interesting comment, as the Ghost Dance ceremony was usually performed without any musical instruments.

dancers from the dust they raised. The Indians were really serious about it, and had full faith in what they were doing. They felt that this new religion was going to rid them of the hated pale-faces who had antagonized them so long.

My father's band had not joined the dancers yet. Two of his brothers-in-law were in charge of them. High Pipe was one of the men, and Black Horn was the other. Father had already moved to Pine Ridge with his family, but had left his two brothers-in-law in charge of the balance of the Indians.

The dust was flying high in the sky every day from the dancing. As the enthusiasm grew, more dancers joined. Then George Wright, the agent, sent for me to see if I would go to my father's band with a message from him. This band was located about five miles west of the agency on the east side of Little White River, so they were only three miles from the dancers across the river. They could both hear and see the dancers easier than ourselves.

I agreed to go, and Mr. Wright furnished me with a team and driver. He was a white man, and when we reached the camp I instructed him to drive up into the center of it before he stopped. The tipis were all in circle. When the wagon stopped, the Indians came out and stood around to listen to what I had to say. There was no excitement, but everyone was curious as to the cause of my visit.

I told my people that I wanted to help them, and that was the reason I had come. I said it would not be right for them to join the Ghost Dancers, as the government was going to stop it, and it would not be best for them to be found there. I told them the government would use soldiers to enforce the order if it became necessary.

The thought that the soldiers were coming disturbed them, but I told them if they felt afraid they could move their tipis in and put them up around my house and camp there. My house was only about a half-mile from the agency. They all agreed to come there the following morning. This pleased me immensely to think that my visit and talk had been a success. When I returned and told the agent, he, too, was very happy.

Just after I left the camp my plans were all "knocked into a cocked hat," as you might say. One of my uncles, Hard Heart, entered the camp from Pine Ridge. When he saw that the Indians were all getting ready to break camp and go somewhere, he inquired the reason of the sudden move. When they told him they were getting ready to come in and camp by my house, he told them not to go. He said that a new world was coming to roll on top of the present one, and that they must either join the Ghost Dancers or perish with those who did not believe. Still, that would not have deterred them from coming to me had not someone come into the camp that night and told them the soldiers were coming. That frightened them to such an extent that they were all packed up and gone long before daylight.[109]

When I awoke the next morning and looked out of my window in expectation of seeing their tipis pitched about my house, I was greatly disappointed. There was no sign of their camp. I looked up the road in the direction they would have come, but there was no one in sight. Then I knew something had frightened them from keeping their promise.

The Indians who had decided to remain at the agency held a council so they could discuss the dance. Like all religious beliefs there were those who believed and there were skeptics as well.

The first thing I knew, all the Indians began to gather at the house of Spotted Tail. He had quite a large residence which the government had built for him after he traded all the northern part of the present State of Nebraska—our hunting grounds—without our knowledge.[110] Although that chief had been dead since 1881, his home was known as the "Spotted Tail House." I still lived in the same house, which my father had bought from the Catholic missionary. It stood down a little slope from that of Spotted Tail, so I could plainly see the Indians gathering for the council. After I had observed several of the leading chiefs going in, I decided to go down and find out what they intended doing.

When I arrived, my brother-in-law, chief Hollow Horn Bear, was speaking, and I stood at the door to listen. He was not a believer in the Ghost Dance, and was talking very strongly against it. All who were in favor of it exclaimed "Hau!" every once in a while. Suddenly, we who were standing near the door saw an Indian riding a white horse coming toward the house as fast as he could urge his pony. He had come from the agency and was headed straight for the council. As he dashed up he leaped from his pony and rushed into the council hall. Hollow Horn Bear was still speaking, but this man, Brave Eagle, interrupted him, exclaiming, "Hey, hey! What are all you men doing here? Don't you know that the soldiers have taken all our women and children away from Cut Meat Creek? Why do you all sit here doing nothing?"

109. There were a lot of rumors going around about soldiers and a possible disarmament. For the effect of these rumors, see Turning Hawk in part 2.

110. This accusation against Spotted Tail is not verified by any other source. This rumor caused jealousy among the Brulés and played a role in the killing of Spotted Tail in 1881. See Standing Bear, *My People the Sioux*, 157–59, and introduction, xvi, by Richard N. Ellis.

This caused considerable excitement, as many of the men had relatives at Cut Meat Creek. The council broke up, and several of the Indians rushed to the agency. My brother-in-law and I started, but first we stopped at my house. My Winchester rifle, with fifty rounds of cartridges in the belt, was standing in one corner of the room, and it was the first thing he spied. He wanted this gun. "Let me have it, and I will go over and see what all this means," he said to me.

When we arrived at the agency, the agent was greatly excited. He was walking the floor, rubbing his head. "I can't understand what has happened," he said to me. "If there is anything wrong, I should have been sent a telegram." He had sent for his Indian Police, who were now arriving. The Indians who had gathered were all ready to start for Cut Meat Creek, and the police were likewise impatient to be off. Everybody was on horseback, and I stood and watched them start on their journey of twenty-five miles, none of them knowing what they would find after they got there. I was to remain at the agency until Mr. Wright returned.

Bad news travels fast. None of the government employees at the reservation cared to work that day. Everybody was just standing around, wondering what was to happen next. Toward evening we saw the men all returning. Their horses were all fagged out from hard riding, and the men were tired, but the news they brought was good for us to hear.

The agent told us that when they reached the camp nothing had been disturbed; that the man who had brought the news had not told the truth. We wondered what his object was in bringing us such a story, and whether he had made it up himself or had been bribed to spread the report. However, the truth never came to light.

My brother-in-law did not come back with the others, but went right on to his band, taking my Winchester along with him. That was the last I ever saw of that rifle. However, he had always wanted a good gun, and that was a very nice (?) way of getting it!

Nothing exciting occurred during the night, but the following day one of my distant cousins, Isaac Bettelgeau [Bettelyoun], a half-breed, came to see me. He was a scout for the government, and was located on the Niobrara River. He told me that all the agencies on the Sioux reserve were to be surrounded in one night by the soldiers. He stated that he could not tell me when it was to happen, but that it was to be very soon. We were doing nothing which demanded the presence of the troops, but they were coming just the same, and we wondered why.

However, this piece of news did not worry me very much and I went to bed as usual. One of my friends, Julian Whistler, was staying with me, accompanied by Frank Janis. We all three slept in one bed, my place being next to the window.

On the second morning, quite early, we heard men marching past. It woke us up, and I raised the shade and looked out. There were soldiers' tents everywhere, and the troops were already up and going through a morning drill. I jumped out of bed and went to the back door. Just as I opened it, I heard the command, "Halt!" I thought it was meant for me until I saw the entire body of troops come to a halt. They were fully dressed, but I was still in my night clothes.[111]

I watched them a minute or two and then went back and woke my friends. They dressed and we started getting breakfast. Soon we saw the soldiers coming over to my woodpile. They began to help themselves, and soon my few cords of wood began to disappear rapidly. I did not say anything to them, not caring to start any trouble. Later, when I was out in the yard doing some work, an officer came to me and told me not to worry about the wood, as the government would pay me for all they used.

The following morning the news arrived of the terrible slaughter of Big Foot's whole band. Men, women, and children—even babies were killed in their mothers' arms![112] This was done by the soldiers. According to the white man's history this was known as the "battle" of Wounded Knee, but it was not a battle—it was a slaughter, a massacre. Those soldiers had been sent to protect these men, women, and children, who had not joined the Ghost Dancers, but they had shot them down without even a chance to defend themselves.

When I heard of this, it made my blood boil. I was ready myself to go and fight then. There I was, doing my best to teach my people to follow in the white men's road—even trying to get them to believe in their religion—and this was my reward for it all! The very people I was following—and getting my people to follow—had no respect for motherhood, old age, or babyhood. Where was all their civilized training?

More of the Indians joined the dancers after the Wounded Knee affair. They felt that they could not meet with any worse fate than that which had been meted out to their friends and relatives.

Always after a trouble of this sort, rumors were apt to be flying thick and fast. As we had no telephones in those days, we had no way to determine

111. The troops arrived on November 20, 1890.
112. Luther Standing Bear's time frame is off, as the Wounded Knee massacre occurred on December 29, not the morning after the troops' arrival.

the truth about the fate of our friends and relatives. All we received were rumors—and they were not of the best. One of the Indians came running into the agency with the report that he had overheard a soldier remark that "they were going to kill all the Indians, regardless of education, because the only good Indians were the dead ones." That sounded pretty bad, but soon came another rumor: "All the Indians who stay with the white people and work with them, will be regarded as white people and are not going to be killed."

It was about two days after the Wounded Knee affair that these rumors began to sift in at the agency. Orders were given that no Indian was to leave his or her house. Everybody's nerves were on edge. My own house was completely surrounded by the soldiers. I did not know whether my own family were alive or dead. My wife and children had gone to her father's before the trouble started.

I talked the situation over with my two friends, Julian Whistler and Frank Janis. We decided to fight if we had to, but agreed that we would not start trouble ourselves. As my brother-in-law had taken my rifle, I was left without any arms. My two friends had no guns. So we went out and each bought a gun and plenty of ammunition, and were ready to fight if it came to a "show-down." While we three were Carlisle graduates, we determined to stick by our race.

After getting these guns we felt much easier about going to bed at nights. We kept the weapons fully loaded, waiting and fully expecting an attack.

One night during a full moon, when it was almost as light as day, we got a scare. We had been in bed for some time, when suddenly we heard the command "Mount!" We jumped from bed, grabbed our guns and went outside. It developed that an officer had seen a lone Indian scout coming over the hill and had given the alarm. The order was given "Forward, march," and off they started. I turned to my friends, and told them when the shooting commenced that we would open the ball ourselves, and keep on shooting as long as we had any ammunition. However, our plans were not carried into effect. The officer had made a mistake. Instead of an Indian scout it turned out to be only a loose horse. The animal was hobbled, and as he jumped along down the hill it made such a queer sound that the officer thought something serious was happening.

We had a few scares of this sort, but nothing serious happened at our agency. Few of the government employees did any work, however, as all were too excited, waiting for all the late news to come in. It kept the agent on the jump, though.

Three or four days later I started over to find out how bad the reports were which we had heard about the fight. My father and mother and their family were at Pine Ridge at this time and I had heard nothing from them. It had snowed in the meantime, and the weather was very cold. It meant a ride of thirty miles on horseback, but I had a good horse, plenty of warm clothing and I did not mind the jaunt.

When I arrived at the place where the fight had occurred between the Indians and the soldiers, all the bodies had been removed.[113] Here and there lay the body of a horse. The tipi poles were broken and lay scattered about in heaps. Cooking utensils were strewed around in confusion; old wagons were overturned, with the tongues broken off. Everything was confusion. It was early in the morning when I reached this place, and the silence was oppressive and terrible.

There were many little pools of water here and there, some with clear water and others red with the blood of my people. I was enraged enough at this sight to shoot anyone, but nobody was to be seen. The place of death was forsaken and forbidding. I stood there in silence for several minutes, in reverence for the dead, and then turned and rode toward the agency.

On the way I met some Indians. My first question was for my father, his wives and my sisters and brothers. They told me that father and his wives were all right, and that my two brothers, Ellis and Willard, were safe. So I returned to Rosebud Agency without seeing them.

All the Indians who believed in the Ghost Dance had now rushed into what was known as the Badlands. It was located in the northern part of our reservation, and was a hard place to enter. The entrance was only large enough for one wagon at a time to pass in. It was an excellent place to stand off an enemy.[114]

Those who had not at first believed in the Ghost Dance ran away with these Indians who were bound for the Badlands. After they had seen what the soldiers did to their friends and relatives, they were not taking any more chances. The few who had escaped the terrible slaughter at Wounded Knee

---

113. The bodies of the dead were removed by soldiers and civilians during the early days of January 1891. Many of the dead were buried in a mass grave at the site.

114. It seems that Luther Standing Bear describes the Badlands Stronghold, but he has made an error in the chronology of events. The Ghost Dancers were in the Stronghold before the Wounded Knee massacre. After the massacre, they stayed around White Clay Creek near the Badlands. They did fortify the camp, but did not return to the Stronghold. However, also Black Elk calls this camp Stronghold (see part 1). There is clearly some confusion about the location of the camp after Wounded Knee.

also fled into the fastnesses of the Badlands, although they had no guns nor anything with which to put up a fight. The soldiers had taken everything away from them before shooting them down. But the other Indians had all brought firearms and plenty of ammunition.

These they divided. They felt sure that now they would have to fight to protect themselves against the white man. *Who would blame them?*[115]

In the Badlands they had plenty of wood and water, but they needed meat. Some of the braves sneaked out in the night and rounded up all the cattle they could find and drove them into their place of retreat. There was no high chief left at the agency now, because Red Cloud, who had always called Pine Ridge his agency, was one of the Indians to run with his whole family into the Badlands.[116]

Everybody in the camp now felt safe, as they had plenty of everything to supply their needs. They could dance when they pleased, and they had no agent from whom to ask permission. They were not under obligations to the government for supplies, as they now had all they wanted. They kept two scouts posted at the entrance to the Badlands day and night, so there was no chance of interference without being seen. The soldiers did not even try to come near them. They knew better!

The troops realized that the Indians who had guns knew how to use them. Those who had bows and arrows were experts in their use. The Indians were really better armed than at the time they wiped out Custer, fourteen years previously. Had the soldiers tried at the time to enter the Badlands, there would have been many deaths on both sides.[117]

General Miles realized all this, so he thought up a plan toward a reconciliation. He called on a few of the chiefs, who had remained at the agency, and asked them if they would not go to their people and try to make peace for them. This was a most dangerous mission to attempt to perform, as the

115. Italics in the original.
116. According to some stories, Red Cloud left because he thought an officer wanted to sell his house, yet others claim that they forced him to join the refugees because they needed him as their leader. See Andersson, *The Lakota Ghost Dance of 1890*, pp. 94–98. For Red Cloud's statements, see part 2.
117. The army officers were indeed cautious about approaching the Indian camp. They were fully aware of their disadvantageous position in attacking the camp. Instead, General Nelson A. Miles who arrived at Pine Ridge on December 31, 1890, decided to encircle the camp and use the tactics of negotiation instead of open confrontation. Gradually the Indians moved toward the Pine Ridge Agency. See Utley, *Last Days of the Sioux Nation*, 251–61; Andersson, *The Lakota Ghost Dance of 1890*, pp. 156–59; Greene, *American Carnage*, 311–32.

Indians had declared they would kill anyone who came to them, regardless of color. The white man had started the fight, and now he wanted the Indian to act as mediator!

My father, who was now the head chief, said he would carry the peace pipe to these Indians if anyone else would accompany him. Nine others volunteered to accompany him. These ten chiefs started off on horseback, not knowing whether they would ever return alive. My father carried the pipe, which all the Indians respected at that time.

When they arrived at the entrance to the Badlands, they were recognized by the scouts on duty, who allowed them to enter unmolested. They all rode their horses in through the gateway in plain sight of all the Indians. Here they dismounted, my father still holding the peace pipe in both hands, straight out before him. Not a word was spoken. The Indians arranged themselves in a circle and sat down. They were making an appeal to their friends to come and accept the pipe of peace. Everything was as quiet as the grave. Among the Indians at that time, there was a strong superstition that if the pipe of peace was brought and not accepted, great harm would come to them or to their relatives.

The sight of this peace pipe made the fighting Indians wild! They were on horseback, and they rode right toward my father and the other chiefs. Not one of the latter moved, but sat perfectly still. One of these Indians had a loaded gun. His name was Ten Fingers. As he came near my father he said, "The white people have killed our people without mercy, and we want to fight them. Why have you brought us this pipe of peace?"

As he finished speaking, bang! went his rifle, the bullet striking the ground between my father's knees and spattering dirt in his face. Father never flinched or said a word of rebuke. He had faith in what he was doing in bringing the peace pipe to these enraged Indians.

You who are Christians—have you ever been in a high temper at a time when someone may have asked you to kiss the Bible? Then you will understand just how these Indians felt toward accepting the peace pipe offered them. However, after a time these wild Indians calmed down, and strange as it may seem, those ten chiefs brought all those hostiles into the agency without a shot being fired! There a peace was effected.

After the affair was over, somebody mentioned to my brother Ellis the incident in which Ten Fingers had fired his rifle between my father's knees while he was holding the peace pipe. This so enraged my brother that after dark he covered his head with a sheet, carried his rifle underneath it, and started out to locate Ten Fingers. He went from tipi to tipi, but could not find him—and it was probably lucky for Ten Fingers that he was not located.

Now that peace was finally restored, who was given the credit for it? Did the Indian who had brought the peace pipe receive any honor for the part he played? No, indeed! All the credit went to General Miles, who was proclaimed the "great peacemaker." Perhaps his salary was raised, or possibly he received a few more stripes to his sleeves. The Indians came to my father about it, and my father, who was the head chief throughout those ceremonies, went to General Miles for an explanation.[118]

He told the General that the Indians thought they (who had remained loyal and at the agency) should have something from the government to indicate that they belonged to the "progressives"—something to show that they had not run away; some sort of emblem for them to wear to commemorate this great peace and the part they had in it.

The General said he would accede to this request of my father's. He secured the names of all the chiefs who had accompanied my father. He must have submitted their names to the officials at Washington, because in a short time some buttons arrived—one for each man. They were about an inch and a half in diameter, and were worn fastened to the coat lapel, much the same as a lodge emblem. On the face of these buttons was emblazoned a rising sun, and in the clear sky above were the words "Peace, Good Will." Below were two clasped hands, on each side of which was a shock of corn; at the extreme bottom was a plough. They were made of some cheap metal, silver-plated.

When these buttons arrived, General Miles sent for my father and gave him the buttons to distribute. The chiefs were greatly pleased to wear them, showing that they belonged to the "progressives." It was a mark of distinction and honor. But I often look back to this incident and wonder, if the general public knows that the men who really settled the greatest trouble between the whites and Indians at Pine Ridge each received a dinky button worth about fifty cents!

---

118. Until quite recently, Standing Bear's mission has been largely overlooked even by scholars, and General Miles has been hailed as the true peacemaker. While we do not know exactly what effect the offering of the pipe had on the final decision to surrender, we should not underestimate the symbolism and significance of the offering of the pipe. It was one of the most sacred rites of the Lakotas and refusing the pipe would have broken the bonds of kinship. For the significance of the offering of the pipe to the Ghost Dancers see Andersson, *The Lakota Ghost Dance of 1890*, pp. 97–98. For a discussion on General Miles possibly using the Ghost Dance to advance his career, see Ostler, *The Plains Sioux*, 301–306, and Andersson, *The Lakota Ghost Dance*, pp. 141–44, 155–60.

Afterword

In May 2000, I sat on the steps of the Wounded Knee memorial, looking around the beautiful South Dakota plains and rolling hills. There was nobody around and I could just sit and listen—listen to the silence and think about those distant days when the horrendous events took place in this stunning landscape. This was my first visit to the Lakota country. All my life I had been reading about the Lakotas, their history and culture, and finally I was here. I traveled around, went to the Badlands, climbed up Black Elk Peak (known then as Harney Peak) in the Black Hills, visited Bear Butte, had a nice taco at a café in a remote corner of the Badlands, and camped surrounded by a small herd of buffalo. At that time, I was writing my doctoral dissertation focusing on the Lakota Ghost Dance, so my trip was not only to look around as a tourist but also to learn—to learn about the people and the landscape, to write a better story of the Ghost Dance. I had read everything that had been written about the Ghost Dance, and I had a nagging feeling that the overall story was missing something. As I toured the Lakota reservations, talked to people, and read more archival sources, it started to dawn on me. What was missing was the Lakota voice—or the Lakota voices.

After receiving my Ph.D., I continued to work on the Ghost Dance with Professor Raymond J. DeMallie, and in 2008 my book *The Lakota Ghost Dance of 1890* was published. I thought then that my journey with the Ghost Dance had ended. I was happy because I felt that I was able to bring forth the Lakota point of view, at least more than anyone else had done by that time. I had put forward a very strong argument to show that the Ghost Dance was not just a demonstration by the so-called nonprogressive Lakotas, and that they had not twisted Wovoka's peaceful religion into a doctrine of war. The Ghost Dance was much more complicated than that; it had a profound impact on the Lakotas, who were struggling with famine, disease, and the loss of land and culture in the late 1880s.

Then I started to write another book—an ethnohistory of the Lakota people in my native language, Finnish. The title of the book translates to *The Lakotas: The People of the Eagle and the Buffalo*. I used even more Lakota accounts of the Ghost Dance and other historical events. My goal was to write the history of the Lakota people from the Lakota perspective, using material produced by the Lakotas as much as possible. During the process the nagging feeling in my head came back: there was still much that could be said about the Ghost Dance from the Lakotas' point of view. Now I felt, however, that I did not want to write another book that would be solely my scholarly interpretation of the Ghost Dance. I wanted to write a book that would truly give a voice to the Lakotas. In the end, there were many divergent approaches to the Ghost Dance among the Lakotas, and I wanted to give as many of them as possible a chance to "speak."

Through the documents in this volume, representing a variety of Lakota voices, I want to demonstrate that there were many ways for the Lakotas to approach the Ghost Dance, and that its religious message appealed across the artificial "progressive" and "nonprogressive" lines. That the so-called progressive people did not turn to the Ghost Dance in a unified body does not mean that they denied its potential power. For example, several of the so-called progressive chiefs, like Young Man Afraid of His Horses, were present at the council where Short Bull was chosen to become the leader of the delegation to go west. Little Wound and Big Road were dancers for a while, but as trouble started to mount they decided to abandon the Ghost Dance. Many of those who did not join the Ghost Dance, like Luther Standing Bear, were sympathetic toward it and understood the religious and political motivations of people who joined the dance. Henry Eagle Horse, a so-called progressive Brulé, said that he was curious about the Ghost Dance but was not going to leave the "white man's road" for the dance. Good Voice said it would be foolish to join the dance, and others felt that following the ways of the white men had made them unpopular, which was difficult to bear. Still they remained on the path they had chosen. These could be called practical voices in a volatile situation.

Reading these documents, it becomes quite evident that the situation among the Lakotas was desperate in 1889 and 1890. Several Lakotas noted that they feared trouble unless things improved. They were correct, but it does not mean that the Ghost Dancers twisted the doctrine into a militant crusade. The Ghost Dancers disobeyed the authorities, plundered Lakota homes, and even threatened the lives of, for example, American Horse. Even so, I argue that the Lakota Ghost Dance religion was no more warlike than the Ghost Dance among other tribes. The Lakotas changed the Ghost Dance to match their religious traditions as can be seen in Black Elk's account, but throughout the Ghost Dance, leaders emphasized education, farming, working, and nonviolence, just as Wovoka had taught them. Even the mixed-blood scouts like Louis Shangrau and Baptiste Pourier noted that the Ghost Dancers did not plan any violence. Louis Shangrau quoted Short Bull's words urging people to go to schools and continue working.

Surely, as also seen in these documents, there was talk about a possible war against the whites. As Little Wound said, "We had to make a great noise so that the Great Father would hear us." However, most Lakotas understood that there was no way for them to wage a successful war against the U.S. Army. That is why the promises of the Ghost Dance were so appealing. The Lakotas would need only to pray and dance to bring about a new Indian world.

Militancy, if one wants to call it that, came about when the U.S. Army arrived on the scene on the twentieth of November. The talk about war was a reaction to the military intervention and the threat it posed. Many of the Lakota accounts presented here, both those of Ghost Dancers and non–Ghost Dancers, say that people simply got scared and angered. The Brulés, already on the move due to new borderlines between the Rosebud and Pine Ridge Reservations, stampeded to the Badlands when soldiers came to Pine Ridge and Rosebud Agencies. They did not know where to go, and in their safe haven in the Badlands they resumed dancing and raided livestock for food. Similarly, Big Foot's people, after learning the fate of Sitting Bull, escaped as fast as they could. Alice Ghost Horse, a thirteen-year-old girl, remembered that it was quite exciting to be chased by the soldiers. Their escape ended at Wounded Knee. The militancy, if there was any, was a reaction to the outside pressures; it had nothing to do with the Ghost Dance as a religion, and I believe that the documents presented here make a very strong case to support this argument.

Perhaps those expressing the strongest condemnation of the Ghost Dance were those Lakotas or Dakotas who had fully embraced Christianity. Some of them, like Elias Gilbert, had become ministers. They thought the Ghost Dance was the work of the devil—a delusion that would take the Lakotas back to savagery. Still, even Gilbert was moved when he saw the Ghost Dance in progress: "I heard them cry and therefore my heart was very sad. They know the Bible so why then nobody is able to do [behave] sophisti- cally," he wondered in a sad tone. Sam White Bird warned against believ- ing in false prophets and condemned the dance as a lie and delusion. Their statements echo the sentiments expressed by white Protestant and Catholic missionaries. Considering their background as newly converted clergymen, this approach is not that surprising.

In the end, the internal divisions within the Lakota people and the problems with the whites, not the Ghost Dance itself, determined the Lakotas' different approaches to the Ghost Dance. These internal divisions had long historical, political, economic, and religious roots in the Lakota society. The Ghost Dance brought these conflicts to a head. Still, while the Ghost Dance brought deepening divisiveness, one can recall Turning Bear's words: "We remembered that many of these people [Ghost Dancers] were related to us by blood," indicating that he believed it was worth trying to reach a peaceful solution to the troubles.

After Wounded Knee, in February 1891, a Lakota delegation visited Washington, D.C. The delegation consisted of former Ghost Dancers and non–Ghost Dancers as well as mixed-blood interpreters. In their testimonies, the Lakotas said that "a whirlwind passed through our country, and did much damage, we let that pass," but the real issue for them was not the Ghost Dance; it was the destitution on the Lakota reservations.

The Ghost Dance, while often looked upon as a backward movement, was in fact seeking to discover ways to adapt and to survive. It looked forward, albeit not into the kind of future the contemporary whites were envisioning for the Lakotas. So perhaps the Ghost Dance could be seen as an innovative way of adaptation to the prevalent situation and an innovative way to find a path to a better life. By presenting these differing, often opposing, voices within the Lakota people, I hope to shed new light on the scholarly interpretations of the Ghost Dance. Moreover, those voices may prove helpful to the Lakota people in their quest to understand their past and their ancestors' decisions during those troublesome times.

––––––

In 2009 I had a long discussion with Ernie LaPointe, the great-grandson of Sitting Bull. He was visiting Finland and we had dinner in Helsinki (we ate reindeer) and the discussion naturally turned to Sitting Bull and the Ghost Dance. We had a long and lively discussion on his family stories about Sitting Bull, the Ghost Dance, sweat lodges and saunas, buffalo and reindeer. Another discussion took place in Denver, Colorado, that same year. During lunch with Professor Philip J. Deloria and his mother, Barbara, the discussion shifted, although briefly, to the Ghost Dance and the role Reverend Philip Deloria played in trying to persuade Sitting Bull to give up the Ghost Dance. These discussions made me think about family traditions. I am certain that there are many more interesting stories about the Ghost Dance that have been passed through the generations among the descendants of the people whose stories are now presented in this book. I hope that someone takes up the task of collecting the stories that Lakotas tell today. Together, those stories and this book would really give us new perspectives into the enduring legacy of *wanáǧi wačhípi kiŋ*—the Spirit Dance.

Appendix

Chronology of Events during the Lakota Ghost Dance Period

Summer 1889

- The first news of the Ghost Dance and the Messiah reaches the Lakota reservations.
- The Sioux Land Commission negotiates for the reduction of the Great Sioux Reservation.
- Hunger and other hardships intensify among the Lakotas.

Fall–Winter 1889–1890

- The Lakota delegation is sent to meet with the Messiah.
- The Great Sioux Reservation opens and the Sioux Act of 1889 passes.

April–May 1890

- The Lakota delegation returns, inaugurating the Ghost Dance among the Lakotas.
- Newspapers take notice of the Lakota Ghost Dance.
- A South Dakota settler warns the commissioner of Indian affairs about the Ghost Dance.
- The Indian agents arrest some Ghost Dance leaders.

June–July 1890

- The Ghost Dance is discontinued.
- Congress votes to cut the Lakotas' rations.
- The Lakota agents suggest that "nonprogressive" leaders like Sitting Bull should be arrested; the Ghost Dance is not a major concern of the agents.
- The army learns about the Ghost Dance through Porcupine, a Cheyenne Indian.

August–September 1890

- Hardships among the Lakotas continue.
- The Ghost Dance is resumed with dances on the Pine Ridge, Rosebud, and Cheyenne River Reservations.
- The Ghost Dance causes concern among settlers.
- The first incidents between the Ghost Dancers and the agents occur on the Pine Ridge and Rosebud Reservations.

October 1890

- Kicking Bear introduces the Ghost Dance on the Standing Rock reservation.
- Agent James McLaughlin urges Sitting Bull's arrest and tries to stop a Ghost Dance in Sitting Bull's camp.
- Several Ghost Dance camps are established on various Lakota reservations.
- Newspapers publish excited articles.
- The new Indian agents take charge of Pine Ridge, Rosebud, and Cheyenne River Reservations.
- The agents become alarmed and call for assistance, but Agent James McLaughlin believes he can control the Indians at Standing Rock without assistance.
- Minor incidents take place between the Ghost Dancers and the agents.
- October 31: Short Bull allegedly addresses the Ghost Dancers.

November 1890

- November 13: President Benjamin Harrison orders the military to assume control of Lakota reservations.
- The agents, especially Daniel F. Royer, send alarmed telegrams to their superiors.
- November 20: The military arrives at the Pine Ridge and Rosebud Reservations.
- Newspaper reporters arrive in late November and "war correspondence" begins.
- Panic among the Indians follows the military's arrival, and Ghost Dancers on Pine Ridge move to the Stronghold in the Badlands.
- The army tries to separate the "progressive" Indians from the "nonprogressive," i.e., the Ghost Dancers from the non-Ghost Dancers.
- Lakotas from Rosebud travel to Pine Ridge in order to join the Ghost Dancers there.

- The Ghost Dance causes a sensation in the press.
- The "bulletproof "Ghost Dance shirts are introduced.
- Sitting Bull's arrest is planned by General Nelson A. Miles and William F. "Buffalo Bill" Cody.
- General Nelson A. Miles travels to Washington, gaining support for his military campaign.
- Negotiations between the Ghost Dancers and the army officers on the Lakota reservations begin.

December 1890

- Newspapers continue to spread alarm.
- Father John Jutz visits a Ghost Dancers' camp; negotiations continue.
- William F. Cody's mission to arrest Sitting Bull is stopped by Agent James McLaughlin.
- Agent James McLaughlin launches his own plan for Sitting Bull's arrest.
- In peaceful developments on the Pine Ridge and Cheyenne River Reservations, Little Wound, Big Road, and Hump give up the Ghost Dance.
- Disagreements occur among the Ghost Dancers in the Stronghold.
- Congressional debate on the Lakota Ghost Dance begins.
- December 15: Sitting Bull is killed.
- Big Foot escapes the soldiers and starts a journey toward Pine Ridge. The army pursues him.
- The peaceful developments at Pine Ridge cease when the Indians learn about Sitting Bull's fate.
- December 28: Big Foot is captured and escorted to Wounded Knee Creek.
- December 29: Wounded Knee Massacre
- General Miles personally takes command of the troops in the field.

January 1891

- Fighting follows the Wounded Knee Massacre.
- Debate about Wounded Knee begins in the press.
- Congress orders an investigation into what happened at Wounded Knee, and the army investigation of the massacre begins.
- Negotiations continue between the Ghost Dancers and the army officers.
- January 15, 1891: The Ghost Dancers surrender, ending the Ghost Dance among the Lakotas.

Bibliography

Archival Sources and Newspapers

Aaron Beede Diary, North Dakota Historical Society, Bismarck, N.D., vol. 2.

Additional Provisions for Sioux. 51st Congress, 2nd sess., H. Ex. Doc., no. 37, vol. 25, ser. 2855. Washington, D.C.: Government Printing Office, 1891.

American Horse Papers, MSS S 903, Yale Collection of Western Americana, Beinecke Rare Book and Manuscript Library, Yale University.

Annual Report of the Commissioner of Indian Affairs (ARCIA). 52nd Congress, 1st sess., H. Ex. Doc., no. 1, vol. 2, ser. 2841. Washington, D.C.: Government Printing Office, 1891.

Annual Report of the Secretary of War (ARSW) 1891. 52nd Congress, 1st sess., H. Ex. Doc., no. 1, vol. 2, ser. 2921. Washington, D.C.: Government Printing Office, 1892.

"As Narrated by Short Bull," recorded by George C. Crager, 1891. Buffalo Bill Museum and Grave, Golden, Colo. (MS [1891]).

Bureau of Catholic Indian Missions, Series 1–1, Correspondence, Pine Ridge Agency, Holy Rosary Mission, Rosebud Agency, St. Francis Mission, Standing Rock Agency, Fort Yates, Microfilm, reels 19–20, Special Collections and Archives, Marquette University Archives, Milwaukee, Wis.

Chicago Tribune, April 1890–January 1891.

Congressional Record: Containing the Proceedings and Debates of the 51st Congress, 1st Session, vol. 22, pt. 14. Washington, D.C.: Government Printing Office, 1891.

Congressional Record: Containing the Proceedings and Debates of the 51st Congress, 2nd Session, vol. 22, pts. 1–2. Washington, D.C.: Government Printing Office, 1891.

Council Held with a Delegation of Sioux Indians. House of Representatives Committee on Indian Affairs. 51st Cong., 1st sess. (Unpublished hearing, April 15, 1890). IUL, microfiche, card 1.

Eastman, Elaine Goodale. "Little Sister to the Sioux." (Typescript, n.d.) Sophia Smith Collection, Smith College, William Allan Neilson Library, Northampton, Mass.

Edward E. Ayer Collection (EEAC), MS 3176, Newberry Library, Chicago, Ill.

Eli S. Ricker Manuscript Collection (ESRMC), Nebraska Historical Society, Lincoln, Nebr.

Eugene Buechel Manuscript Collection (EBMC), Holy Rosary Mission, Special Collections and Archives, Marquette University Libraries, Milwaukee, Wis.

Florentine Digman Papers, St. Francis Mission, Marquette University Archives, Milwaukee, Wis.

Harper's Weekly, October 1890–February 1891.

Hearing Before the Select Committee on Indian Affairs. U.S. Senate, 102nd Cong., 1st Sess. (Testimony of Alice Ghost Horse). Washington, D.C.: United States Printing Office, 1991.

Henry L. Dawes Papers (HLDP), Library of Congress, Washington, D.C.

House of Representatives Committee on Indian Affairs. 51st Congress, 1st sess. (Unpublished hearing, April 15, 1890). IUL, Microfiche, card 1, pp. 1–3.

House Committee on Indian Affairs Papers (HCIAP). Records of the United States Congress, House of Representatives, RG 233, NARA, Washington, D.C.

Iapi Oaye, November 1890–March 1891.

Illustrated American, November 1890–January 1891.

The Indian Helper, January 1891.

James McLaughlin Papers (JMLP), Minnesota Historical Society, St. Paul, Minn.

James R. Walker Collection (JRWC), MSS 653, History Colorado, Stephen H. Hart Library and Research Center, Denver, Colo.

Jerome A. Greene Collection, Arvada, Colo.

Josephine Waggoner Papers (JWP), Museum of the Fur Trade, Chadron, Nebr.

Lebbeus Foster Spencer Papers (LFSP), MSS 596, History Colorado, Stephen H. Hart Library and Research Center, Denver, Colo.

Letters Received, Records of the Bureau of Indian Affairs. RG 75, General Records of the Bureau of Indian Affairs, NARA, Washington, D.C.

Letters Sent to the Office of Indian Affairs by the Agents or Superintendents at the Pine Ridge Agency (LSASPR) 1875–1914, M1282, vol. 9, roll 10, RG 75, Records of the Bureau of Indian Affairs, NARA, Washington, D.C.

The New York Times, April 1890–January 1891.

Omaha Daily Bee, April–November 1890.

The Red Man, February 1915.

Report of Investigations into the Battle at Wounded Knee Creek, South Dakota, Fought December 29, 1890, Reports and Correspondence Relating to the Army Investigation of the Battle at Wounded Knee and to the Sioux Campaign of 1890–1891, M983, vol. 1, rolls 1–2, RG 94, Records of the Adjutant General's Office, 1780–1917, NARA, Washington, D.C.

Richard Henry Pratt Papers, MSS S-1174, Yale Collection of Western Americana, Beinecke Rare Book and Manuscript Library, Yale University.

Senate Committee on Indian Affairs Papers (SCIAP). Records of the United States Congress, Senate, RG 46, NARA, Washington, D.C.

Senate Executive Document, no. 51, vol. 4, ser. 2682. 51st Congress, 1st sess. Washington, D.C.: Government Printing Office, 1891.

Sioux Indian Appropriation. 51st Congress, 2nd sess. H. Ex. Doc., no. 36, vol. 25, ser. 2855, Washington, D.C.: Government Printing Office, 1891.

Special Case 188 (SC 188)–The Ghost Dance, 1890–1898. M4728–29, rolls 1–2, RG 75, Records of the Bureau of Indian Affairs, NARA, Washington, D.C., Microfilm publication, 1973.

Walter Mason Camp Collection (WMCC), Indiana University Lilly Library Collections, Bloomington, Ind.

Walter Stanley Campbell Manuscript Collection (WSCMC), Western History Collections, University of Oklahoma, Norman, Okla.

Washington Evening Star, January 1891.

Washington Post, April–November 1890.

The Word Carrier, November 1890–March 1891.

Yankton Press and Dakotan, December 1890.

Books and Articles

Andersson, Rani-Henrik. *The Lakota Ghost Dance of 1890*. Lincoln: University of Nebraska Press, 2008.

———. "Perspectives on the Lakota Ghost Dance of 1890." In *Reconfigurations of Native North America: An Anthology of New Perspectives*, edited by John R. Wunder and Kurt E. Kinbacher, 140–51. Lubbock: Texas Tech University Press, 2008.

Bearor, Karen A. "The *Illustrated American* and the Lakota Ghost Dance." *American Periodicals* 21, vol. 2 (2011): 143–63.

Berghold, Alexander. *The Indians' Revenge; or Days of Horror. Some Appalling Events in the History of the Sioux*. San Francisco: P. J. Thomas Printer, 1891.

Bland, Thomas A. "A Brief History of the Late Military Invasion of the Home of the Sioux," Part II. Washington, D.C.: National Indian Defense Association, 1891.

Boyd, James P. *Recent Indian Wars: Under the Lead of Sitting Bull and Other Chiefs; with a Full Account of the Messiah Craze and Ghost Dances*. Philadelphia: Publishers Union, 1891.

Brown, Joseph Epes. *The Sacred Pipe: Black Elk's Account of the Seven Rites of the Oglala Sioux*. Norman: University of Oklahoma Press, 1989.

Bucko, Raymond A. *The Lakota Ritual of the Sweat Lodge: History and Contemporary Practice*. Lincoln: University of Nebraska Press, 1998.

Burnham, Phillip. *Song of Dewey Beard: Last Survivor of the Little Big Horn*.

Lincoln: University of Nebraska Press, 2014.

Carter, John E. "Making Pictures for a News-Hungry Nation." In *Eyewitness at Wounded Knee*, edited by Richard E. Jensen, Eli R. Paul, and John E. Carter. Lincoln: University of Nebraska Press, 1991.

Clow, Richmond L. "Lakota Ghost Dance after 1890." *South Dakota History* 20, no. 4 (1990): 323–33.

Colby, L. W. "The Sioux Indian War of 1890–91." *Transactions and Proceedings of the Nebraska Historical Society*. Fremont, Nebr.: Hammond Bros., 1892.

Coleman, William S. E. *Voices of Wounded Knee*. Lincoln: University of Nebraska Press, 2000.

Cooper, Courtney R. "Short Bull's Story of the Ghost Dance and Wounded Knee." *The Red Man* (February 1915): 205–12.

Cozzens, Peter. *Eyewittness to Indian Wars, 1865–1890: The Long War for the Northern Plains*. Mechanicsburg, Pa.: Stackpole Books, 2004.

Curtis, Natalie. *The Indian's Book: Songs and Legends of the American Indians*. New York: Dover, 1950. First published 1907. Copy of original at https://ia600209.us.archive.org/12/items/offeringindianlore00burlrich/offeringindianlore00burlrich.pdf.

Danker, Donald F. "The Wounded Knee Interviews of Eli R. Ricker." *Nebraska History* 62, no. 2 (1981): 151–243.

Deloria, Ella C. *Speaking of Indians*. Lincoln: University of Nebraska Press, 1998. First published 1944.

DeMallie, Raymond J. "Lakota Belief and Ritual in the 19th Century." In *Sioux Indian Religion: Tradition and Innovation*, edited by Raymond J. DeMallie and Douglas R. Parks. Norman: Oklahoma University Press, 1987.

———. "The Lakota Ghost Dance: An Ethnohistorical Account." *Pacific Historical Review* 51, no. 4 (1982): 385–405.

———, ed. *Lakota Society*. Lincoln: University of Nebraska Press, 1992.

———, ed. *The Sixth Grandfather: Black Elk's Teachings Given to John G. Neihardt*. Lincoln: University of Nebraska Press, 1985.

———. "These Have No Ears: Narrative and the Ethnohistorical Method." *Ethnohistory* 40, no. 4 (1993): 515–38.

DeMallie, Raymond J., and Douglas R. Parks, eds. *Sioux Indian Religion: Tradition and Innovation*. Norman: Oklahoma University Press, 1987.

Densmore, Frances. *Teton Sioux Music and Culture*. Lincoln: University of Nebraska Press, 1992.

Eastman, Charles A. *From Deep Woods to Civilization: Chapters in the Autobiography of an Indian*. Boston: Little, Brown, 1916.

Eastman, Elaine Goodale. "The Ghost Dance War and Wounded Knee Massacre of 1890–1891." *Nebraska History* 26, no. 1 (1945): 26–42.

Foley, Thomas W., ed. *At Standing Rock and Wounded Knee: The Journals and*

Papers of Father Francis M. Craft, 1888–1890. Norman, Okla.: Arthur H. Clark, 2009.

————. *Father Francis M. Craft: Missionary to the Sioux.* Lincoln: University of Nebraska Press, 2002.

Gage, Justin R. "Intertribal Communication, Literacy, and the Spread of the Ghost Dance." Ph.D. diss., University of Arkansas, 2015.

Graber, Kay, ed. *Sister to the Sioux: The Memoirs of Elaine Goodale Eastman, 1885–1891.* Lincoln: University of Nebraska Press, 1985.

Greene, Jerome A. *American Carnage.* Lincoln: University of Nebraska Press, 2014.

————. "The Sioux Land Commission of 1889: Prelude to Wounded Knee." *South Dakota History* 1, no. 1 (1970): 41–72.

Grua, David W. *Surviving Wounded Knee: The Lakotas and the Politics of Memory.* New York: University of Oxford Press, 2016.

Haberland, Wolfgang. "Die Oglala Sammlung Weygold im Hamburischen Museum für Völkerkunde [Weygold's Oglala Collection in the Hamburg Museum of Ethnology]." *Mitteilungen aus die Museum für Völkerkunde in Hamburg,* 1977.

Hittman, Michael. *Wovoka and the Ghost Dance.* Lincoln: University of Nebraska Press, 1997.

Hoover, Herbert T. "The Sioux Agreement of 1889 and Its Aftermath." *South Dakota History* 19, no. 1 (1989): 57–75.

Howard, James H. *The Canadian Sioux.* Lincoln: University of Nebraska Press, 1984.

Jensen, Richard A. "Big Foot's Followers at Wounded Knee." *Nebraska History* 71 (Fall 1990): 194–212.

————. *Voices of the American West, Vol. 1: The Indian Interviews of Eli S. Ricker, 1903–1919.* Lincoln: University of Nebraska Press, 2006.

Kelley, William F. "The Indian Troubles and the Battle of Wounded Knee." In *Transactions and Reports of the Nebraska State Historical Society,* 4:30–42. Lincoln, Neb.: State Journal Company, 1892.

Kerstetter, Todd. *God's Country, Uncle Sam's Land: Faith and Conflict in the American West.* Urbana: University of Illinois Press, 2006.

————. "Spin Doctors at Santee: Missionaries and the Dakota-Language Reporting of the Ghost Dance and Wounded Knee." *Western Historical Quarterly* 28 (Spring 1997): 45–67.

Kolbenschlag, George R. *Whirlwind Passes: News Correspondents and the Sioux Indian Disturbances of 1890–1891.* Vermilion: University of South Dakota Press, 1990.

Kracht, Benjamin. *Kiowa Belief and Ritual.* Lincoln: University of Nebraska Press, 2017.

Kreis, Karl Marcus. *Lakotas, Black Robes, and Holy Women: German Reports from the Indian Missions in South Dakota, 1886–1900.* Lincoln: University of Nebraska Press, 2010.

LaPointe, Ernie. *Sitting Bull: His Life and Legacy.* Layton, Utah: Gibbs Smith, 2009.

Larson, Robert W. *Red Cloud: Warrior-Statesman of the Oglala Lakota.* Norman: University of Oklahoma Press, 1997.

Maddra, Sam. *Hostiles? The Lakota Ghost Dance and Buffalo Bill's Wild West.* Norman: University of Oklahoma Press, 2006.

Manhart, Paul I. *Lakota Tales and Texts, In Translation.* Vol 2. Chamberlain, S.D.: Tipi Press, 1998.

McDermott, John. *Red Cloud's War: The Bozeman Trail, 1866–1868.* Norman, Okla.: Arthur H. Clark, 2010.

McGillycuddy, Julia B. *Blood on the Moon: Valentine T. McGillycuddy and the Sioux.* Lincoln: University of Nebraska Press, 1990. First published 1941.

McGregor, James. H. *The Wounded Knee Massacre: From the Point of View of the Sioux.* Rapid City, S.D.: Fensek Printing, 1997.

McLaughlin, James. *My Friend the Indian.* Lincoln: University of Nebraska Press, 1989. First published 1910.

Miller, David Humphreys. *The Ghost Dance.* Lincoln: University of Nebraska Press, 1985.

Mooney, James. *The Ghost-Dance Religion and the Sioux Outbreak of 1890.* (Originally *The 14th Annual Report of the Bureau of Ethnology to the Secretary of the Smithsonian Institution, 1892–1893.* Washington, D.C., 1896). Lincoln: University of Nebraska Press, 1991.

Olson, James C. *Red Cloud and the Sioux Problem.* Lincoln: University of Nebraska Press, 1965.

Ostler, Jeffrey. *The Lakotas and the Black Hills: The Struggle for Sacred Ground.* New York: Penguin Books, 2011.

———. *The Plains Sioux and U.S. Colonialism from Lewis and Clark to Wounded Knee.* Cambridge: University of Cambridge Press, 2004.

Paul, Eli R. "The Investigation of Special Agent Cooper and Property Damage Claims in the Winter of 1890–1891." *South Dakota History* 24, no. 3–4 (1994): 212–35.

Powers, William. *Voices from the Spirit World: Lakota Ghost Dance Songs.* Kendall Park, N.J.: Lakota Books, 1990.

Price, Catherine. *The Oglala People, 1841–1879: A Political History.* Lincoln: University of Nebraska Press, 1996.

Red Shirt, Delphine. *George Sword's Warrior Narratives: Compositional Processes in Lakota Oral Tradition.* Lincoln: University of Nebraska Press, 2016.

Richardson, Heather Cox. *Wounded Knee: Party Politics and the Road to an American Massacre.* New York: Basic Books, 2010.

Seymour, Forrest W. *Sitanka: The Full Story of Wounded Knee*. West Hanover, Mass.: Christopher, 1981.

Sickels, Emma. "The Story of the Ghost Dance. Written in the Indian Tongue by Major George Sword, an Ogallala Sioux, Major of Indian Police." *The Folk-Lorist* 1, no. 1 (1892): 32–36.

Smith, Rex Alan. *Moon of the Popping Trees: The Tragedy at Wounded Knee and the End of the Indian Wars*. Lincoln: University of Nebraska Press, 1975.

Smoak, Gregory E. "The Mormons and the Ghost Dance of 1890." *South Dakota History* 16, no. 3 (1986): 269–94.

Standing Bear, Luther. *My People the Sioux*. New York: Houghton & Mifflin, 1928. https://babel.hathitrust.org/cgi/pt?id=ucl.$b306020;view=1up; seq=15.

———. *My People the Sioux*. Lincoln: University of Nebraska Press, 1975.

Steinmetz, Paul P., Sr. *Pipe, Bible and Peyote among the Oglala Lakota: A Study in Religious Identity*. Syracuse, N.Y.: Syracuse University Press, 1998.

Steltenkamp, Michael F. *Nicholas Black Elk: Medicine Man, Missionary, Mystic*. Norman: University of Oklahoma Press, 2009.

Thomas, Trudy Carter. "Crisis and Creativity: Visual Symbolism of the Ghost Dance Tradition." Unpublished Ph.D. diss., Columbia University, 1988.

Ullrich, Jan, ed. *New Lakota Dictionary*. Bloomington, Ind.: Lakota Language Consortium, 2011.

Utley, Robert M. *The Lance and the Shield: Life and Times of Sitting Bull*. New York: Ballantine Books, 1993.

———. *The Last Days of the Sioux Nation*. New Haven, Conn.: Yale University Press, 1963.

Vestal, Stanley. *Sitting Bull: The Champion of the Sioux*. Norman: Oklahoma University Press, 1989. First published 1932.

Waggoner, Josephine. *Witness: A Húŋkpapȟa Historian's Strong-Heart Song of the Lakotas*, edited by Emily Levine. Lincoln: University of Nebraska Press, 2013.

Walker, James R. *Lakota Belief and Ritual*, edited by Raymond J. DeMallie and Elaine A. Jahner. Lincoln: University of Nebraska Press, 1991.

Warren, Louis S. *God's Red Son: The Ghost Dance Religion and the Making of Modern America*. New York: Basic Books, 2017.

———. "Wage Work in the Sacred Circle: The Ghost Dance as a Modern Religion." *Western Historical Quarterly* (Summer 2015): 141–68.

Watson, Elmo Scott. "The Last Indian War, 1890–1891: A Study of Newspaper Jingoism." *Journalism Quarterly* 20, no. 1 (1943): 205–19.

Wells, Philip Faribault. "Ninety-Six Years among the Indians of the Northwest." *North Dakota History* 15, no. 2 (March 1948): 85–143; no. 3 (July 1948): 169–215; no. 4 (October 1948): 265–312.

Wildhage, Wilhelm. *Geistertants-Lieder der Lakota: Eine Quellen Samlung.* Wück auf Foehr: Verlag für Amerikanistik, 1991.

———. "Material on Short Bull." *European Review of Native American Studies* 4, no. 1 (1990): 35–41.

Wilson, Raymond. *Ohiyesa: Charles Eastman Santee Sioux.* Champaign: University of Illinois Press, 1999.

Wissler, Clark. *Some Protective Designs of the Dakota.* Vol. 1, pt. 2. New York: Anthropological Papers of the Museum of Natural History, 1907.

Index